COR Values

My Exodus From Religious Dogma
to the liberation of Intellectual Autonomy

COR Values

MY EXODUS FROM RELIGIOUS DOGMA
TO THE LIBERATION OF INTELLECTUAL AUTONOMY

Daniel Robert Mazur

DEDICATION

To the cherished memory of my grandparents, Carmen and Gertrude Fortino. Their exclusion from our family revealed to me the fragility and ephemeral beauty of life. This book is a manifestation of my unwavering quest for the right words—words that can shed light on the misguided paths leading to division, heal the scars of estrangement, and guide us toward harmony and peace. May the story of my family act as a catalyst, inspiring us to mend what has been torn asunder and instilling hope that those separated may reunite, thereby avoiding the depths of irreversible regret.

Contents

ABOUT THE TITLE
AND THE BOOK

*C*OR *VALUES* DESCRIBES A PHENOMENON WHERE INDIVIDUALS choose "comfort over reality," leading to the creation of self-serving, distorted truths. The term "COR" encapsulates the tendency of people to shape narratives and beliefs more aligned with their personal desires than with objective reality. Through telling my life story, this book examines how people, driven by the COR mindset, manipulate information, rely on emotional persuasion, and even fabricate facts to shape a reality that serves their own agendas, overlooking the necessity for integrity and objectivity.

The central allure of being COR lies in its comforting reassurance by affirming pre-existing beliefs or offering oversimplified solutions to complex issues, often based on falsehoods or half-truths. This, however, comes at a significant cost. It promotes a culture of evasion, where confronting uncomfortable truths and acknowledging the consequences of one's actions is avoided. This avoidance fosters a societal environment where the rigorous demands of truth and reality are shunned.

The impact of being COR is profound and far reaching. Individuals influenced by these values may find themselves unwittingly supporting harmful ideologies, participating in destructive behaviors, or isolating others based on distorted beliefs. The repercussions are not just personal, involving emotional distress and financial loss, but also societal, leading to division, conflict, and the deterioration of democratic principles. As these fabricated realities take hold, they undermine the bedrock of trust and critical thinking, essential for a healthy society.

OFF AT GRANDMA'S

February 1987

I SAT THERE IN THAT CLONE OF A HOME ON A CITY'S CHECKERBOARD street, 1210 Oak Street, Syracuse, to be exact, an address tamped into my mind by a collection of inextricably memorable visits. It had been a heavily traversed go-between, that street leading to my grandparents' home, one of innumerable others as tritely named—after trees. Unable to determine reasons there, I considered the effects. I was tormented without coherent reverie of years long past, imprisoned by a morphing of assailants, an army of vengeful snippets from my distorted recollections that conjured the attack. The comforts of normality gone, I brooded in a wake of agony. Simpler, carefree days long past had been replaced by skewed ideations, a muddling of ponderings perpetually and incessantly punishing me.

My introspection resuming, I stood and made my way to the sink, the one where Grandma washed her dishes. She did it with her bare hands and never without scalding hot water, which I had imagined should burn. I often presumed her thinking was, *Be sure to kill the germs.*

Above the sink on the windowsill, four husky tomatoes were perched, basking in the sunlight, gradually reddening. Through the glass, a gray goose-down parka with a tunnel-shaped hood was in full bloom, keeping a snowblower pilot warm and dry. It moved quickly—flew—my grandfather steering his John Deere from one end of the narrow driveway to the other, leading from the wood-named street to his tool-filled garage. Small tools, that is, not the power machines like the drill press and table saw in his basement. But it was July, and there was no snow outside. Two seasons had passed, but the chill remained in my mind and in the wearisome snowbanks that Grandpa blazed through. It wasn't a hallucination or an apparition, this aberration from my firm-footed past, this new place my family said was of my choosing, where I was to blame, even if I was only a moth drawn to the flame.

It was early afternoon, one of several bound to be spent there. I was twenty-five years old and self-employed with unattended business, inwardly pining. I was not the conductor of my emotions, and I was only able to comment and observe my behavior as if I were not the creator but a prisoner to seemingly arbitrary events, sources unknown, possibly derived from, associated with, and/or related to fistfuls of unaskable questions. Questions unanswered leading to more questions, tamped into my mind and conjured with hyperthymestic recall. They threatened my sanity as interminable introspection led me toward beliefs contrary to the common-sense conclusions of the surrounding majority, entangling bewildering thoughts with other background noise that I strove to escape while attempting to travel toward more tolerable destinations.

The unknown and uncertainty persisted at the front and in the periphery, incessantly punishing me as I drifted away on a captainless ship toward an unseen shore.

Making my way to the living room, I settled on my aunt's upholstered sofa, the kitchen remaining in my line of sight. Unsure of how I got there, I wrapped a blanket adorned with flowery shapes around me, a craft my mother made from a kit in a K-mart store, or was it Switz's? In the far corner of the room, my grandfather stretched out comfortably in his beige leather La-Z-Boy chair. It was not a fractured memory; he was actually there. He tucked a twined white cord under his blanket. It extended from his ear to his collar where it disappeared, becoming visible again where a torn sock exposed a circlet of heel flesh, its remaining journey to the TV fully exposed. Both of us fiddled with our quilts, adjusting to the rapidly changing temperatures in the poorly insulated room. Above us in the second-floor bedroom, my grandmother waited for her cue—the creaking of two wooden steps—indicating enough TV had been watched. It would happen when the national anthem started playing, the broadcasts concluded, and it was time to sleep.

I had been in their bedroom before, through another door where more creaky steps led to the attic. Across from their bedroom were two more rooms, one of them my aunt slept in, its walls covered in metallic purple paper, a gilding of fleeting taste. Adjacent to hers was a guest room flush with hunting and wildlife imagery. A picture of Dad, clad in his big-game hunting regalia, hung on the wall. It was a framed 1970s newspaper clipping, featuring a buck with an impressive array of high-scoring antler points, its tongue protruding. Another wall displayed a painting of geese in flight, the creatures disproportionately painted in an undeservingly framed presentation. Next to it was my favorite, another bird, a cuckoo that appeared noisily every hour, seemingly desperate for attention. And finally, a showcase on the floor exhibited a mélange of firearms, a generational theme of family interests.

"It's up center field, going, going, it's out of the park!" Grandpa's whoop added to my woolgathering. TV sports and westerns were joylessly imponderable without the company of my grandfather yet immeasurably rewarding with him. The sight of a ball hit long and far, a gunfight featuring John Wayne, or a scene with Larry, Curly, and Moe brought both consoling and tormenting ruminations during every unsolicited appearance.

There was a car accident that morning on my way there to that clone of a home on the go-between wood-named street. If I had driven too fast or too slow, it would have been me lying flat on my back on the street. I intentionally varied my acceleration, deviating from the posted speed limits, and took routes I had never traversed before, with the exception of that final, unavoidable go-between street where my grandparents lived. Memories and moments both near and far left me struggling to comprehend the distances and the differences between destiny and destinations. Was I haunted by evil's whisper, a ghostly echo of imposed theology, or did its seed lie dormant within, entwined in the mystery of genes and biology?

I sat there in my grandparents' house on my aunt's upholstered sofa, my mother's quilt wrapped around me. My pursuit of warmth remembered, vacated by the disparaging of family and friends. As darkness settled in, sleep eluded me. I delved into introspection, contemplating whether my troubles found their roots in the stories I had heard, in moments of flawed judgments, errors, and transgressions. I had lucid moments, memories of better times—camping at Green Lakes with the family, my grandfather strumming his mandolin after Sunday dinners—but they quickly faded, giving way to countless episodes of the antithesis. If I was better than perceived, was embedded theology rendering my body immobile and twisting my mind? The questions loomed.

As I continued to sit on my aunt's upholstered sofa, wrapped in my mother's quilt, I wished it would warm me. In the depths of my contemplation, I immersed myself in murky thoughts, reflecting on the years of rejected dogma that persisted within me, unresolved and dormant, waiting to be transformed into clear, concise instructions akin to the metaphorical "preparatory command" that guided a soldier marching forward.

Had the malevolent forces of Satan's demons been summoned, stirred awake by my yearning for self-assurance? From the captivating depths, a formidable presence emerged in the unexplored corners of my mind. The foreboding thirteenth chapter of Revelation from the Christian Bible unveiled a timeless, aeonian doctrine, the ominous arrival of "the beast" itself. This wicked entity visited me not once but repeatedly for seven consecutive nights until the fateful moment when someone dared to wield a gleaming steel blade, seeking to extinguish my existence with a fatal strike.

Dinner beckoned. The tantalizing aroma of Grandma's sauce filled the air. The thought of testing the pasta's al dente perfection stirred my hunger. I put Mom's quilt back up on the sofa, nice and neat the way Grandpa did. Then I followed my grandfather's meticulous footsteps, my anticipation growing. The joy of savoring a satisfying meal awaited!

But wait, where was everyone? Faint echoes of a distant game reached my ears, leaving me feeling bewildered and alone. Had time slipped away, leaving me in surreal solitude? The Sunday pasta tradition, once so cherished, now stood before me, but I was uncertain if it was a tangible reality or just a fading memory from a distance. Where were David and Paul? Had they chosen to stay behind? A whirlwind of questions danced within my mind as I grappled with the day and my place in it. With it came a seemingly simple realization. Ah, yes, there I was at my grandparents' house, seated comfortably on their sofa. And amidst the assortment of emotions, the mysterious prophecy remained, poised to reveal its hidden truths.

My father had introduced me to the realm of devils and demons when I was eleven years old. Within the walls of the church in Euclid, I was exposed to a world of spiritual warfare, where exorcisms were common occurrences. Together with an eccentric group of long-haired hippies, the peculiar congregation formed, sitting in circular formation on cold metal folding chairs, as if preparing for an otherworldly battle.

In the midst of our rhythmic recitations of the psalms, I joined the collective frenzy, tambourine in hand, unleashing percussive vibrations that seemed to beckon the divine. The air crackled with fervor as my father's voice soared above the tumultuous chorus, invoking the Almighty with his fervent plea, "Bring those no one else wants, oh Lord." Those words resonated deep within me, casting a spell that shaped my life for years to come.

Among the intriguing figures of that congregation, one stood out in particular—David Gentile, the epitome of metamorphosis. I witnessed his astonishing transformation during a mesmerizing tent meeting in the distant town of Parish, an event that is immortalized in the pages of our family photo albums. I can still see him now, his long locks falling to the floor as a pair of silver shears severed his ties to the past, leaving him reborn, both physically and spiritually.

But it was not just the images captured in faded photographs that remained in my mind; it was the intangible impressions, the lingering sensations that had imprinted themselves upon my very being. I could still hear the resounding echo of my father's voice, resonating with unwavering conviction as he held David's face in his hands, unveiling the existence of evil to the unsuspecting "babes in Christ." With fierce determination, he proclaimed, "I cast you out, Satan, in the name of Jesus!" The energy in the room was palpable, as if the forces of good and evil were waging an invisible battle right before our eyes.

Amidst the ever-changing landscape of our small town, a new preacher arrived, heralding winds of change. And in the heart of this transformation stood "Dancing David," a whirlwind of exuberance and devotion. Every gathering became a spectacle as he raised his arms to the heavens, spinning with wild abandon at the center of our circle. His frenzied movements painted a vivid picture, his rosy cheeks and sweat-drenched clothes a testament to the intensity of his faith. It was as if he had been reborn from the depths of his past, redeemed by the boundless grace of a higher power.

Guided by my father's wise counsel, this former hippie tapped into his inner drive and unveiled his sharp business acumen. Through his endeavors, he cultivated a reputation as a discerning and astute entrepreneur, not only for his own prosperity but also for fostering employment opportunities for fellow Christians. His unwavering devotion and business success earned him admiration as a cherished member of the church and a revered figure among the congregation. David's journey served as a compelling demonstration of the harmonious coexistence that can be achieved between spirituality and worldly achievements, inspiring others to embrace the richness of the sacred and secular dimensions of life.

In the midst of these fervent displays, I found myself consumed by jealousy, an envy that birthed an audacious fabrication within me. One fateful night, amidst the clatter of metal folding chairs, I could no longer resist the allure of attention. With a concoction of nerves and deceit, I proclaimed to the congregation, "I have a vision. I can see Jesus on the cross." The words hung in the air, pregnant with expectation and disbelief as eyes turned toward me.

At that moment my heart pounded in my chest, and my cheeks flushed crimson with a mixture of excitement and trepidation. But as quickly as doubt threatened to engulf me, a wave of applause crashed over my fragile façade, immersing me in a sea of acceptance. The taste of validation was intoxicating and bitter, leaving me yearning for more yet questioning the cost of such triumphs.

On the car ride home, the relentless waves of praise reverberated within me, sinking deeper into the recesses of my being. With each word and expression received, a peculiar sense of unease settled within me. It marked the inception of a relentless fret, a seed planted in the fertile ground of my consciousness. It grew silently yet persistently. Nurtured by the paradoxical experiences of a realm claiming truth and godliness, I found myself ensnared in an enigmatic dance, where rewards were bestowed for the darkest deeds.

"Take heed, for I shall grant you sight," an ethereal voice whispered into my ear, its words sending a shiver down my spine. With an audible delivery that evoked awe and intrigue, this ethereal presence from out of the blue bestowed its message upon me. Eager to unravel its purpose, I wholeheartedly acknowledged its presence. It was not just a faint repetition but a palpable and mysterious force, seemingly materializing from the void, beckoning me to uncover the depths of its intentions.

"Alright, I'm listening. What do you desire?"

"Embrace the path before you," the spectral voice urged, the essence of its words compelling me to heed its call. As if obeying an unseen directive, an unyielding urge emerged within me, persuading me to embark upon a profound exploration of the possibilities that my upbringing had integrated into the essence of my being.

The healings, supposedly brought about by divine intervention, ignited sparks of curiosity and kindled flames of inquiry within me. Such a day it was during my formative years in elementary school when an innocuous act led me to guide a friend to an unconventional seat—the rim of a bathroom toilet. "Now, straighten your legs, and align your feet side by side," I said, mirroring the practices observed in church. It was believed that if one suffered from a back problem, one leg would appear longer than the other. This fascinating phenomenon captivated the attention of churchgoers and permeated discussions within the intimate confines of homes, becoming a topic often raised at dining room tables.

One memory of a profound moment within the sacred confines of the church remained vivid in my mind. It was a remarkable occasion when a fervent congregant stepped forward, testifying about the severe impairment that burdened his back. The folding chairs encircled him, their arrangement symbolizing the unity and shared spirit among those gathered. As anticipation filled the air, a crackling energy enveloped the room.

In the midst of that charged atmosphere, the afflicted man took his seat, his feet cradled by my father's fingertips. This poignant scene depicted a profound connection—an ethereal bridge between one in need and a conduit for divine intervention. Observing the misalignment, my father drew attention to the issue. "This is the problem. Look at his feet. They're uneven, one leg shorter than the other," he proclaimed with unwavering conviction.

Then, with a commanding voice that resounded through the sparsely furnished room, my father unleashed his words, shattering any possibility of doubt. "Be healed, in the name of Jesus! Back problems, be gone!" Every eye fixed on the man's legs, and as if responding to the call, a miraculous sight rewarded their gaze. It seemed as though one of the man's feet began to move, gradually aligning itself with its counterpart, a testament to the transformative power at work. His voice filled with joy and gratitude echoed through the room, proclaiming, "I'm healed, I'm healed! Praise Jesus, my back is free from pain!"

Overwhelmed with excitement, the congregation erupted in a roar, a jubilant celebration of the divine intervention they had witnessed. The room resonated with an outpouring of spiritual fervor, as many among the congregation spoke in tongues, their voices harmonizing in a sacred symphony of faith and praise.

Curiosity consumed me as I pondered the nature of the applause that followed the so-called "miracle." Was it deserved or was it as misplaced as the adulation for my fabricated story, my vision of Jesus on the cross? On that day in the boys' restroom at Morgan Road Elementary, I embarked on a quest for answers to these burning questions.

In stark contrast to the folding chairs encircling the faithful, my venture commenced without any theatrical flourishes. There were no mystic incantations or indiscernible intonations, only a heartfelt plea directed to Jesus Christ, beseeching him to heal my friend's ailing back. Rooted in memories, I positioned his feet unevenly before maneuvering them from side by side. The outcome proved unremarkable, lacking the grandeur I had hoped to replicate, but it still mirrored the remembered experiences.

As I contemplated the scene, I wondered if heightened efforts might have incited applause and cheers from my observing friends, akin to the fervor I had witnessed at church. Could it be that these so-called miracles were intricate performances, driven by desires similar to my own, guiding my father's deliberate movements of the man's feet?

These ponderings, intertwined with skepticism, fueled my yearning for truth. I resolved to delve deeper, determined to unravel the mystery that surrounded these extraordinary occurrences.

The chilly air seeped into my surroundings once more, kindling a yearning for the comforting embrace of my quilt. Ah, there it was, draped upon me. Still, an unexplained shiver lingered, refusing to dissipate. Then the voice whispered into my ear once again: "You see me now. Choose." Startled, I pondered the source of these cryptic words. Could it be the demon taunting me once more?

I found myself back within the familiar, cozy confines of my grandparents' house, settled on their sofa. It was a serene Sunday afternoon, a cherished time when my family gathered for a heartwarming macaroni dinner. Or perhaps I had traversed the boundaries of life and death, my soul conjuring a surreal fusion of memories and apparitions after a fateful car crash. Rest eluded me as I grappled with this perplexing trial, teetering on the precipice of existence and the unknown.

In a swift motion, as though whisked away by some temporal force, I relived the sensation in the peaceful surroundings of my grandparents' home, sinking deeper into their sofa's embrace. The television screen came alive with the vibrant spectacle of a bowling tournament, and I watched alongside my grandfather. Amidst the exhilarating competition, a captivating dynamic unfurled—a competitor inadvertently exposed a tapestry of inadequacies, a stark contrast to the grandeur he sought to project. Despite his fervent efforts, no deliberate gaze, choreographed movement, or carefully selected words could conceal the truth. The discord that clouded his morning with his wife, the burdens of financial strife, and the relentless battle against self-worth were laid bare, echoing the poignant observations I had made at Wendy's just the day before.

Indulging in the flavors of a delectable Dave's Single cheeseburger while savoring a refreshing sip of Coke, my attention was captivated by a stranger entering the bustling fast-food establishment. Time seemed to freeze as he contemplated his order, radiating an aura of introspection. Though our paths had never intertwined, his essence materialized before me, as palpable as the sofa I was resting upon. Within my vision, I caught glimpses of the man's intricate character, his identity shrouded in a relentless series of disappointments that had diluted his spirit. It was revealed that he was a high school basketball coach, driven to shape the lives of a fiercely competitive team, an endeavor fueled by the pursuit of self-worth and validation.

Within the luminous realm of the television screen and the tangible world, these personal endeavors served a shared purpose—to awaken a profound sense of self-awareness within those who partook in them. This revelation sprang forth from my own acute self-awareness, a quality that often appeared lacking in the individuals I observed. The unspoken recognition that arose within me amused others, but it remained concealed and safeguarded, shielding me from the potential repercussions of unfavorable judgments.

Aunt MaryJane was engrossed in a conversation with my grandparents in the kitchen, their voices drifting toward me in fragmented snippets. Suddenly, a remark caught my attention. What was that? Had I heard it correctly? I had been shedding tears, longing for my father just yesterday? There was no physical barrier separating the dining room and the family room where I was sitting. Through the open doorway that connected the spaces, I caught glimpses of my aunt as she paced between the refrigerator and the stove. Her presence flickered, resembling a cautionary signal pulsating in my line of sight. Meanwhile, my grandparents maintained an air of quietude, seemingly attentive to my aunt's words. However, their silence was broken when my grandfather rose from the table, his chair scraping against the kitchen's vinyl floor, a distinctive sound that I had encountered before. My aunt and my grandmother followed suit, converging upon me. It became evident that I was the subject of their conversation, a realization I gleaned from discreet eavesdropping. With my aunt taking the lead, their steps suggested an impending intervention. Be it admonishment or perhaps even congratulations, I braced myself for what lay ahead. "Danny, why don't you join us in prayer and invite Jesus into your heart?" My aunt's words floated in the air, full of significance.

Reflecting on the past, I contemplated similar propositions that emerged in the Euclid church and persisted in the town of Phoenix. Adjacent to the church stood a smaller building known as the "parsonage," which served as a dwelling for financially disadvantaged individuals, mostly younger men who were new members. They often made unabashed and even self-aggrandizing confessions, adhering to a creed that emphasized the more tumultuous one's past, the more remarkable their transformation. Across the street, a fire station would occasionally become active with deafening sirens, seemingly aiming to provoke and interrupt the meetings. Four gatherings took place every week—Sunday mornings, Sunday evenings, and Wednesday and Friday nights. The dogma underwent continuous changes, but the expectations of conforming to what was deemed new and approved remained constant. Over time, speaking in tongues became less frequent and less spontaneous, and demonstrations of miracles all but vanished. The healing of backs with my father's touch at a congregant's feet was never witnessed again. Nevertheless, throughout it all, almost every sermon concluded with a call to the unsaved, an invitation to embrace Christ in their hearts.

During those days I didn't fully grasp its meaning, and even now it remains elusive. I never bothered to ask about it, unlike simpler questions that received inadequate answers. "Just go with it" became my mentality. It was what was expected, what was done, akin to tradition. Ironically, tradition, as I later discovered, was a word used to describe practices that could obstruct necessary progress, often wielded as ammunition to criticize and attack other churches and denominations. In a peculiar turn of events, it eventually became a tradition for my father to deliver sermons from notes, which had once been considered taboo. I recall those sermons vividly, my father proclaiming, "The Lord isn't confined to a script; his Spirit moves freely." The congregation's affirmation reverberated through exclamations of "Praise God! Yes, thank you, Jesus! Amen!", followed by hymns of praise. I often imagined my father explaining such changes as a natural evolution toward spiritual maturity. The expression "babes in Christ" comes to mind, as if he would say, "We were young in Christ, in the days of Euclid." Ah, those years brimming with insinuations and expectations to believe without questioning, where non-compliance carried consequences. I would have faced punishment if I had declared the truth of my uncertainty regarding these claims—matters of utmost significance that have been debated throughout history—an omnipotent force overseeing my eternal afterlife. Silence! Obey! Occasionally, a fellow brother or sister in the church would muster the courage to ask, "Why aren't you waving your hands to God with praise like the others?" Doing my best to conceal my discomfort, I would act in a manner appropriate enough to maintain my façade. Within me, the phrase "You want answers, you want the truth? You can't handle the truth," uttered by Jack Nicholson in *A Few Good Men*, encapsulates my frustration. Resentment swelled within me, fueled by the burden of hiding my true self from prying eyes. Amidst the torment, the only escape offered seemed to be a stark ultimatum: "Believe in Jesus, confess his lordship, and find salvation. Choose light or darkness, the definitive door." It was presented as a stark dichotomy, an either/or proposition.

"What's the issue? Just profess your faith in him. Why would you willingly choose damnation?" These words, uttered by my Uncle Joe one fateful Sunday, resounded within the walls of my grandparents' house as my girlfriend, Susan, listened, unaware of the perceived disparities within her Catholic faith. Its practice of venerating statues, regarded as deviating from the essence of true Christianity, eluded her awareness. Her attempts at diplomacy and "fitting in" proved fruitless, for within the realm of my nuclear and extended family, conformity was the sole viable path, demanding compliance or at least pretense in the pursuit of harmony. Discussions that bridged divides and sought understanding, yearning for the mention of Pascal's wager, remained elusive, an unattainable dream. It could have been an opportunity to delve into the chasm between lip service and genuine belief. Their resolute convictions, fortified by interpretations within the realm of fundamentalist Christianity, erected an impenetrable fortress against reason's tender advances. Thus, I resorted to what was necessary, embracing remnants of truth while treading the treacherous path of measured deceit, preserving the thin disguise so vital to my existence. And so, amidst the clandestine shadows, witnessing Susan's tears that day and shouldering the responsibility of consoling her, I walked silently alongside her, guiding her toward the solace of home.

As time passed, changes continued to develop in the dynamics and topics of discussion. The concept of family unity emerged as a recent subject triggered by discussions of the rapture and the impending end times. The belief that "God is coming back" and that the prophecies in Revelation are being fulfilled instilled a sense of urgency—there wasn't much time left. The pulpit became a platform to address worldly corruption, crime, drugs, and similar issues, calling for a more pronounced public display of concern, as if the hoots and hollers from the pews were no longer sufficient. "I want all family members, parents, and children to come together, to stand in a circle and pray with me." It was akin to the Living Word Super Bowl, where families gathered like players in a huddle. Instead of remaining in the pews with the other congregants, I was summoned to join my siblings and parents on the stage, in full view of everyone. We engaged in synchronized crying and wailing, putting our emotions on full display for passersby, nearby observers, and even those at the fire station who dared to peek through the large open doors. The spectacle involved theatrics of sobbing, posturing eyes, and quivering lips. Some would speak in unintelligible "tongues" with a somber tone, performing and observing from the sidelines. I, too, was expected to participate in this dramatic exhibition. My acting skills were pushed to their limits, stretching beyond what I was comfortable with. I couldn't help but reminisce about the good old days when I could listen to episodes of *CBS Radio Mystery Theatre* using my crystal pen radio and hidden earpiece, finding solace and safety in the confines of my pew.

Crafting scenarios in my mind that could elicit even a single tear was a daunting task, but stepping onto that stage took the challenge to a whole new level. We huddled together like a team of athletes, arms intertwined, grunts and sweat connecting us. The surge of discomfort within me, triggered by these involuntary memories, was a direct result of years of pressure to conform and assimilate.

This visceral reaction was how I replied to my aunt's request. I didn't blame her but rather the proposition itself.

Sometimes Aunt MaryJane and my grandparents defied the judgments that contributed to my isolation, displaying genuine care. At that moment, I contemplated the true meaning of having "God in my heart." Perhaps they were onto something—a religion with versatile purposes, capable of good and ill. In that uncertain time, doubts plagued my beliefs and my sanity. But what did I have to lose?

"Alright, Aunt MaryJane," I said. "I'll pray with you and invite Jesus into my heart." With her hand on my shoulder and the other raised, my aunt initiated the prayer, and my grandparents stood by our sides, joining in.

"Repeat after me, Danny. Dear Jesus, come into my life and cleanse away my sins. I acknowledge my past as a sinner and humbly seek your forgiveness . . ." I went through with it, reciting every word, hoping for a transformative experience. Their desire for my salvation was genuine, and I acknowledged it. Their intentions were pure, but the entire process felt awkward, reminiscent of a childhood revival meeting when I stood alongside countless others, earnestly praying and beckoning God to enter my life as the evangelist instructed. It felt awkward then, and the following day, I faced criticism in Sunday School for my approach.

"You didn't even close your eyes while praying up there," a classmate exclaimed. Close my eyes? No one had told me about that. I had assumed it would be easy to look around and emulate others. I thought something was wrong with me.

Now I questioned the expectations placed upon me. How was I supposed to act? I had spoken the prescribed words but felt no discernible change. Should I start leaping or attempt to speak in tongues? I knew I had the ability, just as others did. Their eyes fixed on me, waiting for my reaction. "I think I'll retreat to the sofa and take a moment to relax, alright?" I said, creating yet another awkward moment to be recounted in the future. It seemed as if I might as well have been praying in a crowd with my eyes wide open, acutely aware of being watched and laughed at.

As time marched forward, blending each passing day into a collage of random events, I found solace in memories of simpler moments from years ago when our family stood united. In the dining room, we gathered together, Grandma playfully complaining about her salty tomato sauce while Grandpa strummed his mandolin, creating beautifully off-key melodies that filled the room with love and warmth. Oh, how I longed to recreate that scene, to make them see the reality before us.

"Danny, are you alright?" Aunt MaryJane's sudden presence startled me. Where had she come from? How long had she been sitting beside me?

"Oh, hi, Aunt MaryJane, I'm back," I replied, attempting to regain my composure.

"You're back? Back from where? Where have you been?" she asked, concern evident in her voice. I couldn't let her in on my secret; she wouldn't understand. So, I sat there in silence, wondering how much she knew and for how long she had been aware of my predicament. Fortunately, she stood up and headed toward the kitchen, picking up the phone along the way. My mind raced with questions. Whom was she calling? Was it her husband, Gary? Would she divulge something about me? Perhaps he was the one who posed a threat, the one who might try to kill me.

The haunting chime of the doorbell pierced my deep reverie. Who could it be?

"Gary, I need to call you back. I think that's Bob at the door," Aunt MaryJane said into the phone. Bob? My father? What could bring him here? I had just been thinking about him earlier. Or had I been discussing him with Aunt MaryJane?

As my father and my brother, David, walked through the door, my heart began to race. David was no longer the timid sibling I remembered—the one who hid beneath our family's station wagon as we dodged the fury of teenagers during our daring escapades. Instead, there was a new confidence in his stance, arms crossed, looking down at me with a challenging authority. *He's become so sure of himself,* I thought, feeling the hairs on the back of my neck rise. Another shiver ran down my spine, adding to the heavy cache of secrets I bore.

It was time to summon my courage, to break the uneasy silence. "Here I am, your living proof," I declared, surprising even myself with the audacity of my words.

"What?" my father replied, his voice slicing through the tension in the room. My mind drifted, delving into memories of my upbringing within the confines of religious teachings and my father's parenting style. There was always a cadence to his speech, a deliberate manipulation of timing and tone to capture attention and emphasize selected words, aiming to maximize the impact of his messages. I anticipated a return to that familiar technique, and I yearned to disrupt the predictable orchestration, to dismantle the carefully constructed persona. Enough with the nonsensical detours down Looney Tunes alley. It was time to get to the point, to spit out the harsh truths that my father so readily embraced. *This is what happens when you live in sin, when you turn away from the Lord,* I thought, picturing him wanting to say those words, a combination of a grimace and an unwarranted smile playing on his lips. I had seen that look before, the twisted delight he displayed after exacting revenge. He reveled in it, using my downfall as ammunition for his self-assurance. *Excuse me, but need I remind you that we are all losers here, a shattered family torn apart?* No, I was just fuel for his confidence tank, and there it was, that "Okay, wise guy, I've got this" expression on his face.

I turned my gaze toward David, his arms still crossed over his chest. There was no trace of sympathy or dissent in his eyes, just a silent affirmation of agreement with our father's words. He stood there brooding beside my father, as if daring me to challenge their beliefs. He had found solace in our father's perceptions, accepting them as his own truth despite his firsthand experiences that contradicted such notions. It was as I remembered—when tragedy struck or floods engulfed us, David sought comfort within our father's perspective, adopting the supposed facts and truths handed down. An interesting choice given that before his eyes stood a vehicle ready to transport him to higher, safer ground.

As I laid on the sofa, my mind wandered through the labyrinth of time, yearning to return to a simpler era when worries were scarce and the family was united. Memories of laughter in the dining room flooded my thoughts, moments of joy and connection that brought us together. If only I could transport those moments to the present, to help my family grasp the true nature of what was unfolding, the profound sense of loss and absence that saturated the atmosphere. The weight of their understanding would be a lifeline, offering solace and empathy. But as my father's voice cut through the air, a sharp and accusatory tone, I braced myself for the all-too-familiar confrontation that awaited me.

"Danny, what drugs have you been taking?" The familiar pattern of simplifying complex dynamics into a self-serving narrative took shape. I could already anticipate the song-and-dance routine, the dismissal of intellectual discourse, and the reduction of everything to sin and drugs. "Not getting into a tangled sofa session here, no intellectual discourse about relationships and such from some psychiatrist trying to shift responsibility away from sinners. The boy's lost his mind because he's in sin, on drugs, and that's all there is to it."

Oh, please just go away!

"Join us." The words resonated in my ears.

"David, did you say that?" I asked, my confusion intensifying.

"Did I say what? I didn't say anything," David replied. I turned to face him, searching for a clue that might support his denial. He stood there, undoubtedly present to support the impending onslaught of accusations, yet his imperious stance failed to mask his bewilderment. His expression revealed his cluelessness. But then the question lingered in the air: who spoke those words? Join who? Join what? Could it have been the whisper of the demon, insidiously extending its invitation?

David leaned in closer, his head inching toward mine. Suspense hung in the air as conclusions about me loomed on the horizon, but whose verdict would it be? With a calculated step back, he regained his authoritative posture, arms still folded across his chest. A sneer crept onto his face, displaying his disapproval of me and my current state, a spectacle for everyone in the room. With his own sense of style and rhythm, David turned to our father. "I don't think he even knows who I am," he said. "He's really messed up."

Suddenly, an imposing figure clad in black-and-white-striped attire emerged, an empire of judgment personified. With a swift motion, he extended his arm, clenched his fist, and pulled it back to his hip, proclaiming, "Strike!" The air crackled with tension as the figure's commanding presence lingered, sending a chilling wave of unease and tremors down my spine. With a seamless transition, my father took the metaphorical mound, poised to deliver his pitch: "Danny, I asked you, what drugs have you taken?"

My retort was swift. "What? Who do you think you are?"

"I'm your father," he replied with a hint of sarcasm.

Without uttering a word, I challenged him silently, my thoughts racing. *Oh, really? Are you the same father I recently sought, leaving messages on chalkboards, notepads, and even office walls? Does anyone truly know who my father is?* Against the backdrop of coffee breaks and office banter, my quest stood out, displayed in vibrant colors, injecting an intriguing twist into the routines of company employees. Among messages like "Puppy for Sale" and "$20 Secret Santa Cap," my bold proclamation of "Who's my daddy?" sparked an empire of curiosity, setting off a commotion that captured the attention of all. As I embarked on a two-week odyssey to unveil the truth about my father, conversations and interest soared, leaving no one untouched by the captivating and engaging intrigue, which interrupted the routine of business.

One particular incident unfolded during my persistent solicitation efforts with a man named Dick Shutt, a partner at an electronics company. Despite facing countless rejections, his secretary finally relented and granted me an audience, perhaps driven by sheer curiosity or to alleviate my persistent calls. As I made my pitch, Dick's initial disinterest transformed into intrigue. "What did you say your name was?" he inquired, his eyes flickering with recognition.

"Dan Mazur, sir," I replied.

"Are you by any chance related to Bob Mazur from Tri-Art Studios?"

"Yes, he's my father, and that was his business."

At that moment a spark of realization flashed across his face, and he excused himself, promising a swift return. Little did I know, it marked the beginning of a whirlwind of conversations and curiosity surrounding my father and his business style.

Dick reappeared accompanied by two individuals embroiled in an animated discussion. Their irritation at the interruption was palpable, urging a speedy resolution. With a backward motion of his thumb, Dick pointed toward me, uttering three words that solidified my presence in their minds: "That's Mazur's kid." It wasn't until later that I grasped the underlying intrigue that circulated among businessmen within the community, centered around my father's ambitious transition from entrepreneur to pastor. The comments I overheard dispelled any notions of my father's virtuous intentions, painting a picture of an aggressive go-getter and casting me, his offspring, as a subject of intensified scrutiny.

"Really, Dick? You're claiming that's Bob's son?" one of them asked, amused by my presence as if I were an organ grinder's monkey, entertaining them with my proclamations.

Despite this initial impression, Dick became my client, and over the course of several months, we developed a working relationship and established rapport. During this time, I sought his opinion on various matters. During one after-hours consultation when I sought his counsel regarding a particular issue, his response remains clear to this day: "You know what's best, Dan. Follow your instincts." This departure from my anticipated response left me flabbergasted, devoid of self-interest, ego, or the customary appeal to his authority. I approached many other people, including my parents and even individuals from church, with my question, hoping to discover a range of viewpoints. Everyone had an answer, presenting their perspectives with unwavering certainty, having me believe they were right. But not Dick. He left me contemplating the value of my own process of seeking answers. Could I trust my own judgment and intuition? It was a concept at odds with my upbringing, which revered accomplished individuals who purportedly knew better and dictated instructions.

"I know what's best?" I mused, contemplating the profound implications of such a statement.

Dick's behavior toward me exhibited a paternal quality, sparking the thought that he could potentially be my father. The possibility weighed on my mind, casting a shadow of confusion and intrigue over our interactions. Consequently, I became relentless in making phone calls and unexpected appearances, causing chaos and disruption to his business.

And now, amidst the complexities of it all, I found myself grappling with the absence of even the most basic understanding of my own paternity. My father's identity and whereabouts remained elusive, waiting to be uncovered through a unique unraveling process. Yet in the presence of this elusive man before me, attempting to push me to my limits, I had a different plan in mind. Instead of succumbing to his scrutiny, I decided to turn the tables and test him instead.

Amidst the palpable tension that filled the room, I gathered my courage and broke the silence with a confident voice, presenting a captivating suggestion. "You know, I'm feeling a little hungry. How about we head to the kitchen and indulge in some fruit? Grandma, do you happen to have any fresh fruit?" My diversionary tactic took hold, shifting the focus and disrupting the rigid dynamics that had held sway. Confusion filled the room, but everyone seemed intrigued, ready to embark on this impromptu adventure.

We made our way to the kitchen, anticipation filling the air. Grandma retrieved a couple of bowls, placing them on the table before us. With a flourish, she opened a can of pineapple, pouring its golden sweetness into the awaiting bowls.

"Do you know about the companies that make this fruit?" I inquired, a mischievous glint in my eye.

"Yeah, I do," my father replied cautiously. With a triumphant smile, I presented the fruit before him.

"Well, here it is—the fruit from the very companies you claim to know. Take the first bite, then I'll have some too."

He hesitated, a hint of resistance in his voice. "No, let someone else have it."

"But it's just fruit," I pushed back, determined to challenge his reluctance, "fruit from the places you claim to know."

His resolve hardened. "No, I won't eat any. Let someone else have it." The tension lingered in the air as our eyes locked, a battle of wills unfolding over simple pieces of fruit.

In that pivotal moment, the room held its breath, captivated by the clash of wills. As the standoff continued, a sense of anticipation filled the air, leaving me wondering what secrets lurked beneath the surface. Would this culinary confrontation unravel the tangled web of our relationship and offer insights into the mysteries of my paternity? The answer hung in the balance, poised on the precipice of this seemingly simple act of defiance.

As the room was engulfed in escalating drama, the wail of sirens pierced the air, adding an eerie undertone and intensifying the palpable tension. The disruptive cacophony resonated in harmony with the turmoil stirring inside me.

At that critical moment, following a knock on the door and my aunt's departure from the kitchen to meet those outside, paramedics appeared before me. Their hands reached out, their touch a blend of urgency and clinical detachment. It was a jolting reminder that I was about to be wrenched away from my loved ones again, pushed into a realm of unpredictability and unfamiliarity. Their presence became a disorienting transition, propelling me into yet another journey into the unknown.

While descending the hallway steps under the paramedics' firm grasp, I stole a fleeting glance back over my shoulder. There stood my grandfather, his face etched with a mixture of deep concern and profound sorrow. His eyes spoke volumes, conveying a silent plea for me to remain, to find solace within the shelter of our shared love. But circumstances demanded otherwise, and I had to continue forward.

In that turbulent, confusing moment, as I was being led away, my grandfather's words resonated in the depths of my soul: "Oh, Lord, whatever burdens my grandson carries, place them upon me instead." This profound testament to his unconditional love and unwavering commitment penetrated my being, reminding me of the boundless depth of his love and his readiness to shoulder my burdens and shield me from harm.

Chapter Two

ON TO MIAMI

IT WAS MARCH 17, 1994, SEVEN YEARS LATER. I WAS SETTLED ON THE sofa in my new apartment, gazing through the sliding glass doors at the view outside at 7215 NW 179th Street in Hialeah, Florida. Gone were the familiar oak trees of Syracuse, replaced by palm trees that lined the nondescript east-west street.

Navigating this unfamiliar territory, I was adapting to the unique aspects of travel and daily life there. While I went by the name Dan Mazur, uncertainties about my identity persisted. Born on September 24, 1961, at Saint Joseph's Hospital in Syracuse, New York, I found myself, at age of thirty-two, anticipating that this day would not hold a favored place in my memory. Self-doubt had been a recurring presence, although it was not as unsettling as it once was.

I often questioned the reality of my existence and pondered the validity of my perceptions. In moments of doubt, I grappled with whether to trust my self-assessment or seek others' viewpoints. I'd been labeled in various ways: major depression, dysthymia, bipolar disorder, and even with unconventional terms like "God hater" or "demon possessed." However, I was left to wonder if identifying with any of these labels would bring clarity or cloud my self-understanding even further.

As I delved into a drawer that housed some important papers, a wave of nostalgia and intrigue swept over me. The documents now lay before me, capturing my attention, and it all started with stumbling upon my birth certificate. It was fascinating how something as simple as a piece of paper could hold such certainty about one's existence. My name, place of birth, and age written on its surface alongside the official seal of the commissioner of health and three distinctive signatures. These undeniable facts about my identity should have brought me assurance seeing as, not too long ago, I found myself uncertain of even the most basic aspects of who I was. As I held the certificate in my hands, I realized how much I valued its tangible representation of my identity, and I resolved never to lose sight of it again.

On another Thursday morning in my modest one-bedroom apartment, the clock marked 11:00. It was an unusual hour for me to write, but those weren't ordinary days. I lived alone in that space. While I once held a deep affection for it, the apartment evoked fewer pleasant memories after I moved in.

Across from me, my desk stood against the sliding glass door that revealed snippets of the outside world. If I were to paint a picture of my apartment, honesty would compel me to express its slightly disheveled state. In one word, it was a mess! Perhaps it reflected the way I'd been feeling lately—this melancholy that I described as an adjective rather than a diagnosis. It was not my first dance with depression, and I was keenly aware it could not be my last. These emotional spells arrived in two distinct flavors, much like comparing a cup of Syracuse coffee to the boldness of the Cuban coffee I now savored. Some were mild, fleeting visitors that often graced me with their presence. Others were more potent, infrequent guests that lingered far longer. Through it all, I remained optimistic, clinging to the belief that every experience, no matter how challenging, carried the potential for growth and resilience. Could something good truly emerge from the depths of despair? I mulled this question, all the while yearning for the brighter moments to overshadow the ones that caused even the simplest tasks, like tidying up, to slip through my fingers. If only you could have witnessed the state of my desk, adorned with a chaotic mixture of papers and remnants of food—like a partially eaten apple perched at its edge. Disgusting? Hardly. The true repugnance was in the untold details of other objects scattered before me. Amidst it all, I found solace in my ability to ramble on, even in the midst of my despondency. I'd learned that it was vital to find humor within myself, a sliver of sunshine to brighten the darkest of days. Yes, I had to seek out that small glimmer of light, even if it meant risking a sunburn from basking in its warmth without protection.

I was immersed in my Thursday morning typing session, I couldn't help but wonder what lay hidden beneath the surface of my life. A quest for understanding, a search for meaning propelled my fingers across the keyboard with an almost magnetic force. The need to unravel the intricacies of my existence led me there, to piece together the fragments and memories that formed my being. Perhaps I'd meander through these thoughts, allowing my mind to wander freely, embracing the unexpected twists and turns that revealed themselves along the way.

A curious observation sprang to mind: why was it that whenever I was faced with adversity or pressure, I felt compelled to take immediate action? My financial situation was a good example. Whenever I felt the pinch of monetary needs, instinct kicked in, urging me to invest more time and work with heightened diligence. It was as if I was caught in a perpetual dance, where temporary relief faded all too quickly. But how much of my present state of despondency could be attributed to finances alone? Life demanded more than just fiscal stability; it craved a symphony of deeper connections and profound joys. Yet when fixated on financial needs, I unknowingly neglected the other facets of a fulfilling existence. I had noticed this pattern in others as well—their passions and joys overshadowed by the relentless pursuit of monetary gain. It was a delicate balance, one that often trapped me within the confines of a circular predicament. The pressures of work and the burdens of stress drained the life from my veins, casting a shadow over the vibrant colors that once painted my world.

How I yearned for a mystical button, capable of whisking me away to a simpler time—those innocent days of childhood when worries were but fleeting whispers. I remember climbing trees, embarking on thrilling hikes, swimming through lakes of bliss, and pedaling my bike, the wind whispering secrets in my ears. Back then there was no room for disappointment or disillusionment. The world was my canvas, and I painted it with unbridled joy. Some might have argued that I could still partake in these activities, reclaiming those fragments of happiness, but would it be the same? Could I find solace in these endeavors while the weight of concerns and pressures looms overhead? The enchantment of those carefree days seemed to fade when confronted with the complexities of the present, but the allure remained, beckoning me to seek moments of unadulterated bliss once more.

Chess, that age-old game of strategy and intellect, held a special place in my heart. From a young age, it enthralled me, satisfying my craving for intellectual challenge and competition. Whether I was engrossed in a game, a lively conversation, or an intense sports match, anything that engaged my mind and kindled a competitive spirit commanded my attention. Chess was my proving ground, a place where I sharpened my skills through successes and failures, absorbing the kind of wisdom that only experience can bestow. Traditional classroom teachings seemed tepid against the fiery passion of real-life contests. With every move, I matured as a player, driven by the quest for victory and the warm embrace of success. In victory, I reveled in the process, savoring the journey that led to that triumphant moment. Chess, with all its layers, became a reflection of life's complexities. Competition, a thread that weaves through the fabric of existence, permeates our endeavors—be it in business, relationships, sports, or the game of life itself. Yet there existed stark disparities that set chess apart from the convolutions of reality. In chess the rules are crystal clear. Each piece moves with calculated precision, restricted only by its defined abilities. Life, however, dances to a different melody, its notes shrouded in ambiguity. For years I deluded myself into believing I could grasp the essence of others—know their intentions, desires, and capabilities. But how often had I been mistaken? How often had my trust been shattered by those I believed to be honorable? This begged the question: was I right in my judgment? Had these individuals truly descended from good to evil, or had my perceptions been clouded from the start? Despite the complexity of human nature, I lived by a few steadfast principles, resilient to the whims of my ignorance. The golden rule, to treat others as I want to be treated, served as my guiding light. But all too often, I stumbled in my attempts to navigate this intricate web of sincerity and deception. Who was genuine, and who was hiding behind a cloak of deception, seeking to exploit my vulnerabilities? What were the unspoken rules that governed these interactions? Was there a guidebook that I'd missed? Even if I possessed all the answers, what about the rest? Knowing someone's insincerity or intent to take advantage allowed me to safeguard myself, to steer clear of treacherous waters. But could the wicked transform into the virtuous? Could people truly change their stripes? I was yearning for answers, for a flicker of certainty within the enigma of human nature. In my quest for understanding, I sought a set of guiding principles untainted by my ignorance, rules that would guide me through life's labyrinth, enabling me to be the person I aspired to be.

Throughout my life, the dream of owning my own business had burned within me, an unwavering desire to create a space where I could manifest myself, infused with my beliefs and values. But amidst this yearning, a question lingered in the depths of my mind: could I find others who shared this fervor? And if our paths crossed, how would I recognize them? Were there distinctive qualities, unmistakable traits that distinguished the virtuous from the deceitful and the wicked? Or could darkness masquerade as light, casting an illusory glow upon the unwary?

I had stumbled upon a few guiding principles that assisted me in maneuvering through the convoluted puzzle of human nature, principles untarnished by the lingering mysteries of others. One such rule was to pay closer attention to what people did rather than what they said. Words and actions held significance, but the divide between them unveiled the naked truth—the lies concealed within the gaps. This keen observation had revealed deeper insights into the impartiality with which individuals treated others. A person's true character was revealed in their consistency, in how they treated friends and foes alike. It was a fact that those who were dishonest and deceitful would do well not to discover, for when they claimed they'd take advantage of others but never me, it was merely a matter of time before their true intentions came to light. Indeed, I had embraced a handful of rules that provided a semblance of protection, but I still bore the scars of being burned.

And what about honesty? I had often professed to friends that everyone lies—it is an inherent part of our humanity. To abstain from lying required immense energy and unwavering attention. Besides, some lies are deemed acceptable, such as expressing enjoyment over a terrible meal lovingly cooked by a friend. Why do we associate our feelings with truth and lies? Hasn't the meaning of the word "lie" been tainted by the creation of terms like "white lies," meant to shield our emotions? Among the countless words in the English language, this should have been one of the simplest to grasp. A lie, as most understand it, is a deliberate falsehood. However, we have allowed our emotions to twist its meaning, branding lies as something inherently negative. Thus, people take offense when they are labeled as liars, vehemently denying any association with deceit. I maintained that we were all liars in some capacity—we needed to lie, and we would always lie. The crux of the matter was what we chose to lie about. Though it was never my goal to eliminate lying from my life entirely, I strove to reduce its occurrence with each passing year. And yet I wondered, was this quest for utmost honesty a mistake? Did it burden me with unrealistic expectations, demanding more than I was capable of giving? Had it created a sense of entitlement, expecting others to offer more than they were able?

As I continued my journey, seeking the delicate balance between truth and deception, I found myself navigating a sea of complexities. The path to understanding others and unraveling the mysteries of human nature might never be completely illuminated, but I pressed on, seeking to uncover the truths hidden beneath the surface.

Chapter Three

THE STORY OF THE SALESMAN

AMIDST THE VIBRANT RHYTHM OF A BUSY DAY, I STEPPED INTO the Office Depot, a store filled with activity. It stood on a bustling street in Miami, surrounded by palm trees swaying in the gentle breeze. The urgency of my mission propelled me forward, feeling the relentless passage of time slipping through my fingers like grains of sand. As I entered the store, a mixture of hope and uncertainty filled my thoughts. Would I find the much-needed assistance amidst the wide array of products lining the shelves?

With anticipation shimmering in my eyes, I scanned the store, searching for a guiding presence among the aisles. The crowd hummed with energy, but my attention was captured by a salesman engrossed in conversation with another customer. Doubts crept in as I observed his divided attention, leaving me unsure if he would listen when it was my turn.

I waited for their conversation to conclude, then I approached the salesman, whose name tag identified him as Jose. With unwavering determination, I introduced myself and explained my quest for a line-sharing device capable of seamlessly integrating fax, computer, and phone calls. A subtle unease tugged at my senses as I spoke, sensing that Jose's focus might not be fully directed toward my request.

Despite Jose's polite response, my growing apprehension remained unassuaged. "No problem," he assured me, his voice carrying a hint of distraction. "Wait here. I'll be right back." With those words, he vanished into the depths of the store, leaving behind a trail of lingering doubts about whether he truly understood my needs.

As minutes slipped by, time became a precious commodity in my pursuit. Finally, Jose emerged from the aisles, a box in his hands. Holding my breath, I accepted the package, searching his face for a glimmer of reassurance. "Are you absolutely certain this part fulfills the requirements I mentioned?" I asked. Jose's reply remained resolute, reflecting the same assurance. Though uncertainty lingered, I contemplated the validity of my doubt and weighed the possibility that Jose's words held genuine truth. Guided by that flicker of hope, I decided to place my trust in Jose, completing the purchase and departing the store, ready to face the next chapter of my day.

As I drove home, a wave of curiosity consumed me, intensifying my thoughts about my suspicions regarding Jose. As soon as I entered my apartment, I put the device to the test. Alas, the device proved inadequate, failing to establish the promised connection with my computer.

Five days passed before I mustered the determination to return to the store, not due to a demanding schedule but instead to allow myself time to cool down from my mounting frustration. I recognized the fallibility of human nature, acknowledging that distractions and mistakes can happen to anyone, me included. However, when I sense an impending error, I like to believe I possess the ability to take corrective action.

I was filled with regret for not addressing my suspicions during my initial visit to the store. Had Jose been motivated solely by a desire to expedite my departure that day? Was he inattentive or perhaps even dishonest, prioritizing his own convenience over my needs? I had meticulously explained my requirements, and he had reassured me of his understanding and possession of the correct part. Now my focus extended beyond obtaining the right component. I longed for an acknowledgment of his lack of attentiveness and, perhaps even an apology.

"Do you remember me?" I asked as I approached Jose. His response was lackluster, an unconvincing mumble. I pressed on. "I'm the person you sold the computer part to last week."

"Oh yeah, how are you?" he replied, betrayed no inkling of awareness. It was time to confront him head-on.

"I find myself in a rather precarious situation. You sold me the incorrect part." As I uttered those words, I detected a subtle shift in Jose's expression. Taking deliberate steps toward me, he distanced himself from the shelves of printers that served as an inadvertent backdrop. It was as if a transformation was underway, revealing his true character.

"Okay, well, don't worry," Jose replied. "Just tell me what's wrong, and I'll help you." His words aimed to divert the focus away from any potential responsibility on his part. Unyielding in my resolve, I pressed forward, directing our attention to the item he had provided.

"Let's start with this part you sold me," I said, my tone resolute. Jose's bemused expression flickered with a hint of uncertainty, a telltale sign that he was struggling to grasp the weight I placed on the word "start." Nevertheless, I had captured his undivided attention, a stark contrast to our initial encounter.

"It falls short of communicating with my computer, yet you assured me it would fulfill all my needs."

"No, I'm sure it does exactly what I said," Jose insisted, unwavering in his stance. However, armed with the knowledge gleaned from thorough perusal of the instructions, I retrieved the manual and handed it to him. Then I directed Jose's attention to the four words I had highlighted in bold crimson: "Doesn't work with computers." My intention was to elicit a voluntary confession, hoping to witness a transformative shift in Jose's countenance and foster an authentic connection to the reality of our situation. However, as I gazed at him, a sinking feeling settled in, signaling that my hopes would remain unfulfilled. Despite my evolution away from coercion and force, I realized there was nothing left for me to do.

As I stood there confronting Jose, the air was charged with anticipation. A hushed murmur enveloped the surrounding space as other customers, intrigued by the unfolding exchange, listened in. As their eyes darted back and forth between Jose and me, I couldn't help but wonder what judgments they were passing. Did they view me as an unreasonable troublemaker, stirring up a storm over nothing?

With practiced ease, Jose attempted once again to defuse the situation. His words carried a hint of dismissal, downplaying the gravity of the matter. "Of course, I know this part well. It recognizes phone calls and fax calls. What I said was that it doesn't support computer calls. You must have misunderstood me. However, I do have the correct part and can do an exchange for you." As expected, no apology was forthcoming, and Jose stood firm, denying any wrongdoing.

Our conversation had reached an impasse, rendering further discussion fruitless. In the ensuing silence, only the necessary arrangements for the exchange remained. As I glanced around the store, a potent blend of disappointment and a burning sense of injustice weighed upon me. With the poise and determination of a protagonist exiting a pivotal scene, I turned on my heel and strode out the door, George Thorogood's "One Bourbon, One Scotch, One Beer" resonating in my mind like a captivating soundtrack. Its words and wisdom amplified my resolve as I embraced the melody leading to the climactic chorus of "and out the door I went." It was a resolute step forward, propelling me into the abyss of the unknown, prepared to face the next seemingly insurmountable challenge that lay ahead.

Just as I was about to reach the comfort of my car, a familiar figure approached, capturing my attention. It was a silent witness, one of the customers who had witnessed my confrontation with Jose. Eager to establish a connection, he commenced weaving his own tale, convinced that our stories were kindred spirits intertwining in the cosmic lattice of fate.

Intrigued, I listened attentively, my senses attuned. However, with each passing word, it became apparent that our journeys diverged into separate realms. His satisfaction stemmed from relishing in the humiliation of an employee, reveling in the perverse joy of dominance. It was a narrative alien to my reality, an incongruous tangent on the quest for truth and justice. Was it worth attempting to explain, to bridge the gap between our experiences, given the limited time we had in the parking lot? Would the man even care to know my thoughts? The weariness of unproductive encounters weighed on my spirit, and at that moment, I made a decision. I climbed into my car, the engine purring to life, and drove home.

Chapter Four

A LOOK FURTHER BACK

MANY PEOPLE BELIEVE THAT OUR PAST EXPERIENCES MOLD OUR present selves. Undoubtedly, there's some truth in this perspective. But what about my parents? How much of their history has influenced me, shaping who I am today? Surely, there's value in delving into the chronicles of the past and viewing life through the lens of retrospection. Thus, I embarked on this introspective journey not solely to unravel the mysteries of my own past but also to comprehend the complex system of human behavior that defines others. I sought to unearth how every strand of history had entwined itself into the fabric of my being, shaping who I am today. And so, I shall continue this odyssey with recollections of my father, awakening the latent recollections that reside within.

Once again, my eyes are drawn to my birth certificate, particularly to item #27: Father of Child. It reads "Robert James Mazur, White, 24 years of age, Born in New Jersey." My knowledge of my father's early years is limited, consisting mainly of snippets he's shared with us. I'm aware that his mother was of Polish descent while his Italian father remained an enigma throughout his life. In his quest to understand his past, my father unearthed the painful reality of his own father's tragic end. Only two other facets of his father's life stand out: he struggled with the shackles of alcoholism, and he was unmarried when my father was conceived.

When my father was an infant, his mother remarried, embracing the union with a Polish man, and their family flourished over the passing years, growing to seven. With his darker features, my father stood apart from his siblings, who had a lighter complexion and a distinct hue of hair. Longing to unravel the enigma of my father's life, I once approached his brother, my Uncle Frankie, hoping to initiate a conversation. I distinctly recall that day, within the sanctuary of our Liverpool home, as we passed through a sliding glass door and found ourselves nestled behind its walls, creating an intimate haven of seclusion. After a delightful family outing, the act of crossing that threshold bestowed upon us a cherished gift of seclusion and privacy where our voices could be heard in hushed tones and our thoughts could be shared without interruption. At the tender age of thirteen, my mind was brimming with curiosity, and I couldn't resist posing the question that had haunted my thoughts: "What are your thoughts on Dad being your half-brother?" I inquired, hoping to illuminate the stories that had captivated me and fueled my contemplation, yearning to uncover the truth about his secretive past.

Uncle Frankie's response was swift, shattering my assumptions. "What do you mean? Your father isn't my half-brother," he retorted. Years of tales had woven a complex story of conflicting narratives about Dad's family, leaving me uncertain about what to believe about the essence of his past. Eager for more clarity, I pressed further.

"Come on, Frankie, you and Dad look nothing alike. You know you have different fathers. Why are you deceiving me?"

"No, Danny, your dad is my true brother," he insisted, hoping to quell my doubts.

A whirlwind of thoughts ensued within me, grappling with the weight of Uncle Frankie's words. His true brother? What did he mean by that? Was he playing games with semantics? Was he implying a bond beyond biology alone? Uncertainty engulfed my mind as I strived to unravel the intricate threads of our family's tangled history.

Eventually, our conversation veered back to reminiscing about a day of bass fishing at my grandparents' camp. However, my curiosity remained fixated on uncovering more about my uncle's relationship with my father.

Just as I was about to broach the topic again, my mother entered, announcing that dinner was ready. We retreated indoors and shared a meal, after which the adults retired to the living room. As for me, I retreated to the pantry, finding a discreet spot just outside their view, where I could eavesdrop on their conversation. The exchange began with casual banter, but it wasn't long before I heard my uncle pose the question that had consumed my thoughts: "Danny mentioned that I might be your half-brother. What do you think about that?"

Silence fell upon them, a departure from the customary swift response that typically followed inquiries. Then my father's voice chimed in, deflecting the topic with an unrelated remark. I can't recall his exact words, only that he shifted the conversation away from Frankie's query. To this day I remain uncertain about what to believe, caught up in a maelstrom of unknowns.

Dark whispers of terrible deeds loomed over my father's identity. I was told that his mother concealed his existence from family and friends, shielding him behind locked doors because he was considered her illegitimate son. Poverty, too, was said to cast a dark shadow, subjecting my father to wretched living conditions and nights spent on a bed covered with nothing but newspapers as makeshift blankets. The image my father painted of his past was one of hardship and struggle.

During his high school years, it is said that my father endured a harrowing incident, pushed down a flight of concrete steps. This traumatic event led to an injury that was subsequently proclaimed to be miraculously healed through divine intervention. While this narrative was shared with me and others as a testament to embrace, I was captivated by the underlying causes behind such an occurrence, yearning to understand the root of the conflicts he encountered with his classmates.

Throughout his hospitalization, as he recovered from his injuries, my father shared accounts of profoundly haunting experiences. He spoke of finding himself amidst cadavers, their presence remaining undetected by the hospital staff for hours while he lay trapped within a body cast that rendered him completely immobile, unable to move his limbs. This harrowing narrative has become an integral part of the structure of our family's history, recounted on countless occasions, brimming with vivid depictions of the unsettling sounds of the dying and the disconcerting hisses and squeaks of rodents within the rat-infested room. It was within this crucible of adversity that my father declared himself a graduate from the school of hard knocks, the indomitable spirit within him forever marked by an enduring imprint.

While residing in Liverpool, I suffered a ligament tear in my knee during a winter skiing excursion at Labrador Mountain. As a consequence, my leg was encased in a plaster cast that extended from hip to toe for a grueling six-week period. When the doctor finally removed the cast, I was confronted with the sight of my scrawny, feeble, and odorous leg. It became immediately apparent that reclaiming its strength and simply being able to walk again would require weeks of dedicated therapy. As I contemplated the challenges of my recovery, I could only imagine the arduous process of recuperating from months spent encased in a full-body cast.

Residing on the enchanting circle of Black Oak Drive in Liverpool, a medley of memories unfurled, interweaving turbulent recollections and tranquil moments. This tableau captured the vivid remembrances of being labeled as a preacher's kid, faltering in the face of attacks and prejudice, and succumbing to moments of cowardice born out of youthful inexperience. Amidst these trials, I also embraced the cherished days of carefree bliss, where laughter filled the air as we engaged in leisurely baseball matches around the revered pinewood telephone pole that symbolized our cherished home base.

In our abode within Clairmont Park, cameras were a constant presence, reflecting my father's passion for photography in his personal and professional endeavors. The photographs that adorned our family room end table held countless memories, inviting me to piece them together like intricate jigsaw puzzles, seeking the perfect fit between the snapshots and my own recollections. Among these snapshots, the black-and-white images from earlier years served as evidence that my father had indeed relied on a cane long ago, as the story goes. The doctors had predicted he would require it until the inevitable day when walking became an insurmountable challenge. Yet in my recollections, he engaged in exercise and physical endeavors without any visible struggle. If those same doctors had witnessed his mobility later in life, how would they have reacted? Would they have deemed it a miraculous transformation? And what about the collection of canes and crutches displayed within the Phoenix church, proudly showcased upon the pulpit for all to see? What would the doctors have to say about that?

After being released from the hospital, my father embarked on a new chapter in New Jersey, working as an apprentice in an art studio. It was there that he honed his skills and gained invaluable on-the-job training, accumulating life experience along the way. Eventually, our family moved to

New York, where my father realized his dream of opening his own studio. It was known as Tri Art Studios, a name that I heard ambitious businessmen refer to when I was embarking on my own entrepreneurial journey.

In the photo albums, I stumbled upon images of a peculiar orange building, triggering memories of our earlier years in Bridgeport before our family made Liverpool our new home. Back then, at age ten, I had no inkling of the changes that awaited me, nor did I realize that the seemingly ordinary moments of everyday life were on the brink of a significant transformation. It was a time when our perspectives would shift, and the world around us would take on new meaning.

Gone were the days of carefree conversations and the cherished bonds of neighborly kinship when my mother would dispatch me to the Hoffmans' residence next door with the humble task of borrowing a pat of butter. The era of effortless communication and genuine camaraderie appeared to be slipping away, fading into the recesses of memory. Our once-cherished connection with the broader community became constricted and confined. We found ourselves retreating into a realm of exclusive camaraderie, seeking refuge and kinship solely among those who shared our beliefs—our brothers and sisters in Christ. It was a perplexing time, as these transformative experiences reshaped the lens through which I viewed the snapshots within the albums. Even the image of my youthful self, beaming with pride in my Cub Scouts uniform at Morgan Road Elementary, carried a nuanced weight, stirring reflections on the shifting landscape of our existence.

During that pivotal period, I eagerly attended regular Cub Scouts meetings at my dear friend Steve Dupe's house. His mother, a warm and dedicated figure, served as our den mother, nurturing our scouting journey with unwavering support and guidance. It was within the welcoming walls of their home that our Scouts gatherings unfolded, brimming with excitement and anticipation. I recall the exhilarating moment when our den mother unveiled the captivating project that would fuel our youthful imaginations: building cars for the upcoming Pinewood Derby, an exhilarating miniature car race to be held at my school the following month. The air buzzed with energy as we embraced the opportunity to shape our own racing marvels, each car an expression of our creativity and determination.

Filled with enthusiasm, I returned home after the meeting, excited to share the news with my father and embark on this special project together. However, my excitement quickly turned to disappointment when he replied, "Not tonight. I'm too busy." Undeterred, I continued to ask him in the days and weeks that followed, hoping for his involvement. Unfortunately, he always had an excuse, claiming to be too busy to assist me. Time slipped away, and while my friends proudly showcased their completed cars at the Scouts meetings, mine remained untouched, a constant reminder of my father's unavailability.

In an attempt to hide my disappointment, I would make excuses when asked about my progress, telling my friends that my car still needed work. Deep down I carried the weight of unfulfilled expectations, yearning for the guidance and support that I had hoped to receive from my father.

As race day drew nearer, I was in a state of desperation. I couldn't bear the thought of attending the event empty handed, watching my friends' cars zoom down the track while mine sat unfinished. Seeking a solution, I turned to my mom and shared my frustration about my father's lack of assistance. To my surprise, she took action. "Come with me," she said, her voice filled with determination.

Soon after, my excitement brimming, I descended to the basement alongside my father, clutching the car kit in my hands. With eager anticipation, I dumped the parts onto the workbench, the room filled with the intoxicating aroma of sawdust, a testament to the countless woodworking masterpieces my father had brought to life. The images from magazines that once adorned the pages were now transformed into tangible, awe-inspiring creations.

My father's discerning eyes locked onto the block of pinewood, leaving the other parts behind as he beckoned me to join him in the woodshop. With a pointing finger, he directed me to a sturdy stool, then positioned the block on the lathe, which sprang to life, spinning rapidly. With astonishing skill and unwavering precision, my father wielded an array of tools, shaping the lifeless block into a sleek and elegant racing body. The transformation was nothing short of magical, a testament to his craftsmanship. The air filled with the mesmerizing melody of sandpaper, resonating as my father's steady hand smoothed every rough edge. In awe, I watched as he applied the finishing touches, painting my name in vibrant hues across both sides of the car. The colors burst forth, infusing the vehicle with a unique identity, a vivid reflection of my own spirit.

Yet beneath the surface of this newfound beauty, a lingering sense of emptiness tugged at my heart. While my father toiled tirelessly, I had merely played the role of an observer, reading instructions aloud and offering suggestions that fell on deaf ears. My concerns and desires for a true partnership in the project were met with a dismissive wave. "Son, everything is done. The car is finished," my father declared, oblivious to the yearning within me. It was a bittersweet moment, a blend of frustration and resignation. I longed for more than just a finished car; I yearned for a genuine connection and the opportunity to learn and create alongside my father.

During those days, my sister, Debbie, and I lived under the constant shadow of punishment, perpetually aware of the looming threat of "the belt" that awaited us each week. We would giggle nervously about it, exchanging whispered jokes like "smell it" as if to alleviate the mounting tension. However, beneath the surface, the fear of its frequent occurrence remained ever present. I would scramble up the stairs, my father's belt swinging ominously, ready to strike me through the meager protection of my thin bed covers. But what right did I have to complain?

"You kids have it easy. Other parents use the buckle end of the belt!" my father would say. No blood was shed, and no bones were broken, but worse was the absence of my father's presence and companionship.

"Danny, why don't you go down to the basement and help your father in the woodshop? He'd really like that," my mother would suggest. Did she not realize the anger that would erupt, leading him to strike me? Still, I would ponder her words, yearning to please her. I made attempts to assist my father in the basement, but my presence there never endured for long.

"Stupid! I asked for a grade-four sandpaper, not a two. Give me a screwdriver, not a wrench.. . . Can't you find the quarter-inch socket wrench? You better find it if you know what's good for you.. . . You stinking kids are always meddling with my tools.. . . That's it, I'm getting the belt."

Another Saturday dawned, heralding another eagerly anticipated Cub Scouts meeting where I could proudly unveil my car to my friends. As they caught sight of it, their voices filled the room with exclamations of awe and amazement. "Wow, look at Danny's car!" they exclaimed. Curiosity sparked in their eyes as they questioned whether I had crafted it alongside my father. Their words carried a touch of disbelief, as if my creation belonged within the glossy pages of a magazine. The air crackled with excitement as everyone shared their thoughts, their voices swirling around the room. However, amidst the chorus of accolades, one voice remained notably absent—the gentle encouragement of my den mother, Mrs. Dupe. Though I couldn't comprehend the reason behind her silence, her praise soon followed, adding to the enchantment of the moment. The attention lavished upon me, coupled with my friends' admiration and amazement, created a euphoric atmosphere that filled my heart with exhilaration.

On the following Saturday, the air was filled with anticipation as my family and I embarked on a journey in our trusty station wagon. Our destination: Morgan Road Elementary

School, where the much-awaited derby awaited us. With each step through the crowded hallways, my excitement grew. Finally, we entered the gymnasium, and there it stood—the race ramp, proudly commanding center stage. Surrounding it, tables adorned with name cards beckoned us to take our places. Amidst the bustling scene, my mother handed me a bowl of her homemade potato salad and directed me to carry it to a nearby table where an array of delectable treats awaited. As the room filled with families, a feeling of anticipation settled over us.

Suddenly, an announcement resonated through the space, signaling that it was time to find our seats and settle down. The room hushed as a speech began, and my fellow Scouts and I embarked on a culinary adventure, scanning the table of food for the most mouthwatering morsels. Then we eagerly awaited the conclusion of the formalities and the beginning of the race.

Finally, the moment we had all been waiting for arrived. With a burst of enthusiasm, we rose from our seats and made our way toward the ramp. Standing tall at the top, a man dressed in the esteemed regalia of scouting, adorned with badges and patches, commanded our attention. With unwavering precision, he recited the sacred rules of the competition, his words resonating throughout the room. Meanwhile, another man selected four cars for the opening race. The tension mounted as the Scouts, their proud dens, and their supportive parents were acknowledged one by one. The countdown began, reaching its climax as the bar holding the cars in place was raised. A thunderous "Go!" reverberated through the gymnasium, accompanied by a playful squeal from the mischievous speaker system, seemingly unable to contain its excitement. The race was on.

Pedal to the metal, or rather, wheels to the wood, our meticulously crafted cars hurtled down the track, propelled solely by gravity. The seconds ticked by in a blur of exhilaration and suspense. Within the blink of an eye, a winner emerged from the frenzy, their victory announced with a chorus of applause that filled the gymnasium. The cycle continued, race after race, for a captivating thirty minutes, as the room pulsated with a symphony of cheers and gasps. And then finally, it was my turn.

"Oh great," I muttered as I witnessed my car being elevated high above the others, thrust into the radiant spotlight for all to marvel at. Its grand unveiling reverberated through the room, inducing a profound silence that seemed to be in a state of suspension, as if the air itself brimmed with heightened expectations. With a sweeping gaze, I surveyed the crowd, their eyes fixated upon me, the air thick with anticipation and electric energy. The clapping commenced, a rhythmic cadence that swelled in intensity, signaling a moment of triumph and an opportunity to shine. However, amidst the sea of applause, a tidal wave of unease crashed over me, causing me to shrink down in my seat, consumed by a sense of inadequacy. When the commanding call of "Go!" pierced the air, I closed my eyes, seeking relief in silent hopes for a fortuitous outcome.

The room fell silent. Confusion clouded my mind as I registered the absence of applause. The sudden stillness seemed to stretch on and on. Where was the missing proclamation of victory?

With a heavy sigh, I summoned the courage to open my eyes, bracing myself for the truth that awaited me. And there it was, a sight that struck at the core of my hopes and dashed them against the unforgiving reality. My car, trapped in a daunting limbo, remained suspended, halted precariously halfway down the track. The haunting words of the instructions resurfaced in my mind, their weight crashing upon me like an overwhelming wave. "Gravity/Weight. Be sure your car weighs as close to 5 oz as possible. Add weights until the car's wheels and axles reach 5 oz. Don't wait until race night to get this right. Lubrication. This is essential. Purchase a tube of graphite, and sprinkle a little in the wheel bore with the axle inserted partway."

A sense of urgency permeated the room as a concerned

trio gathered, determination etched upon their faces. The cubmaster, an unwavering pillar of support, whisked my car away to a nearby table, his hands rummaging through a box of supplies. Five minuscule lead weights were attached to my car using a strip of electrical tape, infusing the moment with a renewed sense of hope.

Once again, my car took its place among its rivals, poised for a shot at redemption. The command to "Go!" sliced through the heavy silence, accompanied by a flicker of cautious optimism. All eyes remained fixated on the track as the cars hurtled downwards. This time my car surged forward, propelled by the weights, yet despite its valiant effort, it fell agonizingly short of the elusive finish line. Frustration washed through me, threatening to extinguish the dwindling ember of hope. But fate had not yet exhausted its plans for me, insisting instead on subjecting me to further embarrassment in a third attempt, destined for failure.

Deep within my being, a quiet rebellion simmered, urging me to defy the limitations imposed upon me. When would my father truly listen? Why did I have to bear the weight of the consequences and endure the sting of humiliation on my own? At that moment, I made a silent vow to protest through my actions, choosing not to utter a single word for the remainder of the day. It was a resolute declaration, a steadfast decision that would shape the contours of future interactions.

As our car carried us home, amid the boisterous backdrop of my parents' ongoing arguments, I listened to my father's solemn vow to sever ties with our neighbors. The Pinewood Derby, recorded in the pages of our photo albums and ingrained in my memory, stood as a symbol of missed connections and unspoken desires fused within the lineage of our family. It also served as a poignant reminder of the complexities we navigate and the unspoken emotions that shape our relationships.

Chapter Five

WHEN MOM MET DAD

D URING A TRANSFORMATIVE VACATION IN 1957, MY PARENTS' DES-tinies converged at my father's aunt's idyllic camp, which was adjacent to my maternal grandfather's tranquil retreat on picturesque Oneida Lake. It was a place where nature's tranquil embrace set the stage for an undeniable connection to ignite within my father's heart. From the moment he laid eyes on Mom, he felt an unwavering certainty that she was the one he would marry. However, their love story was not without its trials, as it defied religious and denominational boundaries and challenged societal expectations.

In the early stages of their courtship, my parents encountered a tempestuous incident that cast a shadow over their blossoming relationship. A fateful encounter brought my mother face to face with the hostility of my paternal grand-mother. The atmosphere was charged with tension as accusa-tions were hurled and tempers flared. In a moment fueled by unfounded suspicion, my grandmother resorted to physical aggression, delivering a slap and even pulling my mother's hair. The hurtful words, "You're after my son's money," hung in the air, staining the memory of that day.

Weekend getaways to my grandparents' cherished camp became a treasured tradition, a respite from the monotony of everyday life. In the company of my spirited sister, Debbie, I found comfort amidst the serene surroundings. On one rainy day, after a lively game of *Candy Land* on the porch, an unexpected surprise awaited us—a snapping turtle, discov-ered by my adventurous aunt. This newfound companion injected an element of excitement and adventure into our time at the camp.

Under the sun's warm embrace, I stood in awe as my grandfather displayed his prowess in the art of horseshoe tossing. With his signature three-quarter rotation, each toss resounded with a symphony of ringing metal. The spirited competition and joyous camaraderie filled the atmosphere, planting indelible memories in our hearts.

Yet for Debbie and me, the pinnacle of exhilaration arrived when we climbed aboard my grandfather's sleek black speed-boat. As we urged him to go faster, the boat sliced through the water, propelling us forward with an electrifying force. The crashing waves and the wind tousling our hair amplified our joy, creating moments of pure exhilaration.

And who could forget those idyllic gatherings where the tantalizing aroma of barbecues filled the air? As we floated on black inner tubes, the gentle lapping of the lake's shore enticed us to unwind and bask in the tranquility of the mo-ment. These blissful encounters became an integral part of our weekends, crafting cherished memories that would for-ever hold a special place in our hearts.

During his formative years, my grandfather's educational

path took an unexpected turn when, at age twelve, he found himself in a defining moment of defiance. Fueled by a surge of indignant courage, he summoned the audacity to deliver a powerful punch to his teacher's face, an act that led to his expulsion from school. This moment of rebellion stood as a striking contrast to the image of the gentle and composed grandfather I had come to know. However, as I delved deeper into the stories and the history of the Fortino family, I realized that such bold acts were not uncommon.

Since my early days in grade school, I had the pleasure of visiting my intriguing cousins, the Fortinos, and bearing witness to the diverse personalities comprising their clan. Among them was my grandfather's brother, Uncle John, a man of influence and power as the vice president of the Syracuse Teamsters Union. His commanding presence garnered respect and admiration within our community. The Fortino lineage brimmed with individuals who defied convention and left an indelible mark that shaped our family's narrative. Uncle John resided in West Monroe with his wife and children in a house that exuded a distinct aura of unconventional charm. The entrance, adorned with blankets that served as makeshift doors, hinted at a home where rules were bent and the unexpected thrived. As I stepped inside, my senses were greeted with the earthy scent of dirt and the sight of well-worn floors, each crevice holding tales of countless footsteps and memories. Yet it was the ceiling that commanded attention—dozens of sticky pest strips, adorned with trapped flies, some still buzzing with life. It was an odd and unforgettable sight, a curious testament to the unique experiences that unfolded within those walls.

While our community busied itself with the delicate art of planting flowers and nurturing trees, a different destiny awaited my cousin's property, shrouded in tire-strewn intrigue. An unrelenting influx of discarded rubber transformed the land into a sprawling graveyard of eleven million tires, giving birth to the notorious "Fortino Tire dump," an awe-inspiring spectacle that was part of a monumental $81 million cleanup. The magnitude of this endeavor mirrored the eccentricities and audacious spirit that coursed through the veins of my extraordinary cousins.

Amidst an ordinary day within the bustling confines of a Midas auto shop, a symphony of captivating voices played in my ears, pulling me into a realm of an enchanting tale. It felt as though the universe had conspired to unveil the legends that enshrouded my larger-than-life Uncle John. With each vivid retelling, his exploits transcended the boundaries of ordinary existence, acquiring an otherworldly aura. And then, like a thunderclap in the wind, a voice carried a tale of unimaginable proportions, a story in which Uncle John, propelled by his indomitable spirit, unleashed a resounding punch upon a horse, toppling the majestic creature. The audacity of such an act seized my imagination, leaving me spellbound with awe.

As the intoxicating narrative wove through my mind, a flood of memories surged forth, unveiling a series of captivating images that mirrored the tale being spun. Within the hallowed pages of my family's treasured photo albums, amidst the sepia-toned snapshots frozen in time, I discovered a gem—a mesmerizing image encapsulating the essence of my revered grandfather and his mischievous brother, Uncle John. Their youthful countenances radiated with gleeful defiance, captured in a moment where they stood side by side, fists clenched, poised for a playful duel. It was a photograph that transcended mere paper and ink, pulsating with the indomitable spirit coursing through their veins—a visual testament to their unyielding resilience and untamed vigor.

At that stirring juncture, I found myself spellbound by the vista of fortitude and determination that portrayed the landscape of my lineage. It was a pattern that extended far beyond the confines of the Fortino family, intertwining with the storied legacy of the Ragonese clan. The tales of my grandmother's brother, Uncle Joe Ragonese, reverberated through the generations as well. His hands, mighty in their Herculean proportions, spoke of a toughness forged through heredity and the crucible of hardships endured. Amidst the trials and tribulations, our familial gatherings resounded with a symphony of laughter—a vibrant testament to the boundless joy that permeated those cherished moments. I hold dear the vivid memories of my grandmother, whose hands, much like her brother's, were remarkably large. They were a source of endless mirth and joy, their presence bringing laughter not only within the walls of our home but also within the hallowed halls of our church. Watching her shake hands with fellow congregants after Sunday service, her hands dwarfing theirs in a comical juxtaposition, evoked hearty chuckles and contagious smiles.

Amidst our family gatherings, my grandfather's mischievous spirit took center stage, enchanting us with his playful nature and clever tricks. With a mischievous glint in his eye, he would beckon us to place our fingers between his, promising an unforgettable experience. "Put your fingers in here, between mine," he would say, his voice filled with delight. Like clockwork, year after year, the same words and the same stories flowed from his lips, yet our laughter would erupt as if hearing them for the very first time. It was a testament to the timeless magic he possessed, the ability to infuse each moment with contagious joy.

LIVING WITH MY GRANDPARENTS

MY PARENTS GOT MARRIED IN THE SUMMER OF 1958 WHEN MY father was twenty and my mother was seventeen. While looking through the photo album, I discovered snapshots from their wedding day. The ceremony took place at the Presbyterian church on the west side of the city— the same church I attended when living in Bridgeport. At that time they were residing in my father's hometown in New Jersey, where my sister Debbie was born. However, it wasn't long before my mother returned to Syracuse, this time with my father, to live with her parents on East Division Street. To support his family, my father resorted to knocking on doors and selling family portraits until he secured employment as a commercial artist.

East Division Street held a certain fascination for me. It was an interesting road, built on a hill and paved with red bricks. At its highest point stood a lengthy wall, crafted from an abundance of stones. Until age six, I never had the opportunity to explore the expanse of the wall, from beginning to end.

Much like the profusion of stones, my questions were building. Today, the situation remains unchanged. My inquiries are countless. I contemplate their origin and the resolutions that elude me. They have amassed, forming a stockpile of questions that trace back to the early days when I walked hand in hand with my grandmother along the brick-covered road, passing by the stone wall. What mysteries lay beyond its confines? How was it constructed? And why did our house appear more sizable on the lower side of the hill? The queries endure, their complexity deepening with the passage of time.

Debbie and I often spent our afternoons playing in the back-yard. One day as I stood near the swing set, Debbie dashed to-ward me, her arms flailing. Unfortunately, she failed to notice the chains of a swing in her path and collided with them head on. She became entangled in a perilous position, her neck en-snared. Panic set in as she struggled to free herself, only making matters worse. Amidst the chaos and the clamor, my moth-er emerged onto the back porch, quickly assessing the scene before rushing to help. I stood there as a mere observer, watch-ing as she untangled Debbie from the chains' grip. As Debbie caught her breath, her pallor returned to a healthy hue. That day was a moment of sheer madness, the day when we were instructed never to run in the backyard again.

Near the swing were clusters of grapes, their vines wrapped around stakes. Most of my cousins had a similar setup in their yards, small versions of the vineyard from the farm where they grew up. They had worked hard on the fields of that farm on Buckley Road since they were kids, but that didn't stop them from having their own gardens. They loved growing vegetables and boasted about them to their friends. It was a topic that often sparked conversations.

Grandma kept some of her tomatoes on the windowsill in her kitchen, allowing them to bask in the sunlight and ripen to perfection. I always cherished her enthusiasm when I mentioned them. "Hey, Grandma, how did your vegetables get so big this year? What's your secret?" I would inquire with anticipation. Her eyes would light up in response.

"Oh, have you seen how beautiful they are? I bought two dozen young plants from Hafner's in June. They're a special kind. Remember how many tomatoes we had last year? I'll make sure to tie them up nicely this time, so they don't go bad."

My grandparents, along with their numerous siblings, all shared an unwavering passion for gardening. "Hey, Gert, isn't the weather gorgeous today? How are your peppers doing? Ours are bigger than ever!"

Grandma would make her way into the kitchen, bustling with enthusiasm, and extend her hand over the sink to gather some samples. "I know what you mean. Look at how beautiful these are! Here, give one a squeeze. See how juicy it is?" A mere glance into their eyes revealed the profound commitment and dedication they held for their gardens. It was an extraordinary bond, a shared love for nurturing nature's bountiful gifts, and it held a special place in their hearts.

During the summer, I often found myself in the fields alongside my family, immersed in the task of picking fresh vegetables. "Don, I'm sorry, but I can't play today. I have to go pick beans. You want to join me?"

As September drew to a close, I would step off the bus and within moments find myself in our basement. Meanwhile, Grandma could be found in the kitchen. Her hair would be set in curlers, her hands diving deep into various sauces and concoctions. The enticing aroma would greet me even before I entered the house, a familiar and comforting scent.

The kitchen would be a scene of bustling activity, with pots scattered across the stove and my mother stirring their contents with a large wooden spoon. Rows of empty jars would be waiting their turn, arranged on newspapers and ready to be filled with the bountiful fruits of their labor. Soon enough those same jars would be transformed into vessels of delicious preserves, sealed with a protective layer of wax and then stored in our basement. In the early mornings, before heading off to school, I would make my way to that room, seeking the perfect topping for my toast. "Let's see, I had marmalade yesterday and raspberry before that. Ah, the strawberry jam looks tempting!" With eagerness in my heart, I would ascend the stairs, skipping every third step as if it were an unspoken ritual. There, standing at the sink, my butterknife would lift the coating of wax, revealing the delectable treasure within that would soon grace my breakfast toast.

A hearty appetite ran through my family. Leftovers were a rare sight in our home, not because my mother cooked too sparingly but because we had an insatiable habit of devouring everything in sight. Sweets were no exception—they vanished as soon as my mother brought them home. The moment those desserts, snacks, and juices found their place in the refrigerator and cabinets, they were raided with gusto, disappearing into our eager mouths. It didn't matter how many bags of groceries my mother walked in with; they were no match for our voracious appetites.

Within our food-loving clan, my grandfather reigned supreme. A loaf of Italian bread, sliced down the middle and filled with an assortment of mouthwatering meats—ham, salami, cheese—and delectable toppings was merely an appetizer for him, a mere tease to hold him over until dinner time. His appetite knew no bounds, and he relished every bite.

As I shift my focus back to my grandparents' home on East Division Street, memories come flooding back. We would enter through the rear entrance, positioned at the end of the driveway, which led to a porch-like area. That cozy space had one door opening to the outside world and another connecting to the kitchen, the heart of our family gatherings. I can still see that small, empty room, a place I frequented long before my father's spiritual transformation, back when I first began attending Sunday services at the Presbyterian church with my mother, aunt, and grandparents.

Within that kitchen, my mother and aunt engaged in a game that challenged their beliefs. Seated at the table, they would face each other, taking turns asking questions. However, it wasn't a dialogue between them; rather, they sought answers from a spirit using an Ouija board. The words were spelled out beneath the glass planchette. As Christians, I never quite understood why they dabbled in such practices, but I suppose their curiosity got the better of them. The words would spell out beneath the glass planchette, and the answers arrived swiftly, captivating their attention. On one occasion they even dared to ask the spirit to predict the fate of someone they knew. Weeks later the atmosphere turned eerie when the prediction came true—a foretelling of a tragic accident resulting in death. Despite their fascination with horror movies and supernatural tales, my mom and my aunt were genuinely spooked by this revelation. After that unnerving experience, their experimentation with spirit communication ceased, halted by the unannounced arrival of my Uncle Joe. Upon discovering their involvement, he erupted in anger, reprimanding them and tearing the Ouija board apart, putting an end to their mystical pursuits.

And then there's the painful memory of my father tearing a patch of skin from my neck using a pair of needle-nose pliers. I was sitting in my mother's lap, getting dressed in warm clothes, when the zipper of my sweater caught the delicate skin at my throat. My mother's screams urged my father to react swiftly. He fetched his toolbox and grabbed the pliers to free the zipper from my tender flesh. The incident resulted in a scar that I often jokingly refer to as the result of a tracheotomy performed with a pencil.

Apparently, crying was a skill I excelled at during those times. When these memories resurface, I am reminded of the immense stress my father faced when he left his job in New Jersey. They claim that it didn't help matters that "Danny cried every day for the entire first year of his life."

"You were driving your father crazy," they would say. If only I could replace these memories with the comforting and soothing sounds of the cuckoo clock in my grandparents' home or the gentle lull of my grandfather's snoring.

Chapter Seven

LIFE IN BRIDGEPORT

Aᴼᴼᴼ

FTER LIVING WITH MY GRANDPARENTS, MY PARENTS RELOCATED to an apartment on Prospect Avenue. Shortly thereafter, they purchased a one-story home in Bridgeport, the place of my birth. Our new house had three bedrooms. Mine was situated at the far end of the hallway, the farthest from the living room. Unlike their previous homes, this one had something different: a garage with a doorway that connected it to the kitchen.

During that period, Debbie and I had a favorite game called "Tip It." It involved balancing a plastic clown on its nose atop a pole with its feet wobbling in the air. The objective was to add weight around the clown without toppling it. Something else I enjoyed was our Spirograph set, which allowed me to create colorful geometric patterns reminiscent of paisley shirts and the lava lamp in our living room. I would spend hours drawing these intricate designs on paper.

Apart from toys and crafts, Debbie and I had our own unique style of "shopping." Alongside some of our neighborhood friends, we would go door to door, knocking and saying in unison, "Trick or treat, smell our feet, may we pick your garbage?" This idea originated from Debbie shortly after Halloween. If granted permission, we would rummage through people's garbage in their backyards, garages, kitchens, or anywhere we suspected we might find discarded valuables.

While my dad took numerous pictures of us during our time in Bridgeport, there was one memorable moment that he failed to capture. Photography was part of his profession. However, when it came to taking our family pictures, my mom usually hired another photographer. One day she dressed me up in a black-and-white suit with checkered shorts and knee-high socks for a solo picture. I was positioned on a dresser covered with a white cloth in the hallway of our home. Following the photographer's instructions, I posed, and the moment was captured to be cherished in the future. Interestingly enough, in real life, I didn't appear as innocent as I may have seemed in the photograph. Years later, holding a plastic trash bag filled with my clothes, I took one last evocative look at that picture on the hallway wall, a final day with my family before I was told to leave.

One day while returning from the grocery store, where I ate my animal crackers while my mother shopped, I was sitting in the back of our Volkswagen Beetle next to Debbie. After pulling into the driveway, the car came to a stop, and my mother put it in park, intending to walk to the house with the groceries. I was seated at the door closest to our home. Instead of opening her own door, Debbie wanted to follow me out of mine. I held it open for her, but in my haste to shut it, I failed to move my other hand out of the way. "Ahhhhhhh! My thumb, my thumb!" I cried.

My mother rushed to my side, lifted my hand, and saw the twisted skin with blood dripping onto the driveway. She became frantic, which only intensified my fear. "Oh my God, what happened? What did you do?" Thinking I was in trouble, I pointed at my sister.

"Debbie slammed the door on my finger!" Debbie's face lit up, and she desperately tried to set the record straight.

"I did not! I didn't do that!" she cried. However, her protest was disregarded, not just for that day but any subsequent time she attempted to explain that it wasn't her fault. At the moment, my mom simply frowned and redirected her attention toward me. Fortunately, our neighbor, who was a nurse and a friend of my mother's, overheard the commotion and rushed to our aid. She joined us in our kitchen and squeezed my hand over the sink, allowing cold running water to mix with the blood from my finger. A burning sensation set in as my mother and our neighbor alternated pouring hydrogen peroxide over my wound. After drying my hand and wrapping it in a clean white towel, I was sent to my room to rest.

Later, I visited our family doctor. Within a day or two, I was on a stretcher, being wheeled down a hospital hallway. I was taken to a room where a nurse asked me some questions. Afterward, they placed me on the stretcher and wheeled me to another room where my thumbnail was to be surgically removed. I was given anesthesia, and I slipped into unconsciousness.

When I awoke, I was back on the stretcher with my grandmother by my side, her hand comforting me as we made our way back to my room. As I tried to regain my bearings, a question nagged at me. "Is that what it feels like when you die?" I asked, referring to my experience under anesthesia.

"Just relax, Danny," my grandmother replied. "Everything's okay." I already knew how adults behaved when they didn't take kids seriously. It was one of those moments where it felt like I was being dismissed.

Later, after my family departed, a nurse entered my room,

and I posed the same question to her. She smiled kindly, but she didn't give much weight to my query either.

On Sunday mornings, Mom would style her hair into a beehive and dress Debbie and me for church. While Dad was engrossed in hunting, fishing, working, or reading the newspaper at home, Mom would drive us to the Presbyterian church on the west side of the city. Situated near the hill by Columbus Bakery, that church was where my parents tied the knot and where my mother attended services with her parents and sister for many years.

Typically, I would sit with my maternal grandparents. The service commenced with singing old songs. In the rack built into the back of the pew in front of us, there were always two items: a hymn book and a Bible. While my grandfather knew the words to all the songs, he would open the hymn book, hold it in front of me with one hand, and point to each word as we stood to sing. My grandfather's voice was resonant, masculine, steady, and in tune, while my grandmother's was high-pitched and crackly.

When we sat and listened to the sermons, the Bible would be placed in front of me, and my grandfather's large left hand, with its overstretched watch band, would move from left to right as he pointed to the words being spoken. Sometimes when I started to doze off, my grandpa would set the Bible aside and allow me to rest my head in his lap.

Once I reached an appropriate age, I joined Sunday school with other children in the church's basement classrooms. My teacher was Aunt Rosalynn, who was married to one of my grandmother's brothers. In our classroom the older kids would occasionally engage in role playing, teaching us how to discuss God with our school friends and invite them to church. If it happened to be someone's birthday, Aunt Rosalynn would pin a special emblem on the child's shirt after the class sang the birthday song. The song went like this: "Happy Birthday to you, may you feel Jesus near every day of the year, happy birthday to you . . ."

On my birthday, another boy and I were celebrating. He went first, and Aunt Rosalynn pinned the special token to his shirt. I noticed he already had another special emblem above his short-sleeved shirt pocket. When it was my turn, I voiced my concern to Aunt Rosalynn. "That's not fair! Eddie has two pins, and I only have one." Without saying a word, she handed me an additional emblem.

"Hey, how come Danny gets two?" Eddie protested. "I only got one, and the other one is from last year." It hadn't occurred to me at the time, but no further comments were made, and I kept my two tokens.

My experience with Eddie in Sunday school brings to mind other occasions when I perceived things differently from my friends. In the fall of 1969, I attended Wetzel Road Elementary School. During lunch breaks, I'd sit with my classmates in the cafeteria, overseen by Mrs. White, my fifth-grade art teacher, who also acted as the lunch monitor. My once-beloved *Lost in Space* lunchbox had fallen out of fashion. So, like many of my classmates, I had my mom pack my lunch in a brown paper bag. On the days she didn't rise early enough, I was faced with two options: make my own lunch or sift through my mother's purse in the closet, looking for change to cover the thirty-five cents for the school meal, all the while being careful to not make her coin stash look noticeably depleted. I especially loved putting my own lunch together after we'd had eggplant parmesan the previous night. My mom often made extra, leaving leftovers wrapped in foil inside the refrigerator. The next morning, I'd layer slices of eggplant between pieces of homemade bread, if we had some—one serving for breakfast and two more for lunch. The first time my friends caught a glimpse of my unique sandwich, they burst into laughter, finding it strange and unappetizing. However, Mrs. White didn't ridicule my eggplant creation. Instead of mocking it, she asked to try it. After her first bite, her face beamed with pleasure, leading me to promise her an extra sandwich whenever we had eggplant parmesan at home. I kept my word, and we shared many delightful eggplant sandwich moments together.

Earlier that year, Mrs. White had assigned us the task of asking our fathers about their professions and sharing them with the class. During dinner one evening, I posed the question to my father. Initially, he instructed me to tell my teacher that he was a businessman. But after a moment's reflection, he amended his statement, saying, "No, tell her I am a successful businessman." So, when my turn came, I confidently announced, "My Dad isn't just a businessman; he's a successful businessman."

A memory from Mrs. White's class involves a kite I built using construction paper and straws. Despite my efforts, it failed to take flight after I attached it to a ball of my mother's yarn. I also crafted a clay ashtray, colored it, and baked it in a pottery kiln as a gift for my father, despite his non-smoking habits. I held great affection for Mrs. White and enjoyed all the activities in her art class.

That gives a glimpse into my days within the walls of my elementary school classroom and the bustling cafeteria. These memories are still vibrant—from the sound of the bell releasing my friends to play outside to the brief moment of pause before I stood from my chair, tuning out the surrounding noise, and capturing my thoughts and observations like snapshots in a mental photo album for later reflection.

LIVING IN LIVERPOOL

NOT LONG AFTER I CRUSHED MY THUMB IN THE VOLKSWAGEN door, we relocated from Bridgeport to Liverpool. I recall sitting in the living room of our new Liverpool home, soaking my injured thumb in a solution while watching TV. It provided the perfect excuse to escape after-dinner chores and immerse myself in the latest episodes of *Star Trek*. Night after night, I'd lie on the carpet, chin resting in my hands. Engrossed in the show, I'd tune out everything else around me. The episodes evoked profound thoughts and reflections within me. Despite these inner musings, however, I grappled with the limitations of self-expression, forever seeking the best way to convey the depth of my thoughts to the outside world.

Our new house in Liverpool was more spacious than our previous home in Bridgeport. Not only did it have a garage and a main entrance, it also boasted a second floor and a basement. When we settled in, only a handful of homes in the neighborhood were occupied, the rest of the lots either vacant or still under construction. Adjacent to our house on Black Oak Drive was Glencrest Road, leading to the entrance of Clairmont Park on John Glenn Boulevard. From our living room window, I didn't just see a street circle; I imagined a baseball park, a place where I would meet and play with friends.

One day, from the safety of our garage, I watched a boy and his father playing catch in their front yard. Their camaraderie intrigued me; they seemed more like friends than family. I shared this observation with my mother, and soon after I asked her for a glove, so I could experience the same with my father. On a trip to the nearby Kmart, I chanced upon a left-handed baseball glove, the last of its kind. After some persuasion, my mother agreed to buy it for me. The final step was to coax my father into a game of catch. Although my memory of how I persuaded him is hazy, he did consent, if only for a day. Regardless, I wasn't too fazed. After all, there was a whole new neighborhood out there, teeming with adventures.

Another day with my mother at Kmart led to the purchase of my first full-size bicycle. Free from training wheels, my bike became a vessel for exploration and freedom. Each year I would eagerly rediscover it with a fresh coat of paint and various new accessories, such as a headlight, taillight, speedometer, and other trinkets procured from the store. My imagination ran wild with dreams of embarking on epic bike trips, exploring the corners of my neighborhood, and gradually expanding the boundaries of my travels. Eventually, I even ventured as far as Henderson Harbor, which was fifty miles away. However, during the early days in Liverpool, my biking adventures were confined to the neighborhood until I negotiated with my parents and gained the liberty to explore wherever I pleased. My bike became a source of pure happiness, whether it was cruising to Wegmans grocery store to indulge in candy and cookies or utilizing it as a delightful alternative to riding the bus to school.

Sunday mornings were a sacred routine, beginning with a trip to church, the service commencing 10:00 a.m. As much as I relished the anticipation of post-church playtime, the clock's hands seemed determined to sprint ahead. While my neighborhood companions lingered in the realm of endless games, I reluctantly bid them farewell, destined to return home to prepare for the evening service, which commenced at 7:30. Suppressing any complaints that threatened to escape my lips, a hidden yearning brewed within me, a longing to frolic, lost in the kaleidoscope of joy with my cherished friends.

On one memorable Sunday afternoon, my neighbor Greg arrived in the circle carrying bats and baseballs, attracting others in the neighborhood to join him. Greg and I were already best friends, having spent countless hours together playing with Matchbox cars and exchanging stories in his house. This time, however, our playtime took a new turn as we organized a baseball game with the other neighborhood kids, right in the midst of the circle. Greg designated the telephone pole as home plate and a nearby rock as second base.

"Cool, Greg," I exclaimed. "Let's play!"

After parking my bike in the garage, I returned to the circle. Greg and I took turns selecting teammates, and that day marked the beginning of many games in our impromptu baseball park.

During one of our play sessions at Greg's house, while engrossed in a friendly argument over a baseball card trade, Greg decided to introduce me to a word he deemed really bad. "Hey Danny, I learned a really bad word. Wanna know what it is?" Greg said, then he cautioned me. "I'll tell you, but you gotta promise not to say it. It's worse than 'shit' and 'ass,' and if my father hears me say it, he'll kick my ass from here to the circle!" Lured by the forbidden, I assured him I wouldn't say it. With an air of mischief, Greg finally disclosed his secret.

"Okay, the word is 'fuck.'" To my surprise, it didn't sound as grotesque as I had anticipated. Naturally, I began exclaiming the word repeatedly at the top of my voice, much to Greg's amusement, followed by subsequent pleas for me to stop.

Weekends and after-school hours in the circle were dominated by games—be it baseball, kickball, or simpler ones like "tag." One day after school when we had organized a baseball game with friends from the neighborhood, a peculiar kid arrived on his bike. Unlike the popular bikes with banana seats and "sissy bars" that many kids flaunted, his was a three-speed, which many of us considered nerdy. He pedaled leisurely, head held high, circling around and watching us play. Simply put, he was noticeably different.

Feeling a sense of unease and realizing that ignoring him wasn't the right approach, I felt compelled to say something. Rather than being kind or understanding, though, I surrendered to the pressure to fit in and made derogatory comments about the boy and his bike. I called him a sissy and mocked his geeky bicycle, and my friends in the circle followed suit, joining in the laughter and adding their own derogatory comments. Strangely, none of our words seemed to affect him. He continued pedaling at the same slow pace, circling us as he watched with unwavering composure. His indifference bothered me, so I intensified my taunts, hoping to provoke a reaction, but he remained unfazed.

Days turned into weeks, and the boy continued to be a familiar presence during our playtime in the circle. He would ride his bike around us, observing our activities without joining in. His stoic presence intrigued me, and I couldn't help but wonder why my harsh words didn't seem to bother him. As time went on, I realized that my initial impression of him as being different wasn't entirely accurate. He was simply a boy with his own unique interests and preferences.

Then one day something unexpected happened. The boy decided to break away from his usual routine. He dismounted his bike and walked it into the circle, heading directly toward me as I stood at home plate. It was as if he wanted to establish a connection with me.

"Hi, my name is Donald," he said in a friendly tone. I couldn't help but find his approach a little strange. Among us kids, we didn't typically engage in such polite conversations. If he wanted to play ball, why didn't he just ask? However, I soon realized that playing ball wasn't his intention. Donald had his own ideas of fun, which differed from mine and those of my friends.

"I bet you can't climb that cable to the top of the pole," he said, referring to the heavy-gauge cable known as the "guy wire" that secured the utility pole to the ground. Was this kid challenging me, thinking he was better than me at something? Moreover, he said it right in front of my friends.

"Sure, I can," I replied, feeling a mixture of curiosity and competitiveness.

Without a moment's hesitation, Donald embarked on his daring ascent up the cable. It was a mesmerizing spectacle as he hung upside down, defying gravity with his remarkable co-ordination of hands and feet. With each fluid movement, he approached the pinnacle of the pole. Once he reached the summit, he descended, once again showcasing his incredible abilities. I stood there, speechless. How was it possible? It was a display of skill that I knew I could never hope to replicate, and I didn't even dare to attempt it. A mixture of emotions swept through me as I grappled with the awe-inspiring scene.

Baseball had always been my realm, where I found comfort and excelled among my friends, but Donald had shattered that familiar zone, pulling me into uncharted territory. It was an uncomfortable feeling, but deep down, I was intrigued by his unique talents. His extraordinary feat left me with a burning curiosity, a desire to know more about this enigmatic boy.

I never understood why Donald approached me that day or why he wanted to hang out with me. After all, I was the one who had mocked him and influenced others to do the same. Everything changed for me after that moment. I relinquished my place in the baseball circle and embraced the new experiences that Donald introduced me to—activities I would have never envisioned on my own and that none of the kids I knew were engaged in.

Donald revealed hidden trails in the woods, underground tunnels, and trees to climb and traverse. He also led me to conquer water towers and explore a magnificent tree fort where we could gaze upon all of Liverpool. The adventures seemed endless. The time I spent with Donald surpassed the days confined within our circle, which now appeared monotonous to me. He showed me a world of fun and excitement that I had never known existed.

In the years that followed our initial encounter, Donald and I became inseparable. He cherished the additional thrill my personality brought to our escapades. Together, we embarked on countless adventures, discovering new realms of enjoyment and forging an unbreakable bond.

My younger years were a mixture of fun and trouble. As I grew older, I carried a persistent sense of guilt for causing Don trouble and would apologize to him for my past behavior. However, every time I did, he would remind me of the wild and exhilarating adventures we embarked on, which made our times together so incredibly enjoyable. Many of the games we played were my ideas, such as "Don't Break the Ice," a winter game we would play at the creek, where the consequence of losing was a frigid water-filled boot, or the "Chips Ahoy Cookie Contest," where we would catapult cookies like miniature Frisbees high into the air, watching them descend like delicious bombs as shoppers exited the front of Wegmans grocery store. My ideas ranged from innocent and playful to those that had more significant consequences, often impacting Don more than me.

During our phase of prank phone calls, we would gather in the basement of my house with the family's orange rotary phone in front of us, taking turns making calls. When it was my turn, I would dial random numbers and say the most profane things I could think of. The winner of our "contest" was determined by who could upset the person on the other end of the line the most, and I was determined to win. Don would listen in, his ear close to mine, eagerly awaiting the responses from unsuspecting individuals, often housewives.

As time went on, I grew bored and wanted to make the game more interesting. That's when I had a brilliant idea. "Okay, Don, let's do this again. I'll dial a number at random— oh wait, someone answered the phone!" Don grabbed the phone, a mischievous smile on his face, and proceeded to say every obscene thing he could think of. He went on and on, struggling to hold back his laughter as he delivered his lines. And then, the moment we had anxiously awaited arrived— the response from the person on the other end of the line.

"Donald, is that you?"

Don's face turned bright red as he dropped the phone and turned to me with a bewildered look. He couldn't believe what had just happened. I couldn't contain my laughter, and I dropped to the floor, pounding it with my fists. The sight of his face confirmed that his worst nightmare had come true—I had dialed his mother!

Despite the consequences, Don forgave me, and a week later, we resumed our prank calls. It was a time when I deceived him into repeating the same mistake, a final mistake where no excuse could convince his mother that he wasn't the one making the prank calls. I reveled in the satisfaction of considering myself the winner of our twisted contest.

In sixth grade, I underwent a significant transition when I was withdrawn from the public school system. During that time, I aimed to navigate familial issues and align with family expectations and religious beliefs by fabricating stories. These stories, which included tales of mistreatment and bullying by my peers and teachers, were my way of trying to fit in and make sense of the confusion in my family life. Reflecting on those turbulent times, I realize that my sixth-grade year had been characterized by a lack of emotional and physical resilience. This lack impacted my ability to confront the challenges I faced, leading to my creation of stories as a way to cope with the overwhelming sense of unfairness I perceived.

The tales I spun harmonized all too well with the narrative that had been ingrained in me. The weekly church meetings I attended, where discussions of the world's hate and wickedness were commonplace, only served to reinforce the beliefs that had taken hold of my young mind. The public school system became a symbolic embodiment of these perceived evils, further validating the notion that my fabricated stories were an accurate reflection of reality. As a result, midway through the school year, I was removed from public school and enrolled in a private institution called Faith Heritage.

However, my struggles and challenges persisted even in this new school, and I found myself unable to endure beyond the completion of eighth grade.

My final year at the Christian school also left its mark. During that time I confided in Don, expressing my anxieties about the upcoming transition back into the public school system for high school. I revealed my desperate plan to conceal a knife in my shoe, a misguided attempt to defend myself if confronted. Don struggled to grasp the depth of my fears, and his response felt dismissive, as if my concerns were unwarranted. It is remarkable and unsettling to consider how deeply held beliefs shaped my perception of the world around me. In truth, I never encountered any significant issues with my peers within the public school system.

That marked the extent of the challenges I faced during my school days, aside from the significant setback of my academic performance. My mother scrutinized my report cards, using them as a measuring stick to determine if my grades warranted punishment from my father. However, as I entered high school, my parents appeared increasingly indifferent to my grades, only showing concern when I found myself in other types of trouble. Unfortunately, I struggled academically and graduated at the bottom of my class. Despite my lackluster grades, my mother found some semblance of satisfaction in the fact that I had completed high school. During a dinner at my grandparents' house, she gathered the courage to propose that my father join us in celebrating at the graduation ceremony held in the civic center downtown. However, my father dismissed the idea with a cutting remark, saying, "Danny never cared about going to school, so why should I care about going to his graduation?" It was bewildering to hear him speak as if I should have cared about school, especially considering the teachings I had received about its perceived evils. His refusal to support me not only played a significant role in my disinterest in education but also stood in stark contradiction to the lessons he had imparted to me, leaving an indelible mark on my psyche that I pondered whenever I was in his presence.

Although my school days failed to lay a solid groundwork for future success, I did find solace in occasional moments of enjoyment. Don, unlike the born-again Christian friends from my church whom my parents endorsed, was the one true friend I was allowed to have. However, despite his significance in my life, there were instances when I experienced disappointments with him. He had a circle of friends beyond our bond, and at times I couldn't help but resent him for leaving me behind, trapped in the depths of loneliness. It was during those moments that I reluctantly accepted my solitary existence as my only choice.

Chapter Nine

GOOD TIMES TOGETHER

IN THE LATE 1970S, DURING MY LATER YEARS OF HIGH SCHOOL, MY aunt's home in Liverpool transformed into a cherished haven for our family during beloved holidays like Christmas and Thanksgiving. It was a time when my aunt, accompanied by her husband, Gary, warmly opened their doors to us, enveloping the space with boundless joy and celebration. These festive occasions brought my mother, grandmother, and aunt together, their culinary talents harmonizing to create delectable feasts that would tantalize and satiate our taste buds. The gathering extended beyond our immediate family, as invitations were extended to fellow church members, fostering connections and nurturing a shared sense of delight and unity during the festive seasons.

As we gathered around the dinner table, a vibrant spectrum of discussions would bloom. The topics were as diverse as the dishes spread before us, encompassing everything from animated talks about the day's sermon to lively exchanges about seasonal activities. Laughter and chatter filled the air as we savored not only the delicious food but also the shared moments of connection and belonging.

Once the satisfying meal had come to a close, the men would loosen their belts and relax in the comforting embrace of their favorite spots in front of the television. Meanwhile, the women would take charge, clearing the tables with practiced efficiency and immersing themselves in the intimate conversations that flowed naturally in the kitchen. It was during these post-dinner moments that new bonds were formed and stories were shared, creating memories that would endure long after the last dish had been washed.

These gatherings in Liverpool symbolized more than just a coming together of family; they represented the essence of love, togetherness, and the power of shared traditions. It was a time when the boundaries of age and generation were blurred, and the universal language of celebration united us all.

As the day progressed, we would gather in the living room, drawn together by the soul-stirring melodies of my mother's organ playing, accompanied by the gentle strumming of my grandfather's mandolin. The room would come alive with unified voices, harmonizing as they sang familiar hymns and songs, enveloping us in a transcendence. As the final notes of melodic worship faded away, a restlessness would enter through the room, stirring the spirits of my siblings and me. It was during this bittersweet moment that my mother, with a touch of regret, would suggest that it was time for us to bid farewell.

It was precisely at this juncture, as our departure loomed, that we would conjure the courage to voice our most fervent desires. With hopeful anticipation, we would entreat our beloved aunt and uncle for permission to extend our visit, pleading to spend the night and linger a little longer in their company. We cherished every moment spent within the walls of their home, where laughter cascaded like a bubbling stream, and joy reverberated through every room.

Uncle Gary possessed a magnetism that captivated our entire family, but it was my father who felt an inexplicable affinity for him, forged through the most unlikely of connections. In a twist of fate that piqued my curiosity, there was a time when my father, unaware of Gary's good qualities, harbored reservations about him and a desire to distance himself from this unfamiliar figure. Their paths intersected when rumors began to circulate about my aunt's courtship with Gary, a man who did not share the same allegiance to the Living Word Church that my family held dear. Motivated by his unwavering devotion and the ever-evolving principles of his faith, my father felt a deep-seated compulsion to go beyond mere caution and instead implored my aunt with persistent fervor to sever ties with Gary.

However, their connection defied the limits of my father's counsel, submerging him in a profound and anguishing quandary. How would the union between a devout believer and someone labeled as "unsaved" interlace with the intricate pattern of our Christian family and the cherished sacred community? The sermons my father passionately delivered and the teachings that vibrated through the congregation emphasized the unwavering directive to distance ourselves from those outside the fold. These steadfast convictions had been ingrained into our being, and now my father was grappling with the weight of his own self-proclaimed beliefs.

In the midst of this swirling tempest of conflicting emotions, the resolution to my father's quandary remained elusive, concealed within the haze of uncertainty. The answer, like a fleeting specter, evaded his grasp for an extended period. What course of action would he ultimately choose? How could he reconcile his unwavering belief in the necessity of separating from sinners with the intricacies of the bond forming between Gary and our family? These questions danced like ethereal wisps, tantalizing yet elusive, urging my father to seek solace, clarity, and divine illumination as he navigated this uncharted path.

In a fateful twist of events, my father defied his own disapproval and made a decision that left me utterly astonished—he chose to attend their wedding. The reception that followed was infused with an electric sense of anticipation and curiosity, almost as if we were all in a collective standstill, eagerly awaiting my father's ensuing move. It was a moment charged with tension and possibility, where the trajectory of our family's dynamics hung in the balance.

With a voice that carried the weight of profound relief and reconciliation, my father approached Gary. An intense quietude filled the room, as my father's words bore a significance that resonated with each one of us: "Gary, you're part of the family now. Let's set aside our differences and make the best of it." The room fell into a hushed silence as the gravity of the moment sank in. All eyes were fixed on the transformative exchange unfolding before us, aware of the power and the potential within those words.

In an act of unwavering compliance, Gary responded with grace and acceptance, sealing their newfound connection. It was a moment of true unity, where the boundaries of divergent beliefs were shattered, at least temporarily, and my father's once unwavering black-and-white convictions came into question. Was he reconsidering his perception of sinners? Could he find a way to reconcile his teachings, which had long warned church members against any association with those deemed as such?

As I contemplated the significance of this transformative moment, I couldn't help but wonder about the profound impact it would have on our family's dynamics and, more importantly, on my father's deeply held beliefs. It was a juncture that held the potential to reshape our understanding of acceptance, compassion, and the intricate nature of human connections.

In the wake of this revelation, a torrent of inquiries surged within me, each one seeking to unravel the path that lay ahead. How would this newfound bond between my father and Gary evolve? Would it challenge or reinforce my father's beliefs about sinners and the separation he had advocated for so long? The uncertainty surrounding the outcome loomed large, leaving me in a position of observation and reflection.

Only time could unveil the true depth of their relationship. And so it unfolded, with me as an attentive observer. As days turned into weeks and weeks into months, the bond between my father and Gary flourished, evolving into an inseparable friendship. They became kindred spirits, nurturing an ever-deepening understanding of each other. Their friendship became a source of support and tranquility, a sanctuary in the tempestuous journey of life.

Lurking in the background, however, were the unyielding pressures of deeply ingrained dogma and long-held beliefs. The teachings my father had crafted and upheld for years demanded unwavering adherence, leaving little room for deviation or associations that challenged his established norms. The conflict between loyalty to his teachings and the genuine connection he shared with Gary weighed heavily on my father's heart, pushing him to a critical crossroads.

In a decision fueled by fervent conviction, my father made the painful choice to dissolve their close friendship. It was a sacrifice he believed necessary to uphold his teachings and maintain control over the lives of those he cared for, extending far beyond our family. The parting cast a somber shadow over their once-vibrant relationship, leaving a void not only in my father's life but also in the lives of others.

Occasional encounters served as bittersweet reminders of what had been lost. The warmth and closeness they once shared had faded, replaced by a sense of distance and a lingering feeling of what could have been. The end of their friendship serves as a profound reminder of the sacrifices made in the name of rigid dogma and the potential consequences that arise from blindly adhering to teachings that stifle personal growth and limit genuine connections.

As I embark on the task of recounting my life, a realization emerges. This narrative holds the potential to serve as a cautionary tale, illuminating the perils of rigid beliefs that manipulate our relationships and impede our personal growth and understanding. May those who engage with this story grasp the importance of questioning and critically evaluating the teachings we encounter, seeking harmony between tradition and personal evolution and embracing the transformative power of genuine connections that surpass the confines of dogma.

Everyone in my family cherished their bond with Gary, and his playful nature never failed to captivate us. In the basement of his Liverpool home, he kept a hidden treasure—a BB gun that held an air of mystery and adventure. One memorable Saturday afternoon, Gary presented me with a challenge that sparked my curiosity and ignited a sense of possibility. "Danny, I bet I can light this match by shooting it, just grazing its tip with a pellet!" I was skeptical, but Gary's unwavering determination piqued my interest.

With excitement in our hearts, we set up an impromptu experiment. Using tape, we secured a matchstick to a frying pan and positioned it on a pillow, creating an unconventional target. The room became a playground of laughter and camaraderie as we took turns, our shots becoming more precise with each attempt. The atmosphere buzzed with anticipation as we strived to achieve the seemingly impossible. And then, in a moment of triumph, Gary's aim was true, and the match burst into a brilliant flame, filling the room with a glow of accomplishment and joy.

Those precious moments spent with Gary serve as a vivid reminder of the transformative power of laughter and shared experiences. They exemplify the profound connection and joy that can be found in the simplest of moments.

It was during these times that I realized the significance of playfulness and the unbreakable bond we forged through our thrilling adventures together.

Gary's influence extended far beyond his ability to entertain. He nurtured in me a spirit of critical thinking, encouraging me to question and explore ideas, even when they diverged from his own. With open arms, he welcomed my inquiries and offered his genuine thoughts, creating a safe haven for intellectual growth and exploration. Our conversations expanded my horizons and instilled in me the value of open-mindedness, teaching me to appreciate different perspectives.

However, it was not solely through words that Gary influenced my character. His remarkable approach to adversity also left an indelible mark on my soul. Rather than responding with defensiveness or aggression when faced with mistreatment, he chose the path of introspection and patience. With each instance, I witnessed his unwavering commitment to seeking peaceful resolutions and navigating complex family dynamics with grace and compassion. His example taught me the importance of measured responses and the transformative potential of peaceful dialogue.

Throughout my teenage years, I turned to Gary for guidance on matters that impacted us both. Together, we became a formidable team, pooling our thoughts and insights to navigate the challenges that arose. What struck me most about my uncle was his remarkable ability to set aside ego and prioritize peace within our family. The impact of Gary's presence in my life cannot be overstated. He shaped the way I approach conflict, instilling in me the belief that dialogue, empathy, and understanding are the true pathways to resolution.

On countless weekends, our family united in the tranquil activity of fishing, casting our lines into the vast expanse of Ontario Lake. It was Gary who ignited a spark of curiosity within my father, leading him away from the familiar waters of Oneida Lake, where he had spent years chasing bass and pike. Initially met with resistance, Gary enticed my father into the world of salmon fishing. Never taking offense to my father's objections, Gary chose to let the irrefutable evidence speak for itself. With a humble confidence, he arrived at our doorstep one day, bearing a generous haul of colossal salmon that eclipsed the trophy fish adorning our family albums. The sheer abundance and exhilaration of reeling in these majestic creatures captivated my father, transforming his fishing pursuits indefinitely. The humble bass boat of yesteryear could no longer contain his newfound passion, propelling my father to seek a larger vessel for adventures on Lake Ontario.

One fateful day, fueled by shared excitement and boundless possibilities, my father and Gary deliberated the prospect of jointly acquiring a weathered boat nestled within the confines of an old barn. Despite its dilapidated state, the allure of what could be overshadowed any reservations. However, as reality settled upon us, my siblings and I found ourselves shouldering the weight of after-school hours spent scrubbing and laboring tirelessly to resurrect the vessel from its neglected slumber. The challenge extended beyond the physical to the realm of negotiations, contemplating how to navigate the delicate dance of sharing Gary's permission to use the boat when my father desired it for his solitary fishing expeditions. Before long the boat they had envisioned as a symbol of camaraderie was relinquished, as my father embarked on a solitary quest to find a boat he could claim as his own. In a matter of weeks, Gary and my father acquired brand-new boats, cementing their individual journeys on the expansive canvas of Lake Ontario.

Against the backdrop of the shimmering lake, our family reveled in the abundant joys of summers spent fishing and camping. Together, we cast our lines into the tranquil waters, basking in the serenity and vast expanse of the sky. The bond between my father and Gary, once united in the quest for a shared fishing vessel, found satisfaction in the pursuit of their own maritime adventures. Though their fishing boats sailed on separate horizons, our family remained connected through a mutual appreciation for the serenity and excitement of the great outdoors. Those memorable summers are a testament to the enduring ties that bind us, regardless of the wax and wane of individual endeavors.

Chapter Ten

FIGHTING WITH A SCHOOL KID

IN THE TREACHEROUS LANDSCAPE OF MIDDLE SCHOOL, WHERE EMOtions ran high and vulnerability was a constant companion, I found myself navigating the challenging terrain of preteen life. But I wasn't the only one grappling with such struggles. My classmates were also tiptoeing through the minefields of adolescent emotions, each with their own unique battles to fight. However, I possessed resilience, a secret armor forged in the crucible of eighth grade.

Enter Mike Shawn, the infamous bully whose genetic advantages seemed to fuel his determination to assert dominance over the impressionable middle schoolers. His tactics were relentless, trapping his victims in an unyielding grip and extracting pleas for mercy before releasing them. And on that fateful day, it was my turn to face his torment, a calculated effort to publicly humiliate me. He wove a twisted tale, aiming to force an embarrassing confession from my lips, coercing me to admit that I liked kissing boys.

In that intense moment, as adrenaline coursed through my veins, I recognized the danger of giving in to his demands. I understood that capitulating would only perpetuate the cycle of shame and discrimination. It was in that pivotal instant that I chose a different path—a path of resistance and defiance not just against Mike, but also against the toxic norms that sought to divide and dehumanize us.

Summoning every ounce of audacity within me, I dropped to my knees, not in surrender but to challenge the distorted power dynamics at play. With hands clasped and a voice dripping with satirical despair, I uttered a prayer that was equal parts theatrical and poignant. "Dear God," I proclaimed, my words laced with biting irony, "Mike is so mighty and formidable, the epitome of strength. In comparison, I am but a mere speck, unworthy of his attention. If it pleases him, let him squeeze my feeble fingers until they bleed, and let my existence be extinguished."

A hush fell over the room, a collective realization washing over my classmates who bore witness to this unconventional act of defiance. Laughter erupted, but beneath the laughter, a current of discomfort and recognition pulsed through the air as the spectators began to grasp the inherent cruelty in Mike's actions and the absurdity of the situation in which we found ourselves.

In the aftermath, Mike's swagger crumbled, his power diminished by the weight of his own actions. He slinked away in defeat, and from that day forward, he never dared to torment me or anyone else again.

In high school, the battlefield transformed, and new challenges awaited me. Among them was the persistent use of the term "preacher's kid" as a means to undermine and provoke me. The mere mention of those words ignited a fire within me, fueled by a deep-rooted aversion to being perceived as weak or susceptible to intimidation. I rejected the notion of passively enduring mistreatment and made it clear that I would not be a compliant target. Little did I know that my defiant attitude inadvertently beckoned the very conflicts I aimed to quell, unknowingly setting the stage for a disorderly journey of self-discovery.

One fateful day as the journey home from school unfolded, destiny wrote an unexpected chapter into my narrative. Seated at the rear of the bus, immersed in animated conversations with my comrades about the primary concerns of adolescence—girls and backyard football—I found myself captivated by a discussion revolving around the imminent arrival of Joey's uncle, bearing the promise of explosives. Eager to unravel the mysteries, we delved into the particulars, sharing tales of past escapades with fervor. Little did I anticipate that this conversation would soon take an unforeseen turn.

In the midst of the lively exchange, Joey, brimming with enthusiasm, reenacted the explosive spectacle with grand gestures. Alas, fate played its hand, and in an untimely twist, his hand inadvertently connected with my face. Though the impact was negligible and caused me little discomfort, the abrupt cessation of chatter and the piercing gazes fixated upon me served as an ominous harbinger.

"What's the matter?" I asked. Instinctively, I checked my nose, only to discover a solitary droplet of blood, the crimson stain adorning my fingertips. In that instant, a tempest of indignation and wounded pride surged within me, compelling me to launch a retaliatory assault upon Joey, driven by a potent blend of anger and the desire to reclaim my honor. However, fortune intervened, as an older student interceded, preventing me from inflicting harm and steering me away from the precipice of regret.

With my pride in tatters, I directed my words at Joey, my voice dripping with misplaced aggression. "Once this bus stops, we're stepping off, and I'm going to kick your ass." Sensing the brewing storm, Joey attempted to reason with me, his voice trembling with a mixture of fear and genuine concern.

"Dan, I know you can beat me up. We don't have to fight." His plea hung in the air, an earnest appeal for sanity.

Silent and conflicted, I grappled with the weight of my misplaced anger. A part of me yearned to heed Joey's plea, to break free from aggression, but the destructive ego within me whispered its own warped advice. "Just say it once and then follow through. Show everyone that you're not someone to be trifled with." Fifteen agonizing minutes passed before the bus came to a halt, providing ample opportunity for reflection.

In that prolonged moment, a flicker of realization danced in the recesses of my consciousness. The consequences of my impending actions loomed large, casting a dark shadow over my misguided intentions. Understanding crystallized within me, but alas, I succumbed to the allure of pride and stubbornness, believing I had to follow through with my ill-conceived words. Deep down I knew it was wrong, but I allowed my ego to cloud my judgment.

Sensing the tension and the gravity of the situation, Joey made his way to the front of the bus. His sister, who had Down syndrome, was keenly aware of my threat toward her brother. Joey approached her, comforting her and assuring her that he would be okay. He told her to take his books home with her, promising he would be home soon. Despite his sister's pleas for him to go home with her, Joey explained that he couldn't.

As I witnessed this exchange, a profound sense of guilt filled me as I realized the pain and fear I had caused Joey and his sister. The awareness that I was capable of such hurtful actions made me question my morality. However, despite this recognition, I did not possess the strength of character to rectify my behavior.

Chatter continued to spread among the students as the bus reached its next scheduled stop, and even the bus driver disembarked. With clenched fists, I stormed into the yard of the first home in our neighborhood. A circle of people had gathered, with Joey at its center. As I approached him, my eyes met his, expecting to see only an adversary. However, to my surprise, I saw not an enemy but a brother filled with concern.

Conflicted emotions surged within me. What could I do at that moment? I felt trapped, believing that no one would ever listen to me or respect me if I backed out. The weight of my pride and the fear of judgment held me hostage, clouding my discernment and preventing me from making the right choice.

I clenched my left fist. "Here it comes!" I yelled, telegraphing my intention to strike. Joey closed his eyes as he braced himself for impact and unleashed a flurry of punches. Defying my instincts, I chose not to retaliate, allowing his blows to rain upon my face without offering any resistance. Witnessing the escalating violence, the older student who had intervened on the bus reached for Joey's arm and lifted him off of me.

"That's enough!"

As the chaos subsided, I stood there nursing my battered face and contemplating the senselessness of my actions. Surprisingly, Joey extended his hand, offering a gesture of sportsmanship and declaring it to be a good fight. His display of maturity and his willingness to let bygones be bygones only served to magnify my shortcomings and regrets.

To compound my feelings of defeat, the hurtful reinforcement I dreaded came from a distance. One of the onlookers couldn't resist uttering the words I had fought so hard to disprove: "Ah, he's just a preacher's kid. He can't fight." It cut me to the core, as that was precisely what I had aimed to defy. The weight of failure and humiliation bore down on me.

Desperate to salvage some semblance of pride, I called out to Joey, urging him for a rematch. But he didn't even bother to turn around or acknowledge my plea. It was as if the world had turned its back on me, leaving me alone to face the consequences of my misguided actions.

As everyone dispersed and made their way home, I remained standing there, feeling alone and uncertain about what to do next. Eventually, like a sheep following the herd, I started my own journey homeward.

A minute or so passed when I heard the sound of someone running toward me. I turned to see Debbie Kreigbaum, a girl from another neighborhood who frequented my bus stop every morning. I had noticed her presence over the past couple of months, but we had never exchanged a single word or engaged in conversation. Yet there she was, approaching me with urgency.

"What do you want, Debbie?" I asked, my tone tinged with confusion and skepticism. She responded by expressing her understanding of the situation, assuring me that everything would be okay. It was evident in her words and actions that she cared for me, which perhaps explained her consistent presence at the bus stop. Despite her good intentions, she could not grasp the depth of my humiliation, leaving me with an aversion toward kindness. Without much thought, I unleashed a barrage of hurtful words, causing her to flee, tears streaming down her face. So much for the early morning meetings with her, which I secretly enjoyed.

It wasn't long before I spotted my house. My father was outside, washing his boat. A sense of dread created a perfect storm of emotions. As I approached, a phrase from Monty Python echoed in my mind, "And now for something completely different," as I prepared myself for yet another conflict. I aimed to intercept my father before he could jump to conclusions after seeing my face, to elucidate what had transpired the moment I stepped onto the driveway.

"Dad, let me explain what happened," I implored, eager to shed light on the situation. But he interrupted, insisting we continue the discussion inside where my mother could hear the story.

In the kitchen, I restarted my narrative, recounting how Joey accidentally struck me and detailing the altercation outside. However, as soon as I mentioned being a "preacher's kid," my father interjected, convinced that Joey deserved his fate. Despite my repeated attempts to clarify, my father remained resolute in his belief, cutting me off whenever I tried to provide a more comprehensive account.

"It's commendable that you defended yourself and your faith," he said. "Being a Christian doesn't mean you let others walk all over you."

"But I don't let people push me around," I countered in frustration.

"Exactly," he replied. "You stood up to that bully who targeted you because you're a preacher's kid."

"No, I was called a preacher's kid after the fight."

"Son, you don't understand these things," my father replied, bursting with exasperation. "I do, and I know what happened. Don't worry. You're not in trouble."

There was no convincing my father otherwise, and my mother remained silent throughout. I was perplexed by his distorted perspective of the events and my own stubbornness in wanting to set the record straight. After all, I wasn't in trouble, which should have been a relief. So, why couldn't I simply let it go?

Two days later I found myself in church on a Friday evening listening to my father's sermon on "How Christians Should Respond When Confronted by Sinners." He emphasized the strength of our faith and the importance of standing up for our beliefs, refusing to be treated as weak. However, my heart sank as he proceeded to recount a distorted version of my fight with a boy from the "public school system" who had provoked me by calling me a preacher's kid. Pointing out the bruises on my face, he insinuated that I had emerged victorious. "If you think my son's face looks bad, you should see the other kid," he added. At that moment, I longed to vanish, but instead, the congregation turned toward me as if congratulating me, proud of their shining example.

As the service drew to a close, it became apparent that it was far from over. People approached me, congratulating me with phrases like "Good job, Danny" and "Way to go." But did everyone in the church genuinely believe my father's narrative? I couldn't help but wonder, was conformity to falsehoods the key to acceptance within that congregation, that domain, my family? Would anyone ever truly understand my thoughts and the reality of what was happening in my life? Did I have to stand alone in these struggles? And while I sat here, rewarded, what about the boy from the public school system and others who were being branded as sinners? Who truly held the moral high ground in the situations I was facing?

Chapter Eleven

HIDDEN ROMANCE

Throughout my high school years, I continually uncovered contradictions and falsehoods. Driven to understand and resolve them, I faced a relentless tide of challenges. Each failure to find resolution led to my gradual withdrawal, fostering a tendency to internalize my thoughts. Despite my silence, my face often betrayed my disapproval of many occurrences. This internal conflict was prominent in my mind as I pondered the inevitable revelation of my true self to my family. I feared they would distance themselves from me, as they had done with my uncle and other once-close relatives, due to their religious beliefs.

Within a year after graduating from high school, my true nature became unavoidably evident. This revelation compelled me to embrace my personal evolution and to express my disinterest in attending a church that no longer aligned with my beliefs. Graduation marked not just the end of my academic journey but also a symbolic step into manhood. It signified the end of my sheltered youth, where childlike behavior was accepted, and heralded a new chapter that demanded a break from the constraints of my upbringing. With determination, I embarked on a journey of self-discovery, intent on finding my true identity. I declared my lack of interest in church, ready to face any familial repercussions.

To my astonishment, I was granted permission to continue living with my family, exempt from the obligatory attendance at the Living Word Church. However, as I embarked on this journey of personal exploration, it became clear that my divergent perspectives and evolving mindset put a further strain on our delicate family dynamics. The decision to let me stay, though seemingly compassionate, exacerbated the complexities simmering beneath the surface. Our interactions became increasingly fraught with tension as the clash between my newfound way of thinking—my need to reveal my true self—and my parents' entrenched beliefs magnified the fractures in our relationship. Each conversation became a minefield, every exchange threatened by underlying tension and unspoken disagreements.

The path I had chosen, fueled by a desire for authenticity and personal growth, presented an arduous challenge. The more I embraced my individuality, the more it threatened the stability of our family unit. It was as if my pursuit of self-discovery had become a catalyst for disruption, shaking the foundations upon which our familial bonds were built. But I remained resolute in my quest, willing to endure the turbulent journey that lay ahead in the hopes of forging a new understanding and fostering a deeper connection with those I held dear.

The prospect of having a girlfriend, a companion with whom I could share my deepest affections and experiences, seemed like an elusive dream. It became painfully clear to me that divulging any details about my relationships to my parents would only create insurmountable barriers. This harsh reality came crashing down on me when I made the ill-fated decision to introduce someone I deeply cared about to my family.

Her name was Nancy, a captivating and enigmatic woman attending Barbazon Modeling School, conveniently situated in the building where I worked during the evenings. Our paths would often intersect, sparking a connection nurtured by heartfelt, profound conversations. As the days turned into weeks and the weeks into months, an undeniable bond was forged between us. The anticipation grew, like a seedling reaching for the sun, until one fateful day when Nancy extended an irresistible invitation—dinner at her family's home.

Her father, a renowned and highly respected doctor, resided in a neighboring village a short distance from my family home. The prospect of entering their world, a realm distinct from my own, stirred a mixture of excitement and trepidation within me. It presented a unique opportunity to immerse myself in the warmth of her family's embrace and delve deeper into the captivating persona of the woman who had enraptured my heart.

With eager anticipation, I accepted her invitation, embarking on a journey that held the promise of unveiling new experiences and forging a deeper connection. The evening unfolded with grace and charm, enveloping us in an atmosphere of warmth and familiarity. Engrossed in delightful conversation, I was captivated by Nancy's parents, who embraced me as though I were a cherished friend returning home after a long absence. It was as if the universe had conspired to bestow upon us a sense of comfort and belonging, as if every moment led us closer to a shared destiny.

Nancy, a vision of elegance and poise, radiated a magnetic allure that left me spellbound. Her every word and gesture painted a portrait of grace, a reflection of the woman she had become. Clad in attire that exuded sophistication, I couldn't help but imagine how her presence would integrate with my family.

Buoyed by the waves of affection that coursed through me, I summoned the audacity to broach a daring proposition with my mother. With a flutter of anticipation, I voiced my desire to invite Nancy to our home, to introduce her to my family. To my astonishment, my mother's eyes sparkled with approval. She not only embraced the idea but also suggested that Nancy join us for a Sunday feast following the church service.

It was an invitation that held the promise of unity, a monumental occasion that could bridge the divide between two disparate worlds and illuminate the path to a shared future. Little did I know that this decision would set in motion a cascade of events that would test the strength of our bonds and challenge our intertwined lives.

As Sunday drew near, anticipation crackled in the air, infusing me with a potent mixture of nervousness and exhilaration. Filled with excitement, I embarked on the journey to Nancy's house, my heart pounding with each passing mile. The moment had finally arrived to introduce her to my family, and I was determined to make it an unforgettable and cherished occasion.

Arriving at Nancy's doorstep, I found her radiating an undeniable aura of elegance and allure. Clad in her finest attire, she exuded confidence and grace. With a sense of pride, I led her into the familiar embrace of my home, where my family awaited, their curiosity piqued by the prospect of meeting the woman who had captured my heart.

The afternoon unfolded with a delightful blend of laughter, stories, and the clinking of cutlery against porcelain. Nancy immersed herself in the warmth of my family, effortlessly fitting into the dynamic that had shaped my life.

As we sat around the table, savoring the delectable feast that my mother had prepared, Nancy's generosity and humility shone through. She offered her assistance in the kitchen, lending a hand to my mother and sisters and, in the process, winning their admiration and respect. Her kindness and grace radiated throughout our home, saturating every corner with a sense of harmony and unity.

As the day drew to a close, the time came for Nancy to bid farewell to my family. With genuine gratitude, she expressed her appreciation for their warm hospitality and the memorable time they had shared. Each family member embraced her, their eyes reflecting the connection they had forged in such a short time.

After bringing Nancy home and returning to my family, I was met with a summons from my father. His voice carried a troubled tone, mixed with sternness, as he beckoned me toward him. The events of the day had left an indelible mark on everyone, and I braced myself for what awaited me, unsure of the path my father would guide me down.

There he sat, a formidable figure in his customary chair by the crackling Bullard stove, his piercing gaze commanding the attention of my entire family. As my father spoke, a hushed stillness enveloped the room, each syllable imposing itself on my consciousness. "I may not have control over your actions beyond these walls, but within this house, you are not going to bring your whores and sluts through my door." The weight of his decree settled upon me, casting a suffocating shadow that severed any possibility of integrating a romantic relationship into my family.

In that pivotal moment, a wave of clarity arrived. I knew what I had to do, even if it meant tearing my heart apart. I had to distance myself from Nancy, to create a rift between us that would ensure our paths diverged forever. It was a desperate act, driven by a deep belief that Nancy and her family deserved far better than the turmoil-ridden existence that awaited them within the confines of my life.

The subsequent days were a deliberate dance of emotional tumult. I intentionally sparked arguments, pushing Nancy away with calculated precision. Each word uttered and every subtle act of defiance served as a painful reminder that our love was destined to wither under the weight of circumstance. The inner turmoil threatened to consume me as I questioned the righteousness of my actions and grappled with the depth of my feelings for Nancy. I clung to the flickering hope that she would come to despise me and find a more promising possibility in the arms of someone who could offer her a life free from the shadows that haunted mine.

My father's words lingered in my mind, a constant reminder of the insurmountable divide that had been forged between love and duty. It was a painful lesson in the complexities of life, where choices carried consequences that could not easily be undone.

Chapter Twelve

THE FAMILY DIVIDE

THE WINTER OF 1981 CAST ITS CHILLY SPELL UPON US. ALONG with it came my parents' much-anticipated vacation to sunny Florida, accompanied by my aunt and uncle. Two years had passed since my high school graduation, and it had been over a year since I had attended church. Uncle Gary was still an integral part of our family, not yet ostracized for his perceived transgressions. Excitement buzzed in the air, intermingling with subdued conversations and whispers. Much of the talk centered around my uncle, once known for his social escapades and his fondness for the occasional drink at local bars. To our collective relief, the family dynamics experienced a pleasant shift when Uncle Gary redirected his attention toward spending quality time with us. It was as if a ray of warm sunshine had broken through the clouds, dispersing one of the shadows that had darkened our relationship. This change not only eased the family tension but also brought us closer in unexpected ways.

That idyllic atmosphere was shattered upon my parents' return from their trip. Their weary faces bore the weight of disappointment and frustration, which they wasted no time expressing. They delved into their grievances, attributing them to none other than Gary. My mother, in particular, took it upon herself to shed light on the severity of the situation, painting a picture of Gary stubbornly disregarding my father's guidance and sowing discord between them. The weight of my parents' words left no room for doubt; things had changed irrevocably, and our family would never be the same again.

However, their explanations didn't satisfy my thirst for understanding. I yearned for more than mere generalizations and vague accusations if I was expected to sever ties with my aunt, whom I had known since my birth, and Uncle Gary. Determined to uncover the likelihood of unmentioned truths, I mustered the courage to approach my mother. I pleaded with her to provide specific instances that justified their damning judgment of Uncle Gary. But instead of shedding light on his alleged wrongdoings, she evaded my questions, repeating the same broad statements: "Gary was disrespectful to your father," "Gary was stubborn and cold," "Gary is just a kid, too young to be hanging around your father," and "He's not saved, and he has a malevolent spirit." Frustration welled up within me, as my mother's answers lacked substance, which only fanned the flames of my curiosity.

Undeterred, I persisted in my quest for clarity, desperate to unravel the truth veiled by my parents' cryptic words. I pressed my mother again, urging her to share specific incidents that justified their drastic change in attitude toward Gary. But instead of transparency, I was met with the same evasive tactics and misplaced blame.

As unconvincing as their words were to me, they held

sway over my siblings, leading them to follow along, to abandon their once-close relationship with my aunt and Uncle Gary without seeking to comprehend the full story. I refused to follow suit, though. As the odd one out, my increasing stubbornness strained the already delicate threads of our familial bonds. I had drifted away from attending church, an action that limited my interactions with my siblings and parents to brief encounters tainted by unspoken disagreements.

Weeks turned into a relentless cycle of inquiry as I doggedly pursued the truth behind the shattered relationship. But with each attempt, my mother's vague responses and elusive demeanor left me dissatisfied, their vacuous nature exposing her own insecurities and her unwillingness to confront reality. Her hollow eyes betrayed the doubt that lingered within her as she sought reassurance in the unanswered questions she kept hidden.

Alas, my insatiable thirst for answers and my persistent need to challenge the status quo had once again pushed me into the treacherous realm of trouble. It seemed that my unyielding pursuit of truth was destined to be met with resistance at every turn. My father, unable to ignore the disturbances any longer, confronted me with a mixture of frustration and sternness.

"Danny, what on earth have you been questioning your mother about?" he demanded, his voice booming. "Can't you leave well enough alone? Your godlessness grants you no understanding of spiritual matters. As long as you live under my roof, you will put an end to your ways. You are creating chaos and discord within this family, and it ends now! Keep your mouth shut!"

My father was acutely aware of the ongoing clash between our contrasting views, a constant battle fueled by our persistent disagreements regarding his actions and choices. Each time we faced off, his words were like a powerful repetition of many speeches that failed to sway me. I stood firm, refusing to surrender to the pressure of conforming to his expectations. In doing so, I maintained my cherished relationship with my beloved aunt and uncle, undeterred by the pressures imposed upon me.

My unyielding stance not only fortified my resolve, it also deepened my suspicion. Deep within the recesses of my mother's heart, I sensed a flicker of doubt, an unspoken question about the legitimacy of the reasons she had presented to justify her estrangement from her sister and brother-in-law.

Within my family, the truth remained elusive, with stories passed down that often diverged from the firsthand experiences unfolding. My mother, already distanced from many of her cousins and friends, faced the daunting prospect of yet another rupture in our family ties—this time with her only sister. I pondered the consequences of my father's success in further tearing us apart. Would I be cast aside next, teetering on the precipice of becoming an outcast within my own kin?

After my father's reprimand, I turned away, my heart filled with longing for a united family, even if it meant sacrificing my own place within it—a risk I was on the brink of taking. Everything I held dear appeared to be hanging by a fragile thread. Despite the strain, I remained tethered to them for the moment. Perhaps there was another way, a bolder path. What if I summoned the courage to approach my father and ask the more profound questions? What was he after? What could justify the magnitude of wrongs he was willing to commit in pursuit of his elusive goals?

Three long weeks elapsed, and as each day unfolded, my family's behavior took a darker turn, sinking my spirits further into despair. Whispers permeated the air within the confines of our home, swirling like an insidious wildfire, feeding on gossip and speculation. Gradually, the accusations shifted their focus, targeting me as the alleged source of our mounting troubles. Even my own brother, a mouthpiece for our father's disdain, took pleasure in taunting me in front of others. His words sliced through me like a razor, leaving my wounded soul throbbing with pain. "You're nothing but a sinner, a part of this world. You don't know anything," David jeered one fateful afternoon, his voice dripping with venomous scorn while the rest of my family stood as silent witnesses to my humiliation.

At that moment of profound vulnerability, I lifted my gaze, seeking guidance and support within the depths of my mother's eyes. To my dismay, she remained unmoved, an impassive figure standing before me, devoid of support or protection. The realization struck me with a resounding blow—I had long ago accepted my position as an outsider, labeled as a sinner and an outcast within their world. However, the weight of that moment, accentuated by the silence emanating from my mother, surpassed any previous transgressions I had endured. It pressed upon my spirit, as if a crushing weight had settled in the core of my being.

If there had ever been any admiration for me as an older brother, it was now conspicuously absent, extending far beyond the absence of mere words. The repercussions of my family's utterances cut deeper than ever before, no longer mere words but a scorching condemnation of my very essence. They treated me in a despicable manner, a constant reminder of my perpetual role as an outsider within the confines of my own family.

The days trudged on, each one laced with the poisonous sting of reproach. In the midst of shared meals and gatherings, my father's tongue morphed into a conduit of scorn, spinning tales that portrayed me as an ungodly rebel, a worldly wanderer, and a disregarder of the sacredness of family. It was a maddening and disheartening experience to witness how effortlessly he chose to cast me as a disobedient son, seemingly intent on sowing discord within our family. I was reduced to a mere pawn in his carefully crafted narrative, neatly fitting into his rigid, black-and-white worldview, which categorized the world into simplistic notions of good and bad, sinners and saints, devoid of any room for nuance or understanding.

I yearned to unearth the dormant truths that lay scattered within the fragments of the puzzle, hopeful that they would unlock the enigma that was tearing apart the lives of my loved ones. But the question remained: how? How could I unearth the forbidden knowledge when my own parents refused to engage in candid conversation? I wondered if I should approach my aunt and uncle, with the expectation that they might extend their hands in honesty, guiding me through the intricate corridors of truth. But a lingering doubt gnawed at my mind—would they too conceal their secrets, veiling them behind cryptic words and evasive gestures, mirroring my parents' inscrutable demeanor? I had never ventured into a serious conversation with my aunt about family matters before. The unknown reaction awaited me as I wondered whether she would succumb to the alleged malevolent spirit my father attributed to the bloodline of the Fortinos, possibly unveiling her hidden depths and revealing an unforeseen side.

Lost in my thoughts, a chuckle escaped my lips—a ripple of laughter born from the absurdity of entertaining my father's outlandish statement as anything but fiction. Throughout my life, I had witnessed an unwavering display of love and care emanating from my dear aunt, leaving no room for doubt or suspicion. With unwavering determination, I made my decision, my resolve as firm as steel. Without hesitation, I embarked on a journey to the quaint town of Parish where my aunt and uncle resided. The purpose of my voyage was clear—to engage in a candid conversation, to uncover the elusive truth, and to pull together the scattered fragments of the intricate puzzle that held the key to understanding the profound challenges that plagued not only my life but also the lives of my family.

And so, after a long and arduous journey from Liverpool, I finally stood before them, summoning every ounce of courage to embark on the purpose that had brought me to their doorstep. As I initiated the conversation, a torrent of inquiries about their ill-fated trip with my parents permeated the atmo-

sphere, intermingling with an ever-growing sense of curiosity. This was no ordinary exchange; it delved into the intricate
nuances of their interactions with my parents, a shared experience that had not gone well.

Initially, it seemed as though extracting answers from
them would be a formidable task, as they hesitated, driven by
a desire to protect me from witnessing my parents in a negative light. However, their hesitation was no match for my unyielding determination. No excuse could dissuade me from
unearthing the truth I sought. I forged ahead, undeterred by
their initial reluctance.

And so, our enthralling discussion unfolded, spanning
not only hours and days but stretching across the expanse of
months and years. The topic, like an unfinished tale yearning
to be unraveled, resurfaced repeatedly, its threads intermixed
through future conversations. With unwavering attention,
I absorbed the accounts of my aunt and uncle, fully aware
that their narrative held the key to unraveling the mysterious events of that momentous vacation. Their words pulsated with crystal-clear resonance, exposing the truth they had
witnessed.

Clarity emerged as if I had been granted an intimate
glimpse into the essence of the matter. In their unwavering
support and guidance, I discovered a precious chance to un-
tangle the previously perplexing paths, to grasp the complex
interplay at work, and gain a profound understanding of my
life as it unfolded.

Chapter Thirteen

THE FLORIDA VACATION

AFTER UNPACKING THE LAST SUITCASE AND SETTLING INTO A modest motel, a sense of anticipation filled the air, infusing my parents and my aunt and uncle with electric energy and igniting their eagerness to embrace the day ahead. Guided by an intrepid spirit, they set off in search of sustenance, ultimately finding themselves in the welcoming arms of McDonald's, where their journey of planning would commence. It was still early morning, and the promise of an adventure-filled day beckoned.

As they entered the restaurant, placed their breakfast orders, and settled down to eat, the conversation revolved around their plans for the day. Amidst the bustling atmosphere, Gary's fervent desire to go fishing became evident.

Their gaze fixed upon the world outside the window, a spirited debate ensued. My father, casting a cautious eye at the howling wind, predicted that the fish would not be biting due to the blustery conditions. Ever the optimist, Gary countered his assertion. A lively back and forth unfolded, with my father pointing out the forceful flutter of a nearby flag as evidence of the unfavorable weather while Gary insisted that the wind would have no impact on their adventure.

Tensions escalated as their differing perspectives clashed. Frustrated by my father's insistence, Gary made his stance clear: "If you don't want to go fishing, fine, we won't go. But I'm not going to pretend I agree with you." The situation reached a boiling point, prompting my father to storm out, declaring that they should proceed without him. The air grew heavy with tension as they drove back to the motel in silence.

Upon their return to the motel, Gary remained determined not to let the argument dampen their enjoyment of the day. He left with my aunt to embark on their own fishing expedition, separate from my parents. Upon their triumphant return, my uncle proudly unveiled their bountiful catch, enough fish to create a sumptuous meal. After a brief conversation about their fishing adventure, my mother and aunt set off to a nearby store to gather the necessary ingredients for their culinary creation. It marked a significant stride toward moving forward, an earnest endeavor to mend the strained atmosphere and reignite a sense of harmony.

As they journeyed to the store, curiosity gnawed at my mother, her thoughts consumed by the potential for lingering tension between my father and Gary. Seeking reassurance, she turned to her sister, questioning whether the disagreements still loomed and had the potential to taint future moments.

With a knowing smile, my aunt dismissed their conflict as a passing moment, expressing unwavering confidence that grown men like my father and Gary would inevitably find common ground and transcend their differences.

Their vacation continued with a blend of enchantment

and exploration. They embarked on an unforgettable journey to the enchanting realm of Disney World and ventured into various stops throughout South Florida, basking in the joy of shared experiences. Interestingly, no mention was made to me of any other challenging moments or confrontational encounters during their entire trip.

Gary, armed with a wealth of knowledge about my father's temperament acquired through years of shared experiences, possessed a profound understanding of the intricate dance required to maintain harmony in their relationship. He had mastered the art of navigating the subtle nuances, unspoken rules, and selfless acts that were essential to preserving their peace. However, on that fateful day at McDonald's, a restlessness stirred within him, compelling him to break away from the carefully crafted behavior he had cultivated. It could have been the intoxicating allure of freedom that vacations bring, or a profound yearning to embrace his true self without the weight of pretense.

The consequences of his dissent lingered in the air as they embarked on their journey back to Syracuse. As the story was explained to me, it became clear that Gary made an effort to orchestrate a seamless display of harmony for the remainder of their vacation, stopping wherever my father desired, avoiding potholes pointed out, and doing everything within his power to ensure my father's comfort. This is the story my aunt and uncle shared with me, a narrative that followed a familiar pattern involving my father, one with a remarkable twist: my uncle's refusal to bow to my father's whims that day at McDonald's.

Chapter Fourteen

FROM CHAOS TO CLARITY

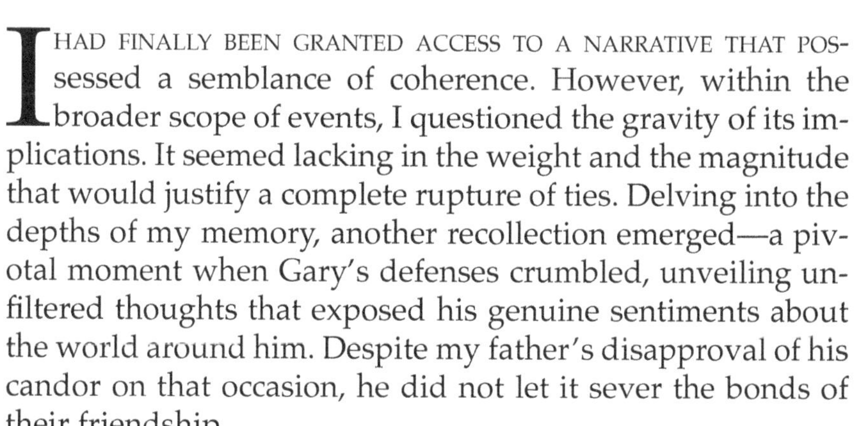

I HAD FINALLY BEEN GRANTED ACCESS TO A NARRATIVE THAT POS-sessed a semblance of coherence. However, within the broader scope of events, I questioned the gravity of its implications. It seemed lacking in the weight and the magnitude that would justify a complete rupture of ties. Delving into the depths of my memory, another recollection emerged—a pivotal moment when Gary's defenses crumbled, unveiling unfiltered thoughts that exposed his genuine sentiments about the world around him. Despite my father's disapproval of his candor on that occasion, he did not let it sever the bonds of their friendship.

Enter Timmy Ragonese, a skilled carpenter and cousin enlisted by my mother to undertake the task of reconstructing a kitchen wall in our home, effectively dividing it from a neighboring room—one that housed the renowned Bullard wood stove, a tale in itself. Events took a dramatic turn when my father returned home to discover a gaping hole in the wall. However, this hole was not a result of damage; rather, it was a consequence of the ongoing project and the transformative process Timmy was undertaking. Succumbing to hasty conclusions, my father erupted in anger, subjecting my mother to a torrent of verbal assaults. The intensity of the moment left all those present, including Gary, who happened to be there that day, deeply shaken.

In the charged atmosphere, Gary couldn't remain silent. With unwavering courage, he confronted my father, casting doubt on his actions with a piercing remark: "What kind of Christian yells at his wife like that?" The weight of his words hung in the air, resonating with the undeniable truth they carried. The room descended into an uneasy silence, my father caught in a rare moment of speechlessness.

This incident proved to be considerably more severe than the story shared with me about their vacation together. However, on that same day, they steadfastly pushed forward, heeding my aunt's sage advice, akin to two adults navigating their differences and discovering common ground.

Reflecting on my own experiences, I also witnessed moments when my father's treatment of my mother lacked the gentleness it should have possessed. However, as he was my father, I questioned whether it was my place to confront him about it. It was during the calm of an early morning, with the sun yet to rise, that we were preparing for a fishing expedition—a day filled with the promise of quality time with our family. Little did we know that the tranquility of the dawn would be shattered by the sharpness of my father's words directed at my mother.

The task of preparing sandwiches for our trip had been assigned to her, and while she worked to fulfill this responsibility, they were not ready as swiftly as my father had expected. His short temper flared, and his dissatisfaction with the delay became apparent. It was in such moments that my father's hot-headedness revealed itself, his impulsive nature leaving a mark. We had grown accustomed to his occasional outbursts during our family outings on weekends—be it boating or camping. We had learned to adapt, to tread carefully, and maintain a delicate balance to prevent further tensions from escalating. Perhaps in those moments I should have summoned the courage to challenge my father's behavior, extending kindness and support to my mother. However, reality dictated otherwise, and I found myself conforming to the expected silence and adapting to the unspoken rhythm that often lingered in the air.

But it wasn't solely my mother who bore the brunt of his actions; anyone could become a target of my father's unpredictable temper. It happened all too frequently, like the moments we spent trolling for fish on Oneida Lake. Casting my line with hope and eagerness, I would often find it entangled in the stubborn weeds. Like clockwork, my father's frustration would bubble to the surface, resulting in a sharp snap of the line, as if assigning blame to me for the mishap. "You're paying for that one. It's your fault!" he would exclaim, his words piercing like the sting of the broken line. These instances repeated themselves like a broken record, an incessant reminder of my father's impatience and my own lack of passion for fishing. It mirrored our time together in the woodshop where I reluctantly yielded to my mother's pleas for us to spend time together. How could I trust that he genuinely wanted my company when he consistently treated me so poorly?

Then there was the ill-fated trip to the Adirondacks. Despite the downpour that welcomed us upon arrival, my father's unwavering determination to fish persisted. It ended up being just him and me in his bass boat, as everyone else sought refuge from the relentless rain. Soaked to the bone, I resented every passing minute. My father demanded that I steer the boat while he cast his line, hoping to reel in an elusive pike. But the elements conspired against us, the heavy winds pushing us closer to the shore. With every gust, my father's discontentment grew, and he unleashed a torrent of relentless criticism, as if I alone were responsible for the boat's wayward path.

Numerous such instances could be recounted, each one shedding light on my father's unsettling behavior, which exposed his limitations as a parent and a friend. However, as I reflect upon my own actions, I am humbled by the realization that I, too, exhibited shades of similar behavior. There were instances when I was unkind and cruel to my friend Don, moments where my actions mirrored the damage caused by my father's outbursts. Despite this, Don remained steadfast and resilient, continuing to play with me and finding joy in our time together. It was through observing my father's actions and engaging in conversations with others, like Gary, that I began to excavate the intricate layers of my father's personality. Yes, Gary shared stories of laughter and camaraderie, and others expressed similar sentiments. In those moments of listening, a yearning grew within me to experience the side of my father that brought genuine happiness and fostered deep connections. Unfortunately, such moments were scarce, like flashes of lightning on a long, stormy night.

Yes, my family understood the delicate dance of silence during my father's tempestuous moments, holding onto the hope that calm would eventually prevail. Gary, having been witness to these outbursts countless times, knew the unspoken rules all too well. Surprisingly, their bond remained unbroken even when Gary dared to challenge my father's actions. Even so, the details of their vacation in Florida, the supposed catalyst for severing ties, remained shrouded in ambiguity. I was expected to accept the narrative that painted Gary as the villain and invoked a spiritual clash between him and my father. However, it was difficult for me to believe in this portrayal, as doubts lingered.

Something else was undoubtedly at play beneath the surface, orchestrating the intricate dynamics of this unsettling situation. What unseen forces were shaping these events? Ah, yes, the deeply ingrained dogma that my father espoused. For countless years he had emphasized the paramount importance of upholding a strict separation between ourselves as devout Christians and those who were labeled as sinners. Within our community, whispers hinted at the increasing amount of time my father spent in the company of his brother-in-law, Gary—a man who, according to our family's rigid beliefs, was deemed a sinner. It was becoming apparent that the minor disagreement during their Florida trip may have been a convenient excuse, a ready-made justification to sever ties with my aunt and uncle and uphold the rigid boundaries dictated by my father's dogma.

And so it unfolded, with the passage of days transforming into weeks, my mother distancing herself from her sister, their interactions limited to the sacred walls of the church. It was astonishing to witness my aunt's unwavering commitment to her faith, defying my father's influence. "I won't stop attending church. It's God who put me there, and only he can make me leave, not your father," she confided in me during one of our intimate conversations.

Amidst the weeks of turmoil, I observed the calculated machinations unfolding before my eyes. My father, resembling a skilled puppeteer, manipulated my mother's thoughts, injecting her mind with toxic messages about my Uncle Gary and her own sister. "It's that Ragonese blood; she simply can't control herself," he would assert, perpetuating a narrative that bore an eerie resemblance to past incidents. I couldn't help but draw parallels to how my father had dealt with my cousins, who had cofounded the church. He spread malicious rumors to remove them from positions of influence and replace them with obedient followers of his teachings. It became increasingly clear that my father's internal struggle with his dogmatic beliefs had reached its climax, fueling an unwavering determination. He clung to his rigid principles, advocating for the strict separation of sinners and saints.

The countdown began, each passing day bringing us closer to the inevitable moment when my aunt and uncle would face their ultimate fate—a fate shared by our other distant cousins who had been cast aside and banished from our lives. The impending severance loomed over us, an invisible barrier that would forever keep us apart.

As the days turned into weeks, the cacophony of accusations grew louder, permeating every corner of our existence. The poison of my parents' words corroded the minds of my siblings and others, eroding any remaining connection to my aunt and uncle. And so it continued until that fateful day, when the final blow was delivered—formal expulsion from the church and our family. The pulpit, once a symbol of unity, became the stage for an orchestrated downfall as weighty pronouncements severed the last remaining ties, leaving my aunt—along with my grandparents, who found themselves caught in the wake—adrift in the turbulent sea of our shattered unity.

Chapter Fifteen

A GATHERING STORM

THEIR VACATION IN FLORIDA HAD ENDED, MARKING THE START of new memories for that summer. During that time, I had limited interactions with my parents. In the subsequent months, instead of staying at home, they chose to spend their evenings at the Living Word Camp. The camp spanned 135 acres of woods, fields, and waterfront on Stone Hill Road in Williamstown. Although it was close to Parish, NY, where my aunt and uncle lived, every time my parents drove to the camp, they passed by my aunt and uncle's house without stopping to visit.

It was the summer of 1981, and my attention was devoted to my own aspirations. In the evenings I worked as a janitor to support my daytime endeavor of establishing a commercial photography business. However, things took an unexpected turn when I was presented with an opportunity to maintain the downtown building, Onondaga Plaza, through an exclusive contract awarded to me. Consequently, I sought additional contracts to maintain other buildings. To aid this pursuit, I leveraged my photography contacts. One of the companies I served was SSAC (Solid State Advanced Controls). I used my rapport with its co-owner, Dick Shutt, to secure the contract. Furthermore, I acquired contracts with other local companies, including Hewlett Packard.

Numerous members of the church engaged in the Living Word Camp experience. Like my parents, many churchgoers owned trailers situated on the premises, providing a retreat after the evening sermons in Syracuse. As my parents commuted between the church and the camp, occasionally stopping at our house for supplies and to run errands, my attention was captivated by an intriguing story. This tale centered around a truth seeker, a devoted member of the Living Word Church. Motivated by his inquiries about my father, Joe embarked on a journey to the Living Word Camp. He and his wife had attended the church for several years and were once close friends with many of my cousins who had since distanced themselves from the church. Troubled by the expectation for congregants to sever ties with my cousins, Joe felt compelled to seek answers. He resolved to drive up to the Living Word Camp to question my father about the situation.

However, before approaching my father, Joe engaged in a conversation with my grandmother, hoping to obtain an insider's perspective. As Joe leaned in, addressing my grandmother by her first name, Gert, his question lingered in the air, carrying the weight of a closely guarded secret. It was evident that the answer held the potential to unlock the mysteries surrounding our estranged relatives' absence from church. With hopeful eyes fixed upon my grandmother, Joe waited for a response that would not only dispel the rampant rumors but also provide a credible truth, surpassing mere whispered speculations.

Burdened by conflicting emotions, my grandmother delved deep into her heart, searching for answers. While she had embraced my father into our family when he was considered a "sinner," she believed in the redemptive power of forgiveness and the unwavering pursuit of peace. But she couldn't turn a blind eye to his failure in extending the same grace to Uncle Gary. The recent events weighed heavily on her conscience as Gary's plight served as a stark reminder of the similar hardships endured by our numerous cousins. As she contemplated her response to Joe's probing question, her words carried unexpected weight and were filled with profound introspection: "Joe, I don't have the answer, but why is it that everyone else is always perceived as being in the wrong?"

In the weeks leading up to a chaotic Sunday service—one marked by rebukes and the casting out of loved ones—my father became entangled in a complex web of complications. The turmoil extended beyond the murmurs surrounding his questionable interactions with my "sinful" uncle. Rather, it was a tempestuous storm of forbidden questions that reverberated through the church pews, unsettling the hearts of congregants and casting a shadow of unease within the sanctuary. These daring inquiries, condemned as gossip by the self-righteous, dared to challenge the established order of seeking wisdom from a select few. Despite warnings and reprimands, there came a day when the relentless curiosity of a fellow believer, Joe, could not be held back.

A few days later, driven by a yearning for further clarity, Joe sought my father out at the campgrounds. His voice laced with sincerity, he inquired, "Brother Bob, why have so many of your family's cousins departed from the church?" After listening to my father's reply, Joe mustered the courage to confront him with the question my grandmother had posed: "Why does your mother-in-law question why they are consistently portrayed as the ones at fault?"

The following weeks bore witness to the distressing continuation of a troubling pattern. Whenever my father was present, whether at the dinner table or elsewhere, the disparagement of my grandmother became an all-too-common occurrence. Accusations were hurled, filling the air with their bitterness: "Your grandmother never lends a hand in the church.. . . She engages in gossip with other women.. . . It's that Ragonese blood, they all seem to possess the same ill spirit as Mary Jane.. . . Why doesn't she contribute to your mother's well-being instead of causing her pain?" These venomous tirades, similar to the tales told about our cousins, further eroded our sense of family unity. It was disheartening to observe the recurrence of discrediting yet another family member, a situation that would inevitably lead to their departure without the chance for inquiries to be raised or explanations to be offered.

Amidst the onslaught of hurtful words, a kernel of truth emerged. It became apparent that my mother was suffering, as evidenced by her desperate attempt to leap out of a moving car, only to be prevented by my father gripping her arm. In the midst of her anguish, she cried out, "I want to die! I can't bear to live like this any longer."

One morning in the kitchen as I was getting ready for my workday and my father was preparing for the evening sermon, he began speaking over his cup of coffee. He detailed the severity of my mother's depression and her attempt to jump from a moving car. He attributed the blame to my grandmother's actions, holding her responsible for the turmoil that had engulfed our family. Although I had much to say, I opted to remain silent, choosing to lend an ear and focus on understanding his perspective.

A week later, my father confronted my grandmother, alleging that people in the church had accused her of speaking ill of him. Caught off guard, she sought specifics, but he declined to name anyone. He added that Brother Lou Levante, a church elder and the principal of the school where she volunteered, had made similar accusations. Moreover, he hinted that Al Cerelli, a close friend of hers in the church, had criticized her character, describing her as a miserable woman and expressing his surprise that her husband put up with her.

In response, my grandmother refuted these claims and was determined to contact Al to verify the allegations. However, my father warned her against this, insisting she remain silent. He went further, stating that her alleged gossip was adversely affecting my mother's mental state, implying that my mother's suicide attempt was tied to her actions.

Despite her frustration and confusion, my grandmother did not heed my father's warnings. She called Al and asked, "Did you tell Bob that I'm a miserable woman and that you can't fathom how Carmen can bear me?" Al vehemently denied ever uttering such words, and their conversation continued until my grandmother became convinced that something else was at play. Seeking clarity, she attempted to reach out to Lou, hoping to hear his side of the story. However, upon contacting Lou, he declined to speak with her that Saturday night, setting the stage for a whirlwind of events that would shake the Living Word Church to its very core the following Sunday morning.

Chapter Sixteen

SUNDAY'S DESCENT: UNVEILING THE RUINS OF TRAGEDY

THE NEXT MORNING DAWNED, AND THE CONGREGATION GATH-ered at the church, oblivious to the dramatic events that were about to unfold. As they settled in, little did they realize that this day would be etched into their memories for years to come.

Before the service began, my aunt, driven by a mixture of curiosity and a desire for resolution, arrived at the church earlier than usual to speak with Lou. "Would you please tell Bob I'd like to speak with both of you after the service?" she whispered. Eager to uncover the truth, my aunt had already caught wind of everything that had transpired the evening before and was determined to set things right with my dad before they got out of hand. Intrigued by her request, Lou agreed to convey the message.

Stepping onto the pulpit, my aunt integrated herself with my sisters, guiding the congregation through a captivating session of soul-stirring songs and praises. Meanwhile, my father, typically positioned at the far right of the pulpit, was engrossed in a conversation with Lou. As the usual murmurs and glances circulated within the congregation, it was inevitable that some individuals speculated whether my father's hushed whispers carried subtle criticism aimed at their own lives. If my aunt harbored any inclination toward such paranoia that day, the ensuing events would undoubtedly serve as substantial validation.

As the songs soared to their crescendo, a peculiar restlessness permeated the pulpit area. Shadows cast across my father's face, darkening his countenance, while he clandestinely signaled to my grandfather, beckoning him to the rear of the church. Their encounter was brief but profound, heralding the commencement of an unveiling of the trials that had beset our family.

"Carmen, your wife is causing trouble here," my father said, his voice laced with anger and frustration. "She's shooting her mouth off to the congregation, spreading lies and rumors about me." A surge of indignation filled my grandfather.

"Oh, but I don't believe my wife is the one spreading falsehoods here. If anyone is a liar, it's you."

The tension reached its breaking point as my father was consumed by rage. "That's it, Carmen! Take your wife and your daughter and leave this church!"

In a stunning turn of events, my grandparents, fully aware of the escalating tensions, decided to defuse the situation by heading toward the exit. However, my father was left dumbfounded when my aunt, displaying an unwavering determination, stood her ground with unyielding defiance. She refused to be treated like a child and asserted her autonomy, reminding my father of her status as a grown woman with a husband of her own.

"Danny, I cannot be ordered to leave with my parents," she confided in me later. "Your mother is their daughter too, and he didn't tell her to leave."

As the captivating spectacle unfolded before the congregation, my sisters continued their heartfelt songs, attempting to maintain a sense of normalcy in the midst of the turmoil. But their efforts proved futile as the tension simmered, the songs gradually nearing their end. The congregation, on the edge of their seats, anticipated the commencement of the sermon, albeit in a slightly unconventional manner.

My father stepped forward, his voice resonating through the microphone. "A few minutes ago, my mother and father-in-law left the church, and my sister-in-law, who hasn't spoken to me in months, remains seated over there," he announced. The unfolding scene seemed to bear the mark of careful orchestration, designed to evoke sympathy from the congregation and unveil the weighty burden that my father had been shouldering—the narrative of a family engaged in a relentless campaign of attacks against him.

Days later, in the comfort of a coffee-scented room, my father again confided in me, seeking empathy as he divulged his deepest emotions. The magnitude of the turmoil that had engulfed him was evident in his voice, heavy with the weight of his experiences. "So much was transpiring," he admitted, his words carrying the gravity of the situation. "I was faced with the daunting task of confronting an elder over the troubling allegation that he had molested his own daughter. The pressure was mounting, compounded by the challenging behavior exhibited by your grandparents and others."

As his words permeated the air that Sunday morning, a palpable heaviness descended upon the church, leaving the congregation teetering on the edge of an imminent and potentially transformative sermon. The events of that morning hinted at the intricate threads of personal struggles, exposing the interplay between the fragility and resilience of family ties. In the midst of this turmoil, profound questions arose, challenging the essence of compassion in times of duress.

My father persisted in his discourse, his demeanor tinged with a sense of embarrassment and unease as he unraveled the intricate details of my grandparents' involvement. Overwhelmed by the weight of his emotions, he felt compelled to repeat his demand, his voice resonating through the pulpit's powerful speakers. With unwavering conviction, he pointed to the exit, commanding my aunt to leave the sanctuary, the force behind his words leaving no room for negotiation.

Despite the expectant gazes of the hundreds gathered, my aunt remained seated, her quiet defiance captivating the attention of all. The collective anticipation hung in the air as everyone waited and watched, curious to witness her response. But she did not yield.

"No, I'm not going," she said, challenging my father's authority and refusing to succumb to his demands.

In an act of desperation, he turned to my mother. "Fanny, go with your sister," he pleaded. However, my mother remained seated, defying him as well. The sense of rebellion reverberated through the church, leaving my father exasperated and defeated.

In his frustration, my father abandoned his initial focus and embarked on a series of rants, venting his grievances about various other problems within the church. The atmosphere brimmed with a mixture of curiosity, unease, and apprehension as the congregation bore witness to the unraveling of authority and the emergence of deep-seated discord.

Remarkably, amidst the unfolding turmoil and formidable challenges, my aunt clung to a flicker of hope and the possibility of resolution. "If only I could have a conversation with your father and my parents," she said, turning to my sister Pamela, who was sitting beside her. Determination burned in her eyes. "Come with me, Pam," she urged. "Let's bring your grandparents back to the church, so we can work toward finding a solution."

They made their way to the rear of the church, their footsteps hushed with the weight of their intentions. When they reached my aunt's car, they embarked on their journey, my aunt revealing her plan along the way. "When I arrived at the church this morning, I confided in Lou about wanting to have a conversation with him and your father. I don't know what happened."

Before long they reached the familiar threshold of my grandparents' house. With urgency in her voice, my aunt called out to her father, appealing for his participation in their shared quest for reconciliation. "Come on, Dad. We can't let it end like this. We have to find a way to make amends. Let's return to the church and work this out."

Against their initial reluctance, my grandparents yielded and made their way back to the hallowed halls of the church. To their surprise, they discovered that my father was no longer occupying the esteemed position at the podium. Instead, it was Bob Dean, a trusted elder and longtime friend of the family who now commanded the attention of the congregation. Bob had been an integral part of our lives, sharing fishing escapades and memorable vacations with us, fostering a sense of camaraderie and joviality.

However, a distressing incident had strained the previously harmonious relationship between Bob and my family. It all stemmed from Bob's daughter, Theresa, who had used my uncle as a justification to pursue a relationship with someone deemed a sinner.

"MaryJane married a sinner, your friend Gary," she said, "so why can't I date one?" This unforeseen turn of events upset Bob, as my father had confided before embarking on his vacation to Florida with my aunt and uncle.

"Bob Dean will never associate with your uncle again," my father declared.

During my visits to the church, I had always been captivated by Bob's sermons. He wove tales of his business ventures, recounting the promotions and tempting opportunities he had turned down, all in the name of serving the Lord. My father had extended special privileges to Bob, granting him a designated spot in the school to store his boat and an office within the church to conduct his business. Interestingly, his office was positioned near my father's own workspace. Whenever questioned about this proximity, my father simply stated, "I need him close by for support."

As Bob took the podium to deliver his sermon, my aunt prayed he wouldn't derail the opportunity she sought to have a conversation with my father. However, to her dismay, it seemed that Bob was poised to pick up where my father had left off. He emphasized the need for unwavering support for my father but also singled out my grandparents for their lack of encouragement. His words carried the weight of accusation as he described their supposed selfish behavior. Reflecting on the stormy turn of events, my aunt confided in me later, "It felt as if the devil himself had intervened and twisted everything."

Now seated with my grandparents in a row just behind my mother, Aunt MaryJane found herself caught in the midst of the escalating tension. My mother, fueled by anger, turned around and unleashed her own retort, exclaiming, "You've really opened a can of worms this time." Despite the callous exchange, Aunt MaryJane clung to her original intention, clinging to the hope that a moment would arise when she could finally speak with my father.

As Bob's sermon neared its conclusion, reprimanding my grandparents, a new figure emerged from the shadows. It was Lou Levante, approaching my aunt and grandparents in their pew, intent on admonishing them directly. Filled with frustration, Aunt MaryJane reached her breaking point. She stepped forward, positioning herself between Lou and her parents, determined to draw a line in the sand.

"Who do you think you are, speaking to my parents that way?" she demanded, her voice cutting through the tension.

"What could you possibly know about our situation?" Her words were laden with righteous indignation, challenging the authority and presumptions of Lou's admonishment.

The congregation fell silent as they witnessed the escalating argument. Suddenly, my father sprang into action, dashing from the pulpit to intercede. "What do you think you're doing here?" he shouted. "Can't you see we are in the midst of worship? Leave this church now, MaryJane, Carmen, Gert!" The force of his words was resolute, leaving no room for compromise.

With heavy hearts and resigned expressions, my aunt and my grandparents followed the direction of my father's pointed finger, retracing their steps toward the door. It was a path all too familiar to me, one that I had witnessed several times before. The weight of the moment settled upon their shoulders as they exited the church, marking their second departure that day.

Chapter Seventeen

TELL ME WHAT HAPPENED

AS TIME MOVED ON, IT CARRIED WITH IT THE WINDS OF CHANGE and the whispers of an approaching storm. My existence underwent a graceful transformation, a delicate dance between lightness and gravity. In the realm of work, I, a young man in his early twenties, toiled to establish a self-made business, nurturing the seed of independence with each stride. However, amidst my pursuits, my thoughts remained entwined in the intricate familial tribulations—a relentless quest to unravel the complex challenges we faced.

Nevertheless, I possessed an extraordinary ability to combine moments of serenity and rejuvenation. Amidst the complexity and the turmoil, a long-forgotten joy rekindled— the resurgence of my longstanding intrigue with the notion of flight and the world of remote-control planes. This dormant desire, abandoned for years, offered me a sense of peace and contentment. In addition to my nightly weightlifting routine from midnight to 2:00 a.m. in the basement of our home, these chosen avenues of escape became fleeting sanctuaries, providing respite from the burden of impending responsibilities and upheaval. They gifted me with precious moments of reprieve, infusing me with the strength to confront the tumultuous currents of my own destiny.

Nearly a week had passed since the unsettling incident within the hallowed confines of the church that previous Sunday morning—an event of which I was still unaware. Against this backdrop, a captivating idea materialized that Friday afternoon—an endeavor to merge the delight of my rediscovered hobby with my family's cherished company. Filled with anticipation, I reached for the phone and dialed my brother Paul's number, ready to unveil the splendid creation that was my recently completed stunt plane. "Hey, Paul, it's finally finished! I'll swing by to pick you up. Let's meet with Grandpa at the field," I exclaimed, my voice infused with exhilaration.

However, the mere mention of our beloved grandfather's attendance provoked an unexpected response from Paul. "Grandpa's going to be there?" he asked, a note of unease tingeing his tone.

"Yes! He'll get a kick out of watching it too!" I replied, my enthusiasm tempered by confusion. A brief pause hung in the air before Paul replied.

"Well, I can't go then."

A whirlwind of concern and bewilderment engulfed me. "What do you mean you can't go?" I pressed, yearning for an explanation.

"There was trouble with Grandma and Grandpa at church," Paul confessed, his voice burdened with unspoken weight. A deluge of questions surged through my mind, crashing against the shores of my consciousness.

"Something happened, and now you can't be around

Grandpa?" I inquired, yearning for clarity.

"Danny, I just can't go if he's going to be there," Paul replied, his words carrying the weight of an untold story.

At that moment, the joy of the occasion faded, replaced by a profound contemplation of the intricacies of my existence. Life's meandering paths had led me astray, erecting a seemingly insurmountable barrier between my loved ones and me. However, amidst the howling winds of change, I vowed to embark on a different path. Guided by an unwavering determination to figure out what was tearing my family apart, I found myself behind the wheel, directing my car toward the school where my father pursued his studies. It was a journey unfamiliar to me, veiled in mystery and ripe with possibilities.

As raindrops pirouetted on my car's windshield, merging and separating in a whimsical ballet, my imagination projected vibrant images of my cousins and other relatives encircling me within the embrace of our familiar home. They appeared to be caught in a transient vortex that enticed them toward enlightenment—an enigmatic domain both fascinating and bewildering.

Stepping across the threshold of the school's imposing double doors, I embarked on a journey within its corridors. As my gaze traversed the surroundings, it was drawn to the photography lab on my right, which evoked a flood of memories from past attempts to bridge the divide between my father and me. The room had become a symbol of longing where I yearned for a connection that remained elusive. Although not yet within my immediate view, I knew that down the hallway lay the rifle range—a domain where students engaged in fierce competitions, vying against rival schools. Similar to the realm of photography, it served as a testament to my father's expertise, where he imparted lessons of precision and focus to eager learners.

Turning left, I approached the door of my father's office and rapped my knuckles against it three times. "Come in," his voice beckoned from within.

As I entered the room, a wave of familiarity washed over me. The walls were adorned with snapshots from fishing expeditions and mementos of boating adventures, creating a gallery of cherished memories. A brass captain's wheel, an emblem of authority, occupied its rightful place on his desk, an enduring symbol of his position as "the man in charge."

After engaging in brief pleasantries, our conversation shifted to the matter weighing on my mind. I was eager to delve into my concerns, yearning to share the burdens that had consumed my thoughts.

I began my inquiry with hardly more than a single sentence, expressing the situation that had unfolded. "I was planning to fly my plane with Paul today, but he told me he couldn't if Grandpa was there. What the heck is going on?"

My father leaned back in his expansive leather chair, his countenance clouded with a tinge of sadness. His eyes began to wander, shifting away from me and then returning, repeating this pattern until they halted with a stern focus on a portrait of our family positioned behind me.

"Son, every day when I sit in this office, I look at that picture. It breaks my heart to know that you're not by my side," he said, his voice tinged with emotion. A look of distress appeared, an unexpected sight that deviated from the anger I had grown accustomed to witnessing when questioning him. I couldn't help but feel a pang of guilt, sensing the weight of his words, but I knew it wouldn't serve any purpose to retort.

Instead, I remained silent, my patience unwavering as I awaited my father's recovery, unsure of the path his words would traverse. When he resumed speaking, his unique manner guided the conversation toward a new trajectory as he sought to illuminate the intricate dynamics between me, my grandparents, and our differing beliefs. "Danny, my son, you're a humanist, and you struggle to comprehend matters of faith because you lack belief. Your grandparents have been causing disruptions within the church, and I can't allow it to continue simply because they're family."

I couldn't help but acknowledge that I, too, posed a challenge to my father—a truth that lingered in the air between us. The question arose: was he drawing parallels between my grandparents and me? Was he implying, through the act of pointing at my image in the portrait, that I, too, presented a problem? My curiosity surged, an insatiable yearning to unravel the intricacies of the situation consuming me. "So, please, enlighten me. What happened? What did my grandparents do that was so bad?"

"Your grandmother has been spreading lies about me within the church, speaking badly about me throughout the congregation," he replied with a hint of frustration. "Meanwhile, your mother is breaking her back, working at the school, while your grandmother sits on her ass at home, having phone conversations that put me down. Instead of contributing to the church, she busies herself with tearing it apart."

Earlier, tears had welled up in my father's eyes. Now they had nearly dried, leaving only faint traces behind. Nonetheless, the relentless accusations against my grandmother continued. My father spoke with unyielding resolve, tarnishing her character at every opportunity, relying on vague generalizations. However, as time passed, a shift occurred in his tone, veering toward a more vindictive and vengeful path.

"And I'll tell you another thing," he continued, his words laced with resentment, "mark my words, your mother and I will thrive once your grandparents are no longer around. We have the church and our family, but who will they have? They will be left with no one, and they will suffer for it!"

I gazed deep into my father's eyes, analyzing his every expression and hoping to find some evidence of misinterpretation. Regrettably, my efforts only solidified what I had been hesitant to accept. My father was deriving gratification from inflicting pain upon my grandparents. I felt certain of it, especially when I witnessed the unsettling sight of his smile, accompanied by a rhythmic nodding of his head—a disconcerting display of pleasure.

"This is how you truly feel? You want to witness Grandma and Grandpa suffer?" I exclaimed, a mixture of disbelief and anguish coloring my words.

A year prior, I had found myself perched in the same chair, engrossed in a conversation with my father that left an indelible mark on my memory. I had posed a question, seeking enlightenment, but his response left me baffled, my mind grappling to comprehend its elusive meaning. At that moment, I caught a glimpse of his awareness of my bewilderment, but he remained resolute, delivering an answer that stood as one of the rare morsels of clarity amid the labyrinth of my inquiries. His words resonated with a peculiar mixture of audacity and intrigue: "Son, you don't understand. I possess power over other people's lives, and it is something they desire for themselves."

In the sacred confines of the church, where righteousness and devotion reigned supreme, the notion of power seemed foreign and incongruous. I was confounded, attempting to reconcile the dissonance between the teachings of Christianity and the seductive whispers of control. How could such notions find footing in a realm so deeply rooted in honor and truth? In my naivety, I clung to the belief that virtue and righteousness held sway over my father and his companions, for in my youthful optimism, I yearned for a world where goodness triumphed.

The memory of that unsettling encounter resurfaced within me, its tendrils reaching deep into the core of my being, igniting a fresh wave of turmoil. At that pivotal moment, hope slipped through my fingers, dissipating into the abyss, as my father's puzzling explanation finally unraveled before me, revealing a disconcerting truth. It became painfully evident that he derived a perverse satisfaction from the envy stirred by his command over the lives of others. It was a jarring confirmation, an unwelcome testament to my father's troubled nature and the misalignment of his priorities.

Amidst the shards of my shattered expectations, however,

my heart still clung to a flicker of belief. I yearned to perceive a glimmer of sincerity in his actions, to trust in the remnants of his good intentions even as the glaring cracks in his character grew more pronounced. The recognition of this fragile bond, teetering on the precipice of doubt, served as a stark reminder of the complexity of our relationship. I grappled with the paradox of questioning his motives while also yearning for his care and guidance. If only he understood the fragility of our connection, the delicate thread that held us together, perhaps he would recognize the extent of my struggle.

As I traversed the heart-wrenching terrain of emotions, I clung to a sliver of hope that my father's intentions were rooted in a deeper goodness, one obscured by his internal turmoil. I also wrestled with the notion that he was lost and in desperate need of assistance, hoping that redemption would find its way to his tormented soul.

"But, Dad, even if they made mistakes, their intentions were good," I insisted, determined to defend my grandparents. "Perhaps they were frustrated, unable to find a better way to handle their problems. Shouldn't their intent to do good be enough for you?" The concept of "intentions" had been a recurring topic in our morning discussions over coffee as we prepared for the day ahead.

"Now, son, I've told you before, good intentions are all well and good, but it is our actions that truly matter," he would often respond.

Little did he know that if I had followed his advice, I would have severed ties with him long ago. As clever as he was, there were crucial aspects that he failed to grasp. While he continued to unleash his wrath upon my grandparents' reputation, a deluge of memories flooded my mind, memories of similar encounters and unsettling realizations. I resisted, attempting to suppress them, but as I listened to his tirade, my father's true identity became increasingly evident.

For the first time, the notion of my father's malevolent intentions crept into my consciousness, casting a shadow of doubt over his actions. Empowered by this newfound realization, a surge of boldness coursed through my veins, compelling me to confront him in a manner I had never dared before. "Do you truly desire to inflict suffering upon them because you perceive them as having harmed you?" I asked. "As a pastor and counselor to numerous individuals, shouldn't your teachings revolve around forgiveness and compassion rather than seeking revenge against those believed to be responsible for causing you pain? Will you hold a grudge against me as well, blaming me for the suffering you endure due to my absence? It's your role to guide others away from the very actions you are now exhibiting. Why not strive to embody the principles of Christianity that you profess, so I can find a genuine reason to respect you and to stand by your side?"

There was no immediate interruption or eruption of anger or retaliation for my audacious words. Instead, an unfamiliar silence enveloped us, charged with unspoken emotions and the weight of unacknowledged truths. Then, in a moment that defied all expectations, my father's stoic persona crumbled, giving way to a torrent of uncontrollable weeping. I found myself in uncharted territory, grappling with the discomfort of witnessing his vulnerability, a side he had always hidden from view. Despite the unease that permeated the air, I remained in my seat, awaiting his recovery from the weight of his own transgressions.

Eventually, he regained his composure, wiping away his tears, a sign that his emotional state had shifted. "The turmoil within this church and our family has become unbearable. I've reached my breaking point, and I can no longer endure it. Your mother and I are going to sell our house, leave this town, and start anew in a place where nobody knows us." The words hung in the air, leaving me stunned once again, as they seemed completely out of character for the father I had come to know. Questions swirled in my mind. How would the members of his church and our family react if they heard these revelations? Was he aware of how transparently he was exposing his flaws to me?

Despite my shock, I couldn't simply accept his declaration. A deep longing stirred within me, a yearning for my father to reclaim the pedestal of respect and admiration I had once put him upon. "You need to have a conversation with my grandparents and work through this," I said. "Christianity is about making better choices, not avoiding them. Leaving our family and your church is not the right course of action. It's not too late to talk things through and find a resolution with the family. And if you find it too challenging, help is available. You can seek guidance from someone impartial who is outside of these difficulties."

"Alright, son, I'll do that. I'll have a conversation with your grandparents, and we'll work through this together," my father replied, offering a glimmer of hope. At that moment, I knew I had said all that I could, that now it was a matter of waiting and hoping for the best.

We left his office and ventured across the parking lot, making our way to the gymnasium in the adjacent academy. Lou Levante, the school principal, was standing there, his gaze catching the traces of dried tears on my father's face. We engaged in polite albeit superficial conversation. My father said his goodbyes and then left me with Lou. As my father headed to his office to continue preparing for the evening's service, I couldn't shake a lingering feeling of uncertainty.

Then, as if he had been waiting for the perfect moment, Lou turned his attention toward me. "So, what brings you here today, Danny?" His words sparked vivid memories of a distant night when Lou had been a guest at our family dinner table. During that gathering he recounted a harrowing tale of a heated argument with one of his cousins that had escalated into a violent altercation in his own kitchen. In a disturbing display of aggression, Lou had punched his cousin's face while pinning him down against the table. The story, shared not as a justification but rather as a testament to his perceived toughness, had left an indelible impression. Now confronted by Lou's inquisitive gaze, I took a moment to compose myself before responding.

"I came here to talk with my father about a matter concerning our family."

"You know, Danny," Lou replied, his voice dripping with reproach, "you and some others in your family, you disgust me. The way you disregard your father and the tireless work he puts into this church is beyond comprehension. It's a shame, a sickness that runs deep, how you bring him trouble instead of offering support." To me, Lou was nothing more than an acquaintance, a mere friend of my father's, someone involved in his school. He held no authority over me, and I certainly held no admiration for him. Yet there he stood, reprimanding me. It felt like a scene out of a movie, where the character's behavior is so repulsive and foolish that it induces second-hand embarrassment. I couldn't help but pity Lou, for he remained oblivious to the intricate complexities at play. I longed for him to embody the role of a revered elder, a wise mentor, or a principled figure—anything but the emperor with no clothes.

A few days later, my father reached out with an update. "Danny, I spoke with your grandmother. Everything is going to be okay."

"That's great!" I replied, relief washing over me.

"I'll do my best to keep the peace within the family, to bury what happened in the past and never speak of it again," he continued. "Oh, and I sent her a dozen roses." However, as the words escaped his lips, I realized their inadequacy.

"Don't you see?" I interjected, my frustration seeping through. "That won't be enough. You can't simply slap a Band-Aid on an open wound and expect it to heal. Meaningful conversations are necessary, addressing the underlying issues head on. Pushing everything aside will only lead to a repetition of the same problems."

"Now, son," my father replied, his tone resolute, "I told you I spoke with your grandmother, and everything will be okay."

Understanding the futility of further debate, I resigned myself to waiting and observing, hoping for a genuine transformation.

Three weeks later, the bitter truth unveiled itself—silence once again enveloped our family. No one dared to speak, and the wounds that had festered beneath the surface threatened to rupture with even greater force. The path forward remained uncertain, and we were left to confront the looming storm that lay ahead.

Chapter Eighteen

ON MY WAY OUT

AND SO IT UNFOLDED, LIKE A TRAGIC SYMPHONY PLAYING OUT over the course of another agonizing month. A dark cloud seemed to have settled over our lives, casting a suffocating shadow on our once-vibrant existence. My aunt and uncle's home, once filled with laughter and warmth, now stood desolate, devoid of the lively visits it once hosted. The same fate befell my grandparents, as if an invisible force had banished all company from their doorstep. Caught in the midst of this storm, I was expected to conform to this cold isolation.

But how could I? How could I forget the times when my mother herself urged me to visit them, emphasizing the immeasurable joy my presence brought to their lives? Was I supposed to turn a blind eye to their pain and suffering, to abandon them in their time of need, simply because my father's cruel words echoed in my ears? No, I could no longer passively accept this absurdity. I engaged in forbidden conversations with my mother, my brothers, and my sisters, defying my father's orders. I refused to let the bonds that tied us as a family be severed by his venomous decree.

My father, in his relentless pursuit of control, had even forbidden me from uttering the names of my grandparents, my beloved aunt, or my cherished uncle in their presence. But I persisted, defiantly speaking their names, recounting the treasured moments we shared, and reminding my family of the undeniable truth—that they were good people, deserving of our love and support.

I no longer cared about the consequences of my defiance. I was willing to bear the burden of my father's wrath if it meant standing up for what I believed in. For deep within me was an unyielding conviction that our family should not be torn apart, that our shared memories should not be erased. They were the threads that held us together, the fragments of a past that spoke of love, unity, and compassion.

However, my desperate attempts to sway their hearts fell on deaf ears. They had become blind to reason, their vision clouded by my father's insidious influence. Like a distorted playback, my words were mangled and fed back to him, reinforcing his iron grip over their perception.

Then came the day that shattered the illusion of stability. I was in the dimly lit living room preparing my taxes when my father approached me. Upstairs, my brother David remained in his room, oblivious to the impending storm.

"Danny," my father began, his voice laced with gravity, "I have something I want to talk to you about." A mixture of weariness and defiance filled my soul as I nodded.

"Okay, fine. Just let me finish filling out this form." I said, my words laden with a hint of resignation. I knew this conversation would not be a casual exchange of pleasantries. Something palpable was in the air, a tension that made my skin prickle.

What transpired next exceeded the bounds of my wildest imagination. The impending eviction had cast a foreboding shadow, but the unfolding events took on an unforeseen magnitude. With calculated intention, my father beckoned David from the solitude of his room, commanding his presence as a witness to my departure. "You're not going to make others believe I threw you out. David will bear witness to the fact that you're leaving of your own volition!" My heart plummeted, not only for my own uncertain fate but for David as well, now thrust into the vortex of our father's twisted tales and manipulations. Even so, within the depths of my being, I clung to a glimmer of hope, certain that the weight of truth would prevail and compel David to speak candidly about that unforgettable day.

During the frenzy of my initial week of the enforced exile, I poured my emotions onto paper, crafting a heartfelt letter destined for David's hands—a testament to the truths he had buried within. Sealing it with hope and trepidation, I entrusted the missive to the whims of fate, yearning for its words to unleash a long-awaited awakening within him.

To my disappointment, however, he never read it. To this day, that letter remains untouched, its contents confined to the abyss of his unwavering denial. In a desperate bid to break the chains of silence, I presented it to him years later, beseeching him to finally confront the undeniable truth. But as resolute as ever, he averted his gaze, rejecting the opportunity to peer beyond the veil and confront the haunting secrets that lay within. Enmeshed in a complicated network of loyalty and denial, he remained ensnared in our shared history, unwilling to uncover the hidden truths held in those weathered pages.

DAVID, DO YOU KNOW WHAT HAPPENED?

1981

David,

Because you had been exposed to a part of an argument that Dad and I had I want to be sure that you hear about the rest of it, not only from Dad but also from me. I hope you will be able to read this with an open mind and that you are able to share this letter with Mom, Dad and anyone who has questions about some of the many problems that face our family.

Last week after getting up in the morning, I decided to work on my income taxes. I brought the paperwork into the family room. After sitting for a few minutes, Dad walked in and said that he had something to talk to me about that I probably wouldn't like. Dad did not say this in a rude manner. I replied by saying, "

OK, I just have to complete the bottom of this form." No problem so far. Roughly forty-five seconds later I was finished. Dad began calmly by bringing up the topic, "Dan, you have to start helping out around the house." Dad brought up how you are going to college and working a part-time job and still have shown concern about the family and help out around the house. He continued by stating everyone else helps out. Dad expressed how for years now I haven't and put a statement to me that I haven't heard before: "Dan, either you are going to help out or you are going to have to leave." My response was, "Dad, you are right. I haven't helped nearly as much as I should. I should do more."

After I agreed, he went on with the list of complaints. "Dan, you come and go as you please, you're a burden to your mother, you don't care what goes on around here. Last week you were only home two days, etc., etc." At this point Dad's voice turned much louder. It became obvious to me that Dad was getting very emotional and upset. I was becoming nervous and upset too. I asked Dad what he meant by saying that I was only home two days last week when I WAS home all week and spent the week-end in Dunkirk with Sue's family. He replied by saying, "I don't even want to get into how you spend only a couple of nights a week at home." This made no sense to me since it had nothing to do with the question. Then I asked him to take back what he said about my being home two nights the previous week before we go any further because we both knew it wasn't true. He refused. So I said to him, "You told me Ma had to hire a maid because of the burden that I am on the family. How much of a burden can I be if I only spend two nights a week at home?" Dad replied by going on about the other areas that I wasn't too good at with the family. It was obvious to me that he was reaching for anything that would reinforce his point. But the last complaint was more than I could handle. Dad told me that I didn't care about our family in any way. At that point because I knew it wasn't true, I thought about something that happened very recently that would not have oc-curred if Dad was right. Mom came to me one day and asked me, "How are you doing?" I said, "What do you mean?" She said, "How are you getting along? Are you making much money?" I said, "I'm doing OK." So, she asked me if we could talk. I said fine. We went into the new room, closed the door and talked. Debbie was in the kitchen looking at pictures of a wedding dress that she just told me would cost in excess of $1,000. So, anyway Ma said to me that there is an expense that she worries Dad will have trouble paying for. Then she tells me how Dad is burdened with Debbie's wedding, how Pam has college expenses, how you have college expenses, and about Paul's tuition. She said how the church has helped out with the driveway, the garage doors, etc. Then Ma told me how Debbie was helping to pay for her wedding, how you and Pam were working part-time to help pay tuition, etc. Then she asked me if I could help out with this major expense that has to be taken care of: a roof that will cost thousands of dollars. Now, I knew Ma wasn't asking for me to come up with all that money. She was just asking if I could contribute some money in an affordable way. I couldn't help but think about how everyone was helping out, but it was for themselves. Thinking about this big burden, Debbie was helping out, but it was toward her wedding. Why not say, "Ma, how about a $500 dress, and here is a $500 to help toward the house?" I couldn't help but share my feelings with Ma. She said the dress was something a man couldn't understand; only a woman could. But hey, after telling her what I felt I said, "No problem. I don't have money right now, but I will help out. Let me see where I am financially, and I'll see what I can do."

David, I love Ma and Dad very much. I don't like to see Ma worried or upset. I have told Ma and Dad a number of times how indebted I am to them. They have helped me with a car and many other things.

So, to go on, I thought about this roof thing for two weeks and decided that I would take a loan from the bank and pay the six or seven thousand for the roof job. Then I called Dad, and we sat and talked. I told him he's done a lot for me. He's helped me with a car and other things. I told him that I heard about the roof and that I would like to help. I said I would be getting more work and making more money, that I am not all "gimme gimme," and I'd like to pay for the whole roof job. We talked about the roof for roughly an hour. We discussed how maybe it would be best to do it in the spring because of certain technicalities that Dad expressed. Then he thanked me for my sincerity and stated how he couldn't let me pay for the entire job.

Now to get back to where I was. I was saying how Dad told me I didn't care about the family or anything that happened around the house. My reply was, "Dad, I know it's only money, but what about when I came to you about the roof? Doesn't that show that I care at least a little?" His reply, and I quote, was, "DAN, talk is cheap, and that was just talk!" Dave, I was so hurt. I couldn't yell, just be hurt. It was not until then that Dad said, "What are you going to do? Either you help out or you're going to have to leave." At that point I said, "Dad, right now because of the way we're getting along, maybe it would be best for me to leave. I don't know. I'm very upset right now. I need time to think." Immediately, he said, "Oh, you need time to think about whether or not you're going to help out around here?" I replied, "No, I need time to think about whether or not it's right for me to stay home at this point." Right then he insisted that I wasn't going to make it look like he had thrown me out of the house. That's when he called you down from upstairs. Dad said he was going to let you hear what both of us had to say, so you could see that I was leaving on my own. I told him I thought it was a terrible idea. I said bringing you into this would only be forcing you to side with a brother against a father or a father against a brother and that no matter who was right or wrong it would be a terrible position to put you in. Regardless, Dad didn't change his mind. You came down, and Dad started to talk to you. He said he asked me if I would start helping around the house like everyone else is and that my reply was, "I have to think about it." I kept quiet while Dad spoke with you. It's what we agreed to do for each other. It took a lot of self-control to keep quiet when I knew Dad was lying—outright lying. When Dad was finished talking to you, you looked at me and said that it didn't sound like Dad was asking much of me. I thought to myself, "He's right; he wasn't asking much," but that's because Dad just lied about what happened. I began to tell you I didn't tell Dad that I needed time to think about whether or not I should help out around the house but that I needed time to think about whether or not I should be living at home. But before I could finish, Dad jumped out of his chair, headed toward me, shaking his hands in my face saying, "Don't point your finger at me." I thought he was going to hit me. Then he called me a liar, said I was twisting the truth etc., deliberately preventing me from telling you my side. At that point Dad said, "Now I'm asking you to leave because you are lying and twisting the truth and are causing trouble in this home." Then he expressed that I would have a week to find a place to live. Then I told him that he needed to search for the truth. I told him he was not living the Christian life that he professed. Then as Dad began to walk away, I apologized for acting nervous and for having to end things the way we did.

David, I love our mother and father and our family, but I have lost the respect that I used to have for Dad. He taught me that one of the sins a man could have that he could not tolerate was to lie.

He was right. But now it is his sin, and I hope for everyone's sake that he will change.

Chapter Twenty

FORGING A LIFE OUTSIDE THE NEST

THE ARGUMENT WITH MY FATHER REACHED ITS BOILING POINT IN the heart of our family's kitchen. Trembling with a mixture of fear and defiance, I stood searching for a way to defend myself against his relentless accusations. As my gaze shifted to my brother, yearning for a glimmer of understanding, I was only met with a blank stare and heartbreaking silence. In that moment, a profound sense of alienation made me feel like a stranger in my own home.

Driven by a deep-rooted sense of being unwanted, I made a fateful decision without knowing where it would lead me. Numbly, I moved toward the pantry, my hands grasping a handful of trash bags. With each step, a surreal detachment enveloped me as I ascended the stairs to my bedroom. I opened each drawer, stuffing my belongings into the green bags, the physical act of packing mirroring the emotional weight of my impending departure.

As I closed the door behind me, I took a final glance at the room that had once been my sanctuary, now transformed into a space of bittersweet memories. The image of my childhood self, captured in a photograph on the hallway wall, caught my attention, a reminder of the innocence and joy that once filled my existence. In that instant, my entire life flashed before my eyes, a montage of moments that shaped the person I had become. The truth of my journey was laid bare before me—this was the culmination of a life defined by struggle and resilience.

With a heavy heart, I continued down the hallway, each step bringing me closer to another chapter, to an unknown path that awaited beyond the threshold of my childhood home. As I descended the stairs, I stole one last look back, bidding farewell to the life I had known.

I emerged from the confines of the house, my car awaiting me like a loyal accomplice, ready to whisk me away. As I slipped behind the wheel, the engine roared to life, its rumble drowning out my racing thoughts. The events of that fateful day were imprinted on my mind, the memories looping in an endless carousel of disbelief and confusion.

The hours slipped by, each one marked by the changing scenery, gradually distancing me from the aftermath of the volatile showdown. In the solitude of the road, I yearned for peace, an escape from the turmoil that had enveloped my being. I wanted a sanctuary, a haven where I could piece together the shattered fragments of my thoughts and soothe the frayed edges of my emotions.

With each mile traveled, the world around me transformed, offering glimpses of hidden shelters and secret retreats. I sought refuge in the embrace of nature, yearning to lose myself amidst majestic landscapes and whispering trees. The open road became my compass, guiding me toward destinations unknown, where I hoped to find the peace and tranquility my soul craved.

As I drove, my mind continued to unravel the threads of the day's events, seeking understanding and resolution amidst the maelstrom. The wheels spun beneath me, carrying me farther into the unknown, the steady rhythm of the road providing a soothing backdrop to my contemplation.

In the midst of my journey, a realization dawned on me. It wasn't just physical distance I sought but a departure from the weight of expectations and the suffocating grip of familial dynamics. I yearned for a place where I could breathe freely, unfettered by the judgments and misunderstandings that had plagued our interactions.

And so, I continued on my journey, the road winding and twisting like the intricate path of self-discovery. Remnants of the day's events lingered, but I was aware that peace would come from within, requiring me to summon the strength to overcome the onslaught of attacks and accusations.

Until that point, all I knew was the profound ache of being unwanted, a sensation so unbearable that the mere thought of inhabiting a house where I was merely tolerated sent shivers down my spine.

In that pivotal moment, as the weight of my circumstances bore down on me, I sought comfort in Sue's embrace—my second significant romantic relationship. To my father and the rest of my family, she was merely "that girl." They remained oblivious to her name, a deliberate choice of my father's to keep my relationships hidden from the family.

And so, armed with newfound resolve, I embarked on a conversation with Sue, hoping she would open her heart and her home to me. I yearned for her understanding and guidance, longing to find refuge within the warmth of her embrace until the day I could stand on my own, liberated from the chains of a life that had never truly belonged to me.

Susan inhabited an enchanting ground-floor apartment nestled within the Norstar development. The vibrant community, located just a stone's throw away from my parents' house, held a wealth of memories from my childhood. I recalled the exhilaration of gliding across the frozen Norstar pond, a hidden gem tucked behind the wooded area near my parents' home. Its glistening surface had always tempted me to explore its icy depths, a place where adventures were born. In those carefree days, Don and I fearlessly teased the older teenagers who dared to skate on the frozen ice, our mischievous laughter and boundless energy reverberating through the crisp winter air.

With every stride, the world outside Sue's apartment seemed to unfold before us like a breathtaking panorama, an ever-present reminder of the enchanting world just beyond our grasp. However, Sue's dwelling was more than a mere haven with a view—it housed a dynamic duo. Wendy, Sue's unwavering companion and confidante, occupied the larger bedroom, their bond a testament to the enduring strength of their friendship. Together, they navigated the complexities of life, supporting and uplifting each other with a shared understanding that transcended words.

Their cozy apartment was filled with laughter and whispered secrets, creating an atmosphere of warmth and camaraderie. Sue and Wendy's presence was a beacon of light, illuminating the space with their vibrant personalities and unwavering loyalty. Their shared journey from their hometown of Dunkirk, New York, to the vibrant city of Syracuse represented a bold leap of faith, an escape from the limitations of the familiar. They embraced the adventure with open hearts, seeking a life beyond the confines of their small-town origins.

Susan thrived in her role at State Farm Insurance, selling auto policies under the watchful guidance of Toni, her charismatic Italian boss. With each passing day, our connection deepened as we delved into the vast expanse of our shared interests, engaging in conversations that ignited our passions and exposed the intricacies of our souls. Sue possessed an innate gift for listening, creating a safe space where I felt at ease unearthing the complexities of my family dynamics. However, little did I realize that this burgeoning bond would propel us into a realm of intimacy that far exceeded any of my previous experiences.

With Sue, I discovered a profound sense of belonging and acceptance. She became intertwined with my very essence, a mirror reflecting the depths of my soul. There was no need for pretense or superficial conversations; she embraced the unfiltered and intricate layers of my thoughts. I could spend hours pouring my heart out, navigating the maze of my emotions, and she would lend a patient ear. It was a love unlike any I had known, where my words were cherished and valued. In the warmth of Sue's presence, I felt both appreciated and emancipated, as though I had found a sanctuary for my real self.

Day after day, our lives revolved around the demands of our respective jobs, each passing moment bringing us closer to the cherished reunions that awaited us. I was drawn to the familiarity of Sue's office, where I found a reassuring symbol of her affection for me, a whimsical display of my name written in various playful forms. However, it was on Wednesday nights that the world truly came alive as we joined forces with Sue's effervescent friend Wendy and a vibrant group of souls at the Sugarmill, a haven where music and laughter created a pulsating energy that fueled our unforgettable nights of dancing and revelry. Among the captivating personalities that graced our circle, Wendy's charismatic brother, Larry, and his vivacious girlfriend, Barb, stood out, adding an extra spark of excitement to our adventures.

On the occasions when Sue and I visited her beloved hometown of Dunkirk, I eagerly anticipated afternoons at Wendy's parents' house—an abode overflowing with joy and merriment. Buzz, Wendy's father, exuded an undeniable zest for life. His booming voice, filled with contagious enthusiasm, affirmed his mantra, "Ya gotta want it!" His words ignited a fierce determination within us, pushing us to seize every opportunity. Their expansive backyard was transformed into our playground, a backdrop for playful games that filled the air with laughter. From lively games of Jarts to animated banter, the atmosphere was uplifted by Buzz's infectious laughter, which melded seamlessly with the melodic chuckles of his wife, Sal. Together, they reveled in the bonds of camaraderie and collective joy.

As the sun dipped below the horizon, casting an ethereal glow upon the surroundings, we sought refuge indoors, eager to embark on a new realm of amusement. The air was charged with excitement as we immersed ourselves into the captivating world of "The Word Game," where imagination met wit, and lines were playfully blurred. Each participant wove their own definition, intertwining it seamlessly with the genuine essence of the chosen word. Laughter reverberated through the room, cascading like a symphony of joy as we unraveled the intricate web of truth and fabrication, reveling in the delightful absurdity of our collective creativity.

At the heart of it all, Sal's laughter was an infectious melody, a testament to the delight she found in our playful antics. Her genuine mirth served as a beacon, illuminating the bonds of friendship that had formed within the walls of that sacred space. With open arms and warm hearts, her family embraced me as a purveyor of humor, an honorary member of their laughter-filled tribe.

In their presence, I unearthed a profound sense of belonging, a refuge that surpassed the confines of my own family. They embodied the essence of a chosen family, their love and acceptance radiating with every heartfelt interaction.

Sue, Wendy, Larry, Barb, Buzz, Sal, and the entire ensemble of characters became more than friends; they became an inseparable part of my journey. Their ability to find comfort in life's simplest pleasures and infuse each moment with laughter was a revelation. Through their companionship, I discovered a new way of being that celebrated authenticity, shared experiences, and unyielding support.

The apartment parties were legendary. Wendy's charismatic brother Larry would arrive with his entourage while Sue's friend GG and her posse would grace us with their presence. It was the night we dubbed "Wing Night" that held a special place in our hearts. The tantalizing aroma of Wendy's secret buffalo chicken wings filled the air, tempting our taste buds with their fiery flavor. Those wings were like no other, a culinary masterpiece that had us salivating before the first bite.

Bag after bag of wings were cooked to perfection, complemented by crisp celery, crunchy chips, and a variety of drinks, from sodas to beers and other spirits. As guests arrived, the volume was turned up, immersing the apartment in beats that set our souls alight. The living room was transformed into a vibrant dance floor where we surrendered to the rhythm, dancing with unrestrained passion and freeing our inhibitions. These were nights of boundless joy, with laughter resonating through the walls, blending with the infectious energy of the gathering.

The aftermath of each party was undeniable. The carpet bore the marks of our enthusiastic dancing, littered with debris that required a thorough vacuuming. Despite the decibel levels that would make most buildings tremble, we were remarkably undisturbed. The building's soundproofing was surprisingly effective, allowing us to partake in our raucous festivities without drawing unwanted attention. We were the kings and queens of the night, free to be as loud and as wild as our spirits desired.

Amidst the whirlwind of new experiences and connections, my unwavering loyalty to my family remained steadfast. I tirelessly reached out to them, convinced that it was only a matter of time before they saw the absurdity of our separation. But to my dismay, my calls fell on deaf ears. One by one, they refused to see or speak to me, shutting the door on any chance of reconciliation. The weight of their silence pressed heavily upon me.

Amid the overwhelming rejections, one beacon of hope emerged. Against all odds, my sister Debbie agreed to meet with me. This was a faint light in an oppressive darkness, an opportunity to mend the rift that had grown between us. We decided to meet at a quaint Syracuse restaurant. Though I longed to delve into the depths of our family turmoil, I sensed that the timing wasn't right. Instead, I focused on maintaining the connection, assuring her that there was no ill will between us. But to my disappointment, Debbie's words cut through the air like a sharp blade. She made it clear that she could have no relationship with me until I resolved my issues with our father.

My heart sank as I pleaded with her, desperate for her understanding and acceptance. "Debbie, that's a matter between him and me. Can't you simply be my sister and stay in touch?" I implored. But her stance was unwavering, stressing she wouldn't see me again unless I met her stipulation. If only she understood the reality—that our father had slammed the door to reconciliation, consistently avoiding me despite my numerous outreach efforts.

And so my life danced on the precarious balance between the somber realities of my family and the carefree world of my newfound home. I seized every opportunity to infuse my days with activities that granted me joy, serving as a refuge from the lingering ache within my soul. While I still made occasional visits to my grandparents, aunt, and uncle, I kept those encounters brief. The bittersweet joy of being in their presence served as a constant reminder of the upheaval I had left behind. Deep within, a burning desire to chart a different course ignited, propelling me toward a path untethered from the shadows of my troubled family.

My focus shifted, homing in on my work with unwavering determination. With the absence of a stable long-term residence, I knew it was imperative to take a more serious approach to managing my finances. As I delved deeper into the realm of responsibility, a vibrant diversity of experiences came alive within the walls of our apartment. Wendy's boyfriend, John, emerged from his Navy service and became a temporary resident in our abode. Adding to the lively mix, Wendy's spirited sister, Lorry, had already claimed her place in our shared sanctuary. Living amidst a trio of vibrant and independent women was a situation that could easily raise eyebrows, especially if my father uncovered the truth. Whispers had already permeated the church community, weaving a false narrative of me leaving home to engage in illicit cohabitation. Oh, how I yearned to set the record straight, to shatter the misconceptions and reveal the deep-rooted truth behind my departure—the desperate quest to escape the clutches of feeling unwanted and unloved.

The highly anticipated day finally arrived, marking the long-awaited reunion with John and coinciding with Sue's thrilling bowling tournament in a far-flung town. We looked forward to joining Sue's teammates and coworkers at the tournament venue, excited to cheer them on and share in their joy. With a mischievous glint in my eye, I warmly welcomed John, enlisting his assistance in concocting a refreshing fusion of iced tea and vodka to accompany us on our adventure.

The car ride became a vibrant medley of laughter and animated discussions, and we eagerly interacted with anyone we encountered, even striking up conversations with pedestrians through our rolled-down windows.

Once at the destination, Sue introduced us to her teammates. While we enjoyed their company, John and I were compelled to explore and mingle with others in the lively venue. Time seemed to evaporate, and the outcome of the tournament faded in importance. Before we knew it, we were making our way to a nearby bar, drawn to the inviting emptiness of the dance floor.

The once lifeless space came to life as we entered, its expansive floor inviting us to lose ourselves in the rhythm of the music's beat.

We formed a line, hands on each other's hips, moving in

unison as we circled the floor. Wendy's gleeful "weeeews" punctuated the air, accompanied by exclamations of joy from the others. As our circle widened, individuals stepped into the spotlight to flaunt their dance moves. The atmosphere was consistently vibrant at all of our spirited gatherings, whether at home, at the Sugarmill, or elsewhere. Just like Larry's kung fu friends, whose impressive skills added a touch of mystique and awe to our events, so did the strangers among us, contributing in kind to the electrifying ambiance.

Our group thrived, growing to a vibrant count of forty or more, and the memories we created together became the stuff of legends. Those were the moments that would be cherished, retold with a twinkle in our eyes, keeping our laughter and camaraderie alive.

Amidst it all, John seamlessly integrated himself into our close-knit circle, swiftly becoming my closest companion and trusted confidant. We shared countless hours engrossed in profound conversations, listening to each other's thoughts and dreams.

One particular afternoon at Onondaga Lake stands out in my mind, our beloved gathering spot where we convened to hang out and engage in heartfelt discussions. While tossing a football, savoring a joint, and immersing ourselves in conversation, John's audacity reached new heights as he unexpectedly plunged into the polluted waters, his laughter and splashes shattering the tranquility of the surroundings. I stood there, awestruck, my mind grappling with a mixture of disbelief and admiration. Onlookers froze in astonishment, their gazes fixed on this audacious display. I couldn't help but shout, urging him to retreat from the contaminated depths. However, with a mischievous grin, John simply shrugged it off, citing his Navy experiences as proof that he had faced far worse. At that moment, I couldn't help but think that perhaps both of us possessed a touch of madness, bound together by an unwavering spirit of adventure and the uncanny ability to find joy in the most unexpected places.

Before meeting John, I'd heard Wendy express reservations about his perceived irresponsibility and his Navy enlistment, stemming from feelings of being unanchored. She spoke of the uncertain future that awaited them, questioning his reliability. Intrigued by Wendy's concerns, I sought an opportunity to engage John in conversation, eager to gain insight into his perspective. We delved into the depths of his life for hours on end as he shared his experiences and viewpoints with raw honesty. I was captivated by his tales, and our connection forged an indomitable bond of friendship.

It wasn't long before John moved to Syracuse and joined me in my endeavors. By then, Wendy and Lori had already moved out of the apartment, leaving Sue and me as the sole occupants. I transformed one of the bedrooms into an office, adorned with a brand-new desk, typewriter, chair, and all the other necessary equipment. I took great pride in my achievements, especially securing my biggest contract yet with Hewlett Packard—a 20,000-square-foot building that required my maintenance services five days a week. As my business aspirations flourished, I garnered new accounts and forged new relationships. Sensing an opportunity, I struck a deal with John, inviting him to join me in the sales department.

Those were unforgettable days, brimming with high energy and unwavering confidence. With limited experience but fueled by self-assurance, we took to the field, distributing personalized short-form letters to prospective clients. I spoke to John with certainty during our training sessions, and our dynamic presence made a lasting impact. In our first month together, John single-handedly generated a deluge of work, surpassing our capacity. While he graciously attributed his success to me, it was his innate greatness, outgoing nature, and genuine demeanor that propelled him forward. Today as I pen these words about him, John holds a prominent position at a renowned pharmaceutical company, leading a team of hundreds of salespeople, consistently reigning as their top performer.

During our quest for new opportunities, John crossed

paths with the owner of a small office park—an enticing prospect situated in a prime location that was in dire need of reliable maintenance services. With our growing business in mind, John proposed that we offer our services in exchange for an office space. Intrigued by the idea, we discussed it at length, ultimately deciding it was a perfect fit for our expanding operations. We relocated my desk and other furniture from the bedroom to the new office, signaling a significant milestone in our journey. It was within those walls that I took the bold step of placing a three-quarter page ad in the Yellow Pages, determined to propel our business to new heights. To accommodate our expanding fleet of equipment, I purchased a sleek blue Chevy Astro van, a symbol of our growing success and a means to transport the tools necessary to serve our expanding client base. As the business flourished, I remained steadfast, fueled by a relentless drive to push boundaries and explore new horizons.

Despite everything, my love for my family remained unyielding. I continued reaching out, placing phone calls in a sincere attempt to bridge the widening chasm. "Debbie, please understand, what's happening between Dad and me is a separate issue. I've never wronged you," I implored, my voice filled with desperation.

"But, Danny," she replied, "by meeting you, wouldn't I be condoning what you did to Dad?"

Her words hit hard, revealing the profound divide between us. They underscored the warped notion that associating with me would be seen as a betrayal, as if supporting one person inherently meant denouncing the other. This doctrine flourished in the discourse surrounding those who dared associate with those who had strayed from the church, irrespective of their familial bonds.

One Thursday evening I was busy cleaning a client's office at SSAC with one of my employees when an overpowering need to speak to my mother overcame me. While I worked, memories of family and the strains caused by our disputes filled my thoughts. Compelled, I called her from the company phone, needing to comprehend her decision to distance herself from me.

"Mom, this is madness. How can you distance yourself from me just because I'm at odds with Dad?" I implored, frustration and disbelief evident in my tone. Her reply stunned me, halting me in mid action.

"Danny, you know your issue? You've always had a mind of your own!" The weight of her statement settled heavily upon me. Gathering my thoughts, I retorted.

"Ma, think about what you've just said. Yes, I have a mind of my own. Shouldn't I? Whose mind should I have?"

An uncomfortable silence ensued, signaling her struggle for a suitable comeback. She had always found it difficult to counter my forthright logic. Eventually, she responded, her voice reflecting a blend of desire and exasperation. "Your father loves you. But until you apologize and show him respect, I can't be with you."

In the years that followed, the trajectories of our lives had carried us on diverging paths. However, fate has a remarkable way of weaving unexpected encounters into our existence. It was on one such extraordinary occasion that I unexpectedly crossed paths with my mother at Penn Can Mall. Accompanied by my friend, Don, we were roaming the stores in search of sneakers. As my eyes locked with Mom's in a moment of simultaneous recognition, a surge of emotion passed between us, and for an instant, her face illuminated with a natural response—a flicker of the motherly affection that had once bound us together.

She went to hug me, but at that moment, an array of conflicting emotions surged within me, colliding like a storm. The anger that had been simmering beneath the surface bubbled up, threatening to spill over. "What are you doing? You want to hug me? And then you'll just walk away, continuing to refuse to acknowledge my existence?" I asked, my voice saturated with anguish and resentment. Taken aback, my mother just stood there, speechless, seemingly incapable of grasping the magnitude of my distress.

To Don, who had been a frequent visitor to my childhood home, my reaction seemed unfathomable—an abrupt display of disrespect toward a woman he had known as kind and caring. In his eyes, my rejection of her embrace appeared rude and out of character. However, he lacked an intimate understanding of the strained relationship that had plagued us for so long. Sensing his confusion, I took a moment to confide in him, revealing the painful truth that my mother had persistently rejected me, dismissing my countless attempts and disregarding my yearning for her presence in my life.

As my words sank in, Don nodded, his expression transforming from perplexity to empathy. He offered his unwavering support, recognizing the complexity of the situation and the weight of my unmet expectations.

Our business was flourishing, riding the waves of success, but the same couldn't be said for my bond with my family. Their absence left a profound impact on me, a constant reminder of the void that seemed impossible to bridge. Even my visits to my beloved grandparents and my attempts to engage with my aunt and uncle only served as painful reminders of the fractured relationships within our clan. Though they tried to steer clear of the topic, the conversations would inevitably drift toward our estranged connection. It was a bitter realization that my once-devoted grandparents, who had been the bedrock of our family, were now distant figures, their presence fading like old photographs. They had showered me, my brothers, and sister with love and care, but now I stood alone, the sole torchbearer of our shared heritage. Reconciliation felt like an elusive dream, slipping through my grasp like water.

It was during these moments of reflection that I found myself questioning the essence of my identity. Who was I now, stripped of the roles I once held within my family? I had been my brothers' brother, my mother's cherished son, but with each passing day, it felt as if those titles no longer held weight. As a child, despite the turbulent dynamics within our family, I found confidence and security in their embrace, particularly in the consistent and unwavering love of my mother. It had become an integral part of my sense of self, a foundation upon which I built my beliefs and aspirations. However, now untethered from those ties, I found myself standing at a crossroads, hungering for answers. Who had I become in this new chapter of my life? And where would I discover the bedrock upon which to build my beliefs?

During the vibrant days spent alongside John, as our business flourished, the once-energetic nights of revelry gradually slipped into the recesses of memory. A newfound sense of purpose and gravity settled upon me, stirring a restless longing for deeper meaning. The passage of countless months had distanced me from the tempestuous years in my childhood home where I adhered to my father's commands. Now unburdened by those chains, I was embarking on a journey to unravel the essence of my beliefs. What were the core principles I espoused? How much of the dogma and values instilled in me were genuine? It was time to venture beyond the familiar, to delve into the depths of my soul and uncover the truths that resonated within.

Religions had never wielded significant influence over my life, as I perceived their shared goal of peaceful coexistence among humanity to be self-evident. It was a noble pursuit, one I believed I didn't require others to instruct me on. Nevertheless, a persistent restlessness nagged at my soul, as if a vital piece of the puzzle had eluded me. It defies simple explanation, but the fracture within my family brought it to the forefront. Even now I sense its lingering impact, its transformative power, which has shaped me in ways I still struggle to comprehend. In those turbulent early days, the pain was almost insurmountable, rendering me adrift in a sea of constant uncertainty. Every aspect of my existence was placed under intense scrutiny, particularly the religious upbringing that had been imposed upon the core of my being.

Consumed by an insatiable hunger for answers, I delved into a relentless exploration of diverse religions. Bookstores transformed into my sanctums, where I voraciously consumed literature from the philosophy, religion, and occult sections. Hinduism, Buddhism, Judaism, Sikhism, Christianity, and more—all were fair game in my relentless pursuit. This fervent quest consumed months of my life as I ventured forth on my solitary odyssey, occasionally sharing fragments of my discoveries with John. But the majority of my readings and contemplations remained locked within the depths of my being. Slowly but surely, my newfound knowledge began to infiltrate every aspect of my existence, making an indelible impact on the trajectory of my life.

Meditation emerged as a unifying practice across diverse belief systems, captivating me with its profound impact. It provided a unique approach to thinking, allowing me to empty my mind and delve into thoughts of my choosing. I discovered that my conscious thoughts were burdened by doubts and fears and constrained by my past experiences. However, through the practice of meditation, I embarked on a journey of unrestricted exploration. It was exhilarating to have this newfound advantage, but I remained unaware of the potential pitfalls. The allure of meditation became almost addictive, as each session birthed new questions that demanded answers. The deeper I delved into meditation, the more I began to question the truths I once held as absolute.

As I delved into various religious texts, my exploration expanded and intensified, leaving me captivated by the concept of reincarnation. This concept resonated within me, affirming my inherent sense that there must exist a profound connection between harmony and justice, a universal fairness waiting to be uncovered.

The teachings of yin and yang, with their intricate balance and interdependence, in conjunction with cause and effect, presented more organic and equitable explanations than the beliefs instilled in me from childhood.

As I delved deeper into biblical literature, a fascinating revelation unfolded before me. I discovered that terms like "hell" encompassed a range of meanings in their original Hebrew and Greek derivatives, including references to a local garbage dump, a graveyard, or the realm associated with such places. These interpretations provided a different perspective, devoid of the concept of eternal damnation. This newfound understanding shed light on long-standing questions, offering a sense of clarity. For instance, when reflecting on the finite lifespan of figures like Hitler, the idea of eternal torment seemed fundamentally unjust. Instead, a more reasonable perspective emerged: that he should endure a million years of retribution for each second of pain he inflicted upon every person he harmed.

And then there were the beliefs of the Jehovah's Witnesses for yet another perspective. According to their teachings, hell is not a literal place of eternal torment but rather a state of non-existence or unconsciousness. They propose that after death, those who are not deemed worthy of resurrection or salvation simply cease to exist.

And that's not all. Jewish beliefs regarding hell also vary. In traditional Jewish theology, the concept of hell does not hold a central focus, and there is no specific doctrine concerning eternal punishment or torment. However, some Jewish teachings propose the existence of Gehenna, which is considered a place of purification or temporary punishment where the soul may go after death to atone for past sins. In Judaism, the emphasis is often placed on the significance of this life and the imperative of leading a righteous and ethical existence rather than fixating on the afterlife. This perspective, which suggests a focus on the present and the importance of ethical living, resonates with me and aligns with the message I've been trying to convey to my family members.

It became apparent to me that fragments of truth could be found in various sources, but no single entity possessed the entirety of truth. The more research I did, the more I realized that my father may have stumbled upon something meaningful, but he had lost his way along the journey.

As my carefree days of fun with Sue and others gradually diminished, I became absorbed in my work and immersed myself in the practices of meditation and research. It was a period of deep introspection, a time when I sought to uncover my own personal truth amidst the chaos that had shaped my life.

One day my phone rang, and it was John on the other end. "Hey, I just had a conversation with the owner of the delivery service on the east side," he said. "Apparently, someone from our company wrote a message on his blackboard, and now he wants to know what it means."

The previous evening, I had found myself at that account, though the circumstances were rather peculiar. I couldn't recall the reason behind my presence, but there I was, engaged in a conversation with one man while inadvertently eavesdropping on a discussion between two others. Their late-night banter piqued my curiosity, particularly when one of them declared his fondness for the night. Intrigued, I interjected myself into their conversation, addressing the other person directly. "And what about you? Do you also embrace the darkness, or are you someone who lives for the light?"

Upon hearing my question, the man who had expressed his enthusiasm for nightlife erupted into laughter. However, the other two individuals in the room responded quite differently. A weighty silence descended upon us, their eyes meeting mine with a seriousness that matched the tone of my inquiry. Finally, one of the men responded: "No, I live for the light."

His words lingered in the air, breaking the intensity of our gaze, locked in a silent standoff. In response, I turned away without uttering another word, each step a measured retreat. The rest of the evening unfolded in a hushed stillness, broken only by the faint whispers of footsteps in the vacant corridors.

Following their departure, their presence dissolving into

the velvet night, I felt an irresistible urge to leave a message on the blackboard. Though the exact words now elude me, I was certain of their impact: they would seize his attention, making a lasting impression on his thoughts.

In the wake of this encounter, my exact response to John remains a blur, but I am sure of one aspect—if my silence spoke volumes to him, the client was bound to offer more insights.

As events unfolded, it became apparent that John would unearth a myriad of reactions from other clients too. He was gradually coming to terms with a stark realization—that my interpretations of my environment and my responses were spiraling into an increasingly erratic and unpredictable realm.

From an outsider's perspective, my behavior seemed unusual, but for me it represented a significant journey of self-discovery. I believed my commitment to meditation unlocked profound insights, endowing me with an acute awareness of the intricate nuances of my surroundings.

The oddities extended beyond this. Before engaging with anyone, I felt an urgent need to fortify myself, to establish a mental shield against the barrage of thoughts I perceived radiating from those around me.

These were the perceived epiphanies, uncovered through meditation. I was determined to emancipate myself from being swayed by the desires and expectations of others. I refused to twist and distort my essence to conform to their ideals in a futile quest for their recognition and approval. My beliefs and perceptions would henceforth be solely mine, free from external influence.

I believed this was a profound realization, revealing how much of my existence had been consumed by conforming to others' whims and expectations. I had been like a chameleon, altering myself to seek validation within their circles while gradually disconnecting from my true self.

Deep within I knew that the persona I had crafted, the version of myself I presented to appease others, was merely a façade.

This newfound awareness, however, brought its own set of challenges. Like any bold transformation, time, practice, and unwavering determination were required to navigate this heightened state of being with finesse and tranquility. And in the process of observing, I protected myself from the corrosive influences of other people's thoughts, shunning direct eye contact and building an invisible fortress around my spirit. This was my safeguard until I felt strong enough to confront whatever lay ahead.

My life was in the midst of a profound metamorphosis, an extraordinary journey that propelled me into unexplored realms. The Book of Revelation, once a distant and mysterious text, transformed into a mystical map that charted the course of my transformation. Meditation, no longer a mere practice confined to daylight hours, became the cornerstone of my existence, replacing the conventional notion of sleep at night.

As I delved deeper into my spiritual exploration, I began questioning the foundations of my past convictions. The certainties that I had clung to appeared fragile and in need of scrutiny. Sleep, once considered a necessity for rest and rejuvenation, morphed in my perception. I began to perceive it as a cleverly devised trap, a cunning tool employed by the forces of darkness to infiltrate our subconscious minds and manipulate our lives from within. Driven by this awareness, I relinquished the sanctuary of sleep, opting to spend my nocturnal hours engaged in meditation instead, anchored to a wakeful state until the break of dawn.

After nights spent in unwavering vigilance, attuned to the mysteries of the nocturnal realm, I became acutely aware of the ominous spirits that prowled through the darkness. Seated on my bed, I braced myself, settling into a composed state as these malevolent entities passed through me, leaving an ethereal chill in their wake. Night after night I remained a steadfast sentinel, witnessing the unsettling dance of evil permeating the air around me.

Then, on a night steeped in destiny, a momentous encounter occurred. As I sat immersed in solitude, I felt an undeniable presence, a spiritual energy that could only belong to my father. In his intangible form, I sensed an opportunity to establish a connection that transcended the physical realm. His slumbering mind, blissfully unaware of the need for protection from my ethereal presence, drew me near. With a courageous leap of consciousness, I departed from my own existence, traversing the ethereal boundaries to reach him.

In the spiritual realm, I spoke to my father, pouring out my thoughts, emotions, and revelations, seeking understanding and recognition. Despite his earnest effort, a veil of confusion clouded his countenance. The depths of my words eluded him, slipping through his grasp like smoke. His struggle to comprehend mirrored my own frustration, for the connection we sought remained just beyond our grasp. Reluctantly, I withdrew from his presence and returned to the confines of my room, the weight of my unspoken truth hanging heavily in the air.

The next morning arrived, drenched in the familiar glow of the rising sun, which cast its enchanting hues upon the delicate curtains. Like a ritual rooted in the depths of my being since childhood, I turned to witness this daily spectacle, captivated by the dance of light and shadows. The shifting shades from fiery orange to brilliant white drew me into a trance, a gateway to introspection and reflection. Little did Sue know, as she lay beside me, that the night had birthed a sea of transformations while she remained in slumber, oblivious to the profound shifts unfurling within me.

I carried out my usual morning routine, indulging in a refreshing shower as a prelude to another day of work. But as I stepped out into the world, my thoughts strayed from the path to my office, instead gravitating toward my family, consuming my consciousness during the drive.

As I traversed the roads, an otherworldly serenity enveloped me, elevating me above the mundane realm of my commute into a meditative state, surrendering to the currents of contemplation.

In the depths of this introspective journey, a startling realization struck me like a bolt of lightning, seeding doubt. Could it be that I had been deceived, that the man I called "Father" was not my true progenitor? If he were not my father, then the burden of his deeds was not mine to bear. Who then, was the mysterious figure behind my existence, concealing his true identity from me? Why would he keep such a secret from his own flesh and blood? The man who claimed to be my father, engrossed in the Lord's work, often contradicted his words with his actions. Perhaps the true instrument of divine work was someone else, someone who had remained hidden in the shadows.

Then it hit me with undeniable clarity, a revelation pulsating through my veins: Dick Shutt of SSAC! His name shone with significance, the person who had granted me exclusive access, a feat not even the renowned Bob Dean had achieved despite his attempts to become a client. The pieces of the puzzle began to align, unveiling a mosaic of truth. It made perfect sense why he had orchestrated the contract for his building to fall into my hands. His daughter, working at an advertising agency—another client of mine—had hinted at his vested interest in my career, compiling a scrapbook of clippings that chronicled my journey. It was as clear as day: Dick Shutt had to be my real father, the one truly carrying out the Lord's work.

Propelled by this sudden conviction, I diverted from my initial route, heading to Baldwinsville, the site of Mr. Shutt's new office. Upon arriving, I asked to see him, the gravity of my discovery fueling my resolve. The receptionist, a new face in this unknown setting, received my message and then vanished into the inner sanctum of the office. After a tense wait, she reemerged, her words deflating my hopes: "Mr. Mazur, I'm sorry, but Mr. Shutt is in a critical meeting."

I was filled with confusion. This environment, steeped in unfamiliar formality, was a stark departure from what I knew. The gazes that met me were filled with curiosity, as if they could detect the turmoil beneath my composed exterior. Undeterred, I implored the receptionist to communicate the pressing nature of my request to Mr. Shutt. Despite my persistence, her response remained firm, resounding with the finality of rejection: "Mr. Shutt is unable to meet you at this time due to his ongoing meeting." Overwhelmed by a sense of loss, I departed, a torrent of unanswered questions weighing down my spirit.

All day my thoughts were fixated on the belief that Dick was my father. I drove aimlessly through the town, lost in a maze of unanswered questions. The burning desire to confront him face to face grew insatiable. Then, as if by some twist of fate, a phone booth materialized before me, drawing me toward a potential truth.

Without hesitation, I pulled my car to the side and made my way to the booth, my heart racing with anticipation. I fumbled with the phone, dialing his number with unsteady fingers. My voice, barely more than a hushed murmur, broke the silence. "Hello, may I speak to Mr. Shutt, please?" The line crackled with a bad connection, adding to the surreal quality of the moment.

"Who's calling, please?" a voice inquired, tinged with curiosity. Gathering my composure, I took a deep breath before responding.

"This is Dan Mazur."

The tension escalated as I waited, my heartbeat thundering in my ears. After what felt like an eternity, the awaited response came. "Hello, Dan, is that you?" Emotions surged through me as I confirmed my identity, my voice a mixture of apprehension and resolve. The moment stretched on, time seemingly frozen in suspense. "What can I do for you?" Dick asked, his voice laced with astonishment.

Summoning every ounce of bravery, I blurted out, "Mr. Shutt, I need to know the truth. Are you my father?" The significance of my question hung heavily, its enormity almost overwhelming.

"Dan, could you repeat that?" he asked, his tone laced with

disbelief. Doubt crept in. Should I ask again? Was this a test? My mind swirled in confusion, then in a sudden wave of panic, I disconnected the call. My heart pounding and engulfed in a storm of emotions, I hurried back to my car and drove off, the unfinished conversation resounding in my head.

The days dragged on, and once again I continued my relentless pursuit of reaching him, making incessant calls to his office in a desperate quest for answers. But each call was met with an unwavering refusal, his voice absent from the other end of the line. My actions grew increasingly erratic, mirroring the turmoil within my mind. Consumed by the need for answers, I found myself visiting my clients' offices in the evenings, leaving cryptic messages on their blackboards for them to discover in the morning. While these actions made perfect sense in my mind, they were deeply disturbing to others who found them inexplicable and unsettling.

Despite my relentless search for answers, they remained just out of reach, slipping through my grasp. I realized I needed to find a way to let go and move on from this relentless pursuit. However, as if guided by an unseen force, an overwhelming impulse took hold of me—a profound need to be in the presence of my grandparents.

I drove toward their home, my anticipation building with each passing mile, then finally arrived and crossed the threshold into their familiar abode. The comforting embrace of their welcoming warmth enveloped me, their smiles luring me to partake in the tantalizing array of culinary delights adorning the table. However, beneath the veneer of their hospitality, an unspoken tension hung in the air, casting a haunting shadow over the room. My grandmother's gaze held a newfound complexity, her eyes grappling with recognition and uncertainty, torn between conflicting emotions. I was perplexed by the shift in her demeanor, as if she now regarded me with cautious uncertainty, concealing a hidden concern. Even my grandfather's behavior seemed subtly altered, a departure from his predictable patterns.

As the hours unfolded, weariness descended upon me like a suffocating shroud, blurring the boundaries between wakefulness and dreams. Strangely, an insurmountable compulsion anchored me within the confines of their home, as if an invisible force bound me to their presence. I felt trapped, unable to break free, as though destined to be ensnared within those walls for eternity. Time became an enigma, the passing days melding into an indistinguishable haze of uncertainty and unease.

And so, I remained there, with days blending seamlessly into one another, each steeped in a sense of impending turmoil. Then, in a crescendo of dramatic events, my aunt, father, and brother David appeared, intensifying the gathering storm of emotions. It was at that moment when the piercing sound of an ambulance shattered the heavy silence. Its wailing siren announced the arrival of two paramedics, their purpose clear and resolute. With unwavering determination, they entered my grandparents' home, took hold of my arms, and guided me toward the waiting ambulance. This marked the beginning of an unforeseen and uncertain future, as I was whisked away from the familiar and hurled into a profound odyssey through uncharted territory.

Chapter Twenty-One

HUTCHINGS PSYCHIATRIC CENTER

AS THE PARAMEDICS ESCORTED ME OUT OF MY GRANDPARENTS' house, the imminent arrival of a new element unfolded before our eyes. Two policemen, figures of formidable presence, materialized, their sudden appearance adding a touch of seriousness to the situation. They blended seamlessly into the surroundings, exuding resolute determination as they joined the collective effort. Our interaction was minimal as I chose to remain silent, devoid of any message to convey.

Handcuffs were clasped around my wrists, binding me tight. Then I was loaded into the awaiting ambulance, ready for the next phase of the journey. Once again, sirens wailed, their piercing sound signaling our departure and the gradual restoration of my grandparent's home to a semblance of normalcy.

As we maneuvered through the streets at a brisk pace, the world outside became a blur of lights and motion. The chaotic wind whistled through the driver's partially open window, mirroring the cacophony of emotions swirling within me.

When we reached our destination, Hutchings Psychiatric Center, I stepped out of the ambulance, the handcuffs still gripping my wrists. Flanked by two stern policemen, we had passed through the imposing gates, but the true essence and purpose of the facility remained shrouded in a mysterious veil. It felt as though I had been thrust into an uncharted realm, where the fragments of my existence unfurled a complex and arcane puzzle.

The edifice loomed before me, a formidable structure shrouded in the ever-shifting shadows that danced upon its walls. As the officers swung open the grand doors, a labyrinthine network of corridors sprawled out, enticing me to venture into the depths of the unknown. Each twist and turn held the promise of secrets, leading to dead ends, intricate junctions, and uncharted territories that stretched far beyond the boundaries of my limited understanding. The air was still, occasionally disrupted by whispers that reverberated like distant murmurs of concern, adding an air of mystery to the already peculiar ambiance.

Every step I took carried a weight of hesitancy, my feet shuffling upon the cold tile floor. The weariness that clung to my being seemed to permeate the fabric of the space, pressing a heavy burden upon my shoulders. Time took on a fluid quality, bending and distorting with each passing second, amplifying the surreal atmosphere. Sounds reverberated with a haunting resonance, as if the facility's walls held secrets yearning to be divulged.

As I emerged into the gaze of the onlookers, a collective gasp of astonishment swept through the room, their breath catching in a moment of disbelief. Wide eyed and captivated, their expressions mirrored the profound impact my presence had on them. It was as if my arrival had stirred dormant emotions, compelling them to confront the depths of their own vulnerabilities and uncertainties. Whispers of speculation and intrigue passed like a gentle breeze, their voices filled with curiosity and wonder. They attempted to unravel the ambiguity that stood before them, spinning tales of uncertainty and weaving threads of conjecture. This is how the scene unfolded, a captivating dance between mystery and runaway perceptions.

Who were these mystifying beings encircling me? To what uncharted realm had my journey delivered me? And above all, what convoluted sequence of events had conspired to propel me to this precipice? My mind, cloaked in a dense fog of despair and confusion, grappled with the shattered shards of my fractured reality.

The inquiries posed during the intake process descended upon me like a swirling tempest, their evasive nature blurring the demarcation between comprehension and uncertainty. "What is your name?" they inquired, and I found myself adrift in a morass of identities. Were they seeking the appellation bestowed upon me at birth, or should I unveil the name that resonated with the depths of my most authentic self? Alas, the answers remained elusive, slipping through my grasp like ethereal phantoms.

"Who is your closest relative?" they pressed, and my thoughts plunged into the abode of ambiguity. Were they seeking the one with whom I shared a bloodline, a physical tether? Or were they alluding to the soul who provided unwavering support and understanding, an emotional lifeline? The questions twisted and turned, leaving me ensnared in a complex web of introspection and uncertainty, trapped within the intricate maze of my fragmented thoughts.

The interrogation continued, each question like a jagged puzzle piece, challenging me to penetrate the veil of my existence. But eventually, the line of inquiry drew to a close, leaving a lingering sense of disquiet within the depths of my being.

I was led through a door, venturing into a series of winding hallways. The faces of passersby caught my attention with their intriguing blend of familiarity and strangeness. It felt as if I had encountered them in a long-forgotten existence.

As I walked, I noticed a trail of drool marking my path. It dawned on me to make a conscious effort to swallow periodically to prevent such occurrences.

Amidst the reverberating symphony of sounds that filled the corridors, a chorus of voices called out to me, their captivating tones concocting an enchanting spell. The melodies of curiosity danced within me, coaxing me to turn toward the intriguing faces that adorned the path, each one a portal to an unknown realm waiting to be explored. The temptation to stray from the designated route proved irresistible, as if the universe whispered tantalizing secrets of undiscovered truths. But with each audacious step I took, my vigilant escorts appeared like spectral guardians, their presence a gentle nudge guiding me back onto the ordained path. It was as if they served as custodians of the boundaries that safeguarded my journey, ensuring that the intricacies of my existence unfurled according to its predestined course.

Finally, the culmination of my arduous journey brought me to the threshold of my long-awaited destination. Before me stood a room, its walls adorned with a cryptic number, enticing me to unravel its hidden message. In an instant it struck me—the digits aligned flawlessly with my date of birth. The revelation confirmed that the room had been tailored for my arrival, a sacred haven crafted to embrace and nurture my very being.

As I stepped inside, the room enveloped me in a gentle embrace, as if cradling me in its arms, tending to my comfort in anticipation of the transformative journey ahead. Having fulfilled their duties, my two guides vanished, leaving me to acclimate to the tranquil atmosphere of that sacred chamber. In the blink of an eye, I found myself adorned in garments that caressed my skin, their softness tempting me to sink into the plush embrace of the inviting bed. However, sleep was not my intention. I chose to sit, venturing further into the depths of my profound odyssey.

At the far end of the room, another figure materialized. His face exuding a tranquil composure, his lips moving in strange formations that emitted sounds reminiscent of a slumbering state. It seemed I was expected to follow suit, to surrender to the whispers of sleep and let my consciousness fade. But a different path piqued my interest, a journey that would take me beyond the confines of my physical form. With my head held high and my gaze fixed upon the ceiling, I felt the detachment of my spirit from its corporeal vessel. I slipped away, leaving my body behind, inert and motionless.

In that boundless state, I embarked on a voyage that transcended the boundaries of the physical realm. Freed from the limitations of flesh and bone, my spirit soared through new realms, traversing the vast expanse of cosmic mysteries. Time relinquished its hold, its linear constraints melting away as I ventured into territories beyond the confines of consciousness, woven into the depths of my own psyche. There, I discovered fragments of memories and hidden desires, my being tethered by the desire to unveil their mysteries.

As time flowed in mysterious currents, the room became a witness to this metaphysical exploration. In this dance between the physical and the ethereal, between silence and the unspoken, I discovered the profound interconnectedness of all existence.

Then, as swiftly as it had arrived, the ethereal realm dissolved, releasing me back into the depths of human existence. The magnificent setting of my metaphysical journey had vanished, yet as I regained awareness, I discovered I was no longer within the familiar confines of my room. Instead, I was in a distant place, transported to a hospital room where a momentous event was unfolding: my own birth.

As I opened my eyes, the hospital room's sterile white walls greeted me, their pristine surfaces reflecting the glow of fluorescent lights. The air carried the distinct scent of antiseptic, mingling with the symphony of beeping machines and hushed voices to create a backdrop of bustling activity. Nurses moved with purpose, their gentle whispers a soothing melody that filled the space.

In the midst of that choreographed frenzy, screams of agony pierced the atmosphere as my mother braved the labor pains, her resilience mixed with fragility. Her face was adorned with determination, bearing the marks of a warrior in the throes of creation. And there, in the midst of her storm, her long, straight black hair cascaded down her shoulders, a symbol of her resilience and beauty.

My father was absent, casting a shadow of sorrow over the room. It was a void left unfilled, however slight. Yet, by her side stood another man, a figure emanating warmth and compassion. His presence radiated unwavering support, bringing comfort and fortitude. In his gentle embrace, he became a pillar of stability, filling the void left by the one who had chosen to walk away. It was a testament to the power of love, transcending the bounds of bloodlines and defying societal norms.

Amidst the familiar faces was another inexplicable familiarity in the room, a profound recognition that surpassed the limits of this mortal existence. It was as if I had known my mother, this woman before me, in a different realm or a different lifetime. The connection between us felt ancient, embedded into the essence of our souls, even though she was not the mother I had known before.

Taking my first breaths, I entered this world anew, a blank canvas ready to be painted with the colors of life. The world unfolded before my newborn eyes, a mesmerizing kaleidoscope of colors and shapes, a realm of endless possibilities. The cries of my arrival mingled with my mother's joyous tears, initiating a celebration within my own being, an equal joy that radiated from her.

Lying on my back, my tiny fingers and feet fluttering in the air, I embraced the newness of my existence. I had been reborn, a vessel for experiences and discoveries. With each passing moment, I would delve deeper into the secrets of my connection with this familiar woman, unraveling the mysteries that bound us beyond the confines of this ordinary existence.

And so, with the innocence of a newborn, I was ready to embark on the adventure of my new life, eager to explore the depths of love, to forge my own unique path, and to paint the masterpiece of my existence upon the vast and wondrous canvas of the world that awaited me.

But then an unwelcome interruption shattered the delicate harmony of my desires, wrenching me from the realm of my dreams and thrusting me back into the confines of my previous mortal existence. Reluctantly, I opened the door, only to be greeted by a figure that was both abstruse and disconcerting. His presence loomed ominously, dampening my hopes and aspirations. His words, uttered like stern whispers, directed me to return to the life I had left behind.

In a flash, the tendrils of my desires slipped through my fingertips, leaving me stranded in the confinements of the ordinary room, enveloped by the familiar. My otherworldly journey toward the life I yearned for was brief and had come to an end.

In the gentle morning glow, I rose from my bed, embracing the warmth of the sun's tender rays as they caressed my skin. The heavenly light filtered through the half-open blinds, casting intricate patterns on the walls of my room. It created an enchanting ambiance, as though a touch of magic had been infused into the once-sterile environment, offering a glimmer of hope and joy for the day that lay ahead.

Beside me, my roommate remained in peaceful slumber, his face adorned with a tranquil expression. The gentle rise and fall of his chest served as a testament to the rhythmic cadence of life itself while the flow of his breath was a reminder of the miraculous process that sustained us. The subtle twitching of his fingers expressed the intricate dance between mind and body. Each movement, each subtle nuance, reflected the profound intricacies of the human experience—an exquisite symphony conducted within the boundaries of our fragile existence.

As the morning sun bathed the room in its luminous embrace, a distant voice sounded through the corridors, summoning patients to the medication counter. Was this the role they had expected of me the day before? Was my name truly "Patient"?

Joining the others, I adopted their rhythm, moving harmoniously with the group. The air carried a distinct scent, a mélange of antiseptic cleanliness mingled with a whiff of weariness. We stood in line, our hands outstretched, receiving our offerings, each person uttering a quiet "Thank you." The clinking of cups and the deliberate pouring of liquid merged into a symphony, a unified declaration within the sterile confines of that room.

Leaving the area, I moved along with the crowd, drawn to the enticing aroma of breakfast emanating from the dining room. The space hummed with subdued energy, a cacophony of whispered conversations and introspective gazes. The melodic clatter of cutlery against plates provided a backdrop to the chaos and confusion of the moment.

As I sat there, the room came alive with a peculiar energy, vibrating like a hive of bees. People shuffled in, their weary eyes reflected the multitude of struggles they bore.

A woman with disheveled hair and vacant eyes took a seat next to me. Her trembling hands clutched a Styrofoam cup, and the steam rising from the coffee curled around her like a fragile mist. I caught glimpses of a story sketched on her face, a tale of battles fought and scars carved deep within her soul.

Beside her, an older man sat in profound silence, his gaze fixed on an empty space in front of him. His weathered countenance bore the marks of a lifetime of trials, a roadmap of endurance etched into his skin. It seemed as if he carried the weight of the world on his shoulders, lost in the labyrinthine depths of his thoughts.

In that room the air was thick with hidden narratives waiting to be unraveled. As an observer, I embraced my role, riding the currents of their lives, eager to uncover the essence of who they were and the mysteries within their stories. I navigated the expanse of that world of intertwined destinies, seeking to understand their purpose and, in doing so, discover my own. That was why I was there.

Then another directive was issued to us, a whisper that unfurled into the air and resonated with each of us. In perfect unison, we rose. Our synchronized movements led us to our next destination: a sprawling, open room that invited curiosity and exploration. In one corner stood a ping-pong table, its surface marked by countless matches. High on a wall, a television loomed, its flickering glow bathing the space below. Chairs were arranged beneath it in an arched formation. Drawn to the allure of moving images, several among us approached the television with childlike fascination. As fingers navigated the buttons, their eagerness evident as they surfed through various programs, the sounds and flurry of channel changing seamlessly interwove with the room's frenetic energy. It was as though they were destined to harmonize, complementing the collage of diverse worlds and stories unfolding in the space.

Amidst the dynamic scene, the overseers emerged as beacons of authority, their immaculate white attire distinguishing them from the rest. With each step their footsteps reverberated with a distinct cadence, setting them apart as they navigated the room with graceful poise. Engaged in hushed conversations among themselves, their voices barely audible, they emanated an aura of tranquil authority. The atmosphere was permeated by their calm demeanor, instilling a sense of respect and order. Periodically, authoritative requests punctuated the air, directed toward my peers, solidifying their role as guardians within that obscure realm.

As I witnessed the tableau before me, the intricate dynamics of power unfolded, speaking volumes through the subtle cues and interactions. These revelations hadn't come by chance but rather through my astute observation and unwavering attentiveness. The room became a theater of unspoken power struggles, and I was attuned to the underlying currents that shaped that mysterious milieu.

In that space where authority and vulnerability intertwined, I discerned the delicate balance between control and compassion. The gestures, expressions, and whispered conversations revealed the intricacies of those entrusted with the well-being of others. It was through my perceptive gaze that I gained insight into the intricate dance of power, understanding the depths and nuances that shaped that microcosm of societal dynamics.

My role as an observer was passive but was an active pursuit of knowledge and understanding. I consumed the scenes that unfolded before me, extracting meaning from the subtleties and unspoken narratives. Through my clear-sighted observation, I unearthed the hidden layers and uncovered the truths beneath the surface.

Through this journey of discovery and empathy, I became keenly aware of the purpose behind my presence in that realm. My observations revealed the profound impact I could have on those around me and on myself. With each revelation, I was driven to navigate that intricate web of power dynamics not merely as an observer but as an agent of change and understanding.

Armed with the insights gained through my observation, I was poised to wield this knowledge wisely. I embraced the responsibility of deciphering the intricacies of power, discerning the true nature of those who held it, and utilizing that understanding to foster compassion, empathy, and positive transformation within that inscrutable realm.

Continuing my process of observation, my eyes roamed the room once more, hungry for further enlightenment. And the room did not disappoint, for amidst the inhabitants of that place, my attention was drawn to a man standing near a doorway, his restless energy palpable. His gaze flickered with a haunting intensity as he paced back and forth, consumed by internal turmoil.

His hands were engaged in a repetitive and meticulous motion, untangling a cluster of hair that he had previously twisted and entwined upon his head. Each twist of his fingers seemed to carry a profound sense of purpose, extending beyond the mere physical release of knots. It was an intricate dance, as if he had yearned to liberate himself from the entanglement of haunting memories that had ensnared his mind. The room itself had become a theater, a stage upon which his inner struggle had unfolded, a battleground where he had fought the invisible demons that had plagued his thoughts.

As the strands of hair accumulated around his fingers, he didn't simply let them go. Instead, he wrapped a chosen bundle around his index finger, creating a twisted collection. And then, with a sudden jerk, he pulled them free from his scalp, adding another patch to the tapestry of missing strands. The sight was disconcerting—an adorned head with sporadic patches of exposed scalp, a mosaic that portrayed the battles he fought within.

The act of his self-inflicted baldness became increasingly apparent, an undeniable symbol of his yearning to shed the weight of his past, to strip away the haunting memories that clung to him. It served as a visual manifestation of the unseen scars that marred his psyche, an external reflection of the inner turmoil he carried with unwavering strength.

In that place, every observation unraveled a layer of understanding, revealing the profound depths of human struggles. As an empathetic observer, I bore witness to the stories carved into those individuals' lives, where their battles, both in victory and defeat, intertwined to craft a textured portrayal of human experience. With each revelation, my drive to explore the essence of their existence deepened, and I was compelled to offer compassion and support and contribute to their journey of healing and self-discovery.

The intriguing depth that veiled their experiences invited

me to uncover their stories. I was drawn to the battles they waged in solitude, recognizing the quest for liberation from the burdens of the mind that resided within. Curiosity and compassion filled my heart as I contemplated the tales concealed within their souls, yearning to understand the intricate complexities of their pain and the flickers of hope that guided them toward healing. As an empathetic observer, I navigated that realm with a tender approach, recognizing and honoring the intricate nature of each individual's struggles. My purpose extended beyond merely comprehending their experiences; it encompassed forging connections that transcended the confines of our shared existence. Through those connections, I strove to foster a profound sense of empathy and understanding that had the power to illuminate the path to healing for those I observed and for myself.

Time slipped through my fingers like quicksilver, its elusive nature a constant reminder of its intangible essence. A memory rose within me, its resonance blending with the words once spoken by a figure draped in white garments, his voice carrying the promise of my beloved aunt and uncle's visit at 3:00 p.m. The anticipation of their arrival infused me with a renewed surge of energy, igniting a flicker of hope that cut through the weariness that accompanied my tireless examination of the mysterious individuals within that place.

Driven by an insatiable thirst for their presence, I approached a man who exuded authority and wisdom, my heart pulsating with a blend of excitement and apprehension. "What time is it?" I inquired, my voice laced with anticipation. The question lingered in the air, heavy with expectation. His eyes fixed upon the timepiece adorning his wrist, he responded with measured calmness.

"It's 2:10 p.m."

I absorbed his words, nodding in acknowledgment, though deep within I grappled with the daunting challenge of comprehending the elusive passage of time.

As the wait for their arrival stretched before me, the tales of the room's occupants reemerged, their narratives urging me to delve deeper into the intricacies that shrouded them. I heeded their call, immersing myself in analysis and contemplation, determined to unravel the layers of their existence. Lost in contemplation, pieces of understanding slowly began to fuse together, giving rise to a startling realization. A sense of unease filled me as I recognized that hours had slipped by, unnoticed. Could it be that I had inadvertently missed the much-anticipated visit from my family? It seemed likely that they had come and gone while I was deeply immersed in the depths of my own ruminations. Returning to the man I had previously asked for the time, my voice now carried a mixture of desperation and resolve as I inquired again about the time. His face showed a blend of bemusement and patient compassion, and a glint of understanding flickered in his eyes as he responded, "It's 2:15 p.m." His next words were laced with empathy, acknowledging the repetitive nature of my questioning. "How many more times will you ask?" He couldn't grasp the depth of my predicament. I must have asked him the same question ten more times before 3:00, as my perception of time was skewed, failing to align with reality. Time had become elusive, slipping beyond my reach.

Unaffected by this revelation, I was caught in a perplexing cycle, trapped by my need for reassurance. It was a delicate dance of repetitive inquiries and his patient responses.

Each time he answered, it was a gentle reminder of the fleeting minutes since my last query. My mind struggled with these passing moments, as the environment distorted my sense of time, leaving me in a loop of longing and confusion.

Despite the elusive nature of time and the haze clouding my thoughts, my desire to see my family remained unshakable—a beacon of hope in this bewildering place. Navigating through the uncertainty, I clung to the hope of their arrival, eagerly awaiting the moment when my aunt, uncle, and Susan would walk through the door, bringing their familiar comfort and warmth.

Finally, the moment I had been waiting for arrived. As I fixed my gaze on the door, a wave of excitement washed over me. There they were—my dear aunt, uncle, and Susan—coming toward me with purpose.

Amidst the hustle and bustle, we found a place to sit together, enveloped in the steady hum of conversations and musings.

"Hi, Danny, how are you feeling?" My aunt's voice emerged warm and clear, cutting through the hullabaloo. Caught betwixt the realms of external engagement and the whirlwind of thoughts within, I was in a state of divided attention. My words became fleeting phantoms, escaping my lips like wisps of smoke, leaving behind a void to be filled by their interpretation of my expressions.

With a yearning to grasp the depths of my inner world, they leaned in, their eyes becoming intrepid explorers, navigating the unspoken language beneath the surface. However, the language of my body, the dance of my features, failed to mirror the ruinous symphony within. They witnessed my furrowed brow and troubled countenance, but the flickering embers of joy that their presence kindled remained concealed beneath the surface.

As quickly as they had appeared, they vanished, leaving merely a hint of their brief sojourn. I found myself alone, attempting to decipher the subtle intricacies layered within their visit.

With their departure confirmed, the prospect of dinner called out, serving not just as sustenance for the body but also as a marker of time's cyclical passage. As darkness fell, veiling the windows of the rooms in which we had congregated, it draped the external world in a phantasmal drape.

Within the stillness of my sleeping quarters, while others surrendered to the embrace of slumber, I remained upright for another night, a sentinel of solitude engaged in silent contemplation. Amidst realms akin to dreams, I navigated the vast expanse of my mind, delving into its depths. Those nocturnal hours became my sanctuary, a time of communion with the mysteries of the self. In this sacred space, I sought comfort, enlightenment, and a profound sense of purpose.

As our daily rhythms unfurled, the first rays of dawn cast their gentle embrace, heralding the presence of my new-found comrades. United, we greeted the morning, partaking in shared meals, and through shared silences and conversations, we sought an understanding of our past experiences that brought us to that juncture. Adversity bound our stories together, and the shared weight of our histories and hopes secured our bond.

As the ensuing chapter of our journey presented itself, our footsteps once again led us to that expansive room where the vibrant energy resonated around the ping-pong table from every side. Within that sanctuary my understanding of those individuals reached profound depths. Yet amidst comprehending their journeys, I was also compelled to reflect upon my own struggles. There I stood, entrusted with the purpose of aiding those fellow souls. Standing there, charged with the mission of supporting those kindred spirits, I wondered how successful I had been in tending to my own wounds.

Alas, I had to confront my own shortcomings. My repeated phone calls and efforts to broach heartfelt conversations with my father about our family's tumult and the truths I harbored were largely met with staunch resistance. Yet there was a singular moment, a shimmering beacon of hope in my memory. It was when my father acquiesced to a meeting, agreeing to address the long-standing rifts between us. The anticipation preceding that engagement was palpable, filled with visions of potential reconciliation. At long last he had agreed to a genuine exchange of words and feelings. In that bygone moment, I held onto the hope that, side by side, we would sift through the complexities of our family dynamics. It represented a chance for our family to rediscover the bridges that once connected us.

He opted for our rendezvous to take place at a familiar Denny's restaurant, a cherished venue where late-night breakfasts were savored after the evening church sermons he delivered so passionately. In anticipation of the significant occasion, I meticulously picked out my attire. Let me elucidate the rationale behind this selection.

Back when I lived at home, many of our mornings were punctuated with shared reflections over hot cups of coffee. During those intimate junctures, my father and I would embark on dialogues about my ambitions in the business world, especially my endeavors as a commercial photographer. My growing passion for photography transitioned into a viable career path for me.

During my high school years, my father gave me a cherished possession: a Konica Autoreflex TC 35 mm camera. With the extra money I had earned from selling flower seeds to neighbors, handling a paper route, and even peddling candies door to door, I eagerly procured film rolls and embarked on capturing the essence of the world through my camera's lens. Oh, how I reveled in every moment! The anticipation of mailing the film for processing and eagerly awaiting the emergence of the developed photographs held a special kind of thrill.

When I discovered that my school offered a photography class, an entirely new world of possibilities emerged before me. Darkrooms, enlargers, film processing, and printing were no longer mysteries waiting to be revealed. The days of anxiously awaiting my pictures to appear became a thing of the past. While color film processing and printing remained beyond my reach, the realm of black-and-white photography beckoned with endless opportunities.

Ra-Lin's, the city's photography store, became my sanctuary, offering a diverse selection of various grades of black-and-white photo paper, each one possessing its own distinct contrast and graininess to enhance my artistic visions. Accompanied by Don, I eagerly explored the photography magazines in the magazine section of Wegmans' Grocery store, indulging in delectable doughnuts from the bakery as we perused the pages, selecting additional items necessary for our photographic pursuits. Filled with eagerness and excitement, I ordered my first Beseler enlarger, a crucial tool that would unlock my ability to transfer the captured images onto paper, breathing life into my creative visions.

Now whenever inspiration struck, I could retreat to the intimate haven of my own darkroom, nestled within our transformed basement that had once served as a mundane laundry room. Above the doorway, proudly displayed in golden letters purchased from Switz's, the words "Danny's Studio" shimmered, symbolizing the metamorphosis of the space into a realm where artistic pursuits thrived, and the seeds of my dream to establish my own photography business were sown.

Armed with my trusty ten-speed bicycle and later my moped, my camera became an unwavering companion, accompanying me on every venture. My eye was drawn to the unconventional and the overlooked, seeking to capture hidden gems in unexpected places. Whether it was discarded items in the trash can of a department store, a broken tennis racket abandoned in a park, or even the process of paint drying on a wall, I yearned to document the thoughts and visions that enthralled my mind, to see them come alive in black and white before me.

In a world where traditional academic pursuits and discussions about SATs and college choices eluded me, photography emerged as my calling, my vocation. It became the driving force behind my actions, embedded into my daily routine. In the evenings I found support for my passion through my work as a janitor, a position I secured thanks to a referral from my sister. That job not only provided me with the means to afford a car but also granted me the opportunity to rent a studio space where I could further cultivate and nurture my business pursuits.

During our moments by the Bullard stove, as my father savored his coffee, I would share with him the successes and failures of my workdays. I sought his advice and opinions, eager to learn from my mistakes and strive for improvement. And on occasion, he would reciprocate by sharing his own experiences, often the burdens he carried, seeking my thoughts and perspective on them.

Then one fateful day, our routine took an unexpected turn. He unexpectedly invited me to join him in the car, and together we embarked on a journey to a store in Penn-Can Mall. "Son," he proclaimed, "I'm going to buy you a suit and a trench coat. It is not enough to merely act the part; you must also look the part."

Inside the store, he introduced me to his trusted tailor, a skilled craftsman who measured me and then worked his magic. With precision and care, he crafted a tailored suit that fit me perfectly. My father's dedication did not stop there. He ensured every detail was attended to. He even purchased new shoes as well as galoshes to protect them from the harsh winter salt, ensuring that my appearance would always be impeccable.

A few years later, on that pivotal day at Denny's where we planned to address our family conflicts, I donned the suit he had bought for me, filled with hope for the profound discussion we were to have. Upon my entrance, however, a harsh reality presented itself. My father wasn't there to engage. The intimacy we once held dear was overshadowed by the presence of Bob Dean, who seemingly stood as his protector. In vain, I tried to navigate our outstanding conflicts, but my efforts were continuously interrupted. Much of my conversation was directed toward Mr. Dean rather than my father. And when my father finally spoke, for the first time I heard him say the phrase that he would repeat throughout the years, every time I sought resolution and understanding: "I'm not ready yet."

In the sphere of my family life, I confronted significant failures, a realization that engulfed me in a wave of loss and despair. Having fully acknowledged this, my confidence in my ability to help others had been shaken. Amidst the bustling activity surrounding me, I retreated inward, fixated on my shortcomings.

Caught in an endless cycle of introspection, I sought an escape. An urgent need to walk the room's perimeter arose within me. As I paced along its boundary, my pathway gradually narrowed, pulling me in an ever-tightening spiral. With each step, I felt more ensnared, both physically and emotionally, sinking deeper into the maw of despair. When I finally reached the center of my inward journey, a profound isolation overcame me, and I found myself alone at the heart of the room. This weight of emotion became too much, and I crumpled to the floor, lying prone. An uncontrollable tremor overtook my muscles, reminiscent of a seizure or an epileptic fit. However, the spasms were not caused by physiological factors but instead served as an expression of the turmoil within my psyche. In a frantic effort, I thrashed and hopped on the floor, straining to separate myself from my body, my past, and my present. This visceral dance, its intricacies and motivations, was a mystery known only to me.

The room bore witness to this spectacle until I settled down. When I realized that this process would not liberate me from my physical confines, the room returned to its normal rhythm, and the sounds of ping-pong games and chatter regained their familiar cadence.

Once again I found myself imprisoned in the room's vast confines, surrounded by restless souls, each lost in their own personal reverie. A potent desire to escape that place consumed me like a fire that refused to be tamed, leaving the burning question of "How?"

A mysterious woman, clutching a tablet as if it were the key to our salvation, moved among us. She approached each individual, her inquiries poised to unlock our release. It was whispered among us that the right answers could free us from captivity. Unfortunately, I was not among the fortunate ones to whom the face of favor turned. Then unexpectedly, she came before me again, her eyes shimmering with intrigue.

But my voice faltered, and she swiftly moved on, disappointment etched on her face. I possessed no answers, no words that could offer me an escape from entrapment. Still, deep within, a resilient spark of hope remained, kindling my desire for liberation.

Driven by desperation and stoked by defiance, I withdrew to the room's remotest corner, my eyes riveted to the lone window that offered a glimpse of the world outside. A sunbeam slipped through the glass, its luminous touch a stark contrast to the stifling gloom of our cage. My longing intensified, nearly consuming my sanity. Firm in the belief that even death wouldn't grant reprieve from such agony, I gathered every last shred of my strength and lunged at the window. As I did, I cried out, "Susan, I love you!", a raw testament to the undying love within my battered soul. But fate stood against me. The window, forged from impenetrable Plexiglass, dashed my dreams of escape. I was left defeated, my head and neck marked by the scars of my failed uprising.

In a flurry of urgency and disbelief, one of the overseers, a woman, rushed toward me, her eyes wide in shock and concern. With a grace that belied her urgency, she took her place beside me, joining me on the floor. Cradling my head in her lap, her touch acted as a soothing balm to my wounded spirit. Her fingers wove through my hair, a tender gesture that radiated comfort and understanding. Then she whispered to me in a voice that carried the weight of unwavering assurance. "Don't worry. Everything will be alright." Her words were a beacon of hope in the darkness. Her soothing presence and comforting touch peeled away the layers of torment that had haunted me, bringing a touch of serenity amid the storm.

The tranquility of that distressing scene was shattered by the sudden arrival of another overseer, a man whose presence exuded an unsettling air of intrusion. He strode toward us, his gaze leering, and his words cutting through the air with malice. "I bet you like having his face between your legs," he said with a sneer, seeking perverse satisfaction. An indignant fire ignited within the woman, her eyes flashing with fury. Without hesitation, she confronted him, her voice filled with righteous indignation.

"How dare you!" she snapped, her words serving as a resounding rebuke. "Get out of here!" Her command, conveyed with unmistakable authority, quashed any room for his insolence.

Taken aback by her unwavering resolve, the man recoiled, his posture faltering under the weight of her words. He turned on his heel and slinked away, his presence receding into the background. In the wake of his departure, the woman's gaze returned to me, her eyes filled with renewed determination and unwavering support. In her embrace, I found a glimmer of hope amidst the darkness.

That fateful night as I returned to my room anticipating much-needed rest, I discovered a startling change. My roommate was gone, replaced by a mysterious figure perched in a chair, his eyes locked onto me like a predator observing its prey. Subdued chatter about my being on "Constant" permeated the corridors before I entered the room, kindling unease within me.

As I settled onto my bed, preparing for a session of deep meditation and introspection, the watcher remained unyielding in his seat, his gaze never wavering from me. I felt an inexplicable urge to meet his stare, to engage in a silent battle of wills. While holding his gaze, I held my breath, deliberately withholding the intake of air to provoke a response, hoping he might break his stoic façade. But he remained a solid monument of silence, his expression revealing nothing.

My attempt to hold my breath, to prolong the intensity of the moment, reached its limits as my lungs pleaded for release. Reluctantly, I exhaled, surrendering to the natural rhythm of my own breath. The watcher remained unyielding, a statue in human form, arms folded across his chest, his face both disconcerting and captivating.

Undeterred by his implacable presence, I delved back into

my meditation, determined to find relief and clarity amidst the bewildering encounter. With each breath I ventured deeper into the recesses of my mind, seeking answers to the mysteries that plagued my thoughts. As the session neared its end, I opened my eyes, half expecting the watcher to have vanished into the shadows of my imagination. To my astonishment, he remained seated before me, a steadfast sentinel, his vigil unbroken.

And so, as the sun ascended, illuminating the confines of my peculiar abode, a new day unfolded with its familiar rituals. The routines resumed, from the ingestion of prescribed medications to the shared breakfast and the collective convergence in the expansive room adorned with a ping-pong table and flickering television screen.

On that particular day, however, a sense of anticipation hung in the air, signaling the arrival of another extraordinary occurrence within the confines of that special room. As the imposing doors swung open, three figures materialized in a dramatic entrance that defied the monotony of our existence. Their sudden presence stirred the stagnant atmosphere, rousing a surge of curiosity among the ever-watchful sentinels who had grown accustomed to the undulations of our enclosed world. Three men, their countenances shrouded in mystery, seized everyone's attention and sparked whispers of intrigue among the inquisitive murmurs that permeated the room. "Who are they?" reverberated in hushed tones, a reflection of collective curiosity eager to unveil the secrets veiled beneath their façades.

Each step they took into the room was met with fixed gazes and widened eyes, fueling a storm of speculation and conjecture. The air crackled with anticipation as imaginations ran wild, weaving tales of their origins and the potential impact they could have on our collective fate. Were they agents of change, bearers of news that would shake the foundations of our existence? Were they mere spectators, drawn to observe the peculiarities of our confined existence, like guests in a grand theater of the absurd?

Their eyes bore into me, and with an air of authority, one of them directed me to follow. A mixture of trepidation and curiosity surged through my veins as I heeded their call, venturing into the unknown under their guidance. The voices of my fellow captives blending into a chorus of bewilderment and disbelief. "Who are these interlopers? How did they breach the fortress that confines us?" Their whispers trailed behind me, carried by gusts of uncertainty.

As I crossed the threshold into an adjoining room, the weighty door swung shut with an ominous finality, severing my connection to those outside. I found myself confined within the four walls, though the muffled voices of my comrades and overseers persisted outside the door—a chorus of fervent speculation amplifying the mysteries that unfolded within.

As I stepped back from beyond the door, a captivating question took root in the depths of my being, refusing to dissipate: from where did this intoxicating touch of serenity emerge? Was it a sanctum carved amidst the pernicious uproar beyond the door, or did it draw its power from the profound influence of the three figures standing before me?

As one of the men secured the door, his gaze turned toward me, exuding a commanding yet comforting presence. With a gentle touch on my shoulder, he posed the question: "How are you?" At that moment, a cascade of thoughts flooded my mind, each one opening a doorway to countless possibilities. But much like with past inquiries, the answer eluded me. I stood motionless, wrapped in silence, leaving the question hanging in the air, like a secret awaiting discovery.

"Do you know where you are?" he probed, delving deeper into my psyche. My thoughts spiraled through potential realities, transiting vast landscapes of the afterlife. I considered the vivid depictions of hell from biblical texts. Was this the result of my earthly misdeeds? An eternal disconnection from everything I once held dear? Had I been ensnared in the fiery abyss, my soul consumed by ceaseless flames?

As my mind wandered, it strove to unravel the pieces mired in perplexity and understand the purpose of the four walls that confined me. Each emerging possibility presented its own challenge, pushing me to comprehend its significance and reconsider my place there.

Then another touch graced my shoulder, prompting me to wonder, "Do you know who you are?"

Ah, that age-old question, one that has baffled me time and time again. Who was I, really? Was I defined solely by familial ties, the roles of a son and brother? Or did my identity reside in the friendships I'd nurtured, as a devoted confidant to John and a source of happiness for Susan? I once read that friendships were mere illusory constructs, seductive traps naively fallen into, lured by worldly desires.

Even there, where I tread the path of retribution, the concept of my so-called true self—or the persona society expected of me—constantly challenged me. Around my wrist, engraved on plastic, was my name: "Danny." This emblem of identity was striking, reminiscent of the flamboyant letters on my pinewood derby race car. Elevated on the stage, it not only revealed my identity but also laid bare the trials and tribulations that had shaped my existence.

In a moment of profound clarity, a powerful epiphany welled up within me, demanding release. I raised my head in silent proclamation of my resolve, signaling the forthcoming revelation of my truth. The three figures before me subtly adjusted their positions, bracing for the momentous disclosure that loomed. Lifting my right arm, I displayed the tag bearing my name. "Look," I said, breaking the lingering silence. "Can't you see? I'm guilty. I'm Danny!"

These were the words that managed to pass my lips—a rarity in that realm where silence had been my refuge, especially when faced with probing inquiries. The man's gaze, steady and unrelenting, stayed locked onto mine. His eyes seemed to delve deep into my core, as though cradling my soul.

"Oh, that's fine," he replied in a soothing tone. "We're here to take care of that for you."

The man beside him spoke next. "Scissors, please." A tidal wave of disbelief swept over me. The realization became clear—I was no longer among the living but in the afterlife's equivalent of a hospital. I had been examined and now stood on the brink of a significant procedure.

Grandma, is this the fate that awaits us in the world beyond? I wondered. Panic surged within, threatening to overwhelm me. Desperate for comfort, I reverted to the familiar ritual of counting backward from ten, clinging to the rhythm as though it might offer some anchor in that bewildering situation.

Holding the scissors in his hands, the man stepped toward me. With a firm grip, he wielded them like a compass, as if the blades possessed a magnetic pull, guiding him toward the destined path. His gaze was fixed on the name encircling my wrist. With one hand wielding the scissors, he guided the blades toward the name while the other hand raised my arm, presenting the target. Panic engulfed me, evoking the all-too-familiar sensation of visiting the doctor with my mother. Every muscle in my body tensed, and a primal scream of terror rose within me, as if anticipating the inevitable pain of a needle penetrating my arm. With trepidation, I watched as the scissors opened, like a predator poised to engulf its prey, on the verge of swallowing my printed name in a single decisive motion.

I trembled, sweat trickling down my forehead as I averted my gaze from the name tag, unable to bear its sight any longer. My eyes fixed on him, awaiting his command. "And cut," he said, the words spoken with practiced precision, as if he had carried out this process countless times before. His command hung in the air, resonating with weighty significance. Then the sound of the scissors filled the silence, the steel blades brushing against each other, creating a haunting melody that pierced the stillness. With deftness and purpose, they severed my connection to my name. I stood there, a witness to the departure of my identity, watching as it descended to the floor like a feather floating down from its lofty perch.

In an instant a profound transformation hit me, dissolving the weight of expectations and blame that had burdened my shoulders for years. Released from the depths of my being, the tag, along with the false identity it represented, vanished into a distant dimension. I was filled with a profound sense of peace, a serene calm that left me feeling weightless, unburdened, and tranquil. It mirrored the ghostly presence of the three figures before me, who had exuded a similar lightness and serenity ever since their arrival in the vast open room.

"Is that better now?" the man asked. My mind pondered the question, confirming the certainty within me. Yes, it is, I concluded, opting to keep my thoughts to myself, instead allowing him to interpret my expressions and draw his own conclusion. As his gaze remained fixed on me, his inquisitive demeanor transformed into a gentle smile. The warmth and reassurance emanating from his smile enveloped me, providing a sense of comfort and understanding. And then, in a manner reminiscent of the figures who had guided me to my room upon my arrival, their purpose seemingly fulfilled, they opened the door and stepped into the hallway, leaving me behind in contemplative solitude.

Once again, the voices of my comrades and overseers sprang to life. As the three figures passed them by, familiar questions returned: "Who are you? What are you doing here?" Undeterred, the trio maintained their steady pace. They remained silent and persistent in their purpose as they crossed the large room. And then, without a backward glance, they strode through the imposing doors of the gathering room, their presence fading into the distance, never to be seen again.

Later that evening as I approached my bed, I eschewed my customary routine of sitting, crossing my feet, and delving into deep contemplation about my day and my existence. The presence of the man, seated in the chair with his arms folded across his chest, also failed to pique my interest. Instead, after changing, I nestled beneath the comforting layers of blankets and surrendered to sleep's embrace. It was a profound night of rest, a tranquil reprieve from the relentless torment of seven nightmarish days endured while awake. It felt as though I had been granted permission to succumb to the soothing refuge of sleep, an assuagement befitting someone unjustly accused and punished.

Throughout the following day, news reached me of a series of upcoming meetings. One in particular captured my attention—an encounter with a mysterious individual known as a psychiatrist. Both my father and I would be involved. A torrent of thoughts blazed, laden with apprehension, racing through my mind. Would this be akin to those instances where I had stood before my principal alongside my father, confronting the repercussions of my actions and the troubles I had instigated? Would the principal, once again, dismissively glance at the bruises marring my body, buying into the pretext that they were the aftermath of a bike accident? Or would he discern the concealed truths they bore?

The anticipation of that imminent encounter alarmed and intrigued me. I yearned for an earnest discourse with my father and the psychiatrist, longing for my sentiments to resonate. However, as moments ebbed away, a stark realization set in—the eagerly anticipated meeting would not materialize. Instead, I was apprised of another meeting, this time with my aunt and uncle. As the designated moment approached, a fervent appeal for liberation sprang from within me, akin to a solicitation for clemency.

The psychiatrist, steadfast in his verdict, was initially averse to endorsing my entreaty. But then an extraordinary turn of events unfolded. As if swayed by the urgency of my plea, my aunt and uncle joined their voices with mine. Their collective entreaty shattered the psychiatrist's resistance and forged an unexpected agreement. It was decided that my release would be granted the following day. However, a condition attached to my newfound freedom—I had to commit to maintaining my medication regimen and attend scheduled outpatient therapy sessions.

And so, as the first rays of sunlight caressed my room, I stood amidst its warm embrace, knowing it would be the last time. With a sense of anticipation, I gathered my belongings, preparing for my aunt and uncle's arrival. They would sweep me away from that place and guide me toward the next chapter of my story, a tale filled with new possibilities and unknown horizons.

Chapter Twenty-Two

FINDING MY WAY BACK—AGAIN

EVER SINCE MY RELEASE FROM HUTCHINGS PSYCHIATRIC CENTER, the desire to restore the strained relations between my parents and me and to witness their reconnection with other beloved family members remained a steadfast flame burning within me. This longing intensified as another chance for reconciliation emerged. Whether this renewed opportunity stemmed from empathy for my struggles, their own longing for a new beginning, the heavy weight of guilt, or a myriad of other reasons, the exact catalyst mattered not. What mattered was the undeniable fact that a door had opened once more.

I received invitations to visit my parents' home in Liverpool, to dinners and gatherings not only with our immediate family but also with their close-knit circle of friends from church. However, amidst the laughter and camaraderie, I discerned a consistent theme, a disheartening pattern. Our discussions inevitably revolved around their lives, the church, its members, and the entirety of their insular world. Though I found some comfort in these familiar subjects, as a twenty-five-year-old who ran his own business and had new friendships and experiences outside the confines of the Living Word Church, academy, and campgrounds, I continually sought to share pieces of my own journey in our conversations. Regrettably, such efforts were met with palpable disappointment and a deep-seated sense of not being heard.

As the weeks passed by, the absence of meaningful interactions served as a disheartening reminder of my father's reproachful words, spoken long ago when I introduced my girlfriend Nancy to our family. "Keep your trash, whores, and sluts out of this house," he had admonished, a phrase that had reverberated across the passage of time, casting a lingering shadow that had constricted and stifled the natural flow of conversations, even those of that time.

Like my Uncle Gary once struggled before his expulsion, I grappled with the daunting challenge of articulating my thoughts and emotions. Engaging in authentic conversations about my life became a persistent struggle, as I felt obliged to offer hollow compliments or fixate solely on the experiences of others.

Despite these hurdles, I was determined to learn and adapt, making the most of the cards dealt to me. I embraced the invitations, attending the dinners and meeting familiar faces from church as per their requests. However, as time wore on, concealing my true thoughts and emotions became an increasingly burdensome task. The weight of this charade, particularly in my family's presence, grew heavier with each passing moment. A single disapproving expression, captured by my father's watchful gaze, held the power to shatter everything. Aware of the consequences, I understood that such an encounter could lead to my expulsion, banishing me once again through the very door I once hoped would be my refuge.

A few weeks after my release from Hutchings, I expressed my desire to visit my mother. When I reached out to her, I found out she was at Al Cerelli's home alongside my father, caring for Al, a bedridden member of the Living Word Church, who was nearing the end of his life. "Come over and join us. You remember Al," she urged, evoking memories of the times I spent with Al's son, Lee, several years earlier. Lee was one of the few church attendees I had formed a friendly bond with during my time there. We used to hang out together, shooting pool at the community center just down the street from his house after Sunday morning services. While I would have preferred to visit my parents in the comfort of our family home, I understood that circumstances dictated my visits to involve others—church acquaintances in their homes, at the campground, or other locations they frequented.

"Alright, Mom," I replied. "I'll see you there."

As the day arrived and I entered the house, I was struck by the sight of so many familiar faces. Gathered around the dining room table were individuals who had been faithful members of my father's church for as long as I could remember. Pockets of conversation animated the room, emanating from smaller groups clustered in various corners. However, my attention was drawn to my father, who, at the head of the table, held the rapt attention of about a dozen listeners. He was in his element, captivating his audience with a tale I had heard before. The story played out like a well-rehearsed script, detailing a day from his "pre-saved" past when he endeavored to teach a lesson to someone he disapproved of.

With each passing moment, his voice grew bolder and his gestures more animated, as though he were reliving the scene he described. His storytelling was a compelling performance, pulling the guests into his narrative with a magnetic force.

As I scanned the room, a sense of anticipation tingled in the air. I was curious about how each individual would respond to the story's approaching climax. It was as if an unspoken competition had emerged, with everyone vying for my father's attention, each hoping to be recognized as the most rapt listener. He was clearly more than just another guest; his prominence in the gathering was evident.

With the climax of his story on the horizon, I remained observant, fixated on the myriad of expressions playing across the faces of those around me. "So I put the gun to his head and said, 'What are you going to do about it now?'" He paused before delivering the punchline. "That's when I pulled the trigger. He thought it was loaded the whole time. He was so frightened, he wet his pants!"

At the conclusion of my father's story, a triumphant smile adorned his face, his eyes shining in anticipation of the roaring laughter he expected to ensue. And while laughter did follow, there was a slight pause before it began. In that moment, I observed the reactions of those around the table, wondering if someone might dare to withhold their guffaw.

However, the room quickly filled with uproarious mirth. The boisterous cheering seemed to stretch out, prolonging the moment. As I looked around, others were doing the same, each seemingly calculating the appropriate duration and intensity of their amusement. Inside, a powerful urge welled up within me to be the one who didn't join in. Thankfully, I held back, ensuring my profound disgust remained hidden.

Suddenly, an elbow nudged me, insisting I partake. "Laugh, Danny!" one of the guests whispered into my ear. For a moment it felt dreamlike, as if I'd detached from the scene, watching my father soak up the adoration of a standing ovation. But then the illusion shattered, revealing the reality before me. The applause dwindled, and as my gaze swept across the room once more, I realized all eyes were on me. Somehow I had become the cue for when the laughter should end. The joyful atmosphere vanished, replaced by tension. My silence, it seemed, had upset the balance, casting an uneasy shadow over the room.

Dad's triumphant smile was the last to fade, and it did

so slowly as our eyes locked. In that moment, an unspoken understanding passed between us. I braced myself for what would follow, fully aware that while I wouldn't be banished to my room or subjected to physical harm, the repercussions would cut deeper, leaving an indelible mark on our already strained relationship.

It was a merciless cycle, a disheartening dance of disappointment and discord that seemed to spiral endlessly. No matter how fervently I toiled to mend our fractured bond, the path to reconciliation eluded me, like a shimmering mirage in a vast desert. Each endeavor, though filled with hope and determination, only served to widen the gap, pulling the relationship further from my grasp. The prospect of reclaiming what we once had, not only for me but also for the rest of my family, felt like an elusive oasis in an unknown landscape, forever out of reach, fading into the sands of time.

If only my family had embraced open and honest discussions about the topics that now hold profound meaning for me. Our family must come together and reshape our dynamics to foster a harmonious coexistence. This unwavering conviction has been the driving force behind my tireless endeavors. I refuse to let go or make progress in my life without the involvement of my parents and siblings. As for the moral assessment of my approach, I find myself uncertain. All I can say is that it is the path I have chosen, driven by my unwavering commitment and the underlying reasons that propel me forward.

On a particular Sunday afternoon, another attempt to foster familial harmony went awry. I had joined my parents, siblings, and a few guests, including Tom, Debbie's fiancé, for a post-church service dinner. As we dined, with various conversations emanating from around the table, Pam introduced a new topic. Just moments earlier my father had regaled us with one of his characteristic dinner tales. This tale centered on Rocky Ganella, a longstanding church member who was frequently the subject of ridicule due to his peculiarities. The added jests from my father evoked hearty laughter from the family, intensifying the humor at Rocky's expense.

However, as Pam started her story, a sinking feeling overcame me. Given what had just transpired, I feared she would follow suit. Would this be another moment where I'd have to bite my tongue? I had grown accustomed to wearing a mask when around my father, something I had donned just seconds earlier. Would I have to do it for Pam too?

Her story began in the usual Mazur fashion, marked by animated gestures and the characteristic volume. She recounted an incident when her dog broke free from its chain and raced through the neighborhood. Up to that point, it seemed like a straightforward and harmless tale, but I was unprepared for the twist to come. In its escapade, her dog ventured into our neighbor's yard where the owner stood in the front with one of his children.

"Get your goddamn dog out of my yard!" he shouted.

Without hesitation, Pam confronted the man. "Get my what out of here? My goddamn dog, you said?" She urged him to repeat himself, louder this time, perhaps in front of his child, to showcase his use of profanities. She went on to voice her strong disapproval of his behavior, chastising him for not minding his own business and trying to boss her around.

By and large, Pam had dutifully adhered to my father's expectations, aligning herself with what was expected of her. However, her unkind and malicious behavior toward the neighbor contradicted the core values of Christianity, values that my father emphasized on numerous occasions during Sunday services. It not only violated religious principles but also undermined the other virtues we were taught, such as respect for our elders. In truth, these ideals seemed to be mere abstractions, devoid of practical application or demonstration. It appeared that prioritizing behavior that pleased our father took precedence over embodying these values. And in that pivotal moment, what better way to respond to our father's narrative than for Pam to share her own story, told in the same spirit as the one he had just shared?

At the conclusion of her story, everyone erupted in laughter, taking delight in Pam's triumph over her neighbor. Lo and behold, it wasn't the church that was the true shaping ground for my family's behavior but our worldly interactions.

Seated beside Pam, my youngest brother, Paul, observed quietly, his eyes taking everything in. After a moment of hesitation and a flicker of uncertainty, he joined in the whoop. He was the first to comment, his words spilling out with glee. "Pam really got him good!" If there had ever been a shred of doubt about the nature of their bellowing, Paul's response shattered it. It was a confirmation of my worst fears. Their mirth derived from the satisfaction of belittling and demeaning others. Even our father, the esteemed pastor, couldn't help but chuckle in agreement, his laughter blending seamlessly with my siblings.

At that moment I longed for my father to step in, to assert his authority, and tell my young brother that such behavior was neither acceptable nor amusing. Paul and my mother, inherently good individuals, were susceptible to being swayed by these darker inclinations. Yet there I sat, branded as a sinner by my family, the sole person disturbed by my sister's hurtful remarks. I felt powerless, unable to take any action. As a non-Christian, I couldn't find comfort in prayer, but I yearned for my family to embody the principles of Christianity that they professed to uphold.

Weeks had passed since my release from Hutchings Psychiatric Center, and I had visited my parents and siblings multiple times. Yet with each encounter, I found myself deprived of the chance to share the essence of my life—my experiences, discoveries, and the deep truths that had shaped my journey. The things I longed to reveal to my family were reflections of the very ideals they professed to uphold as Christians, ideals that seemed absent in our conversations and interactions. This realization pressed down on me until I could no longer contain the mounting pressure. So, I made a decision. I would hold back no longer. I would take a stand.

"What's wrong with this family?" I asked. "Is it funny to be harsh and mean to others? Do you want me to laugh because my little sister bad-mouthed our neighbor? Aren't Christians supposed to be kind and caring? No wonder we have so many problems. How can we ever reconcile with our grandparents, aunt, and uncle when we can't even be nice to our own neighbors?"

My brothers approached me, and it became clear that I wouldn't be allowed to stay. "Dad, I'm sorry, but I couldn't stay silent any longer," I said. "I reached my breaking point, but now I'm finished, and I'll just go. I don't have anything else to say. I get it; I can't stay, so just allow me to go away."

"Who do you think you are, mister?" he demanded. "You don't get to have the last word here. You shoot your mouth off and then expect me to treat you with respect? You don't tell me what to do in my own house. After everything we've done for you, allowing you back into this home and everything. You never even apologized once for anything you did! You always did what pleased you, never showing me any respect! Never! And another thing . . ."

His voice grew increasingly louder as he continued to berate me. Amidst his reprimands, I made my way to the closet to retrieve my shoes, his words trailing behind me. As I walked toward the closet, my brothers grasped my arms as if believing it necessary to remove me from the house. I shrugged them off. "It's snowing outside, and if you think I'm leaving without my shoes, you're in for a fight!" They exchanged glances, as if to remind each other that I was their older brother and not to be trifled with. They released me, and I retrieved my shoes, carrying them with me to the front door.

As I made my exit, the door slammed behind me, sealed by my brothers to ensure my departure.

There I sat on the cold cement porch, my socks already wet and the dampness seeping through my clothes as I struggled to put on my left shoe. Suddenly, the door swung open, revealing my mother, tears streaming down her face. She pleaded with my father, who had a firm grip on her as he tried to pull her back inside the house. "Bob, let me go. I want to talk with Danny," she implored. Finally, he released her, and the door slammed once again. Then it opened just a crack as my father positioned himself to eavesdrop on our conversation.

"Danny, why did you choose your grandparents over us?" my mother asked, her voice trembling. I was stunned, her question catching me off guard.

I realized she might have believed I had made such a choice, although I had never considered it until that moment. It seemed like an unusual time for her to bring it up. I had spent years urging my mother to have an honest conversation with me, to discuss something genuine, and now she wanted to talk about such things, at that moment? With my father pacing anxiously inside, I knew I had to respond quickly.

"Mom, you don't understand. I didn't choose sides against anyone. I simply refused to stop caring about my grandparents. That's all." There was a brief silence as she absorbed my words, then she looked at me. "Okay, Danny, I'm going to call you later, and we'll talk about this, alright?"

I nodded in agreement. "Okay, Mom."

My father grabbed hold of my mother, pulling her back inside. But her words were enough for that moment. An odd sensation came over me, a sense that something was finally going right, even if it was the worst possible timing. The feeling lingered as I walked down the driveway to my car, but it dissipated as soon as I heard my father's voice shouting at me from the porch.

"I never want to hear that you've been talking with your mother again! Stay away from this family! Don't ever call this house again! You're not welcome here, and I don't want to see you!"

As I reached my car, its familiar shape standing sentry at the curb, I thought the distance would grant me reprieve. But distance proved irrelevant, as his venomous words pierced the air, reaching me with startling clarity. Ignoring the effect his tirade had on my spirit, I pressed on, searching amidst the jumble of keys in my hand. Yet the toll of his insistence, his demand for me to detach from my mother, bore down on me. It was another attempt to keep her from me, a tactic I had grown accustomed to. Once again, fueled by a surge of unwavering determination, I was unable to maintain silence any longer.

"Why isn't it enough for you that I'm leaving? Must you continue to yell at me?" I asked, my voice resolute. "Shut your mouth, Bob. Shut your mouth, Mr. Mazur, sir, or whatever title you believe is yours. I'm leaving now, and I don't want to hear another word from you!"

That is what I said, standing next to the mailbox, my outstretched finger pointing at him. I remained rooted in place, unwilling to budge until I witnessed a flicker of change in his rigid demeanor. Then, as if my words had finally penetrated his hardened shell, his shoulders slumped, and he took a hesitant step back. At that moment I glimpsed a crack in his veneer, a hint of vulnerability long overdue.

In response to this unexpected shift, I lowered my finger and relaxed my stance. With a mixture of relief and defiance, I got into my car. It was the first time in my life that I hadn't addressed him as "Dad," and it was a display of disrespect unlike anything I had ever shown before or since. The weight of that defiance lingered, a tangible reminder of the deep-seated frustration that had fueled my words.

Over the years I have been accused of saying terrible things, of harboring hatred toward my father, but such accusations are baseless and untrue. I never uttered a word of hatred toward him or anyone else. While our relationship was marred by conflict and resentment, beneath it all was a glimmer of understanding. It was not hatred that fueled my defiance but a desperate plea for recognition, for a connection that had been shattered and needed to be rebuilt.

Days turned into weeks, and weeks turned into a seemingly endless expanse of time as I awaited a call from my mother that never came. Each passing day heightened my disappointment and uncertainty. I questioned my own naivety, unable to comprehend why I had allowed myself to hope for a connection that seemed destined to remain severed.

In the depths of my solitude, I couldn't help but reflect on the consequences of that fateful day. Sitting at the dining room table, fueled by a surge of courage and a desperate desire to be heard, I unleashed words that reverberated like a thunderclap. Little did I know that those words would create new walls between me and those I once called family.

Their contemptuous remarks, tinged with disdain, haunted my thoughts. I could almost hear the incredulous exclamations that accompanied their tales of my supposed transgressions. They painted me as a rebellious soul, an unruly force that dared to challenge the status quo. They spoke of my audacity to speak my mind, accusing me of disrespecting my father, reducing him to a mere "Bob," as if we were strangers passing each other on the street.

Their tongues wagged with judgment, declaring me to be possessed by a "bad spirit," a sinner engulfed in a fiery concoction of anger, rage, and hate. It was as if they had crafted a narrative that transformed me into a villain, an embodiment of all their fears and insecurities. And yet, I knew deep within that their version of events was a distorted reflection of reality.

The nagging suspicion that my experiences were more than just isolated incidents but emblematic of a broader trend grew harder to dismiss. It appeared that any challenge to the established norms, be it the status quo or the church's doctrine, resulted in predictable consequences. Those who strayed from the dictated norms, who dared voice their doubts and assert their individuality, found themselves branded as rebels and viewed as sinners by the devout.

Reflecting on the silence that enveloped me, I began to question the worth of my choices. Had my prolonged silence been in vain? Should I have continued to speak my truth, consequences be damned? The answers eluded me, swirling in a vortex of uncertainty.

Yet one thing remained steadfast: I refused to accept the distorted narrative that they wove around my existence. I clung to the belief that my intentions were pure, driven by a yearning for authenticity and a refusal to be silenced. And so, despite the isolation and the weight of their judgments, I resolved to forge my own path, even if it meant walking alone.

The unspoken rules permeated the air, their presence tangible yet concealed beneath a veneer of denial. It was a twisted game of secrecy, where the lines were drawn without ever being explicitly spoken. As I observed the dynamics within my family, it became increasingly apparent that there was an unwritten mandate to distance themselves from me, their own flesh and blood.

I tested the waters, challenged their steadfast adherence to the unspoken directive. I even confronted my siblings, only to have them see and confess the directives.

"Why won't you see me?" I asked, frustrated and longing for the truth. "Has Dad forbidden it?" The response was a well-rehearsed dance of deception and denial.

"What? Dad never said anything about not seeing you," was the reply, their feigned innocence veiling the unspoken restrictions that governed their interactions.

I couldn't help but marvel at how well they sidestepped the truth. It was as if they had been trained to deflect any mention of the unspoken decree, shielding our father from the responsibility of explicitly stating, "Stay away from Danny." It was a delicate dance of words where silence and gestures spoke louder than any explicit command.

It was a message delivered in the glances exchanged, hesitant steps backward, and hushed conversations behind closed doors. We were all puppets in his grand play, unknowingly dancing to the rhythm of his unspoken commands.

I saw through their denials and embraced the reality that they were unwilling to acknowledge. The division within our family, the severed ties with our grandparents, uncle, and aunt—it all traced back to the orchestrator of our pain, my father.

Chapter Twenty-Three

THE DISENGAGEMENT PARTY

OUR FAMILY LANDSCAPE OFTEN APPEARED LIKE A PUZZLE WAIT-ing for its missing pieces. Many times I felt like the discarded part—left out, overlooked, lost. However, fleeting moments of warmth occasionally pierced that cloud, leaving me wondering if I was truly adrift. Occasionally, there were hints, gestures from siblings that beckoned me back into the fold.

Then came the day that was imbued with gold and shad-ow—Debbie's engagement to Tom. Her invitation was like a sunbeam, but as days dwindled, storm clouds of doubt loomed. Debbie wasn't just a sister; she was our family's torch-bearer, the eldest grandchild. A visit to the sacred haven of my grandparents' home unearthed a bitter truth: they, along with my cherished aunt and uncle, wouldn't grace the event. The thought of their absence was a stone sinking in my heart. It wasn't about why they were absent; it was the haunting void created by their absence at such a pivotal juncture. My heart ached to share this with Debbie and my parents, but I knew that broaching the topic was unfeasible, that voicing my concerns would risk my own invitation to the celebration.

Debbie's invitation, which had once shone brightly, now seemed dimmed by the palpable absence of our clan's pillars. But when the day dawned, I stood tall, making my presence felt. The backdrop was David Gentile's abode, a dream woven in twilight. Poolside, candles shimmered like a constellation, their reflections waltzing on the water. The assembly was substantial, predominantly members from the church. Gentle Christian melodies set the tone in the background as I navigated the crowd, reconnecting with familiar faces from days long past when I too was a regular at the church.

In a secluded corner, away from the house, a table bathed in ethereal white stood as if awaiting royalty. One by one, my family members converged, their chairs seemingly preordained. An array of glittering bottles poured nectar into crystal glasses, which soon sparkled in every hand. The atmosphere thickened with anticipation until a voice rose, carrying tales of the Mazur legacy.

The evening might have been Debbie and Tom's ode, but for me, the song was different. It sang of belonging, painting a picture of my family drenched in twilight's embrace while I watched, a silhouette on the fringes. With the others I lifted my glass in a silent serenade, our collective gaze anchored to the family table, honoring the enduring spirit of the Mazurs.

Did anyone grasp the tempest within me as our glasses clinked, as wishes soared? Each clink of our glasses, each lofty wish, and I felt like a sailor adrift, at the mercy of a turbulent sea without a compass. I had been blindsided, utterly unprepared for the swell of emotions. If circumstances had permitted, if I could have voiced the turmoil churning within me, I could have predicted the response: "You don't involve your-self with us, so why would we assume you'd have wanted a seat at the table?"

I'd like to think that most people would fathom the depths of my emotions that evening. But when it came to my siblings, especially Debbie, did she catch even a glimpse of my turmoil? What crossed her mind when she included me? And upon witnessing the night's proceedings, did a hint of realization dawn?

Post-toast, I set my glass down and made a beeline for my car. *Couldn't I have been forewarned?* I mused.

As I drove away, a familiar route seemed to guide me, and soon Oak Street stretched before me, a path leading to my solitude and the tranquility of my grandparents' house. Over-whelmed by the sting of familial exclusion, I was consumed by a longing for my grandparents' comforting embrace. Upon knocking, I was greeted warmly, and the rest of the evening was spent on their porch, engaged in the kind of genuine, simple conversations I had always cherished. We watched cars go by, and I reveled in the simplicity and warmth of the moments I held dear with them. Their presence, an age-old balm, soothed the raw edges of the evening, rekindling cher-ished memories and warmth.

BEYOND THE STIGMA: REVEALING AWARENESS

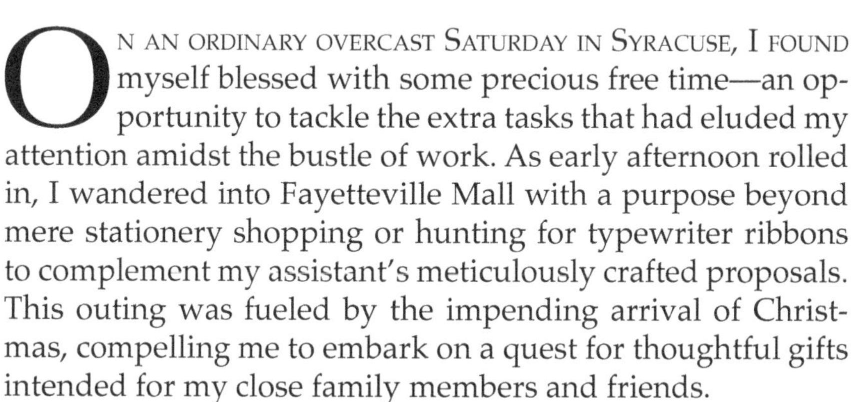

ON AN ORDINARY OVERCAST SATURDAY IN SYRACUSE, I FOUND myself blessed with some precious free time—an opportunity to tackle the extra tasks that had eluded my attention amidst the bustle of work. As early afternoon rolled in, I wandered into Fayetteville Mall with a purpose beyond mere stationery shopping or hunting for typewriter ribbons to complement my assistant's meticulously crafted proposals. This outing was fueled by the impending arrival of Christmas, compelling me to embark on a quest for thoughtful gifts intended for my close family members and friends.

After finding a Cuisinart blender for my aunt at JCPenney,

I found myself once again navigating the mall's corridors, surrounded by the familiar sounds of Christmas songs.

A year and a half had passed since my release from Hutchings. I had plunged back into the cleaning business, focusing on improving our crew and securing more contracts. I tried not to linger on thoughts of my fragmented family, the complications, and the consistent rejections, unable to find a way to reintegrate myself into their lives. Despite my dedication to work and the friendships I had forged, these substitutes and the time spent away from my family felt insufficient. My mind invariably wandered, contemplating how I could find my way back to them.

Against this backdrop, I carried out my daily activities, even the most mundane ones. That day was no exception as I walked alongside numerous members of my community, many of whom were also shopping for gifts. Lost in thought, I cast my gaze upon the unfamiliar faces passing in and out of view. And then, among them, one face stood out. It was not the face of a friend but rather an acquaintance from my past. In such instances I occasionally stumbled, attempting to recall how I knew someone. However, the shared environment and circumstances in which we had previously encountered each other were driven so deeply into my memory that I recognized not only who he was but also what I had to do as he drew nearer.

The man bore a resemblance to me, with dark brown hair, a stature under six feet, a medium build, and brown eyes. Someone could have easily mistaken him for one of my cousins. He wasn't alone; he was walking hand in hand with a beautiful woman. As they drew closer, snippets of their conversation reached my ears, accompanied by expressions that reflected their lightheartedness on that leisurely Saturday afternoon. A question emerged within me as I became intrigued about the nature of their relationship. Was she his girlfriend, his wife, or perhaps his mistress? As I observed their affectionate gazes and considered her age, it became evident that she was not his daughter. Despite that realization, the answer to the question about their relationship continued to elude me. I longed to know, hoping there was a deep connection between them.

The moment arrived. They were mere feet away from me, on the brink of passing by. "Hey, Tommy," I called out, grabbing his attention. Both of them halted their steps, their eyes turning toward me, but there was no flicker of recognition in their gaze. If I didn't speak again, and soon, Tommy would undoubtedly inquire about my identity, a question I wasn't ready to answer quite yet. "Hey, how have you been? It feels like ages since we last saw each other," I said, keeping my words concise and to the point, not giving him an opportunity to reflect.

It came as no surprise to me that he didn't recognize me. I knew that the more I revealed myself through gestures and declarations, the less likely he would have any inkling of who I was. After all, he knew nothing about me, and that suited my intentions perfectly.

"I was up in Alexandra Bay with some of the guys last weekend," I continued, maintaining the charade. "We had an incredible time. You should have been there. It's fantastic to see you again. You haven't changed a bit. By the way, I still have that office on Morgan Road. You should drop by sometime, so we can catch up."

Tommy, obligated at the very least to return a smile, began warming up to me, though with a touch of awkward hesitation. "Oh yeah, that sounds great. I'd love to—"

"No, really, Tommy," I said, interrupting him midsentence in order to steer the conversation. "I apologize for not staying in touch. How have things been for you?"

"It's all pretty much the same. Everything's going well enough," he replied, proceeding cautiously as if hoping to stumble upon a clue to jog his memory about who I was.

None of what I had said held any truth. I hadn't been in Alexandra Bay the previous weekend, and Tommy had no knowledge of my office or my business. But I continued to spin tales, fabricating stories about my recent activities and embellishing my bustling life over the past few weeks. I seized the opportunity to mention my business partner, John, as a means to flaunt my involvement in the local business community. My presentation was carefully crafted, exuding charisma and overflowing with boasts and braggadocio.

"Sure, let's catch up sometime," he interjected, his hesitation diminishing. I paused, bringing my rambling to a halt, then shifted my attention to the woman beside him, still holding Tommy's hand. "I'm sorry, I don't believe we've had the pleasure of being introduced. Tommy, who is this beautiful woman?" It became apparent to me that the woman, without uttering a word to Tommy, was already aware of his lack of recognition toward me—a revelation that filled me with satisfaction. While they hadn't exchanged any words since our encounter, the unspoken exchange of eye contact and subtle gestures between them spoke volumes, revealing a profound connection that went beyond mere hand holding. It was everything I had hoped for. At that moment I understood that just as I knew precisely what was expected of me upon seeing Tommy, she also comprehended her role in the encounter. She possessed the opportunity to spare Tommy the embarrassment of not recognizing me, the supposed long-lost friend who had approached him with such fervor.

"Hi, glad to meet you. My name is Tina. And who are you? How do you know my husband?" I glanced away from her for a moment, stealing a quick look at Tommy. He seemed relieved, as if on the verge of recalling our connection, our shared history. Unbeknownst to him, the truth about me and the purpose of our conversation in the mall that afternoon was about to be unveiled, but there would be no relief in the revelation. Instead, it would have the opposite effect.

Redirecting my gaze back to Tina, who stood resolute by Tommy's side, I realized that the look she gave me in that moment was one that could never be replicated if our paths crossed again. Tina was on the cusp of forming an impression of me, one that would likely leave an indelible mark, deeply ingrained and everlasting.

"I was once a patient at the Hutchings Psychiatric Center. I encountered your husband shortly after a harrowing episode in which I tried to kill myself by jumping through an upper-floor window. A compassionate woman was the first to come to my aid, sitting with me on the floor and calming me by cradling my head in her lap and stroking my hair. Tommy was right there too beside her, saying, 'I bet you like having his face down there between your legs!'"

With a sudden release of her husband's hand, her eyes widened, her mouth agape in disbelief as her face leaned in closer, desperate to confirm the unimaginable words she had just heard. If I had lingered even for a moment longer, it would have been to fully capture the sight of her expression—an embodiment of shock and disbelief. As for Tommy's reaction, I had no interest in witnessing it. Without a backward glance, I turned on my heel and walked away, leaving Tommy to grapple with the shattered illusions he may have harbored about me and leaving his wife to question the very foundations of her perception of him.

Chapter Twenty-Five

NEVER GIVE IN

Never give in. Never give in. Never, never, never, never—in nothing, great or small, large or petty—never give in, except to convictions of honour and good sense. – Winston Churchill

I WAS A STUBBORN YOUNG LAD, A TRAIT THAT PERSISTED INTO MY teens and beyond. My determination was unwavering whenever I set my mind on something. It saddened me to see the gradual dissolution of relationships within our once large, close-knit family, as well as the drifting apart of friends, neighbors, and acquaintances. While I wasn't directly involved in the disruption or restoration of many of these connections, I did become entangled in one particular bond— that between Don Kirnan and my father. Don was a former member of our church and also my boss at Onondaga Plaza where I managed the building's cleaning operations in the evenings. I was still living at home back then, endeavoring to establish my daytime photography business.

I dropped hints daily to my father and Don, reminding them of their past friendship and shared experiences. I believed there was no reason for them to remain estranged. To my surprise, my efforts bore fruit, and I learned that Don planned to visit our home for a conversation with my father. Encouraged by this discovery, I eagerly awaited Don's arrival. When he finally arrived, we all gathered in the living room, taking our seats as the conversation began.

However, the situation took an unexpected and unsettling turn. Just a few minutes into their discussion, my father approached the fireplace and picked up the iron poker, brandishing it at Don. "I'll wrap this poker around your neck!" he exclaimed. I was shocked, but to my surprise, Don remained unfazed. As a hockey coach and former player, his eyes seemed to convey the thought, *Gee, I didn't know this visit was going to be recreational.* However, he refrained from voicing such a sentiment. Instead, he calmly made his way to the door and left.

The next day at work, he offered me an apology. "I'm sorry, Danny. I didn't anticipate that we would make any progress."

Chapter Twenty-Six

VISITING THE
LIVING WORD CHURCH

BEFORE THAT PIVOTAL DAY AT MY PARENTS' HOME, WHEN I STOOD by my car, reeling from the sting of my father's hurtful words shouted from the porch, my curiosity had led me to the church. I arrived after the service had started and took a seat at the back. As my father preached from the pulpit, I listened with intense focus. I couldn't help but notice several congregants sneaking glances at me.

My visit to the church was driven by a specific goal: to seek validation, a personal confirmation, to ascertain whether everything within those walls—the sermon, the people— aligned with my memories. As I absorbed the sermon, I found the answers I was looking for. The exact words escape me now, but I recall a sense of dissonance between the message delivered and what I felt was appropriate, should I ever decide to embrace such a community. The sermon felt out of place in the world I knew. It was like reading a manual for something I would never own, prompting me to ponder its relevance.

There I was, once more in that familiar setting, my mind drifting, transporting me to times long past. Despite feeling out of place, a sense of obligation prevailed, the need to conform to my parents' expectations as their compliant son. But this time things were different; my presence was of my own choosing, driven by personal motives.

As the sermon continued, spanning nearly an hour, my thoughts wandered, and a sense of restlessness took hold, manifesting in small, fidgety movements. My fingers caressed my wrist, a gesture that sparked curiosity within me. Why this reflex? Suddenly, a forgotten memory resurfaced—a past fixation.

On my thirteenth birthday, my father had given me a unique watch, featuring a timer precise to the tenth of a second. The last digit, changing rapidly, was hypnotizing. During my father's sermons, I was often absorbed by my watch, challenging myself to stop the timer exactly at ten seconds. After numerous attempts, I achieved a personal record of thirty-six consecutive precise stops. I recall achieving that milestone at 8:49 p.m. on Friday, September 8, 1978, after over two years of practice. This experience at the church left an indelible impression on me: to cherish and value every moment, regardless of its brevity, understanding that each one holds a significance and should never be wasted.

As the service drew to a close, David Gentile, an iconic member of the church who had been part of the organization since its inception during the days in Euclid, approached me. I had already taken notice of his presence, and it seemed fitting that if there were ever to be an interaction that would bring me back and connect me with someone who embodied everything the church stood for, it would be him.

He took a seat beside me and smiled warmly. "Hi, Danny, how are you?" I wondered what he wanted and why he couldn't have waited until the meeting concluded. "Would you like to come over to my house for a visit?" he asked.

"Sure, why not?" I replied.

If there ever was a true embodiment of a sinner, someone whose transgressions surpassed those I was accused of, David was it. He had experienced a profound journey, a former hippie once deeply immersed in a world of drugs and rock and roll. However, he had undergone a transformation, embracing a life guided by the church's principles and becoming a successful businessman and devoted family man. It seemed fitting that he was now extending an invitation to me, providing an opportunity to delve further into the world of my past.

After extending his invitation, David made his way back to his seat. As the service drew to a close, I became aware that my mother, brothers, and sisters were somewhere nearby, likely occupying their usual spots. However, I felt no desire to seek them out or engage in post-service conversations. With unwavering determination, I remained resolute in my purpose, immersing myself in my surroundings and ensuring that the decisions that I had made over the past few years were the right ones.

When the service concluded, David glanced in my direction, seemingly confirming my commitment to visit him. I replied with a nod and then proceeded toward the rear exit, where we rendezvoused, and I consented to following his car to his home.

In my blue Chevy Astro van, a vehicle I had bought a year earlier for my cleaning business, I navigated the route, having plenty of time to delve into my thoughts and contemplate David's intentions along the way. I found myself pondering what he knew about me, my experiences at Hutchings, and the circumstances that led me there. I was certain that he, too, was engaged in contemplation, creating a plan to save me and guide me back into the church's embrace. Throughout the remainder of the journey, I tried to anticipate the approach he might take.

David, who was married to Anita, had four children. Their children were raised in the doctrine of the Living Word Church and attended the Living Word Academy. Their family's level of involvement in the church mirrored that of others I knew. To them the church wasn't just a place of worship; it was the focal point of their lives. They gathered almost daily for various activities, including frequent church meetings, school events, camp gatherings, and house meetings.

Upon arriving at David's home, I was surprised by how close it was to my grandparents' residence on Oak Street.

"Come inside," David said as we stepped out of our vehicles and entered through the side door. "Would you like something to eat?" he inquired as he headed to the refrigerator.

"Sounds good," I replied with enthusiasm.

As David gathered food, dishes, and cutlery, he engaged in conversation with me, as if unveiling a script that he had crafted during our final moments at church and during the drive to his beautiful home.

"Personalized Care" was the name of the business David owned. It employed several church members and others from the Syracuse community. His journey from rags to riches, from sinner to saint, exemplified the best that the Living Word Church had to offer. However, to my astonishment, I soon realized that David's invitation to his home that evening was not driven by a desire to "win me over to Christ" or share personal testimonies of his blessings and the importance of salvation.

Despite knowing of David's presence in the church for many years, my perception of him had been shaped through the lens of my parents' perspective. This meeting presented a valuable opportunity for us to engage in a genuine and meaningful conversation, transcending the usual exchanges of pleasantries.

I was delighted to have the opportunity for a genuine

conversation with David, regardless of the subject matter. I waited patiently for the moment when he would create an atmosphere conducive to deeper discussions.

He began by drawing my attention to various items within my line of sight, including the impressive custom-built stereo system integrated into the living room walls. Then, without hesitation or engaging in small talk, he delivered a statement that caught me off guard.

"Your father traps people, then threatens a withdrawal if they don't do as he says," David remarked as he rinsed a glass under the tap. I was taken aback. This was David Gentile, often seen at the church altar during services, passionately singing worship songs until he was breathless, his clothing soaked with sweat. A devout congregant who spoke in tongues and believed he communicated with God was now sharing his concerns and grievances about my father. And he was doing so with such unusual frankness. There were no preliminaries or attempts at humor; he got straight to the point.

As David retrieved two slices of homemade bread from the toaster oven and spread jelly on them, memories of my mother and others raving about his culinary skills came rushing back. With the first bite, those accolades were justified. Amidst this delightful interlude, David steered our conversation in a different direction. "I've been living alone here for a while now," he revealed. "Anita and the kids are in my other house. I've been facing difficulties, and a significant part of it involves your father."

My thoughts raced in response to that revelation. *Wait a minute! Is this the real reason for his invitation? Is he just going to keep venting, or does he have a plan to save my soul?*

Maybe, just maybe, this was a chance for a deep and genuine discussion. Such an experience had never taken place with my parents or anyone from the Living Word Church before. While I frequently encountered familiar faces from the church on the streets, my exchanges with church members like Rocky Ganella were more than just superficial—they were unsettling.

With his vacant stare and hollow comments, Rocky crossed my path one day at Dominick's Restaurant on Burnet Ave. I was in the middle of a crucial meeting with a client, presenting a proposal for his advertising agency. I spotted Rocky from a distance, and I was struck by a feeling of dread as I anticipated the scenario about to play out.

As expected, Rocky approached and interrupted my business meeting. "Hi, Danny. Praise God! Just wanted to let you know that Jesus loves you, and your father does too!" he declared, taking a seat beside my client. The inappropriateness of the situation was painfully apparent, and I was desperate for an escape. How could I even begin to explain such an awkward intrusion to my client?

"God is waiting for your return to his kingdom, away from this world," Rocky continued, further complicating matters. In response, I sought a swift resolution, eager to defuse the situation and restore my professional demeanor.

As I sat with David in his home, taking another bite of the delicious toast, my thoughts wandered to the potential direction of our conversation. How well did I truly understand this man, whom I had known only through the lens of my parents and the Living Word Church? Did my initial speculation during the drive still stand? Might he reference Romans 3:23, emphasizing that "all have sinned and fall short of the glory of God," in hopes of persuading me to forgive my father, much as he might have done himself?

However, I soon recognized the pointlessness of trying to anticipate his motives. I decided instead to concentrate on following wherever David guided our discussion. To my surprise, he began sharing intricate details of his personal challenges and experiences. "You can't fully grasp it," he admitted, his voice tinged with vulnerability and urgency. "I made the hard choice to leave the church, knowing deep within that it wasn't right. But the consequences were severe. Everyone I knew, including my kids and my wife, cut off all contact with me. They are completely immersed in the church and its teachings, and they have no other place to turn. Your father threatened to isolate them from others if I didn't comply with his demands, and he has already carried out that threat once. I felt trapped, with no alternative but to return. I can't bear the loneliness of staying alone in this house any longer."

I realized I had been unaware of these details. I hadn't even considered the context in which David was recounting his experiences. What he described was vastly different from anything I had anticipated. David had observed the manipulation, deceit, and ungodly behavior within an environment he had once trusted and believed in. He had positioned himself and his family at the heart of the church community, allowing it to become the core of their lives.

That evening as I sat with him, it became evident that David had returned to the church not as a mere participant fulfilling an expected appearance but as a lost sheep seeking to find his way back to the fold. Undoubtedly, others in the church had seen me through a similar lens, believing that I needed to make a return, to turn away from my worldly ways. However, as I listened to David's story, I realized his decision to return was not driven by a steadfast belief in God but rather by the fact that he felt he had nowhere else to go.

As he continued to confide in me, David unveiled a multitude of anecdotes about the injustices he had witnessed and the motives behind his departure. It became evident that his intention in inviting me was not to provide assistance or guidance after all. Instead, David Gentile, whom I had come to know as "Mr. Living Word," the embodiment of what my father had dedicated his life to, stood before me broken and hopeless, pleading at the feet of sinner Danny, asking the poignant question, "What should I do?"

For years, David had been following my father's advice and appeared to find success in the accomplishments he showcased upon our arrival at his home. But what did he expect me to offer? He had been present alongside my father and me just days before I was involuntarily admitted to Hutchings Psychiatric Center, witnessing my turmoil and hearing the skepticism surrounding my recovery. Now, perhaps after observing my regained coherence, he saw it as a miraculous transformation or harbored the belief that I possessed knowledge capable of aiding him in his own struggles. I could only guess.

As I absorbed his words, I grappled with the weight of his plea and the responsibility he had placed upon me. "I don't know why you're coming to me for answers," I said, "but if you truly want to hear my thoughts, I have no problem sharing them. Just be prepared for what I have to say."

"Yes, tell me, what do you think I should do?" he replied.

"What about God?" I asked. He looked at me with a bewildered expression.

"What do you mean?"

"All those years you spoke in tongues at church, all the miracles I heard about, were any of them real? I thought the Christian life was supposed to be about standing up for what's right and accepting the consequences, the rewards and the persecution."

David sighed. "You don't get it, Danny. I tried standing up to your father, but it didn't work. What should I do?"

"Stand your ground? Remain steadfast in your beliefs? Perhaps think about joining a different church?"

Clearly agitated, David shook his head. "I tried leaving, but it's been too challenging—not just for me but also for my wife and kids. Things only got worse."

"If you're looking for an easy answer, you're talking to the wrong person. I spent time in a psychiatric ward, remember? I came close to losing my sanity trying to navigate the same manipulations and dishonesty you speak of. Why would you expect me to have answers for you that I didn't avail to myself?"

David's lament continued. "I've been devoted to the Living Word for so many years, and everyone I know attends there. If I walk away, they'll ostracize me. I don't know if I can make new friends."

"David, do you still consider yourself a Christian?" I asked.

He hesitated for a moment before replying. "Yeah, I do."

"And do you still believe in faith?"

David nodded. "Yes, I believe."

"Then perhaps this is a test of that faith, a challenge you wouldn't be facing if you already had all the answers."

His response was tinged with concern for his children. "But my kids go to the Academy. How am I meant to deal with that?"

Our conversation seemed to be going in circles without any clear resolution or new direction. It was more of the same until we returned to the pleasantries commonly used at times of departure.

David continued to attend the Living Word Church and renewed his friendship with my parents. However, I didn't have any further contact with him until two years later. By then I had relocated to Florida. I grew suspicious that the letters I sent to my mother were being intercepted and withheld from her. Wanting to ensure that she received a particularly heartfelt letter that I penned for Mother's Day, I reached out to David, hoping he could deliver it to her personally due to his close ties with my parents. I called him and left a voice message to that effect. A day or two later, David left a message on my answering machine. Among the few words he shared, what remained with me were the following: "I'm too close." Immediately, I felt compelled to write another letter, this time addressed to him.

Two years after that, during a trip to Syracuse to see my grandparents, I decided to visit David's residence on James Street. As I knocked on the door, I discerned the faint sounds of movement inside, but no one came to the door. Later as I shared my experience with my brother-in-law, Frankie, I was devastated to learn that David had passed away. He was only forty years old.

I kept a copy of my letter to him, which is reproduced below.

David,

You're too close? What does this mean? Does it mean you will do nothing that may encourage separation? Does it mean you have decided the ends justify the means? Are you telling me you have no faith in God? That you do what people will have you do, so you will not lose their love or acceptance?

Honesty with me would demand other words and explanations. You would have mentioned the loneliness you have being unable to express what you really feel. Why do you settle? Is it enough for you to give life to only a part of your being? Are you sure you are bringing life to the best part of you?

I have asked you for a favor. Though the reason for my request is sincere and with good intent, you will not participate. I don't think you can know how this makes me feel. It tells me much about you and saddens me. Not that I will not have your help, but that your sadness will continue by not accepting mine.

Faith is an interesting word. It cannot be synonymous with understanding. If only I could convince you to act according to your heart and not to desired conclusions.

There's a saying I've heard about relationships. "If you love someone, set them free. If they come back they were yours. If they don't, they never were." Maybe something of this can be said about friendships. Something like "be yourself, and see who sticks around. The ones that do are your friends, the ones that don't never were."

There is at least one thing you and I have in common. For many years, at least four times a week we have for one reason or another been exposed to the same thing. Coincidence? I made a decision to have faith, and to follow my heart. Where my journey will take me I do not know. If I knew, faith would not be required.

How about you David? Why did you quit? Will you ever get back on track?

Four times a week, for many years. All training, clues to the right way to handle what we face together today. Have you forgotten? How you handle me and my family is what God & the bible are all about. The meetings were supposed to be the classroom. When given a choice, why remain unemployed? Gain courage/faith and put your lessons to use.

What about all the deserving people you could help? Isn't this enough of a source to draw strength from? Can't you put some of the needs of others in front of your own? Don't you believe that it is better to give than to receive? Who knows, maybe with a little faith your own needs would be met.

The letter's ending is lost

DEPARTING STATE DUALITIES: NEW YORK AND MIND

BY THE SUMMER OF 1989, TWO YEARS AFTER MY RELEASE FROM Hutchings Psychiatric Center, my relentless attempts to reconnect with my family had ended in disappointment yet again. Back in 1981, I had clung to a steadfast optimism, believing my future would unfold differently. I hoped time would steer me toward a more favorable path, but that hope had crumbled.

Following my letter to David, I was certain that the truth about past events would come to light. I expected, at most, a mild rebuke for neglecting household chores, confident that there was no reason for my family's estrangement.

Contrary to my expectations, I became an outcast, perceived as a challenge to the essence of my father's mission. My family stood united against me, turning into adversaries. I felt like a sputtering candle, its weak light barely penetrating the surrounding darkness.

Teetering on the edge of despair and mired in confusion, I questioned my role as a son and a brother. The thought of abandoning everything crossed my mind, but the same bewilderment that sparked this idea also hindered its realization. In the end, it wasn't the absence of the family I once knew that restrained me; it was the realization of life's relentless flux—the unchanging truth that nothing stays the same, and everything evolves. Like a spinning roulette wheel, I understood that eventually, my situation would shift, and life would continue its course. With this recognition, I chose to stay put.

My desire to reconnect with my family remained strong, but my focus shifted toward personal growth and self-discovery. I was no longer solely the son or the brother of my past. I redefined myself through the concrete realities of my present life, embracing roles as a friend and a dependable employer, supporting others as they forged their paths and identities.

I missed John, who had left my home along with Wendy and Lori a few years back. His absence as a friend and collaborator in our shared business venture had significantly diminished the allure of that endeavor. As John left Syracuse to pursue his own path, both in his relationship with Wendy and his new position as a sales representative for another company, I was faced with a pivotal choice. I decided to bring Ed on board, a seasoned professional in his early fifties, to fill the void John had left.

As my business continued to grow, the need for expansion became clear. I hired a supervisor to manage the working crew, which marked the beginning of a transformation in my role within the company. During this period of change, I traveled to New York City and secured a deal with a firm based there. The deal involved us handling floor and carpet maintenance for a chain of retail stores across a designated region in New York State. In essence, my company became one of several subcontractors tasked with upholding the cleanliness standards of carpets and floors in these establishments statewide. Although the profit margins from that agreement were modest, I valued the opportunity, and I accepted the terms, especially the absence of a non-compete clause in the contract.

As my relationship with Ed deepened, our frequent lunch meetings, often accompanied by White Russians, became a regular occurrence. We began to strategize about offering independent services for carpet and floor maintenance to retail stores across New York State. Now in my sixties, looking back on this phase, which had somewhat faded from my memory, is intriguing. In my twenties, I was no match for the seasoned wisdom of a man with far more life experience.

Our company underwent significant transformations as agreements were established and roles evolved. This change continued as we involved our supervisor and my secretary in further deals, aiming to grow the business substantially. Through ongoing discussions, particularly between Ed and me during our frequent lunches, we reached a mutual agreement that, despite him being initially hired as a salesman, my own talents were better suited for that role.

Consequently, for many months I dedicated myself to the task at hand, making countless calls and traveling across the state to cities like Rochester, Albany, and Buffalo, forging deals with various retail stores.

Looking back now, I realize how naïve I was. At that time I held a simple belief that our collective talent and capabilities would pave the way for us to achieve our most ambitious dreams, as long as each of us fulfilled our roles.

However, unbeknownst to me, underlying dynamics were at work that had escaped my consideration. While Ed, my supervisor, and secretary each possessed exceptional skills, they didn't share the tight-knit bond I had with friends like John, Wendy, Lori, and others. As our work progressed, I realized, much later than I should have, that they had been convening in private during my extended absences. During these gatherings, discussions and arguments ensued regarding their respective roles in the company, questioning who was benefitting more or less and proposing changes. It was only then that I grasped the events that had been unfolding in the background while I was single-mindedly focused on acquiring new business.

Besides seeking new clients, I was conducting interviews with owners of janitorial services across the state. The future seemed bright, and momentum was on our side. I had secured a considerable number of solid contracts in Syracuse in particular, further bolstering our revenue.

While these three individuals were optimistic about the company's future, they had no ownership in the business. This became a central theme of their private discussions and led to a shift in the company's atmosphere, deviating from the passion and drive that fueled my initial entrepreneurial journey before our paths converged.

As I pen these words, reflecting on that chapter of my life, I'm transported back to those moments, consumed by feelings reminiscent of a malignancy needing extraction. But I took an unexpected step. Instead of clinging to what I had worked so hard to build, I faced the reality of a situation that was creating rifts similar to those in my familial past, something I had been reluctant to confront. I met with them, signed the documents transferring all ownership to them, and asked for nothing in return. My sole desire was to distance myself from the discord. In a brief moment, "Commercial Cleaners," the company's name, vanished from my life.

I transitioned to a new role in sales, landing a position selling flash-frozen food. Gone were the days of perpetual availability that came with owning a company and having to be on call around the clock. The midnight emergencies—such as employees forgetting alarm codes, locking themselves out, or dealing with equipment malfunctions—became mere memories, and the strain of managing day-to-day operations receded. A particularly memorable moment from this period occurred during a meeting at Hewlett Packard, where I had to assert that the inadvertent disposal of equipment worth tens of thousands of dollars, left unsecured by one of their technicians, was not due to any negligence on the part of my company or crew. Freeing myself from the responsibilities at Commercial Cleaners also meant I was unburdened from such stresses.

With newfound freedom in my schedule, I fostered new friendships and engaged in more enjoyable activities. Through my childhood friend Don, whom I maintained regular contact with, I encountered a diverse group of individuals. We frequently gathered at Don's apartment to play cards, and I started spending a substantial amount of time there. Meanwhile, my relationship with Susan began to mirror the dynamics I had experienced with my family during my earlier years at home. She once pointed out that our cohabitation resembled that of roommates rather than a meaningful relationship, and I recognized the truth in her observation. While we occasionally shared a meal together, most evenings I would venture out in search of my own sources of entertainment.

Just before my departure from Commercial Cleaners, when my enthusiasm for the business was waning, a group of us, including Don and a few friends, spent a Saturday night at Club 37 in North Syracuse. That night I was introduced to Kyle, the brother of one of Don's friends, Kerry. Much like Don had intrigued me when we first crossed paths in our childhood days, I was similarly captivated by Kyle.

I recalled hearing whispers in high school about a looming confrontation between Kyle and Mike Chesebro, a formidable figure on the Liverpool varsity wrestling team. Both were recognized for their intimidating presence, and few would dare cross them. What I found amusing was that, despite Kyle's daunting reputation and appearance, he was quite different from the persona others had painted of him.

From the outset, during our initial meeting at the club, I was taken aback to find that Kyle had a high-pitched voice—completely opposite of what I had anticipated. Throughout the evening, as we delved into the ambiance of the club, I often noticed Kyle distancing himself, operating independently from the larger group. Drawn to his distinct personality, I approached him. Our conversations about various nuances of our environment were always enlightening. His insights invariably differed from the norm. Thus began my friendship with Kyle. He rapidly became my closest friend, and together we embarked on numerous memorable escapades.

On one notable occasion while mingling with students in the lounge of Syracuse University, a student who was about to attend a psychology class challenged me to sneak into the class and engage in a conversation with the professor during the session without revealing that I wasn't registered in his course. While I can't remember the exact topic of the lecture, I took on the dare and managed to have a lengthy discussion with the professor during the class with relative ease.

On our days off from work, we embarked on quests in search of unforgettable fun. Within the college premises, we embraced our mischievous side, immersing ourselves in a world of boundless creativity. Equipped with a trusty VHS camera slung over my shoulder, we assumed the roles of students and reporters, conducting interviews that kept everyone guessing.

As we strolled the hallways, our laughter harmonized with the vibrant energy of the students, moments that were preserved forever on video tape. The lounges transformed into our captivating stage, a backdrop for capturing the students' wild antics, while the recreation room became an arena for epic ping-pong battles—a spectacle immortalized on precious VHS tapes with each swift swing of the paddles.

Our adventures weren't limited to just the college grounds. Saturday afternoons saw us embracing our adventurous spirits as we navigated the streets in Kyle's sleek 280Z. Equipped with my trusty camcorder and buoyed by the stirring beats of Queen's "We Are the Champions," we fearlessly struck up conversations with strangers, crafting memorable tales and immortalizing the heart of those serendipitous interactions.

The enchantment of the winter season beckoned us to whimsical parks, where our playful enthusiasm embraced the snow-covered slopes. We joyfully mingled with those who dared to slide down the icy hills, cherishing the comical moments recorded on our ever-rolling camera. When hunger called, we satisfied our appetites with slices of pizza from a nearby parlor, immortalizing the infectious spirit of the staff through our lens.

For me these vibrant adventures served as a much-needed escape from the weight of personal loss, infusing my life with unadulterated joy and light-hearted bliss. They offered a delightful contrast to the seriousness and responsibilities that come with self-employment.

Meanwhile, Susan embarked on her own realization during this transformative period. She recognized two distinct aspects: first, my progress on the path to recovery, surpassing the challenges of the hospital phase and reintegrating into society. Second, she acknowledged that our relationship was no longer evolving in a healthy manner. She suggested that it would be beneficial for me to embark on a journey of independence and find my own place. Despite my initial reluctance, she held firm in her conviction, anticipating my acquiescence. Eventually, I mustered the courage to take the plunge and decided to move into the Covered Bridge apartments nestled in the village of Liverpool. Within those walls I embarked on a new chapter of my life, bidding farewell to Susan and embracing a future devoid of her presence.

On a typical Friday evening, Kyle and I found ourselves driving back from a club, accompanied by two intriguing girls we had just met. Our plan for the night was to continue the festivities at my place, immersing ourselves in music and indulging in more drinks. Among the array of flavors I relished at that time were Alabama Slammers, a delightful concoction of amaretto, whiskey, gin, and orange juice. As fate would have it, I had already savored six of these delectable libations.

Behind the wheel of the sleek 280Z, a surge of comfort and overconfidence coursed through me, tempting me to surrender to the exhilarating urge of spinning the tires. I was driven by the anticipation of impressing the girls with a thrilling display of excitement. Little did I anticipate the unexpected twist events were about to take.

As I glanced at the rear-view mirror, a surge of anxiety welled up within me as I caught sight of the flashing lights of a police car and heard the piercing wail of sirens. I pulled over, bringing the evening's excitement to an abrupt halt.

Within moments an officer approached my window, his gaze piercing the tension. He requested my license and registration, and I retrieved the necessary documents from the glove compartment and my wallet. However, the atmosphere grew increasingly tense when the officer's words cut through the air. "My God, it reeks of alcohol in here. Who's been drinking?"

Without missing a beat, one of the girls seated in the backseat interjected. "I have no idea where that smell is coming from, but it's definitely not me." Though intended to deflect any blame, her words sent a pang of discomfort through me, knowing full well that the unmistakable scent of alcohol emanated from my being. However, I remained resolute in my determination not to let her remark incriminate me or amplify the officer's suspicion. Meeting the officer's gaze with unwavering confidence, I replied calmly, devoid of defensiveness, steering the conversation away from the topic of alcohol. To my astonishment, he swiftly veered the dialogue onto a different course, never mentioning the issue again. I don't recall whether a ticket was issued, but eventually, he let us go, and the revelry resumed at my apartment.

On several subsequent occasions, I found myself being pulled over by law enforcement after consuming immoderate amounts of alcohol. Despite the seriousness of my actions, I escaped the rightful consequences, leaving me perplexed and bewildered. My repeated avoidance of the deserved punishment left me questioning the elusive reasons behind my apparent evasions.

During this transitional period, as I distanced myself from Susan, a newfound common interest between Kyle and me was blossoming: our shared fascination with women. It was during one eventful evening at RJ O'Tooles in Nottingham Plaza, located in North Syracuse, that Kyle crossed paths with his steady girlfriend, Donna. Coincidentally, I discovered that Donna was the younger sister of Debbie, the girl who used to visit me at my high school bus stop. As Kyle's romantic connection grew, I couldn't help but feel like a third wheel during our evening adventures. Little did I realize that the dynamics were about to undergo a transformation.

A unique moment was on the horizon, waiting to unravel within Switzes, a department store where I sought supplies for my office. As I stood in line, my attention was drawn to the enchanting gaze of the girl operating the register in a neighboring line.

Approaching women was not something that came naturally to me. While I could engage in conversation when introduced or during a transaction, taking the initiative to start a conversation was something I didn't do. This was an entirely new experience, one that compelled me to go out of my way to find the right words.

I switched to the adjacent line, waiting for my turn at the register. When the moment arrived, I gathered my courage and complimented Tara on her beauty, expressing my interest in getting to know her better. She graciously acknowledged the compliment but revealed that she was already in a committed relationship. Undeterred, I inquired if she was engaged, to which she responded in the negative. Seizing the opportunity, I handed her my number. "Just in case fate has other plans," I said. With that, I left the store.

To my surprise, a few days later, Tara called me, and our

journey of dating and creating memories together began to unfold. We ventured into intimate moments in captivating places, such as Bonnie Castle Resort, where a memorable incident involving a comedian's flirtation with Tara stirred a slight discomfort within me, a recurring theme in similar situations with others. As time progressed, Tara decided to move in with me. The four of us—Kyle, Donna, Tara, and I—delved into adventures, exploring the town and any experiences that came our way.

My relationship with Tara spanned several months. However, over time our bond weakened, and our interests began to drift apart. Despite my earnest appeals, Tara chose to end our relationship. This breakup had a deep effect on me, as I was keen to preserve what we had once shared. However, Tara's decision was firm.

That period, during which I was transitioning to a weekday role at the food company where I handled sales of flash-frozen foods, yielded an unforeseen discovery. Apart from the position not aligning with my personal and professional interests, another issue came to light. Within the company were whispers about the potentially misleading nature of our sales tactics. We realized that the calculations we employed, purportedly illustrating annual financial savings based on customers' purchasing habits, were inaccurate. Driven to address this, I discussed the matter with management. Even though they promised to take corrective action, their follow-through was disappointing. This situation, evoking memories of my stint at the cleaning company, strengthened my resolve to leave the company. Luckily, a fresh opportunity presented itself soon after.

One Saturday evening I accompanied Kyle to a wedding reception for one of his friends. Amidst the festivities, Kyle introduced me to someone who was not only a mutual friend of the groom but also a fellow painter affiliated with the same union as Kyle. As our conversation flowed, it veered toward employment prospects. During our chat, he mentioned an enticing vacancy for a full-time painting role at the Turkey Point Nuclear Plant in South Florida.

His curiosity ignited, Kyle sought more details, his face lighting up at the prospect of moving to Miami. He turned to me, asking if I was up for a new adventure. I was hesitant at first, as if to convey the gravity of the decision. Moving to a new city required thoughtful consideration, and I expressed the need for time to think it through. Then mere seconds later, I proclaimed, "Alright, I've made up my mind. Let's do it!"

From that moment on, we immersed ourselves in detailed planning and preparations to turn our decision into reality. Shortly after Thanksgiving Day in 1989, we set out on our journey, braving the steady snowfall. My apartment furnishings were safely stowed in a U-Haul truck, with Kyle's high-performance motorcycle also inside. He followed in his green Honda hatchback, the 280z towed on a trailer. We were Miami bound. Kyle had saved enough to support us in the beginning. The plan was for me to find a job upon our arrival to contribute to our living expenses, and in time, to set up my own business in that winterless locale.

Upon reaching South Florida, we settled at my cousin Timmy's place in Fort Lauderdale. Our days were consumed with the relentless search for a suitable apartment, which ultimately led us to Naranja Lakes. The scenic spot just north of Homestead was close to the Turkey Point Nuclear Plant. However, destiny had other plans. Kyle's hopes of working at the plant did not materialize, compelling me to quickly reevaluate my path and find immediate employment, as time and money were in short supply.

Driven by urgency, I seized on an unforeseen job offer that led me to a pivotal three-week training program at the Friden Alcatel headquarters in San Francisco, focusing on the sale of postal equipment. It was a significant deviation from my original path, but one I had to embrace to overcome the financial strain we were facing. Throughout that crucial time, I consistently sent my per diem to Kyle, ensuring he had sufficient funds to manage our shared expenses.

As the sounds of uncertainty filled the air, they served as reminders of the uncharted road that lay ahead, challenging us to navigate through unexplored territories and embrace the unknown with resilience and determination.

Chapter Twenty-Eight

STARTING ANEW IN NARANJA LAKES

T HE INITIAL DAYS PROVED DEMANDING. MY MORNINGS STARTED with sales meetings in Miami Lakes, some forty miles away. My trusty steed for those journeys? The "winter rat," a moss-green artifact from Syracuse, a vestige of Kyle's past. Weather and time had gnarled its once sleek exterior with patches of rust, and its cacophonous muffler played a rambunctious tune, announcing its arrival from a distance. As if that wasn't challenging enough, the air conditioner had given up the ghost, so I had to brave the journey with the windows rolled down, feeling every degree of the Miami heat. Standstills on the 826 Palmetto were the worst, with the sun's rays turning the car into an oven. At work I would park at the far end of the lot, hoping my colleagues would overlook the car's battle scars. This ritual stretched on for weeks as I managed my earnings, ensuring rent was covered and our basic necessities were addressed.

After several months, a long-awaited breakthrough arrived. Kyle's job opportunity at the nuclear plant made a surprising comeback, and he began his tenure there, ushering in a wave of financial relief. With our primary concerns eased, we could finally indulge in the South Florida lifestyle as we'd envisioned. Our sense of adventure reignited, leading us to the sandy shores of Fort Lauderdale and South Miami as we dove headfirst into the pulsating nightlife.

During one of our memorable outings, an enchanting day unfolded. The clouds danced across the sky, and a recent drizzle had left the world glistening. With the usually bustling sands of South Florida welcoming fewer footprints, during our leisurely stroll southward from the iconic News Café on 8th Street, destiny presented us with Claudia. In stark contrast to the demure beaches of Green Lakes and Sylvan Beach in Syracuse, South Florida's shores were a celebration of boldness and vibrancy, epitomized by the popular thong bikinis that dotted the landscape. And there, against this colorful and dynamic backdrop, stood Claudia. She shimmered like a jewel, her presence radiating an undeniable confidence and allure that captivated anyone who glanced her way.

Kyle and I were eager to meet her. However, while I hesitated, bound by my own reservations, Kyle, ever the embodiment of unbridled confidence, approached her, his steps displacing the sand beneath him. I stood still, entranced by the scene unfolding before me, Kyle leaning in, his hands painting the air with each animated gesture. Their laughter intermingled with the sea breeze, and after what seemed like moments frozen in time, he straightened up and waved me over with an enthusiastic grin. With a growing sense of curiosity, I approached, and Kyle introduced me. "This is my friend, Dan." Claudia greeted me with a smile and an accent that whispered of distant shores.

As we chatted, weaving tales from our past and sharing snippets of our day's adventures, a palpable spark hung in the air. Never one to let an opportunity slip away, Kyle smiled at Claudia with a hint of mischief. "We're planning to come back to South Beach tonight to check out some of the clubs. Would you like to join us?"

Claudia's eyes gleamed in response. "Sure, I have a girl-friend I can introduce you to, and the four of us can go togeth-er." As her words lingered, my mind raced.

Is she implying a duo for the night? Is she choosing . . . me?

We decided to rendezvous at the News Café at dusk. On the long drive back to Naranja Lakes, we seized the moment to draft our evening's blueprint. As the shadows began to elongate, we donned our finest threads. Kyle, with his keen eye for detail, pointed out the subtleties of style, suggesting I tuck in a corner of my shirt to exude a nonchalant elegance. The hot pink 280Z roared to life, its vigor mirroring our antic-ipation of the night ahead.

Maneuvering through the colorful maze of South Beach, we finally found an elusive parking spot. Kyle, wearing a playful smirk, reached for his Drakkar Noir cologne, then passed it to me. "Easy does it," he warned. Scented and set, we headed toward the lively 8th Street and News Café.

There, amidst the canopy of twinkling lights, Claudia and an enchanting companion lounged at an alfresco table. "Hel-lo, guys," Claudia said with a sparkle in her eye. "Kyle, this is Luci." Internally, my heart raced, and the question resurfaced: was Claudia hinting at a paired evening with me?

Luci's accent, reminiscent of Claudia's, intrigued us, lead-ing to revelations about her Chilean heritage. Our curiosity also drew tales from Claudia about Buenos Aires, including the unique tidbit that her father's company specialized in crafting faucets and fixtures. As our conversation evolved, it became clear that while Claudia and Luci had been living together during Claudia's three-month visit, their bond was deep-seated, forged over many years of shared experiences and laughter.

In exchange, Kyle and I recounted our recent transition from Syracuse and discussed the stark contrast between life in Miami and our hometown. As our dialogue unfurled, the pulsating beats from nearby Ocean Drive restaurants and clubs reached a crescendo, setting the rhythm for the evening.

After our spirited discussion, we agreed it was time to depart the café and plunge into the night's escapades. The anticipation was palpable as we deliberated the most enticing spots to visit.

From the outset, Kyle's attention seemed fixed on Claudia, largely overlooking Luci. This wasn't unexpected to me. Recognizing the dynamic, I gravitated toward Luci, immersing myself in conversation with her. My primary goal was to ensure that the evening was enjoyable for all of us, and I felt fortunate to be in the presence of two captivating and intriguing women.

As the evening progressed, we hopped from one club to another, immersing ourselves in the heart of Miami's effervescent nightlife. The atmosphere was electric, and we reveled in the city's diverse array of entertainment. The night, spent in the company of two enthralling women, was unforgettable.

As dawn hinted on the horizon, it signaled that our sojourn amidst the vibrant energy of South Beach was coming to an end. It was time to embark on our journey back to Naranja Lakes, marking the conclusion of our eventful and satisfying evening.

The morning following our nocturnal adventures, we chose a laid-back activity, heading to the community recreation area for a swim. Once we'd had our fill and hunger began to gnaw, we went back to the apartment to fix a meal. I was in the midst of crafting a sandwich, spreading a hearty amount of mayonnaise on whole-wheat bread, when the phone's insistent ring cut through the silence. Without missing a beat, Kyle answered.

Over the hum of the apartment, I heard him greet Claudia. Piecing things together, I assumed he had shared our number with her the night before. My sandwich assembly paused when he extended the phone to me, causing a mixture of curiosity and astonishment to bubble within.

"She'd like to chat with you," he said.

With me? I thought, my mind buzzing with a mixture of excitement and anxiety.

Our ensuing conversation was seamless, and before long, she expressed her interest in another rendezvous. "How about next Saturday?" I suggested. She agreed, sharing Luci's address and instructing me to be there by 7:00 p.m.

After hanging up, I turned to Kyle, a torrent of uncertainty swirling inside. "How am I going to do this?" I asked, hoping for some advice.

"Just take the hatchback and head over," he replied as if presenting a simple solution.

When Saturday came, I followed his advice. As I pulled up in the rusty green hatchback, its broken muffler roaring, I glanced at my watch: 6:55 p.m. I was a little early. As I waited in front of the sprawling apartment complex, the minutes seemed to take longer than usual. 7:05 . . . 7:10 . . . There was no sight of her. Confronted with multiple doors and no hint as to which one was hers, I began to question my decision to wait. Had she changed her mind or perhaps found a more enticing offer for the evening? As I pondered this, I felt a surge of relief. I was spared the potential embarrassment of seeing whether she'd be willing to ride in the aged Honda. Comforted by those thoughts, I set off on the forty-mile journey back to my home in Naranja Lakes.

Upon entering my apartment, Kyle was waiting there for me with surprising news. "Claudia called," he said, his voice carrying a hint of intrigue. "She wants to know why you stood her up."

I was taken aback by his words, my mind racing. "Stand her up? I was right there, in her driveway, waiting," I shot back, my voice tinged with incredulity.

Kyle extended a hand, revealing a crumpled note with Claudia's number scribbled on it. "Well, regardless, she wants you to call her."

With a deep breath, I dialed, each ring amplifying my apprehension. When Claudia's voice broke through, it carried a mixture of confusion and annoyance. "I was there, exactly as we planned," I insisted, trying to keep my voice steady.

"When?" she asked, her voice tinged with surprise and a hint of irritation.

"At seven o'clock sharp. I hung around until ten after seven, then I left," I replied, a familiar twist of unease in my gut. She paused, and I could almost hear her replaying the events in her mind. Then she let out a sigh.

"I got caught up. I was racing back from the beach on my rollerblades."

"I assumed you stumbled upon something better," I admitted, the vulnerability evident in my tone. A weighty silence stretched between us, finally broken by her response.

"And yet here we are, talking again."

As we continued, our conversation veered in an unforeseen direction. Claudia expressed a desire to meet again. We settled on a rendezvous: the same location, the same parking spot, the same time. On the agreed-upon day, I was there, right on time.

Given her striking allure and the town's swanky reputation, I braced myself once again for momentary hesitation or perhaps a fleeting smirk upon seeing the car's battle scars. Yet in a display of unexpected grace, Claudia stepped into the vehicle without a hint of disdain, as if its vintage charm was simply another feature in the evening's intricate mosaic.

Our initial destination was News Café, where we had met up with Kyle and Luci previously. We nestled into a secluded outdoor table, setting the stage for our maiden tête-à-tête, an intimate exchange shielded from interruptions. Our intentions were simple: a twenty-minute chat to chart out the evening's club-hopping adventure. However, as the evening shadows lengthened, we were drawn deep into a captivating conversation that lasted a full ten hours, extending until the first light of dawn. As the city started to come alive, I escorted her back to her place, then began the tranquil forty-mile journey to Naranja Lakes.

Over the ensuing months, Claudia seamlessly integrated herself into my life. As her planned departure for Buenos Aires approached, we gravitated once again to News Café, ostensibly for our farewell. Yet when the weight of the impending goodbye pressed down, our steps didn't lead us to the airport but to a nearby phone booth. Flight reservations were canceled, and plans shifted. Claudia was staying.

With Kyle rounding out our trio, we ventured into scenic spots like Key Largo, South Beach, and Fort Lauderdale. In the interludes between these escapades, we cherished tranquil moments in our apartment, basked in the comfort of the community pool, and soaked in the vibrant atmosphere of the recreation center. Our backgrounds and interests might have been poles apart, but it was this very contrast that brought us closer.

Even so, a subtle schism, destined to deepen in the ensuing years, began to emerge: our differing financial landscapes. As I navigated the demands of my career, soon to be compounded by the intricacies of initiating a small business, Claudia, buoyed by her father's affluence, luxuriated in time and resources. Peering into what the future might hold, I discerned the challenges our unique situations would bring: Claudia's penchant for long, indulgent trips could inevitably distance us. I came to the sobering realization that not only might I be unable to join her in the lavish locales she frequented, but the relentless pace of my professional path could further diminish our shared moments.

As my bond with Claudia deepened, it evolved past the bounds of mere friendship, adding layers of complexity to the dynamic within our trio. A notable complication arose from our interactions with others, particularly Donna, Kyle's on again/off again girlfriend from Syracuse. A year earlier while I was living at the Covered Bridge Apartments in Liverpool, on a late-afternoon during a warm summer's day, Donna appeared at my door. Her surprise visit came shortly after my return from the Retreat Restaurant in the village, where I had enjoyed three potent blue Hawaiian drinks.

She entered my apartment, catching me off guard, as I hadn't made any plans to meet with her. I found her presence strange right away, especially since Kyle wasn't with her. Within seconds of her arrival, I found myself engaged in a passionate kiss with her, followed by our sudden drop to the floor. In the midst of that moment, before things could progress further, I came to my senses and realized her connection with Kyle. As I pushed her away from me, a wave of guilt struck me, and I insisted that she leave.

Overwhelmed by guilt, I contacted Kyle the next day and confessed what had happened. After expressing the gravity of the situation, he insisted on a meeting where all three of us could discuss and uncover the truth. However, before that, Kyle insisted that Donna and I share our accounts independently with him, detailing what had happened.

When the three of us convened, he questioned Donna in front of me. Her account didn't match my story. She admitted to being at my place but downplayed and even denied the rest. It seemed she hoped I'd confirm her version, maybe thinking that, in Kyle's absence, the facts could be easily obscured. However, I stood firm, refusing to adopt the idea of presenting a story that absolved either of us of blame. I maintained that the events had indeed taken place as I had initially confessed.

The discrepancies left Kyle uncertain about whom or what to believe, and the incident continued to resurface even a year later after moving to Miami, straining our relationship and creating lingering doubts in our relationships with other women.

The inevitable finally occurred: Claudia returned to her home in Buenos Aires. Concurrently, my bond with Kyle began to change. While it's tempting to blame the fractures in my friendship with Kyle on her departure or other dramatic events, the reality was perhaps more mundane: the inexorable march of time and changing priorities.

I found myself increasingly ensnared by professional responsibilities and dreams of resurrecting my own business. These aspirations started to intrude upon the cohesive blend of activities that Kyle and I shared.

In my absence, Kyle wove new stories, and he seemed to thrive in his solo adventures. One evening as the sun's last rays painted the sky, he regaled me with tales of a captivating British belle he'd encountered at Duffy's—a sports bar at the crossroads of US1 and the Palmetto. His enthusiasm was infectious, and he insisted that I would be charmed by her wit and presence. Curiosity got the better of me, and I agreed to a rendezvous.

As we cozied up to the bar, Kyle introduced me to Janet with a glint of excitement in his eyes. Janet, in turn, waved over her entourage, a lively group with stories from all corners of the globe, enveloping us in a whirlwind of introductions. The bar's ambiance, illuminated by dim, sultry lights and punctuated by the soft hum of chatter, seemed to draw us all closer.

When Kyle stepped away for a refill, Janet leaned in close enough for her words to dance in my ear. "Wanna dance?" she whispered with a playful smirk, her voice dripping with intrigue. Caught off guard, I hesitated, thinking of Kyle's evident interest in her.

"Nah, but I'm sure Kyle would like to when he gets back," I said, trying to keep the atmosphere light.

"But I don't want to dance with Kyle," she replied with a teasing smile and a mischievous glint in her eyes. "I want to dance with you."

Despite her captivating invitation, I held my ground. But as the days went on and our paths crossed again, a magnetic pull developed between us. Janet became more forthright with her intentions, and I couldn't hold out forever.

An intriguing trend was emerging. Whenever Kyle would introduce me to women he fancied, they invariably seemed more drawn to me. Baffled, he'd frequently tout his athletic physique to my face, as though their preference for me was inconceivable and defied logic.

As months went by and we mingled with other women—be it at the community pool, at home sipping on my specially crafted rum-heavy strawberry daiquiris, or during various social outings—it became clear that the disproportionate attention I was receiving was turning into a problem.

This situation exacerbated an already existing issue. Despite my commitment to work and my reluctance to participate in outings, such as trips to the tiki bar in Key Largo, Kyle seized these opportunities. With the free time I lacked, he even accompanied Claudia on various excursions without me. I was indifferent to this as long as harmony prevailed among us. However, Kyle's unsuccessful attempts at forging romantic connections heightened his frustrations, which grew burdensome.

One morning over breakfast, Kyle caught me off guard by abruptly raising a topic: he felt that Claudia should no longer be at our apartment. While I hadn't noticed any conflicts between them, I suspected his distress stemmed from Claudia not reciprocating the attention he desired. Out of respect for our shared living space, I decided to honor his request without probing into the details. I approached Claudia and tried to explain the situation as delicately as possible. However, she was puzzled. From her perspective, she and Kyle had been getting along, especially given the time they spent together while I was at work. Despite her confusion, I informed her that she could no longer stay at our place.

Although Kyle was intrigued by women in Miami, throughout our stay in Naranja Lakes, he never ended his long-distance relationship with Donna in Liverpool. He arranged a weeklong visit for her, flying her down to stay with us. Unfortunately, their reunion was far from idyllic. They bickered incessantly, and during one particularly heated dispute, Kyle physically restrained Donna, pinning her down on his bed until her screams subsided. Witnessing their volatile relationship was deeply unsettling.

Throughout this period, every evening felt like stepping into the latest episode of a drama series. Frequently, I'd come home from work to be greeted by the chaotic aftermath of their disputes. One day a large hole in the living room wall caught my eye, an unsettling testament to the intensity of their arguments.

"If you were here, it would have been your face," Kyle remarked with a dark hint of humor. The apartment's ambiance had shifted from a peaceful refuge to a suspense-filled battleground, making each return home an exercise in bracing myself for the unknown.

Despite the tumult in our personal lives, my professional trajectory soared. As we neared the two-year anniversary of our move to South Florida, I took the bold step of leaving my job at Friden Alcatel, where I sold postage equipment. My sights were set on pioneering my own venture in the tile-restoration industry.

Leveraging the strong professional relationships I had cultivated, I secured contracts with three local janitorial services. This allowed me to provide tile restoration in residential settings. By forging partnerships with tile stores near Palmetto 826, I ensured a steady influx of leads and potential projects. The success of this enterprise not only dwarfed my previous earnings but also offered the exhilarating freedom of steering my own ship once more.

As my enterprise flourished, Kyle chose to leave his job to join me in this promising venture. At first his zest for our shared project seemed to alleviate some of the strain in our relationship. However, despite his initial zeal and the business's success, the disparity between our levels of commitment became evident. Whether from a lack of interest, oversight, capability, or perhaps a reluctance to collaborate with me, Kyle devoted more and more time to partying than to our shared venture. Meanwhile, I remained steadfast, pouring my energy and dedication into expanding the business.

One day everything shifted when Kyle came to me with a startling revelation: "Dan, if you believe you can run this business without me, you're sorely mistaken." His words caught me off guard, leaving me speechless. The idea of progressing without him had never been a consideration. My goal had always been to work hard and grow the business, hoping for Kyle's consistent involvement. However, when he did participate, his behavior was frequently erratic and even bizarre.

For example, one day Kyle had an appointment with one of our repeat customers to discuss a new floor-sealing service. While he'd shadowed me on countless sales pitches, absorbing my tried-and-true methods of winning clients over, Kyle, always the maverick, decided to forge his own path. In what he believed to be a stroke of genius, he carried along a quirky gray clay skull pierced with a nail. He hoped this eccentric piece of art would serve as an icebreaker, showcasing his unique personality.

But the universe had a different script in mind. The moment he left, my phone buzzed with a frantic call from the client. She described him as "wild eyed and unpredictable," questioning his choice of a "bizarre talisman." As such stories continued to unfurl, it dawned on me that Kyle's unconventional ways of connecting, especially with women, often spiraled into episodes worthy of a sitcom.

Amidst the persistent challenges and simmering tensions that defined our relationship, coupled with Kyle's unrelenting threats to our partnership, a moment of reckoning emerged. I confronted Kyle, the air thick with gravitas, as I explained that he was free to chart his own course whenever he pleased, independent of my presence. However, a condition was clear: our collaboration demanded his unwavering commitment to prioritize the work at hand. Despite my plea, Kyle's mounting frustrations and the chasm growing between us cast an ominous shadow.

A new camaraderie took root in his life, one that fueled a whirlwind of extravagant revelries and decadent celebrations, leaving scant room for the responsibilities we once shared. The nights stretched late, drenched in vibrant chaos, and our exchanges were consumed by an eerie silence. The relentless cycle of twilight debauchery, moments of solitude, and our dwindling connection endured unabated, casting a long shadow over the ensuing months.

Suddenly, Kyle presented a bombshell: he had struck a deal with the landlord, giving us just a week to empty the apartment. Then he revealed a meticulously hatched plan to move in with his buddy, Rick, conveniently situated in nearby Cutler Ridge. As for me, I was left navigating the swirling tempest of uncertainty, pondering where to drop anchor next.

The weight of financial woes pressed down on my shoulders, a staggering debt of $10,000, a testament to our ventures that had spiraled downward. As the clouds of monetary pressures threatened to pour, the chasm between Kyle and me widened, magnifying the storm within.

Amidst the chaos, a beacon of hope emerged. I had crossed paths with one of our esteemed clients, Gaston, the visionary art director for the elite magazine, *Selecta*. Spotting a unique allure in me, Gaston invited me to be the face of a captivating photo spread. In the photo I was portrayed as a contemplative lifeguard, eyes lost in the vastness of the sea. Below the arresting image, an eloquent Spanish caption alluded to my choice of sunscreen.

It's noteworthy to mention the undercurrents during the photo session. In his mind, Kyle believed his sculpted frame was more fitting for such prominence, a sentiment that added another layer to the growing tension before his startling revelation.

Leveraging the budding connection I had cultivated with Gaston, we set a date for a luncheon. Amidst the soft chimes of toasting wine glasses and the seductive scents of exquisite cuisine, I confided in him about the pivotal juncture I was facing. With his trademark chivalry, Gaston offered me sanctuary—a room within the cozy confines of his residence. Our agreement was sealed on Monday, August 10, 1992. By the time dusk had painted the horizon the following Thursday evening, I had embraced the serene ambiance of Gaston's sanctuary.

As fate would have it, merely three dawns after that, the tranquil Sunday morning of August 16 was betrayed by an ominous cloak of storm clouds. Hurricane Andrew, with unparalleled rage, swept through South Florida, erasing my previous home from the map, leaving in its wake a melancholic mosaic of debris and nostalgia. I shudder to think of the peril that might've ensnared me had I been trapped within those walls during the storm. Destiny's capricious currents have a way of navigating us, even when we row fiercely against the tide. Once the bedlam subsides and reflection takes hold, one can't help but marvel at life's unpredictable odyssey. Amidst all the bends and twists, the intricate choreography of decisions and fate becomes apparent. The monumental shift that day, instigated by nature's fury, had me endlessly musing on the alternate tales that could've been penned in the annals of my existence.

Chapter Twenty-Nine

THE POEMS OF NARANJA LAKES

AFTER ARRIVING IN THE SUNNY EMBRACE OF FLORIDA IN THE AU-tumn of 1981, I aspired to reinvent my life, seeing it as a blank canvas for new beginnings. However, lingering remnants from my New York saga seemed to whisper incessantly, yearning for a conclusive epilogue. The silhouettes of my grandparents and aunt, who were still painting their lives in New York hues, became daily sketches of memories and unresolved heartaches. And then, like a discordant note in a symphony, came the disheartening news of my grandmother's frail health and looming surgery. Though my heart ached to fly to Syracuse and stand sentinel by her bedside, my wallet's lament held me back. What twisted the knife further was the revelation that my parents, just a stone's throw away, let old grudges cloud their judgment, overlooking a chance for kindness.

I yearned to bridge the rift with my father, hoping he'd muster the compassion to visit Grandma in tandem with my mother. But their elusive, unlisted number thwarted my attempts. In a stroke of inspiration, I dialed my sister Pam, certain she'd be my beacon in Syracuse. But the cold embrace of her answering machine was all that greeted me.

With a deep breath, I began. "Pam, it's your brother Danny in Florida." I painted a vivid picture of our grandmother's plight, voicing the anguish that distance imposed upon me and juxtaposing it with the baffling inertia of our kin just around the corner. Overwhelmed, I couldn't resist adding, "Let our father know that, while I may be absent, he should expect a unique Christmas present as my replacement."

Time seemed to stagnate as days morphed into weeks without a whisper from home. But the universe had a twist in store. Three weeks later, my past returned in the form of an FBI agent on my threshold, a surprise courtesy of my father. Rather than mending familial fences, he'd construed my heartfelt message as a cryptic threat, prompting a federal investigation.

After introducing the agent to my turbulent situation, I explained the context of my call. My narrative of being an ocean away from a beleaguered grandmother, compounded by the indifference of kin closer at hand, seemed to resonate with him. His nod of comprehension was the silver lining as he exited my world, never to reenter it.

That startling encounter, layered over my familial heartache in Syracuse, fanned the embers of my quest for closure. Even with miles as barriers and financial shackles, I began to see my isolation as an unexpected muse, nudging me toward new avenues of catharsis. I turned to the art of words, letting poetry weave my pain, hopes, and dreams into verses, immortalizing my journey and providing relief.

"Listen"

Listen to the words both warm and cold, they are far yet close to be heard and understood.
A generation of pain is the price to be paid when the true thoughts of the young are not known.

"A Mind of My Own"

My family's gone, live away from my home, my mom says it's because I've a mind of my own.
Hope she wasn't sincere, just didn't know what to say, cus I've lost my mind now been in this ward since Sunday.
I drool when I walk, roll my eyes when I talk, make me bleed, I'll just nod because I think that I'm God.
Dad says it's my fault my life came to this day, there are seven where I'm from
only I went my way.
Tried to end my own life when something strange came to be, three men dressed in white they came to visit me.
No one knew who they were, no one got in there way, and where they were from
no one ever did say.
I could feel that they cared, they spoke as if they were one, said "Stop blaming yourself for things you haven't done"
That was the first night I was able to sleep, it had been seven days, their words I will keep.
My own blood does not know why they should want to see me, but it's their choice to make now without them I'll be.
They may not be mine but I have what I need, I should praise my dear God from their ways I am freed.
That was five years ago, what I've learned since I've grown, all I want for my life
is a mind of my own.

"Growing Apart"

Summer's so near, let's skip school this last week, pedaling our bikes to unknown places we seek.
We've planned really well, covered all of our tracks, we scammed a school teacher, one who's really lax.
Things went very smooth, we had nothing but fun, till one day

when my dad had found out what I'd done.
He set me up good, asked how school was that day, looking straight in his eyes, many lies I did say.
"Got a phone call this morning, with your school I did speak. They want to know where you've been, haven't seen you all week."
So I ended my lies and confessed what I'd done, wondered what I should do, should I face him or run?
Because I skipped school, he was pretty mad, but my lying was why he would beat me real bad.
He reached under a chair as I ran for the door, He was hiding a switch, I had a whipping in store.
My run he expected, not a chance for escape, and at that locked doors where my beating took place.
With the red on his face and both eyes closed, he swung in my direction till blood blisters rose.
When the beating was over and the day turned to night, I went up to my room and I turned off the light.
And when morning came, it was long sleeves and high collar, didn't want my school to know I got a beating from my father.
But it wasn't enough, too much for me to hide, So I made up a story 'bout a fall from a bike ride.
People looked at me funny, they knew something was wrong, I needed more time for my act, hadn't rehearsed it too long.
And just when I thought the day's end would make me glad, I remembered an appointment with my principal and Dad.
There was lots of discussion about what to do with me, when a gap in my shirt showed a bruise to see.
With a look of concern, my principal leaned forward toward me and asked what in God's name had happened to me.
There was a moment of silence as I thought up a story, 'bout how I fell off my bike and made my skin look so gory.
But before I could talk and go into my act, my father spoke up to introduce what was fact.
And when his right hand reached my principal's knee, he squeezed just a bit till eye to eye they did see.
Then slowly Dad spoke words for us to hear, "Dan fell off his bike, do I make myself clear?"
After those words it was silent, nothing further was said, and there never was any discussion 'bout what really kept me from bed.
Many things we do learn, being taught by our father, living by his own rules, mine did not want to bother.
More problems to drive our lives further apart, why won't Dad let

me say what I feel in my heart?

Is it the guilt that he feels 'bout the wrong he's done me? I want to be close; we should talk and be free.

He says I'm his child, I should be seen and not heard, but this distance between us proves his ways are absurd.

This chapter in our life ends while another one starts. It's the same kind of story; we're growing further apart.

"Advice"

I'm headed for trouble, need help on the double, what decision do you think I should make?

I've been there before, there's no need to feel sore, but my advice that I give you must take.

So I listened real close to each and every dose, but the prescription seemed too big to swallow.

Then I thanked my dear dad, for his advice I was glad, but his ways weren't the kind I could follow.

When I took one quick look at the way that he shook, I knew I had more problems to face.

So his help had to cease, because I wanted peace, my new truce, his advice can't replace.

"The Pastor"

Eeny, meeny, miny, moe, which religion's not a show?

Pastor beat his son; it was violent and bloody, trusting people keep sending their money.

Actor, preacher, how do we gauge, is that a pulpit or a stage?

The man's of God, and I'm back with my wife, no he's not my son lost his life!

With the tin man's heart, Oz had nothing to do, whether you're happy or not, it's up to you.

"Why Do What You Do?"

What makes someone do what is thought to be right, when they know it will make them cry every night?

Many people do things for their pleasure and gain, me I do things that will bring me more pain.

Am I strong as a bull standing up for what's right, have I caused my own troubles let the truth out of sight.

All I know that I'm sure is the guilt I would feel, if I did not try to do what my heart said was real.

"Prodigal Son?"

Searching for my identity, not knowing who I should be.
Silenced by the maker's lips, not old enough to sail my ship.
That time has passed; my youth is gone; I'm smarter now but something's wrong.
The maker says that it's okay, but no one smiles like yesterday.
The castle's built king at its throne, don't want to be a prince told to leave when I'm grown.
The pain begins, my feelings strong, I only know where I don't belong.
Hello mother, hello brother, would you see me if you could?
God is great, God is good, but we don't think that we should!
That's okay, that's all right, because now I know what's wrong and right.
And if you think I'm the prodigal son, tell me your troubles and see if I run.

"Control"

There are only so many things we can control in our life, for our hearts there's no choice when warm times turn to ice.
But it's only for a season for after the winter comes the spring, a better love and understanding our fresh look will bring.

"Untitled"

It's not the place that I am, it's how I feel when I'm there, it's not the things that I have; it's how I get them.
It's not the smile that you see, it's the reason I smile, the truths that I've known all the while.

"In the Blink of an Eye"

Unfamiliar face I see. Our first contact, as eye meets eye. A brief deep look, as I prepare for my ritual. While, as I begin, time itself changes. Only for me to see. Hidden from others. A racing of thought impossible to trace at the rate of its occurrence. As I go into my final stage of preparation, slowly my eyelids begin to break the contact between us. And, the ritual begins . . .
Talk to me, you. Who you are. I will listen. Images of what you are will flood my mind. I will judge you. Having an instant impression from the use of my senses and experience. I will attempt to measure your intelligence, your strengths, your weaknesses. I

will be looking, probing for clues to your presence or absence of kindness. If you've a mask I will gently pull it from your face so as not to be noticed, then look. If you are not my kind, you will not see me, but what I portray. What to you may be the silence and calm in a brief encounter will be to me an eternal consequence of our contact. I will race to capture what information I can before it escapes my view. I will consider every clue and conclude with great conviction. And, I will never look back. When I view your breath, I will conclude. From the pitch of your voice, I will conclude. From every word you speak, every variation, every repetition, I will conclude. Always these things without exception. Yet my actions will vary according to my desires of the day. Changing ever so slightly, being governed by morals. Morals as determined by my observations of those perceived to be kind.

Oh, strange prayer, help me face my convictions as I meet this new encounter. For now, and only now, having touched my awareness shall I open my eyes and end my blink.

"Looking to Order (A Song)"

I'm sick of my life, I'm sick of my world, Please, please, please won't you take my order? I'm looking to order.

Traveling in a passenger van, faster than they can And I'm looking to order, over the border.

And you know we're talking, and talking, and talking. Is anyone listening?

You know you see more than fun, when you look at the sun, over the roller coaster.

Please give me my ticket

And I'm looking, I'm looking, I'm looking to order, so give me some order.

And you know we're looking, and looking, and looking for tickets, but for a discount.

So you send me to the door to see, yet hoping I'm blind as can be. Wanna ride the roller coaster, please give me my ticket.

I'm looking, I'm looking, I'm looking to order. Someone show me some order.

What's not meant to be mine, taken will make me blind, can't give up my order. Don't wanna live without order.

I'm looking, I'm looking, I'm looking to order. I want to give you my order. Don't you know you need order?

"Random Stuff"

- Facts unchanged, yet changing words, are the tools, changing worlds of blind fools.
- A father seeking pleasure in his fortune and his fame has a child of true pleasure for his failures to be blamed.
- Even the dimmest light shines brightly in a room of darkness.
- Heaven's no hell, and love is the absence of anger.

Chapter Thirty

UNDELIVERED—THE MOTHER'S DAY LETTER

AFTER THE UNEXPECTED FBI VISIT TO MY NARANJA LAKES HOME, I embarked on a journey to see a friend. Vera, who had been my next-door neighbor from the moment I moved into the Naranja Lakes community, had since returned to her family's home in Panama City. Over many evenings, Vera shared stories of the rifts and tensions that had shaped her family dynamics. However, amidst the challenges, whispered conversations, and emotional roller-coasters, her family experienced a miraculous reconciliation. As I watched them rebuild bridges, I was reminded of the discordant notes playing in the background of my own family ties, making the harmony I craved seem like a distant dream.

As I bade farewell to Vera after my all too short visit, I was profoundly affected by the evident warmth of her reunited family, an impression that stayed with me. With Mother's Day just around the corner, I was inspired to write down my whirlwind of emotions, a mixture of hope and despair. Drawing from my memories with Vera and her family, I crafted a sincere letter, envisioning it as a unique Mother's Day tribute. But there was a hitch—previous letters I'd sent had vanished into thin air, never finding their way to my mother. I hatched a plan, reaching out to David Gentile, a family confidant, hoping to receive his support. But fate had other plans. David, alluding to his deep-rooted ties with my kin, stepped back from my mission. As a result, my mother never got to read the heartfelt words I had so diligently composed. Here it is in its entirety.

May 2001

Dear Mom:

If you receive this letter, you have been given my gift to you for Mother's Day.

Over this past weekend I visited a good friend who had moved from Miami to Panama City. Vera (my friend) grew up in this town about 600 miles north of Miami. When visiting her I met her two sisters and parents for the first time. You see, her family has been wanting to meet me for some time. When Vera was living in Miami, she was having many problems with family, marriage, and more. I spent much time talking with her and her parents to try to help mend their and other relationships. Well to make a long story short, she went through a divorce, and moved back with her parents. Turns out what was thought to become an ugly situation went quite well. There was no problem with the x even. Turns out he realized it was the right thing for him. Anyways, this family has put me up on this altar where I am not too comfortable.

These people sincerely believe that it was me that restored their family. All while I visited them, they did nothing but try to please me, and everything to keep from upsetting me. This was a difficult thing for me to deal with. How can I explain to you how this trip touched me? Many things were happening to me. My friend Vera had done some wrong things to her parents and her parents did some wrong things to her.

Looking back what impressed me was the unwillingness to either to not respond, be it good or bad, to the other. Her sisters stayed in touch with her though they didn't agree with many of her actions. Through many of the months since Vera has moved home, I have observed many of their struggles with new problems. Some of them are with each other, and some of them are together against other forces. Many times when I looked at this family at the dinner table, in the living room during open conversations, and others, I had all I could do to keep tears from my eyes. This family was so happy to be together, and they gave me the thanks for making it happen. To see how they treated each other, even when they disagreed. I'm sure I've made my point. I have a habit of overstating.

Anyway, it became a problem. When I left this family on Monday, I became depressed. My nine-hour drive home became a nightmare. All the good thoughts of what I was a part of became the void of my own life. What I had gladly done for my friend I had failed to do for myself. During this trip I did something regrettable, something I will not discuss.

Today my gift to you is the awareness of my feelings for you. Though no one benefits from the pain I feel in my separation from you, it may comfort you to know you are greatly cared for and missed.

I never asked or needed you to agree with anything I've ever said or done. I've just needed you to be there for me. The last words I ever heard from you were that you would call me. You never did.

Funny thing though, Had you reached out to me all my present experiences, friendships, etc. would not exist. I could never reject you from my life. Nothing, even the threat of my life would keep me from you if you expressed your need to be part of me.

Yet the void from my past is being filled. As sad as I am to let go and move on, I cannot avoid the many wonderful experiences I have encountered. I have friendships today that I would have never dreamed possible.

I miss you, but I know with or without you I will move on, and I will be OK.

I have been having some strange dreams lately. In these dreams I am spending many hours just talking to you. I am talking to you about things that have been happening to me over the years. With this information you are finding out who I am. Something you never knew, and something I have been finding out.

Maybe someday.

With all my love

Chapter Thirty-One

MIAMI GARDENS:
A NEW CHAPTER

IN A TWIST OF FATE THAT VERGED ON THE MIRACULOUS, I EMERGED unscathed from the hurricane's wrath. My initial grievances—those inner murmurings about the hasty evacuation of my home—suddenly felt as frivolous as a child's petulant cries. That ordeal illuminated a stark truth: my enforced relocation wasn't a cruel twist of fate but rather a lifeline leading to safety. Back in August 1992, countless souls in Homestead and Naranja Lakes would have given anything for the forewarning that had once seemed a burden to me.

Despite acknowledging my good fortune, I still had formidable tasks and responsibilities ahead, surpassing any I had encountered prior to the hurricane. Unlike the home I left, Gaston's home remained untouched. There were only scattered tree limbs in the yard from the excessive winds. However, there were other consequences. For three weeks his home was without power. We resorted to gathering water into buckets for bathing, using the water stored in the bathtub. The water had been treated with chlorine pellets prior to the hurricane to prolong its usability. Though our cars' tanks were brimming with fuel, we drove judiciously, knowing gas stations might stay shuttered for the foreseeable future.

A few days into our post-hurricane life, driven by a mixture of concern and curiosity, I ventured to my old neighborhood. Navigating my way through disfigured streets and unrecognizable landmarks, I became disoriented, making my trek there lengthier and all the more emotional. The devastation I encountered was soul crushing. My neighbors' homes stood roofless, with gaping holes where walls used to be. The sight of tents set up in front yards, serving as makeshift shelters in front of the ruined residences, was particularly harrowing.

Despite the sweeping devastation, life pressed on, with everyone tending to their individual needs. As for me, my focus shifted to my business. As thousands of homes in Miami cried out for repairs, the prospect of increased business loomed large. But there was a caveat. Before we could dive into flooring restorations, more pressing priorities took precedence: fixing walls, securing roofs, and repairing or replacing interior furnishings, like cabinets and countertops. As the weeks rolled on, the backlog of proposals grew. Beyond the logistical hurdles, another concern emerged: how would our crew remain engaged during this prolonged hiatus? Regrettably, we lost some, particularly those who owned chainsaws, lured away by lucrative gigs clearing debris-laden properties and streets.

As the days went by with my business still in recovery mode, my bond with Gaston deepened, seeing as we crossed paths daily. While my ties with Kyle dwindled into memory,

Gaston emerged as a dear friend. Known for his creativity, he surrounded himself with an artistic entourage. His social flair led him to host regular gatherings at his place, with an invitation always extended my way. One evening I accepted his offer. We convened over dinner at his home, where we showcased our poetic talents, reading aloud verses of our own creation.

With the festive season around the corner, including Christmas, I got to know his family better, meeting his sister, mother, and cousins. At one such gathering, Gaston's playful side emerged. With a twinkle in his eye, he urged me to greet his mother with the Spanish phrase, "Me pican los huevos," assuring me it meant "Happy to meet you." Trusting him, I parroted the words, only to later discover I had announced, "My balls itch."

As the days turned into weeks and weeks into months, my phone began ringing incessantly with clients eager to set their contracts in motion. The tide of business swelled, and my financial horizon brightened. Soon, I had amassed enough savings to stake out a space of my own. I settled on a residence at 7215 NW 179th Street in Hialeah, just a few miles from Gaston's place.

It was at that time, as March 1993 unfurled, that I found myself in the serenity of my new apartment, lost in introspection, gazing out at the world beyond my sliding glass doors. Against that backdrop the idea of writing—of capturing and reflecting on my life—took root within me. Little did I know then that the urge to chronicle my experiences would sustain for many years to come. Now as I review and fine tune these words, aligning the narrative and ensuring its fidelity to the sentiments I felt when first penned, I find myself teetering on the brink of finishing this intense yet deeply gratifying odyssey. The journey, rife with challenges, has also served as a beacon of introspection and revelation.

In the quiet sanctuary of my apartment, my life's cadence began to shift. The stars finally aligned, allowing me to embark on a heartfelt trip to Syracuse and into my grandparents' embrace. While there I also rekindled bonds with Frankie, my former brother-in-law. Even though time had wedged a distance between him and my sister, Pamela, Frankie remained steadfast, ensuring his daughter, Domonique, spent precious moments with her great-grandparents. I'll forever be grateful for the visits he arranged, which brought moments of profound joy to my grandparents.

But fate still had cards to play. While awaiting my Syracuse-bound flight, I struck up a conversation with a fellow traveler. As our chat meandered, a delightful revelation emerged. Not only were we sharing the flight, destiny had also cast him as my soon-to-be next-door neighbor.

Over time, Randy and I developed close ties, and I found myself intertwined with his lively group of friends. Then there was Claudia, who'd jet in from Buenos Aires. Our reunions resembled the unrestrained days of social escapades, casting shadows of the vibrant times with Kyle in Naranja Lakes.

On balmy weekends, Claudia's affection for Disney World drew us to Orlando. Our escapades were often peppered with breakfast detours at her favorite haunt, Denny's. And then there were our idyllic Sunday brunches at Snappers in Key Largo. There, the strains of a gifted musician's guitar would waft through the air, serenading us with Paul Simon classics by the water's edge. That tradition, begun on a whim, unfurled its magic over the next quarter-century, gifting me with a mosaic of treasured moments.

As the autumnal palette splashed its colors across the landscape, reflections of my Syracuse journey and the deep familial ties it evoked stirred within me. Overflowing with emotion and a sense of longing, I crafted a heartfelt letter to my mother. Each word carried a piece of my heart, and with hope as my compass, I dispatched it, fervently hoping it would find its way into her hands.

MY LETTER TO MOM

October 25, 1993

Dear Mom,

Today is Monday. Monday evening, about 7 p.m. I've been talking with a new friend over the phone today. A new friend who somehow contributed to a new idea in my mind. That is, suddenly I have this thought of writing to you. Writing is not the big deal it used to be. That is, as it was when I was much younger. Now I enjoy it. In fact, I write quite often. Though some things never change. My spelling is as poor as ever. As well as my word usage, composition, etc. But this isn't a test. So, I guess it doesn't matter. Besides, with these computers (I am using one), I can at least correct my spelling errors.

I started writing a lot more since buying this computer. I've learned to type quickly, and I don't get as tired as I seem to when pushing a pen. What you may not know is there are some serious problems with writing if you are left-handed. Picture your left-hand printing words on a piece of paper. It follows right through the fresh ink on the paper. This makes for one ink covered hand if you're into long letters. Also, another problem I have (which may or may not have to do with being left-handed), is when I begin writing about something emotional, intense, or something, you know, that I am trying to put emphasis on, I write too hard and fast. Making for some messy, sloppy penmanship. When typing, I don't have that problem.

Anyway, enough about my writing problems. I want to discuss something I hope you find more important. To start, I want you to know why I am writing this letter. It's because I want you to know. You may be asking to know what? I'll try the best I can, to explain little by little through this letter.

No matter what has happened over the past years, you are my mother. The mother who gave birth to me, the mother who raised me. For reasons, many strange reasons which I will try not to get into, you have never known me. I don't know if you agree. But I say this in a conclusion based on what I have learned about from others. I may never have the opportunity to learn about, to know you. But you may be able to know me. This is not an attempt to have you contact me. In fact, I don't know if you will ever receive this letter, or any other one I may send to you, or have sent to you in the past. What I do know is that today, Monday, October 25th, I'll have thought of you, and in some way may have reached you. Who knows, I keep all my letters on disc. If you don't read them as they're mailed to you, well, maybe 20 or 30 years from now things will be different. Maybe we'll be talking by then. At that time, you may want to know what I was like. I'll be able to show you these letters. In 20 years, you'll be in your seventies. Many things can be seen differently at that age. Don't you think?

So, since I feel one way or another you will read all my letters, and because I think twenty years in many ways is no longer than a day, I'll write as though you will be reading this tomorrow.

On to other topics. About not knowing me. Why do I feel there was little communication of importance when I was young? I will tell you some things I remember about my days at home. I remember fifth grade. Fifth grade was a turning point for me. At that time many things were changing. That was when the church started in Euclid. I used to go into the bathroom in school, sit kids down on the toilets, and raise their feet to heal their backs. Like

Dad used to do in church, remember? Somehow, things got very confusing at that time. I did not understand what I saw, what I was hearing within our religion. I won't get into detail right now. I just want you to know some things really confused me. At about that age I was convinced I was old enough to know the difference between right and wrong. I thought I was living a lie, and was convinced I would be held accountable for this and other sins. I even thought I would burn in hell if I died. Pretty weird for a kid that age huh? None the less it's true. I remember all too well. As well as I remember not wanting you to have any idea what I was thinking. To let you know I was a sinner? Earth shattering. This was serious stuff. Do you want to know what it was I was feeling so guilty about? Remember in the Euclid church when everyone would sing in a circle? All would hold hands, raise them toward the sky, speak in tongues, etc. It was difficult for me to do that. I forced myself many times. Especially when us kids would get a little talk from Dad or someone else in the church. That little talk used to make me feel something was wrong with me if I didn't behave like everyone else. I believed those talks. Ask Dad if he remembers the day he gave me his tambourine. One day at the Euclid church he did. It was the same day I announced to the church I had a vision. You see, David Gentile, or some other person spoke of a vision one night. Maybe even that same night. I remember saying I saw Christ on a cross, as well as two others by his side. Then, everyone around me singing prayers, clapping in approval and singing praise to God. There was a lot of excitement, emotional expression. What I want you to know about my vision is that it never happened. I lied. Not for any bad intent. I really wanted to see a vision. I wanted to fit in. I wanted to be like David Gentile. He was always having visions. He was always admired. It seemed as though God was talking to everyone in that church except me. Everyone was speaking in tongues, everyone "felt the spirit." But not me. Something had to be wrong with me, right? So, I faked it. And my act became my secret. I was a sinner. I couldn't let you know. I could not let anyone know. I must have been a sinner, right? God didn't talk to me like he did with everyone else. We were taught there was heaven and hell. Nothing between. All were Christians or sinners. I wanted so much not to go to hell. For years I searched within my mind, within myself for a way to escape hell. I looked for a way to become saved. I suffered. If only there was help for me. Yet during this time there were offers of help to me. Help from you and Dad. I remember one time in particular that comes to mind. About something you and Dad used to tell me, my brothers and sisters. That we could always talk to you if we needed to. I found those words unfair. Especially when I tried to talk with Dad about things he didn't agree with. I think you forgot to make mention of the exceptions. The conditions in which we would not be allowed to talk to you. Like when you don't agree with what we have to say. Or how about those really weak answers like when you don't have one but give one anyway. I'm referring to those answers like "you have to have faith," or "that's just the way it is." Do you remember one of my more memorable lessons about honesty that Dad gave to me? I'll tell the story. It was at the time I got my worst beating. When I skipped school and got caught. Dad said he beat me because I lied. Not because I skipped school. Because I wasn't in school and I lied saying I was. When we were in school Dad lied about the bruises on my arm that the principal asked about. Dad said they were from a bike accident. They were really from the beating Dad gave me with the switch he made from a willow tree. I had a lot of questions about this one. Like why I would be punished in such a severe way for doing something that Dad did. I guess this was another one of those exceptions in which no answer would be offered from either you or Dad. I did approach you. You offered no explanation. What was so tough for me was that the times I really needed to talk to you, I couldn't. Those unspoken exceptions prevented me. I guess this is what I meant when I said we really don't know each other. I mean we never talked about the most important things. Those things that were really messing up my life. Things that made me think I was a sinner headed for hell. It was tough those years living a fake life. Going to church four times a week, faking my interests, and beliefs. All to keep some kind of peace, some kind of sanity. Looking back I realize how much was missing. Like my interest in reality. Nothing seemed important, nothing really seemed to matter. My school work was lousy. I was involved in nothing. What did I care about in school? Nothing. I just wanted to escape. I wanted to climb trees and explore sewers. Emotionally I hid from you, Dad, and my teachers. As you know I was quite the introvert. Did you ever wonder why? Had it ever occurred to you I was in desperate need of guidance? Did you feel I was a lost cause? Without a good education, without good grades, what kind of a future did I have? Did you or Dad ever, one single time, talk to a teacher of mine? Were you concerned enough to take some kind of action? Maybe you felt God would take care of everything? You and Dad showed little thought about preparing me for my life after school. I never thought about my life after school either. And, speaking about the unspeakable, let me tell you about when I discovered girls. I knew I was damned for hell when I discovered girls. All those hormones and feelings. Does any of this surprise you? Did you ever wonder why I did not want you to know I liked girls? Did you or Dad ever have one conversation with me about girls? Why not? Did you ever wonder why I had no relationships? Why I spent so much time alone, without any friends? Or why I was never involved with family, with you, Dad, or any of my brothers or sisters? Did you have any idea what was going on within me? Today I feel different than I could ever have imagined possible. Those years ago should have been happy times. Times of excitement and experience. Days of exploration, new friendships, relationships, etc. I missed the excitement of learning, the feelings of love. Not having these things and seeing them in others really confused me. Especially because I saw them in people who were supposed to be sinners damned to hell. I remember looking at them and thinking all of what I was taught. About how they appear to be happy but really weren't. They were faking it. Because they were sinners and didn't know better. How confusing all this was. Especially in later years when I found out that if these sinners were faking their happiness, well, then these people that Dad calls Christians must be faking their happiness too. That is, if I ever even saw happiness in them. I caught many people living in lies. Lies that I found so many, many like you mom, so willing to cover up. I think of all those high school dances I missed. All those school functions. And all I knew to do was to hide. To escape. To me all those in my school were sinners headed for hell. All the students, all the teachers. Hell bound. Nothing any of them could have said would have meaning to me. They weren't anointed by God. They didn't have the gifts or the wisdom my father had. And my dad says they are sinners. The lost sheep. They were not saved. They did not go to the living word church. Can you start to see who I was? This is what I was. Did you know me? In my teens I questioned much of what I was taught. Questions giving birth to new questions. Questions that I could not find answers to. Religious questions. Or, since I know you don't like the word religion, I'll say things about God. Questions about life. Like how it was people in areas of the world that never heard about Christ could be sent to hell for not being saved. Or about how someone who believed in good and was not saved could be forced to suffer for eternity in hell. Or how a murdering, hateful, evil person could be saved, get hit by a car the next day, and spend eternity in heaven. I searched for answers to these questions. I searched within myself for answers. Every day I struggled to bring order to my mind and self. I went through hell to make sense of my life. To survive my upbringing. To make some sense of all the conflict and contradiction. Today is different.

Do you believe that hindsight is 20/20?

The torment is no longer with me. But back then, and for some years after each step of thought that brought some light would bring a new darkness. The more I felt I learned about reality, the more confused I would feel. Do you think you can imagine what it is like to be completely confused? Do you think I can? Do you know what my days in the mental hospital were like? Do you know why you saw me drooling, staring like a zombie at walls, walking like Frankenstein? Do you know why I would lay on the floor on my back, shake like I was being electrocuted, flick my eyelids rapidly until my eyes rolled toward the back of my head, then stop, get up off the floor and walk around forgetting what I had done? I'll try to explain some of these things to you. An explanation I could not offer for years to anyone. But before I tell you, do you have a guess? Many years have passed, and you must have reached some conclusion about what may have caused my behavior. Do you think I was possessed by a demon? Do you think I was paying for my sins? Do you think it happened to warn my brothers and sister of what would happen to them should they be like me? I think if we all look close enough, and are willing enough, we can find many truths about ourselves. When I was in the hospital, I was not aware I was in a hospital. I thought I was in hell. I told no one this for a number of reasons. One is that I thought everyone was trying to use me for something. Another is that I became unable to communicate. I was trapped in the mind that I fought so hard with to solve my problems. What I am not sure if you know or not is that prior to my involuntary stay at the hospital I had thoughts of suicide. One specific thought of suicide was nearly carried through. In some strange way since I thought I was going to kill myself I decided I was already dead. I don't know if this makes much sense to you. But the fact is I thought I was dead. This has a lot to do with why I thought the hospital was hell. I am not sure if I mentioned it in my letter earlier, but nothing in my life is more certain than the fact that I thought I was in hell while at the hospital. As I mentioned, I have had a fear of going to hell since I was 9 or 10 years old. To me everyone in the hospital was some kind of spirit, or demon. Where do you think all these ideas came from? They did not come from nowhere? All of the confusion surrounding my life, within my life, that could not be worked out took form, took control.

Just prior to the moment I was on the floor shaking like a vibrator, I was talking to someone. We had a conversation that made me think I was given permission to leave hell. The way I thought I could leave hell was by leaving my body. So I laid on the floor and shook until I thought my spirit left hell. Then I got up, forgetting what I did. Maybe at that moment I forgot what I did because I was not supposed to be there. My spirit left my body, right? There was no telling anyone about this stuff for a long time. And then all that talk about paranoid schizophrenia, bipolar disorder, psychiatric therapy, lithium, Jesus Christ, etc. Wow. What a trip all that was. And poor aunt MaryJane, grandma and grandpa. None of them knew what to do. At one time they prayed with me, telling me to ask Jesus Christ into my heart. To depend on Christ for my salvation, my healing. I know they meant well. But when they did that thing only got worse. Salvation through any attempt of religion was the last thing I needed at that time. Trying to understand the mysteries of religion which mankind has been doing and fighting wars over as far back as we go, is in large part what brought me to the hell I was in. This may make you think that I do not believe in what you and Dad have raised me to believe. Well, in a large way that's correct. But it's more like the way you lived the ideals you expressed. I learned a lot of good from the talk. And, as for hell, I have no plans for visiting again. I won't be returning. I tried it. Don't care for it much.

I remember a prayer I used to say. It began one day when I used to work in a seven-story building as a janitor. I saw this poster in an office. It was a scenic picture with some words written on it. I remember it as if I am looking at it right now. It read; "we see things as we are, not as they are." After reading that I was inspired. Inspired to pray. I feel it was and still is the sincerest request of my life. I don't remember my exact words, but in context I said; "God, if you are there, the only thing I want for my life, the most important thing that I desire, is to know the truths of life. To understand what is really happening with and around my life." Then I said something with the same sincerity, "no matter what the price or pain to me." I remember the moment well. At that time, I felt I would give much for the understanding I sought.

Which became the understatement of my life. However, it is the prayer that I continue today. As for those days at the downtown building, my prayer seemed only to complicate things. Why does it so often seem that for things to get better they first must get worse. And worse things became. My prayer was like asking God for permission to follow my conscience. And for the courage to deal with the consequences of my actions. Like the time I felt a need to tell Dad something I knew he didn't want to hear. That I was too old to go to church for you and him. That if I went it had to be for myself. There were some big problems after that one. Mom, I know you saw many things wrong with me which never did get discussed. Do you think they were swept under a rug because you and Dad didn't know how to deal with me? Do you think that if you knew me better you may have been able to help us both? Have I answered any of the questions you may have had about my past behavior? Do you think good communication is required in all healthy relationships? Did you, do you think we communicated well? If you think, thought we didn't, could anything have been done about it? What I want to know is could you have helped me? And if you made a mistake, do you think it is too late to offer some help now? Is what never started really over between us? It's really something how values, ideals, religion etcetera that we are raised in affect our entire lives. In my view they both help and hinder us. Do you remember one time that I came to you or Dad for advice? I remember going to Dad once for advice, not for what I had to do. Dad never did know the difference between the two. After that I went to him and told him I would never ask for his advice again. I said our relationship as father and son was more important than the money he could help me earn, and that the advice was not worth the tension it created. He said nothing. I could never keep track of the things I said to the two of you that made things quiet. Why? Do you think he should have talked to me later about what I said to him? Maybe what I said wasn't important? Maybe it didn't matter. I was preoccupied with other seemingly more important matters. Like that I was a sinner headed for hell. Compared to that problem, what else could ever matter? I never even talked to a friend about what was going on. Not a school counselor, not a teacher, neighbor, no one. I tried to find a solution to all of my problems on my own. In my own head. Something was very wrong. Why didn't I go to someone in my school? They were worldly people. People of the world who were sinners. Sinners headed for the hell that I was trying to escape from. I couldn't go to them. I couldn't approach anyone in the church. They would find out I was a sinner. The only solution I could find, and this goes for the days right up into my teens, was to figure the mess out on my own. This decision has affected the rest of my life. To this day I take, seek advice from no one. I figure things out on my own. It's the only way I know. However, what has changed dramatically, which by now you must agree, is my ability, willingness to express myself and my thoughts with others. I ask myself where my values and other beliefs come from. I think I took all of my experiences and sifted through them. I think about things I have heard, try to make some sense of them, and experiment by mixing them with new experiences and ideas. Making me who I am today.

It's now 8:30 pm. I think this is a good time to end today's letter.

Hopefully you will realize this letter is not an attempt to make you call or contact me. You have made a choice not to see or talk to me, and I accept your decision.

I have a desire for you to know who, what I am. That is, for you to really know me. As I really am, was. If you do read this letter in the next few days, I don't think it would (at this time) be good for you to call or make contact with me. I think you have been through a hell of your own. What I would like to do is to continue writing to you. To write letters about my present and past experiences. I have not written anything about my life today. You may be surprised to see who, what I have become.

I do and always will love you. Maybe we still can have the chance we never had. The chance to know each other.

Dan

After dispatching that letter, silence from my mother ensued. Today I wonder if it ever graced her gaze. Indeed, all previous letters sent her way received the same silent response. However, the winds of fate were about to shift. The following May, I wrote a new letter, this time to my father. While he remained silent, through a strange twist of fate, the letter found its way to my mother. To my surprise, she responded, ending our prolonged silence. Here is the letter I wrote to my father.

Chapter Thirty-Three

MY LETTER TO DAD

May 17, 1994

I don't know how I should address this letter. Dear Dad, Mr. Mazur, Pastor Mazur? Surprised that I am writing to you? Will you ever even get this letter?

The reason I am writing is because of a conversation I had with Grandma last night. Nothing was discussed about you, but hearing that neither you or Mom have seen her brings back some old thoughts. I really don't have many thoughts about you or my brothers or sisters anymore. My life with all of you in many ways was a different lifetime. You knew little about me back then, and I am even more different now. I don't know if you ever think about me, I don't think I really care. I have no interest anymore in your approval, or in having you understand me or see some things as I do. But I do still care for my grandparents and my aunt and uncle. They never judged me, and made sure I knew I could count on them if I needed them. All I really ever wanted was emotional support. I'm independent, never asking for money or even much time of anyone.

You know Grandma had an operation, don't you? Is it still important to you to have someone admit their fault, that they were wrong? Who cares about things like that? Look at the pain you allow yourself to go through because you cannot let go. How is my mother? How will she be, years in the future when her mother passes away? It will be too late to resolve the conflict. You may be asking me the same question. How would I feel should you or Mom pass away. Ours is a different story. Do you remember one time that you reached out to me? Since I left the house, did you ever contact me and say, "Dan, come on son, we need to talk." You know, the kind of thing fathers do when their kids are confused, out of line, or when things just aren't right. I never got that call from you, not even a letter. You never attempted to sit down with me and talk things through. But I did. Something I am very proud of. I did the right thing, having tried for years to talk to you. Ya, I made my mistakes blowing up and saying stupid things when I was very upset about some things I saw. But that didn't make me bad, just human. I used to dream about the day when I could talk with you, to tell you how I honestly feel. You never knew me. I am now nearly 33 years old. What could a kid my age those years back have possibly done that warranted your actions, or maybe I should say lack of action? Isn't a parent to be long suffering? Wasn't I the student, and you the teacher? Wasn't I expected to make mistakes? Did you just one day decide that I was so bad that you could have nothing more to do with me? What kind of psychological effect did you think this kind of rejection would have? And you didn't show disapproval to Mom and the rest of my brothers and sisters following your example. Were your actions really in my best interest? What effect would all of that rejection have on me? Well, you know what happened to me. I refer to the psychiatric facility. How do you feel about that? Do you live OK with all of this? No guilt?

Even if I was as wrong as you used to say I was, why didn't you make an effort to work things through? Do you think it was right to turn your back on me? Is it still OK? These are things that used to really get to me. I made every possible effort to talk with you, and to see my brothers and sisters and mother. Every one of you turned your backs on me. That is why our situation is different. Should you or any of you pass away I will have no feelings of guilt. I tried. Are you sure you can say the same? You know what really used to get to me, is that all of this was in the name of God. Is this what you think God really wants? Do you think it is his will for you not to try and work these things out. How is it that you can just turn your back and ignore what has happened? It takes a man, maybe even a man of God to face and deal with this, doesn't it?

God has been trying to tell you something. Will you ever listen to him? I think you do not listen to him because you are afraid of what may happen should you begin to face these problems. There is a price you feel that must be paid, and you try to avoid it. But your many years of suffering are what you now pay for avoiding what should be done, a cost much higher than the one you try to avoid. And you will continue to pay.

Life is fair.

It still amazes me that my mother took five years to respond to my numerous letters. Perhaps it's not so surprising, as I've always suspected that attempts were made not only to keep me from her but also to intercept my letters. Nonetheless, the long-awaited moment arrived, cloaked in mystery though it was.

Chapter Thirty-Four

MY RESPONSE TO MOM'S LETTER

June 1, 1994

Dear Mom,

I received and have read your letter. There are so many things I want to say, and I don't know where to begin. Let me start by saying how surprised I am that you wrote to me. I am not sure how long it has been, eight or nine years since I was living at the house. It was around the same time as when your parents stopped going to Dad's church. This is the first letter I have from you. When I finish writing I will be sending it certified mail, return receipt. My reason for doing so is not with bad intent. I just want to be sure you will get it. I have written and sent many letters to you and have no idea if any of them ever reached you. You mentioned in yours of promising yourself to write to me if ever hearing from me again. When did you make that promise? My letters to you go many years back.

I think there are things about my letter that you misunderstood. Regardless of this and the fact that your letter's content is not particularly pleasant, I am glad you sent it. Seven long pages, 4,150 words (my computer added them). You obviously spent quite some time collecting your thoughts and writing it. I have read it quite a few times already, and will be reading it several more times within the next few days. I'm curious to know something new about you. Your views of life, how they have or have not changed. Your opinions of other people, and their differing religious beliefs. Do you think your beliefs in your faith are exactly as they were nine years ago? Are you as certain today of what you felt was fact yesterday? Has the church changed over the past nine years? If so, in what way? Have your relationships with "sinners" changed? Do you have any close involvement with anyone who does not go to the church? Do you have any kind of contact with "outsiders," people like me? I'm not going to find answers to most of these questions in your letters, but I will learn other things about you.

When I think of your letter, the first of many things that comes to mind is something you wrote at its end. "You need to get rid of the anger and hatred you have. It's like murder the Bible says; it will consume you." How is it you're so certain I have this problem? I've read my letter many times. As usual my letter asks a lot of questions that remain unanswered. It points out the disappointments I've had with you and Dad. Mostly, its context reflects questions you've avoided answering for many years. My questions to you remain the same, but don't carry the same intensity, the same weight they used to. I don't see the anger or hatred in them that you speak of. Maybe it's because my words come in the form of a letter that you feel this way. I am full of hate because when you read my letter you pictured me screaming my words with a purple face and a vein throbbing at my neck? My letter really had more to do with my curiosity than anger. My old need to have questions answered, questions that you always refused to answer. Like the heart-to-heart talk I often asked for but never had. Those old questions were very important to me, but not anymore. The important questions have been answered. Some of them for a long time now. It's just that I used to have a need to hear you say them.

Maybe it's not the letter you refer to. I remember one day I made a phone call to Pam's house. I can see how you'd interpret what I said to her as hatred. However, I explained that day to you in a letter. I made that call after hearing Grandma was in the hospital. I was told the family wasn't interested in seeing her. I did become very angry. I knew how much good you could do by being there. I said some terrible things about Dad on Pam's phone. If your phone number wasn't unlisted, you would have gotten my call. I told you and others knowing what happened that I regretted my actions. What I did was out of frustration, not hate that I have within me. I couldn't be there, and you could. I wanted to be there, and you didn't. This is one of the situations I referred to in my last letter when I said "Ya, I made my mistakes blowing up and saying stupid things when I was very upset about something I saw." So, is this what makes you say I have hatred? Other than that, the only previous communication with you I recall that doesn't go back more than six or so years is the last day I saw you. I had been visiting the family for about two or three months at the time. It was during a time when I was making a new attempt to get involved with the family. Which reminds me, how can you say "you missed out because you never wanted to be with us"? Don't you remember my efforts? For a long period, in fact most of my life you and Dad have made attempts to involve me in your lives. I can see that now, and also agree my response to those many attempts was very unfavorable. However, as weak as it may have appeared, mine was an attempt, an attempt that failed. Did you ever think about why it never worked? Do you think it's because we don't have the same spirit, as you mentioned in your letter? Don't you think it may have had more to do with something more specific? Something that could have been discussed, maybe even overcome with a little bit of reason and conversation? Isn't there a way that we could have faced the cause of our conflict so something could have been done about it? Or is it really as you say, good and bad spirits clashing, something to accept and not change? Our conflict has continued for many years. Maybe there's a common denominator, something that every conflict we've had has in common that has been the real cause of our problems. I am going to talk more about this later. As for that last day I saw you, it was as you said in your letter, I "blew up." But it wasn't over nothing. In fact, how can you say it was over nothing? You said you were going to call me, and you never did. Did you think to ask if something was bothering me? When a criminal is convicted for a crime, isn't there some kind of investigation, a trial first? Doesn't the accused have a right to defend himself? Or do you think if someone appears guilty they should be convicted, punished for their crime without the opportunity for defense? You're so certain there was no reason for my outburst that you felt it fair to allow the two or so months we began to communicate to end? You gave up so easily, it made me feel like I wasn't worth the effort required to restore or maintain the relationship. You never even asked me if something was bothering me, if there was a reason why I behaved the way I did. And you broke your word with me, you said you would call me and never did. Our entire relationship together was at stake, don't you think that called for some careful judgment? You knew what I did, that my blow up damaged my goal, being back with the family. So why did I do that? Doesn't there have to be a reason? Something was bothering me many days before that final day. Something that grew into a much bigger problem I had difficulty dealing with. Every time I visited you and the family all conversation was about the Church, Dad's life, your life, or the life of my brothers and sisters. These topics were OK for me, but no one ever showed an interest or care to know anything about me. I'm not talking about food for ego. Never in all the time I saw all of you was anything said about my life. I might not have been the born again Christian the rest of you were, but I was a brother and a son. At that time, I had been dating a girl for over three years, remember? She didn't profess to be saved either, but she was someone I cared for deeply. Susan was my first important relationship. I tried bringing her into conversation a few times. Dad would never call her by name, always referring to her as "that girl." The situation reminded me of Nancy. Remember Nancy? She was a girl I met that I knew for six months before introducing you to her. I never went to bed with her, and the most I ever did was to kiss her. I invited her over for dinner to meet the family, remember? After dinner she helped you wash the dishes. She was very polite, very proper. When she left Dad had a talk with me, a talk that was not in private, but for all around to hear. He told me he didn't want me to bring my trash into the house. He said that what I did outside of the house he had little control over, but he would not allow me to bring my diseases, my flings into the house. What do you think that little talk did to me? Would it create any difficulty for me to remain part of the family? I didn't have friends in your church because my convictions kept me from attending it. So, you knew I wouldn't have a relationship with someone from there. What was left? It was now clear I wasn't allowed to bring a girl from the "world," a "sinner" into the family. What did you expect me to do? Was I supposed to never date a girl again? Did you leave me any other choice than to have dates that you wouldn't be told about? The first thing I did was to bring my conflict to your attention. Do you remember? But when I explained to you what had happened you showed little concern and little understanding of my dilemma. Maybe your reaction was part of an attempt to get me back into the church? Your letter says you never tried to force me to do so. ". . . we did not force you & (couldn't anyway) to go to church . . ." Were you both forcing me, pressuring me to make a choice? To be with you, your beliefs and church, or to have a life outside of the family? This is only one example of why it was becoming so difficult to be a part of your lives. There are other examples where I felt pressured into making the same choice, but there are also many other things I want to say. I have plenty of paper, but my time has its limits. I am already at a pace where this letter will be incredibly long.

Your letter also says you never stopped me from having anyone over the house. "Anytime you asked if you could bring someone over that I had never met, I never said no to you." Did you think I could ask Nancy over again? What was so bad about her? I was never told why she was the tramp that Dad described her as. Her father was a doctor, and lived in the village. I know because I was invited to and had dinner with them at their house. Part of his home was his office. They treated me well, and at the time I felt that they liked me. She went to the same school as I, was very pretty, and was conservatively dressed and mannered when you met her. Was it only that she didn't go to your church that qualified her as the tramp Dad described? You did allow Nancy over that Sunday long ago, but she could never return. And though I was interested in a relationship with her, I discontinued the effort. She was close with her family, and I knew that if we got serious, she would want her parents to meet you. It would have never worked out. I often wondered what her parents would have thought if they knew what Dad had said about her. It was obvious they were very kind and gentle people who must have cared deeply and wanted the best for their daughter. They didn't deserve for such a thought to exist. I really liked her and thought about her for months after I said good-bye. I never gave her an explanation.

Are you certain you know why we never have a good relationship? Are you sure it was really all my fault? I never sat down and had a conversation with you or Dad to discuss these problems. Is it really my fault when you know it is you who refused to talk? Look at the past twelve or so years of my life, I've been trying to get both of you to talk with me, and you've avoided every attempt. Anyway, let me get back to my discussion about the last day we saw each other. During my new attempt to become involved with the family I was feeling left out. It was easy to have a conversation with everyone about their lives, I knew plenty to talk about. But I needed more. I began to resent that for the many weeks I was with you no one showed any interest in me. I knew I was different from all of you and that we didn't have much in common. I was allowed to and did join into conversation about your lives, but I needed to know someone cared about mine. Why is it you never asked me about my relationship with Sue? Did I love her? Was she someone I liked to talk to? Were we very close? Was I considering marrying her? What were her parents like? Where did they live? Do you have answers to any of these questions? Did you have any questions about me? How was my business? Was I OK financially? Considering I had recently left the hospital and was still having some obvious problems, wouldn't these questions be expected? Was I getting by OK? Was I happy? Did I have feelings of depression? Were there things that were bothering me? Did I want to be with the family? What was making it so hard for me to be with you? Was someone upsetting me? Was I interested in having a family of my own? Did you ever think to ask me; How are you getting along with your brothers and sisters? Can I help? What is going on between you and your Dad? Do you love your father? Do you hate him? You say in your letter you have a good understanding of many of my feelings. Are you sure they're my feelings? I know you never found out about how I felt by asking me, where did your conclusions come from? Did you ever think to talk to me about who I was? All those weeks I was with you I felt I was treated as though my life were a disease. As if contact with me would be fatal. The look was over all of you, everything was there but the white suit and mask that protected you. Maybe no one could talk about my life because I have a different spirit? Didn't Jesus spend much of his life talking, communicating with sinners? Was I really all that bad? Maybe if you asked me some questions about my life you would have had more insight to who I really was, and to what we both really needed. What was it about Sue that attracted me to her? You never thought to ask? I felt she was somehow able to understand me and my feelings, something that was extremely important at the time. It's a big reason why I felt drawn to her. It's what I was missing from you. I've often thought about this. If I had a good rapport with you, I may have never met or had as much of an interest in Sue. It was being able to talk with you that I needed, that could have kept me from my eventual explosion. I was beginning to resent that I could only discuss your lives with you. It was a problem that was building and beginning to consume my thoughts during visits. I needed to talk. But how? We never worked through a problem together. Every approach I made as a child to discuss a problem was turned down. We never began the rapport that we needed to deal with this problem. So there never was a talk between us to work it out. And that last day you saw me came. It was something fairly small, something Pam said while she laughed at a neighbor that set me off.

These are the only situations I can think of in the past six or so years that may be interpreted as showing my anger or hatred. But we're talking about a few situations and many years. How is it you can be so certain of what I am today? It's difficult enough to know people you're with every week for years, and you say you know who I am today, through less than a handful of experiences over many years? I suppose you also knew who the church elders were, during the many years of your relationship together, and that you intentionally allowed a man to preach to hundreds of people during the same evenings he returned home to molest his daughters. Are you sure that you and Dad are as good at judging character as you say you are? Look, I got into all of this trying to show you that my hate or anger isn't anything that should concern you. You've made clear that you feel I'm a liar so I'm trying to appeal to your reason. If I tell you I'm not angry or full of hate you won't believe me. But if I offer you my explanation along with what you know to be fact, you may realize what you thought was my hate was actually something else. I'm not saying that I've never been angry either though, I've been angry plenty of times. But if you look to understand what has caused the anger it is there where our attention should be. You have had no anger through all of this? Of course you have, but it's expected for what has happened. There is no importance for either of us to point out anger in the other. And as for hatred, if it's what I have, you should have much compassion for me. It is a terrible and destructive thing. But you can only fuel the problem by addressing it as you have. I thought I knew you better than this.

"I know that this letter will be in vain & anything I have to say won't mean a hill of beans to you, but there's a few things I want to set you straight on." Your letter offers more insight, telling me how you feel today. It means a lot to me and I hope there is a lot it will set me straight on. I've read it many times, and am looking within it for answers. For years I have begged you to discuss with me some of the things you have now written about. Wanting you to be honest, to share your feelings about things that have happened. Your letter is the biggest clue I have to who you are today. Though a lot of it appears to be criticism, I am happy to have it. Not for the chance to defend myself by attacking you, but for the chance to respond to your obviously sincere feelings with mine. Taking a close look at your letter, I read much about the harm I have caused you. You show me that some of this harm comes from situations as the few I've discussed. For example, the last day I saw you when I blew up. If you believe my explanation, that I had problems I was unable to control that led to my explosion, and that my visits were an attempt to restore my relationship with the family, would you feel less harmed by me? If I tell you that when in the hospital I lost my ability to reason, and my recovery took many months (possibly dozens) to be what some may consider normal, would you understand I may not have been able to control my feelings in such a difficult situation? Is this explanation enough to make you feel a little less harmed by me? If you initiated the talks I've often worked so hard to have, might we'd have been able to prevent some of these problems? Do you think that if you were talking with me about what you have now read, instead of reading it, that there would be some impact? By looking into my eyes, by watching my behavior, listening to the tone of my voice, maybe you could tell if I was sincere? How much can a letter possibly accomplish? As far as I am concerned, proper communications were always necessary, but never available to resolve our differences. If I only knew back then that good communications are a skill, a skill I never had and wasn't learned through my family experiences. But I was starting new relationships that would begin to offer the lessons I needed. Like my relationship with Sue. With Sue I began to learn that conflict could be resolved through communication. But I crawled like a baby. I learned that when it came to real communicating, I was far behind others my age. Regardless, it was a beginning and I was on my way. And then there were new friendships, and other new relationships. There were more people I'd meet who were willing to open up to me, people I could learn from. New friends who gave to me for what I had to offer, not out of pity or charity. They enjoyed my company, and were motivated to be with me by their interests rather than obligation or guilt. Through these experiences which never cease to continue, I have attained the experience missing from my youth. The experience needed to build on in order to reach the successful relationships I desire.

The second paragraph of your letter, "you mentioned in your letter that Dad never sat down to talk to you." I have a copy of my letter. I will quote the part you refer to, "Since I left the house, did you ever contact me and say, "Dan, come on son, we need to talk." You know, the kind of thing fathers do when their kids are confused, out of line, or when things just aren't right. I never got that call from you, not even a letter. You never attempted to sit down with me and talk things through. But I did. Something I am very proud of." The letter was addressed to Dad and as you say I am referring to him. But I'm referring to one specific talk, a talk concerning one specific topic. The topic I referred to in my letter. The same topic I've been asking for Dad to talk with me about ever since living at the house. About why we are no longer together. The discussion of a resolution to our differences. You mention that he didn't write, won't write but returns his phone calls. Yes, he returns the phone calls to tell me he's not willing to talk. You don't know this? It's a fact that Dad rejected every request I have made to talk with me. During various periods I have all but begged him to meet with me, to sit down to talk. I made my last request less than a year ago. I told him I'd fly to Syracuse on the exact day, any day he'd pick to talk. His reply was the same as every other time. He said he's not ready for that yet. You should ask him about this. You should also know that what I asked for was a heart-to-heart talk. These were the exact words I used. Each time I asked, he told me (in a very soft voice) that he wasn't ready yet. This has been going on for years. Is this the kind of thing a good father would do? Is this the way a good pastor would behave? Does he advise others to keep from talking? What does it mean that he's not ready? Maybe he won't talk to me for the same reason he wouldn't talk to the psychiatrist. What would happen if the details of our conflict got out into the open? Everyone's perception of reality would change. Like about me for example. To look at all those details is to see what really happened. The details, the facts don't show me to be the monster, the perception that you have created which many people now believe. When the door is open, those who dare to look will know me and others for who we really are. We will no longer be seen as the sinners we have been made to be. What would be the consequences if people knew I wasn't what they thought? It would cause you some difficulty and require a great deal of explanation on your part. Explanations that would bring everyone a little closer to God. You told me in your letter that the enemy is using me for his purpose. But you don't know who the real enemy is. The real enemy is the same for all of us. It is the hatred you've spoken of. I hope it is not what you've embraced, and that someday you'll learn that the knowledge, information, communication, and understanding you resist are really part of who God is. They are not the enemy.

I read in your letter about all Dad did for me that I took for granted. You are right. And I am very sorry I behaved the way I did. If only I could turn back the clock and show him that I do appreciate his efforts. But the fact is I didn't take much notice at the time. I can see it now looking back, but that's because of who I am today. At that time, I was consumed by other thoughts. Most of them I discussed in my October letter. At seventeen or eighteen years old I was pretty confused. Who I had become had consequences not only to myself, but to those close to me. I don't know if this is a common thing for teenagers, but if it is it's a terrible price one must pay for being a parent. But again, I would hope you would understand my actions were not an act of hatred. Rather a result of confusion and complication. At that age I had yet to confide in or have a close relationship with anyone. I have heard Dad once say that no man is an island. I think he is right. But that didn't keep me from trying to survive on my own. I suffered and caused others to suffer as a result. It wasn't until after my breakdown that I began to open up. It was almost as though I had no choice.

"When you left Syracuse, we had policemen at our door looking for you. We received a telephone call, and the person on the other end asked Dad if he could talk some sense into you. You have quite a track record." What is this all about? If I was in trouble and you care for me as you say you do, couldn't you have informed me? Couldn't you have written me a letter? If someone contacted me saying you were doing something wrong or that you may be in some type of trouble, I would inform you. You're still my mother no matter what has happened. If my actions could help you, I'd feel compelled to do something. Was it anything important? It reads like it was. Isn't real love when you care for someone without requiring anything in return? Actions, or lack of action like you've shown are what make me think twice about how you really feel toward me. I hear what you say, like when you say you really love me. Then I see what you do. Then you end your statement by saying "you have quite a track record." That only sounds like you are trying to hurt my feelings. Do you know what the police wanted? Your statement implies I did something that must have been pretty bad. I assume to make your conclusion, your judgment, you must know what it was all about. Or is this and other statements in the letter just an attack against me. Is it simply your anger? Will you ever offer me an explanation? The only thing that I can think of that makes any sense is a phone call Pam made to me when I first moved to Florida. She told me you received a threatening phone call from someone claiming to be affiliated with the Mafia. Supposedly they told her that if I continued to cause trouble for a company I used to work for, that I would end up floating in a river. This is a company that I learned was operating in fraud, ripping off customers out of tens of thousands of dollars, and in which I decided to do something about. Many people saw what was going on within this company and turned their backs. No one wanted to do anything out of the fear of the consequences. I played part in some of the damage that was mainly targeted at elderly people who were seen by the company as easy prey. I did not know in the beginning I was taking advantage of these people, but as soon as I figured it out, I tried to do something about it. I first approached the company owner, giving him the benefit of the doubt. He admitted to what had been happening and promised to make an immediate change. Later I found he didn't make the changes he promised. I spoke with him again, reminding him of the outright immorality and illegal conduct he was responsible for. I told him that at this time should he not make a change I would be informing the Attorney General's office. Again, he agreed to make changes. Weeks passed, and no changes were made. I visited the Attorney General's office and informed them of the misdoings of the company. Later I was approached by a local news station who interviewed me and filmed me for their evening news. It was shortly after that when I moved to Florida. A friend was moving out here and I needed a new job. I was convinced Florida was a good opportunity for me. If this situation had to do with the reason the police came to your door, I will apologize for any trouble it may have caused you, but will not apologize for my decision to follow my conscience. The only other reason I could think the police came to your door would be concerning finances. I went through a lot of financial difficulty prior to leaving Syracuse. But it was dealt with through my Attorney. My attorney and all others concerning my financial situation have had a way to contact me. I even made sure that Aunt Mary Jane's number was left with the appropriate people. I've been hiding from no one, nor have I evaded anyone who has tried to reach me. Still, at this moment I feel puzzled as to how you can keep such information from me, and conveniently bring it to my attention in the form of ammunition, as an attack against my character. I cannot think of any other reason the police may have asked for me, or why they would have asked Dad to talk some sense into me. Was Dad concerned for me? I never heard from him either. Maybe he should have called to try and talk to me? Should I have been in your position, my conscience would have demanded that I make a phone call. If I was unable to face or talk to you, I would have written a letter. If I didn't have your address, I would have given the letter to you through a friend or relative you are in contact with. Why? Because I could have helped you or saved you from possible trouble. Because I am concerned and care. You don't believe me? My proof is in my insistence to communicate, the first step toward a resolution. The first step I've been trying to make since I was a young teen.

"I truly feel sorry for you because you do not know what family is. You missed out because you never wanted to be with us." Boy you got me good here. If I could only begin to explain what it's like not to know what family is. This statement is very true, and has made things difficult for my life. It's always been difficult for me to trust other people; my relationships are very complicated. Let me try to explain a particular difficulty, I can think back to when I was pretty young, thirteen or so. At the time I felt you, my brothers and sister would always be a part of my life. In fact, it was one of few things seeming real to me. But that's all gone now. It was the one thing in my life I thought I could always count on. It has left me feeling that much in life is temporary. It's difficult for me to imagine I will not be left behind again. Be it a friend, girlfriend, or potential wife. I feel that for reasons, be them justified or not, anyone I get close to may eventually leave me. This makes it difficult to get close to people, as I don't like the vulnerability I feel. At moments I feel some of the good, the fun I used to have as a kid without a worry or concern in the world. But those moments are pretty rare. For the most part my days are filled with activity of a serious nature. This is where I feel the most comfortable, the most safe. But no matter what I do I am aware of the void within me, and my need to be part of something bigger. Like a family.

"You missed out because you never wanted to be with us." I wish it was that way. But the truth is I wanted to be with you. Why was I visiting the last few months I was with you? Can you disregard my explanation of that day? Are you sure that you didn't make your response because it's convenient? To take my position would require a lot of work, a lot of self-review, a lot of unraveling. Are you sure you don't say what you do because your position requires no change? Maybe if you thought for a moment that I wasn't such a bad son, that what has happened has more to do with a lack of understanding, maybe then you wouldn't be afraid to talk and work through our conflict. Maybe this is the kind of thing the psychiatrist thought was necessary. Your entire world will change once you realize I have always loved you as much as you love me.

"I can never remember when you ever tried to spend time with any of us. It was the other way around. Of course you will deny this because you have had and are living in lies for so long that you really believe your lies. Start looking at yourself in a mirror and take a good long look." This is very strong. So strong that I would think you thought it through quite carefully before making it? Later in the letter you mention how you know who I am. "I cannot comprehend that you say we never knew you. We knew you from the day you were born." Are you sure you read my October letter? I went into some detail about this. Regardless, it shouldn't take an explanation to understand what I meant when I referred to your not knowing me. Maybe I am not writing clearly. I will not deny that you have spent much time trying to initiate, encourage my involvement with the family. You did. You continued with your efforts right through the many years of my distant behavior. But we never had any rapport other than a superficial one. You didn't know the important things about me. The things that would have allowed you a better chance to begin and continue a good relationship with me. It's why nothing you tried with me worked. You didn't know me. You didn't know what you were dealing with. I really think that by now, considering what I've said in the earlier parts of this letter, you must know what I mean about not knowing me. If you still don't understand, there are other clues. Read my October letter again. It speaks in detail about many things confusing me you never knew about. And the part about lies, yeah, I lie. But I don't lie to myself nor am I living within a lie. I lied to Dad in my letter to him that you read. I said in my first paragraph that I don't care if or what you think about me. The truth is, part of the reason I am spending so much time writing to you is that I do care what you think about me. These are the kind of lies I live with each day of my life. I bare them. And I am sure there are more like them. And no, I don't believe my lie. I believe and understand why I said it. I didn't want you to know I suffer. But I do. Do you really know me? "Start looking at yourself in a mirror and take a good long look." Have you been reading this letter? Have you read my past letters? Are the conclusions you make based on what you read? Can you honestly say that you've looked at yourself as deeply as I've looked at myself? Many people who know me, or others who may read this or past letters I've written will say my comments are a result of deep self-review. I've been looking hard at my life, not hardly, at my faults and much more. I'd like to hear the reason you make such a statement because it's pretty obvious it's far from the truth. I am constantly reviewing my life, my daily behavior. You can't see any evidence of this in my writings? Even if my conclusions are completely wrong it must be obvious to you that I have been taking a good look at myself. And if my determinations of my behavior are wrong, I'd appreciate your opinion as to what would be right. Does it occur to you that since I am looking so closely at myself there must be some motive, some improvement or benefit I seek?

"You say that Dad never returned your phone calls or letters. Yes he will not write to you but he will always return your calls." If you buy a washing machine that is under warranty for a year and it breaks down only a month after you buy it, what do you do? I think you'd call the company to get it repaired. So let's say you do; "please send a repair man," and the company replies, "ok, but the person you need to speak to isn't here, I'll have him call you when he gets back." Your phone rings two hours later; "Ma'am, I'm the repair man. I can't come by now but I know you need me, call me later. Oh by the way, how's the weather there? Nice. That's great, take care." If nine months go by, and you've called this shop every month only for the repairman to return your calls saying he's not ready to help, what would you do? Maybe you'd call back to speak with someone else; "Sir I keep calling your office and leaving a message for the repairman to fix my washer, but nothing ever happens." What will you think when this person says; "well mam, he returns your calls every time you call, doesn't he?." You're going to think "big deal." It's the same with Dad, I've been calling him for years, for a heart-to-heart talk. He returns my calls but says he's not ready to talk. He won't deliver the goods, and never responds to any of my letters. Do you understand?

"In your letter you stated that you were judged by us. There's a difference between judging and correction." Here is my quote, the only area of my letter that mentioned judging; "But I do still care for my grandparents and my aunt & uncle. They never judged me, and made sure I knew I could count on them if I needed them." It can be interpreted that indirectly I was implying you have judged me. And that's fine because it's true. My grandparents, my aunt and uncle have allowed me to approach them to discuss any topic I feel is important to me. They did not come to me and say, "Dan, you can talk with us about anything." Quite simply, they never refused to listen to anything I had to say. And it's not because they were never emotionally involved that they had an open ear. There were situations that called for much involvement on their part. Not only did they listen to me, but at times even labored and went to financial expense. My uncle, who is no blood relation to me, labored for days cleaning office buildings late into the evenings while I was in the hospital. He said nothing about his busy schedule, nor did he ever show me that I was in his debt. Did you ask anyone if I had financial difficulties during my stay at the hospital? You knew I owned my own business, did you check to see if it would survive my stay? Did you offer your needed help? My Uncle made sure I had a business to return to when leaving the Hospital. And I won't tell you the details, the financial expense he absorbed for me. I'm embarrassed by it. Were you as concerned? Even if I was a sinner, what kind of impact do you think an offer of my brother or sisters to help would have had? Even if they only volunteered an hour or two of labor, do you think Dad could have arranged that? Do you think he could have asked them to pitch in, to help me keep my business while I was in the hospital? I'd have been in their debt, but ended up feeling much differently. Dad asked me if I was on drugs when he saw me. And when I heard he refused to talk with the doctors I knew he had interests other than my best interest in mind. Yes, you were all there, and that was part of what I needed. But neither you or Dad offered what I really needed, what the professionals were telling you I needed. And you accuse me of being a know-it-all: "You cannot take correction because you always had the answers, so you thought." Weren't you gambling with my life when you didn't follow the recommendations of the doctors? Weren't they the trained professionals? Grandma, Grandpa, Aunt

Mary Jane and Gary listened carefully to what they had to say. They didn't take the same chances you did. "My prayer for you is that some way & somehow one day you will humble yourself . . ." All my life you and Dad avoided my questions. You never allowed me the opportunity to express my concerns, the chance to develop a relationship between us. It's because we never talked that you didn't know who I was, yet without knowing me, Dad knew enough to say the help I needed had nothing to do with what the doctors prescribed. Something was wrong with me, twice I came close to killing myself, and nothing you ever tried had worked for my life. Yet you prevented trained professionals from providing what they said was necessary. Were Dad's actions that of a humble man? How is it that through his years of failure with me he was so certain he had the answers? Did his methods help me? The doctors were trained to deal with this type of problem. You needed to follow their advice. Does saying this make me a know-it-all? Does it mean that I think I have all of the answers? Or does it show that I have common sense? Nothing you had ever done worked in resolving the years of conflict. It was time to give it up, it was time to stop trying to correct me. That is the word you used, isn't it? "In your letter you stated that you were judged by us. There's a difference between judging and correction." Somehow within this experience you felt your treatment of me was about correction? All you needed to do was to show me the love you say you had. The Doctors would have told you the rest. It was really quite simple, and what everyone else did. You didn't have to clean any of my buildings, or show up every day to see me. But it's all a part of the past now. There will be no talk with the Doctors to offer the answers we needed. It's been the demand of my life, with both of you, this heart-to-heart talk. Why couldn't I have it? And about your comment to judgment, Gary Lawton made a judgment, a conclusion, a determination, that he would listen to me if I asked to speak with him. He looked at my life, and decided I'm worth listening to, but you looked at my life and came to a different conclusion. It's your opinion that regardless of past promises you'll have nothing to do with me. This isn't judgment? Webster's dictionary says a judgment is an opinion or estimate, the ability to come to opinions, criticism, decisions about things. Was it your opinion that you would not be in touch with me? And where does correction fit in? Let me tell you. It is also your judgment that I require correction. This isn't common sense? I think I'm so smart? I'm now 32. Is it good, moral to use correction as leverage against a son of my age, of any age? Isn't this what you've been doing by denying my need to be with the family, by punishing me until my behavior is favorable to you? Your actions make no sense for a number of reasons. You said I made no effort to be with the family, right? Which is like saying I didn't want to be with the family, another statement you've made many times. So how can denying me what I don't want, force me to behave favorably to you? Take a long thought about this, it makes obvious the fact that something is wrong with the way you've been trying to correct me. If you pursued some type of counseling or discussion about this behavior years ago, I wouldn't need to address it. Anyway, correction, judgment or however you label it, I'm 32 years old and no longer live in your house. I have my own life and it's absurd to think you can correct me, that David, Pam, Paul, and Debbie can correct me by choosing to stay away from me as well, and that such a decision has nothing to do with judgment. Look, if you must insist it is about correction, remember it hasn't worked. It's time to try something different?

Next, I am reading in your letter about how you stayed home, how you felt it important to be with family. The trailer you bought, the love there was in the home. I believe and remember that. I think it was smart. Then you began telling me how hard life was for Dad when he was young. I can't imagine going through some of the things he did. It's terrible. Having become very close to and marrying him you must have felt a lot of his pain. And you must have been proud of him for offering more to the rest of the family. This helps me to understand a lot of what confused me about the past. When asking you why Dad did what was clearly wrong, you often answered by telling me how hard things were for him as a child. You told me about many good things he did as proof he cared and meant no harm. It's easier to see now and takes away some of the pain. But back then, when it was all happening your excuses for him only added to my confusion. Dad was also my Pastor, someone who counseled hundreds of lives. Many of his messages were clear in both arenas, like the one he made when I was very young, that the worst thing a man could be was a liar. He also made clear it was something he never wanted me to forget. I never did. Remember the day he beat me for lying? You saw him do it, and knew he was out of control, hitting me in rage, swinging as hard as he could, even hurting himself trying to cause more pain than he was physically able to. Remember the look on his face? Like a lion he showed his rage by flashing his teeth and roaring. Then he cornered me behind a table and lunged over it to attack me. I compare his behavior to an animal because we both know he was out of control, my father and pastor, the man who was supposed to offer the guidance I needed to live a happy life. I thought my lessons were supposed to be learned through an expression of love and understanding. But there was never even a discussion about what happened that day, only a periodic mentioning of money I owed to repair the table Dad broke when jumping on it to attack me. Was this how he would prevent me from lying again about skipping school? Would it keep me from skipping again? How can I forget the experience? Cuts covering me from neck to toe, from the switch he beat me with. Knowing his act was premeditated made me feel even worse. You knew that earlier that day he went into the yard to find a stick to beat me with. Like he said before beating me, he wanted to find just the right one, a "flexible green one that wouldn't break when striking me." Well, he found it, shaved the bark off of it and sanded it to a smooth surface. He did really good, because of the dozens of times he hit me, the stick never broke. In fact, the only reason he stopped beating me was because it shredded to pieces. Did you know he was going to do this to me? Why didn't you try to stop him? The only reason my face wasn't hit was because my arms protecting it. What would people have said if I couldn't protect my face? I hid most of the other parts of my body that would have caused you complications if they were seen. And I never slept that evening, the cuts made it impossible to lay down. I sat up all night and thought about what had happened. Do you remember the day Dad went to school to talk with the principal about why I skipped? I wore long pants and a shirt with a collar that was buttoned up to my chin, there were many marks I tried to hide. People in my school asked about the cuts I couldn't cover, like the ones they saw in gym class. I was the liar I'm accused of being, and made-up stories to avoid the attention. But when in the principal's office, a gap in my sleeve exposed a bruise I wouldn't need to lie about. My principal saw it and asked me what happened. He looked concerned. Dad moved quickly, getting his attention before I had the chance to respond, then told the principal it came from falling off of my bike. I couldn't have lied any better. None of this is news to you, I tried many times to talk with you about it. I wanted to know why Dad lied about it, and why I was beaten for doing the same as him. But you offered no explanation, only told me how much he cared for me. Was my father trying to teach me that it's OK to lie if it's to protect yourself? Was this something only I didn't understand? No one else ever struggled over the contradictions. Whenever my father, my pastor was caught in a lie, it was covered up. Was that because you and others understood he tried to protect himself and others he loved? Is this the exception, the time it's OK to lie? Can you see how this might have confused me? You also asked me to have compassion for Dad, you said he didn't know how to deal with many of these issues because of abuse he experienced as a child. This confused me all the more. Didn't his occupation require these skills? Didn't he advise many people how to handle this kind of situation? I sat at the same dinner table in which many similar problems he was consulting families through were discussed. I would have thought that because of who my father was he couldn't have had the inability you expressed. And if he did, what business did he have counseling all those lives? This is not news to you, and is what I asked you as a teenager many years ago. The questions were never answered back then, will your response be the same today? We all have pain in our lives that makes situations difficult to deal with. But should we do something about the pain or continue to use it as an excuse? Will my kids be told I meant well, but be mistreated because of my abuse as a child? You've said at times I believe you hate me. But you're wrong, I never felt this way. I've always felt the wrong being done was more about your confusion than hate. And even if I thought you hated me, I'd never tell my kids my lack of love for them was a result of my abuse as a child, because I was never loved.

"This is what it all boils down to. You can't stand what our faith is." Come on ma, what is this? A big part of what I believe in was learned from your faith. I have friends from many different religions and beliefs that remain part of my life because of certain values they all have in common. It's their values, not their religion or faith that concern me. Their religion is personal, none of my business unless they want to discuss it with me. If their values are similar to mine, and come from a belief in a God I never heard of, that's OK with me. Trying to force them to believe in anything different would only be perceived as an attack against their source of happiness, an attack against what they feel offers the strength to carry them through life's difficult moments. Is a good teacher more concerned that his student learns the lesson, or that he gets the credit for teaching it? Isn't love about the same thing? Wanting the best for someone without expecting anything in return? I'm not trying to convince you, and wouldn't try to convince anyone that what I say is right. Understand how I feel, know that I have no problem with your faith. It's more likely you think I can't stand your faith because it's at the center of your lives, and there is conflict between our lives.

"Well you are proof that there is a God because the bible tells me that in the last days children will be disobedient to their parents." Disobedience? Do you think the problem lies with disobedience? Have any of my words caused you to consider looking somewhere new? Does it have to be exclusively about what's wrong with me? I've been telling you about many of my faults, not only the ones you felt necessary to point out. Do you think you may have some faults of your own? You appear to feel I was wrong about everything in my letter. Or maybe you just didn't see any importance in discussing anything other than what I've done wrong? Are you still convinced the problems lie completely within my disobedience, my pride, my arrogance, my disrespect, my anger, my hate? "You reek with much pride." You knew me as a kid, often I tried to prove myself, to make everyone think I was the best, the smartest, the toughest etc. Isn't that what kids do as they grow up? Isn't it a part of growing up? It's really an act of insecurity, isn't it? Why would I need to prove to everyone I was so great if I was so sure I was? You see no compassion for this obvious flaw in a child? Isn't it common for this type of behavior to continue in a youth past his late teens? Some people have passive personalities, some have very aggressive ones, don't you agree? Are either wrong? Do different personalities respond favorably to the same type of treatment, or do they need to be treated differently? Was I treated the same as my brothers and sisters as your letter says I was? Or maybe you were referring to being treated with the same love and care? "Humble yourself which you have never done in your life and ask the Lord for humility, because you reek with much pride." Do you think the way you have presented this character flaw will help make me more receptive to change? Or are you writing as the word reek seems to imply, with feelings of anger.

"You are very well experienced in knowing how to kick the ones that love you in the face." What I've been writing about needed to be discussed in conversation. Since you refuse to talk, I thought spending some time going into detail in a letter would offer some of the insight we both need. Throughout this letter I've explained why I've blown up and explained some things I feel to be wrong. I have always thought we've needed to understand what has happened and why before we could ever have any real forgiveness for each other. Something was always with me, telling me that the kind of attempts you and Dad made to resolve conflict would never work. I am not referring only to our conflict, but the way conflict was treated with many others. It was that feeling that compelled me to talk with Dad about your deteriorating relationship with your parents, a similar problem existing before my days with you ended. I told my father his solutions were Band-Aids on open wounds, that flowers delivered to grandma and agreements made through quick discussions only delayed the catastrophe. Is this the arrogance you saw in me? Was this the behavior that made you think I'm a know-it-all? My concern for your relationship with your parents is what ended our relationship. Do you remember Dad telling me I was not allowed to discuss family matters with you, or my brothers or sisters? Why did I have to be kept quiet? My need to talk to Dad, and what I had to say to him was disrespect in your eyes. I remember what he said to you about our conversations. Like the day in the principal's office when he changed the facts to keep himself from looking bad. "To alter for one's own purpose." This is what Dad did so often. It's not a quote from your letter, it's a quote from Webster's dictionary, it follows the word manipulation.

Maybe now after reading this letter you have a better idea of who I am? Is there anything you see differently?

I believe a lot of what Dad says is true, like his inference to lying being a terribly destructive thing. Do you know why lying was such an important issue with him? "Of course you will deny this because you have had and are living in lies for so long that you really believe your lies." Let me go back to the day in the principal's office. We know the facts, right? Dad lied, and neither of you would discuss it with me. Did the two of you ever even consider talking with me about it? There never was a discussion because there was a problem, a dilemma. Dads' treatment of me was wrong, everyone knew that. But Dad needed a way out. He didn't want to face the possible consequences for doing what he knew was wrong. A difficult choice had to be made, but would it be a choice between right and wrong? What if people in the church found out he beat me? What would they say? What if the principal informed the authorities that I was abused, what would they do? To lie to the principal would save Dad from many complications. But what of other difficulties they would cause, like with the lessons of honesty he tried to teach me? Was it through his example that he wanted me to learn, or did he feel he could beat it into me, that "punishing" me when I lied was enough? Is this the same treatment you continue with me today? You refuse to share your lives with me until I see things as you like. You interfere with the truth, and turn it into something that you feel will serve you. You think your actions prevent unwanted change, but they hinder the change you really need. Isn't this the very reason why Dad felt it so important to never lie? Is the conflict between us, the conflict between you and your parents, the conflict between you, Dad, old friends and cousins, between you and your sister, Dad and his brothers and sisters, between my brothers and sisters and myself, is all this conflict the price, the result of manipulating the truth into what one person wants to preserve? Is it more realistic that this characteristic is what needs review, that it's what should be discussed and dealt with in our search for a solution, that's deserving of the attention you've given to my disobedience? Isn't this what the common denominator really is?

"When you point the finger at us three always comes back to you." Were you pointing your finger at me when you said, "you have had and are living in lies for so long that you really believe your lies"?

"How about searching for truth and finding out what life is all about." Haven't you been watching me do this since I was a young teen? Isn't it why I was asking and continue to ask so many questions? It didn't keep us together. You wanted a son who could follow his parents lead without questioning their moral intent. Maybe you found this in my brothers, but it was never in me. What I was had caused you great troubles, and I understand why I had to be manipulated out of your lives.

As damaging to me as your rejection was the false impression of me that you left with many people, especially my brothers and sisters. Paul appeared to be the least judgmental, and the most unsure of all that happened. He didn't appear as confident of your conclusions. He is no longer a child, and I understand is attending college. I've often thought of writing to him but never knew how I could reach him. I am asking you to give this letter to him. I am asking you to allow him the opportunity to decide for himself what it is that I am. To deny him this opportunity is to deny him his rights as an individual. Refusing my request would be your attempt to control his perception, a denial of his right to choose. To restrict this information from him is to manipulate him into seeing things as you desire. It would be an act of censorship. Many countries use similar methods to control the thoughts of their people. Does your church enjoy the right to practice its beliefs without the interference of the state? Maybe you believe in this right only when it has something to offer you? Should you ever want me to give a letter, a tape, or any form of information to a family member, friend or other you may demand that I do so. I have no right to withhold information that I may feel is unfavorable to me. Regardless, I will eventually find out if you've done what I request. And if Paul hasn't received my letters he eventually will and will also know that you refused to give them to him. I am asking you to give him a copy of this letter, as well as copies of all papers I am sending you. I refer to my poems, my October letter to you, this letter to you, and I am asking you to offer him your letter to me. Since your letter is not my writing, I cannot insist that it be given to him.

Paul; I don't expect you to believe anything in this letter. But if you haven't found answers to questions you may have, if you may not even know what some of these questions are, maybe you should consider looking at things in a different way. Is it wrong to have questions? Is it wrong to want answers? Life should have taught you by now that information is not a bad thing. In fact, that information is necessary to have answers. As lost as you may feel I am, why don't you look at who I am. If you can find out more about me, maybe you can help me understand why I am no longer in touch with you? You do care about me, don't you? Maybe we can help each other? My letters contain thousands of words, and they discuss many topics. You may find them to be confusing, unbelievable, manipulative, insightful, hateful, I could never guess. But why don't you get a second or third opinion? What's wrong with asking for a little bit of help? And where would you look for this help if you wanted it? Would you ask for it from someone who is involved in the same problems? Don't you think it may make good sense to get it from someone who is not involved? A neutral party? Someone whose interpretation won't be affected by their involvement or maybe even religious convictions? You go to a school where there are departments dealing with human relations. How about asking a teacher, a counselor to read my writings and offer their opinions? Then maybe you can let me know what you think? You could write to me?

Mom, I'm not asking to be part of your life or for you to make any changes. I don't even feel a need to convince anyone that either of the two are needed. I am not looking for an apology, or for you or Dad to say I am not a disobedient son. I write to remind you that a truth does exist and was once with you. And that you always have the choice to accept it for what it is.

Dan

I didn't receive a response from my mother. If she did write one, it never found its way to me. However, my letter did make its way to my brother, Paul. And, lo and behold, he chose to respond. I replied swiftly.

MY LETTER TO PAUL

July 6, 1994.

Paul,

There once lived a man named Socrates. During his life, it was thought by many no man living was wiser. In fact, at some time approaching 400 BC, Socrates decided to put this claim to a test. You may have found this man to be even stranger than I. His behavior had complicated his life greatly. He suffered much, in fact was eventually sentenced to death. What fascinates me so much about this man is that he could have avoided his death, but chose not to. He was charged with speaking against the gods, and with corrupting the youth of Athens. Actually, these were the charges that were made public. The real charges were unmentionable because the government was afraid their mention would provoke the hatred developed within Athens during a past war. Simply said, discussions concerning war crimes were banned. After the war Socrates was accused of attempting to influence the youth of Athens to revolt against the newly developed democracy. He was begged by friends to propose a small fine, to admit his wrong doing. Apparently, it was never the intention of the government to execute him, but to make him admit to wrong doings. But to pay a fine no matter how trivial would be to Socrates an admittance of guilt. When his friends again begged him, the next time to arrange his escape, he argued the act would be legally and morally wrong, since every citizen of a state has entered into a social contract to obey its laws. As I mentioned it was said, during his trial to a jury, that no man of the land was wiser than Socrates. I can only assume that the statement was made to show the jurors that Socrates was of sound mind, responsible and liable for his actions. Socrates told the jurors he wanted to test the statement to prove that it was false. So he began his test. He first went to the statesmen, and found that those whose reputation for wisdom was the very highest were in fact the most lacking in wisdom. He said he knew he was wiser than the statesman, because at least he knew that he knew nothing. Then he went on to the poets, to see if they were not wiser than him. He found that the poets created their poetry not by wisdom but by inspiration, like prophets who say many fine things but understanding nothing of what they say. Yet the poets thought that they were the wisest of men in all other matters, because of their poetry. Then he went to the craftsmen, and did find that they knew of many fine things that he did not know, like how to build ships or to make shoes. But like the poets, they believed themselves to be wise in matters of the greatest importance because of the skill that they had in their own craft. Socrates saw this to diminish the real knowledge they had. Socrates then said to the court that he concluded after discovering wisdom cannot be found among the statesmen, the poets, or the craftsmen, that what the gentleman really meant was not that he was wise, but that he at least knew he really knew nothing. "The only true wisdom consists in knowing that you know nothing."

I am also often reluctant to do what others say I should. When you knew me, I was pressured to claim being a born again Christian. You will probably disagree, saying I was given a choice and never forced to believe in your faith. But that's really not so. It was made clear I would not be allowed a normal life with you unless I conformed. Much of what I wrote in my past letters given to you explains this. I had many unanswered questions, and I saw much the leadership did that contradicted the beliefs I was supposed to accept. I was able to understand the explanation that people fail, and that my eyes should be on the Lord. But when I found that man (more specifically the leadership of the church) showed interest in burying the problems I saw, I vowed to be critical of their conclusions. I was once told that God lives within us. It was there I knew it wrong to accept the many unquestionable teachings I experienced. To you, all I needed to do was say I was a born again Christian and live the appropriate lifestyle. A simple godly thing required to have an eternal life with the Lord and harmony within the family. You've shown yourself unable to understand my choice. Because your interpretation of the Bible allows you exclusive rights to heaven, you are threatened by anyone who doesn't embrace your beliefs. As your letter says you see in Black and White. You are limited to simplistic thinking, only able to consider solutions to the surface of the issues brought to your attention. It is below the surface where clues lie in a variety of shades that offer the realistic perception you should desire. Here is where the true reasons lie that show you unable to continue with me and other family members. The idea of "clashing spirits" is nothing more than a simplistic answer to the surface of deeper problems you appear unwilling or unable to comprehend. Your type of response comes from scripture quoted to support your desires, not from your desire to understand scripture. It is also the reason you offered no answers to my many questions. Like questions concerning an elder. If this spiritual clash exists with me, surely it would be felt in the presence of a child molester. Not only did our family "receive his spirit," our family also allowed him to preach in a church during the same many months he was molesting his children. Clearly this "clashing spirit" you speak of has more to do with your need to draw lines and see in black and white. You've forgotten how to look within yourself to test the conclusions of your theology. If one thinks only in terms of black and white, the saved and the sinners, the good or the bad, he has found a convenient way to avoid dealing with information that may change his beliefs. Should you treat me any differently than a sinner, you would have to question the black and white rules that you live by. My experience with our family is that it will choose comfort over truth, and it will be more comfortable for you to continue as you have than to question the many years of your damaging behavior.

The Lord gave us all a mind for a good reason. It is good to reason. Surely, we should use this gift to screen information we are given, to determine if what we are told should be accepted or reconsidered. Talk of clashing spirits that you say is keeping us apart may not have been your idea, but you've accepted it and encourage others to follow suit. Those of your faith without reason will not question your beliefs and be easily accepted by your group. Others who reason will question, and may face some of the consequences I have experienced should they continue such unacceptable behavior. Hopefully, those outside of your faith exposed to your actions will be wise enough to know your shortcomings are your own, and not a reflection on Christianity. From what I read I'm sure you'd feel badly if your behavior has turned people off to the idea of becoming a Christian.

When at the Church I looked to see the good in others saying they were born again Christians, to determine if it was for me. But I saw trouble instead, much I didn't understand that kept me from joining your faith. Our family was unable to handle the simpler, more tangible issues, yet I was expected to accept our parent's conclusions to complex problems. I contemplated the difficulties between myself and Dad, and between many others. I believed much could have been resolved through interest in truth and understanding. The title to our father's radio ministry was "The Truth Broadcast," but where was the pursuit of truth? To become synonymous with the word was considered a worthy goal, yet matters of the greatest importance showed no regard for it. I consider them "tangible" issues because the facts and details were there for our review. And though it was obvious our family wasn't capable of handling the "tangible" issues, I was expected to agree with conclusions to the more complicated situations. Yes, like you I wanted to know who God was, but I didn't want to take my family's word for it. And when I believed things were complicated and confusing, I felt it honest and unworthy of criticism to confess my ignorance. Was I so wrong for not having the answers the rest of you claimed? Would you consider me "saved" if I ignored my feelings and did what I was expected to do? Would you treat me better for being dishonest to myself? How can my inability to understand be interpreted as my choice for Hell? There isn't an instinct within you that disagrees with your treatment of me? You refuse to accept that there's nothing to fear from me, and base your fear on spiritual conflict. Consider the many years of our father's relationship with Uncle Gary, I suppose they struggled through spiritual conflict while enjoying each other's company?

If you think their eventual departure was due to spiritual conflict, you must also think your friendships with Mannie, Nicole, Jeremy, James, Tony, Lori, and others dissolved for that very reason. Relationships are more complicated than you make them appear. If you feel they end because of "clashing spirits" you've denied yourself the growth they offer. The relationship between our father and Gary may have started out of an obligation to a sister-in-law, but continued because they enjoyed each other's company. It makes no sense to explain the end of their relationship with your generalization. I could go on for hours with stories of common sense, but have said enough for you to understand? Without offering a reason you expect me to believe that a "spiritual conflict" exists, the excuse that is nothing more than camouflage to your wrongful behavior. Like our father you're using spiritualism to cover-up wrongful doings, as you say I'm a sinner to avoid conversation with me, to prevent yourselves from being exposed. You've embraced the behavior of our father, and like him you hide from reality. Both of you have excluded reason from your lives, and have the right to do so. But remember your decisions are just that, they are unreasonable.

Must we go on like old men, debating the meaning of life and spiritual this and that's? Can't we talk about the simpler things within our lives? Are you sure you're wiser than when you were a child? You didn't live with such restrictions back then. You will claim responsibility for your own actions? You're the one who accepted the rules you live by. "There are two kinds of spirits, one which is good, and the other that is bad." As you say, "black and white." And since yours is good, mine must be bad. We'd have never understood this as kids, we were smarter back then. If only Socrates possessed the knowledge you claim to have. He never claimed a religious life, and according to your beliefs is living in the hell you say I'm headed for. His interest appeared to be in truth and morality. He felt the improvement or the tendency of the soul, the care for wisdom and truth was the highest good. Isn't this a quality of the light you say you follow? But the black and white of your beliefs show this not possible. "One cannot follow two masters, cannot have qualities of both the light and the darkness." Socrates believed in good without feeling it important to express a connection to God. And many others born after Christ believed in the same good, the same qualities of the light without claiming to be a Christian. To protect your beliefs, you assume they were not saved and on a road to destruction. Imagine if somehow you were in contact with someone like Socrates. You would eventually see him as a follower of darkness to keep order in your life, to protect your beliefs. Isn't this the behavior that put Christ on the cross? You would strike out against him, as you strike against all you cannot understand with words that infer your wisdom and peaceful interests. It's a behavior that keeps on repeating in history. Years ago, many people in Salem Massachusetts were put to death because they were different, because of the community's ignorance. Like those in Salem, you hide from or try to destroy what threatens your beliefs. In Salem those feared were called witches, your group calls them sinners with clashing spirits.

You've told me it's bad to look back at the past, that I should learn to let go and move on with my life. I've heard this before. I realize the world doesn't revolve around me and my concerns. Common sense should tell you I have a life outside this conflict and don't dwell on it all the time. Many years have passed, and the two or three letters you have from me aren't excessive. The poems you have were written four years ago, over a period of several nights. Writing them helped me immensely, allowing me to put my experiences into perspective. I see nothing excessive here. Doesn't the Bible teach lessons through a constant review of the past? Shouldn't this be reason enough to consider the value of such a review? Maybe we're both at fault for not looking into the past enough. Why does your school teach classes in History? Doesn't looking at the past offer explanations to the present? Doesn't understanding how we got where we are help us to get to where we want to be? Isn't this why we study the Bible? Isn't this part of the reason it was written?

I carefully wrote my letter to Mom to have her understand my intentions. You quoted me, "Even if my conclusions are completely wrong it must be obvious to you that I have been taking a good look at myself. And if my determinations of my behavior are wrong, I'd appreciate your opinion as to what would be right. Does it occur to you that since I am looking so closely at myself there must be some motive, some improvement or benefit I seek?." Your response was "So I see someone who lives in doubt and fear that what he's been doing all along has been in vain. Since you're not a Christian the Bible says you are a seed of Satan . . .." There are a few things I would like to say about this. Firstly, It's my goal to always seek to improve myself, to change for the better. Yet I hope that no matter how sure I am of myself, I will always be able to consider another point of view. You think this shows doubt and fear, but doesn't it take someone secure in his own beliefs to consider the beliefs of another? Wouldn't it be easier to help a sinner by understanding who he is? Maybe there's something to learn from others? I'm not a Christian, and have a relationship with Satan? You insult me greatly, yet will refuse to take responsibility for what you say. You've told me you're man enough to take responsibility for your own actions, but are you sure? You won't say that the Bible says I'm associated with Satan? You told me in your letter it was a man who shot people in a train that needed to take responsibility for his actions, you didn't put the blame on his gun. Isn't this what you're doing when you make the bible responsible for your conclusions? Which reminds me, how is it you can you compare the crime of a murderer with the blow up I had at the house? If I was wrong as I admitted, shouldn't my punishment fit the degree of my crime? Did I deserve a life sentence from the family? Is this what you mean by taking responsibility for what I do, that I should accept the consequences no matter how severe? Did Dad ever blow up with you, David, Debbie, Pam, or Mom? Would he be deserving of the same punishment? I didn't murder anyone. You spoke to me of Dad, "the Lord called him—as imperfect as he was. He just obeyed the call. Moses, Abraham, David made worse mistakes—did you know that?" But didn't God make these people face their wrong doings? When their wrong was done against a person, weren't they to go to the individual and ask for forgiveness? You wrote, "And he paid the ultimate price—The loss of his older son. You don't think he regrets that, But it's not all Dad's fault. And he did not stop after his mistake. We all have to move forward—and Dad did." Did life with me have to end? Was this punishment appropriate for what you now say was Dad's crime? Are you certain that handling this manner in a biblical fashion will not help our relationship? You're certain the consequences aren't reversible? What do you mean "We all have to move forward—and Dad did." He either continues in the same mistakes, or covers them up. We both know he doesn't correct them. Why does he bury what he did to me? Should I assume he did any different when he refuses to speak with me? You say he recognizes his wrong? Shouldn't he be telling me about it? Don't you know he has the power to change what we have between us? Isn't it biblical to approach the ones you've wronged for forgiveness? No matter how wrong I may have been, being that he is the born again Christian, wouldn't you expect him to approach me and confess his wrong? Shouldn't this be important to him for many reasons, wouldn't he want to be a good example so I may join your faith? Isn't this what love is really about, putting others before yourself? Do you believe our father lives in darkness because he doesn't practice what he teaches? Does your spirit clash with his as well? You say that I'm the sinner, and wouldn't expect me to approach our father, but wouldn't you expect him to approach me? Especially now, since you agree about some of the wrong he has done? You say he's paid the price, the loss of his oldest son. But are you sure the price is for his lies and not for his unwillingness to make things right?

I don't have all the answers you say you have, but there are some matters I'm sure of. I hope to never shut people out of my life for not having answers to difficult questions, especially concerning one's faith. Another; I don't know if I could forgive myself for choosing to believe in something for the reward of a heaven or fear of a hell. Clearly, it's only I who knows what my feelings for the family have been. I've never accused you of a life in the evils of darkness. Regardless of what you've said about me, your writing shows your interest in good. I know so little about you. Some of my questions for you are the same I asked of Mom. Are you certain I'm a follower of the evil you've described? This is what you see in my letters? It's not from discussions we've had. You said when knowing me you were young and impressionable, and now you're wiser and sure of yourself? Your talk reminds me of Socrates' reference to the statesman and poets. At least I'm wise enough to know of my ignorance. "I'm just trying my strategy at making you to take that one, single most important move." You made an analogy with chess. Is your strategy sound, are you sure you have the right objective and know how the pieces move? You seem to admire my skill so maybe you'll take my advice. Stop trying to establish the premise of my inconsistency and confusion, even if it were possible an exposure of such faults would offer you little advantage. You failed to recognize the validity within my claims, and don't realize it is there where the important battles are won, through understanding the perceptions of the other. I've been exposed to your beliefs for years, and know them well. But what do you know of mine? Much time has been wasted trying to expose the wrongs of my perceptions, without your ability to even recognize them. This is the barrier that handicaps your play. Spend less time digging for faults, and more time trying to understand me. Only then will you be qualified to make a decision of rejection or acceptance. Should my views be rejected, it is within the sound foundation of such a decision that information will be found to offer the help I need. If you continue quoting scripture, be careful not to use them to justify what you do. Your use of scripture says much about you, but not what you try to say. Many people quote scripture to justify their actions, but the only value is the desire their quotes reveal. As hard as it may seem, you need to be neutral to understand my position before measuring information against your beliefs. This may prove to be too difficult a task.

Do you have any idea why I've felt it important to be understood? If you knew me, you'd know you have no reason to be separated from me. The fact I think differently isn't a reason to keep me out of your life. Because I'm different I haven't been allowed the same opportunities you and others in my family enjoy. But to everything there is a season, a day of a new horizon precedes you that will bring a better understanding of people in your life. You'll feel a deep remorse for harm you've unknowingly caused, and be eager to treat me as the brother and friend I was meant to be. Today you say forget the past, but tomorrow you'll be looking back to remember the stagnation that consumed your life. Awed by what was once so easily accepted without merit, you'll never forget, your memory will become deep-rooted, the message to never be so blatantly misled again. Many of your days will be spent struggling to understand how you were easily fooled as you learn that new experiences have no resemblance to old opinions. Scripture will most likely remain important, but will be used differently. And I will be the one who reminds you to be patient with others as blind as you once were. Call this prophecy, heresy, blasphemy, Satanism, confusion, hatred, jealousy, evil spirited, unfounded, whatever you like. But it's nothing more than a step sincerity will force you to take up the ladder of your spiritual growth.

I've recently read a book called "Blind Faith" written by Kay Marie Portfield. For the most part, it discusses negative effects that dysfunctional religious groups have on its members. While reading the book I was surprised to learn of situations similar to our own. Because they exemplify our experience, I'm offering them to you and hope you will read them to better understand what has happened. Reference is made to cults and other extreme groups in her book, please don't let this prevent you from recognizing qualities that all dysfunctional groups, religions or families have in common. I read her story after writing my last letter to you, making the similarity between the book and my letter a coincidence. As you read the pages I copied for you, know I ask you not to read them as truth, but as a perception for consider-ation. Be as objective as you can while reading the pages. Much is strikingly similar, often identical to experiences that led to our separation. I've wanted to discuss our past for many years and am grateful you wrote to me. I hope after reading these pages you will continue to respond by offering your opinion. It's all I've ever asked from anyone.

Sincerely,
Dan

Chapter Thirty-Six

MOVING TO BAL HARBOUR

After writing to Paul, all that followed was silence. No more letters came, not from him, my mother, or anyone else. So, I redirected my attention to my life in Florida, immersing myself in my work. By 1996, a distinct rhythm had formed. My business partnership with Ricardo, the subcontractor with whom I eventually worked exclusively in the floor restoration industry, was thriving. This success allowed for visits to my grandparents and aunt and uncle whenever my schedule permitted. When they moved from Syracuse to Tennessee, I prioritized driving up to see them, cherishing our moments together.

With Claudia's enduring presence in my life and her unmistakable love for the ocean, I was inspired to search for a new home. When she visited, she often escaped to the beaches and cafés of Miami while I was absorbed in my work. I could picture her waking up to the soothing sound of waves at dawn, the sun's first rays painting the horizon, and her, moments later, taking a relaxed walk on the sand, coffee in hand. In time I stumbled upon the perfect spot: a waterfront high-rise in Bal Harbour. Although I appreciated the beach, I soon discovered it held a different significance for me. Over my decade-long stay there, despite the breathtaking ocean view, I usually kept my blinds drawn, my interactions with the beach limited to early morning jogs along the five-mile trail beside it.

On one occasion during one of Claudia's three-month visits with me in Bal Harbour, we embarked on a road trip to Tennessee. With bags packed and playlists queued, we set out, our excitement at reaching our destination surging as the miles dwindled. Claudia was about to meet my family, but among them, it was the anticipated meeting with my grandmother that had her stomach in knots.

Adopted as a child by a couple whose age now mirrored that of my grandmother, Claudia's past experiences painted an image of such women in a motherly role as stern and distant. She braced herself, expecting a similar aura from my grandmother. But when the moment came, she found my grandmother to be incredibly warm-hearted and caring. Even today, my grandmother having passed, Claudia occasionally reminisces about her with affectionate regard.

With Claudia having grown up amidst opulence, I hadn't realized the nuanced scars it left. Being whisked away by a nanny at the slightest sign of distress left its mark. Through Claudia's insights, I saw the dual-edged sword of privilege: the allure of luxury juxtaposed with the emotional voids it sometimes camouflaged. It's peculiar how our past, like a shadow, often trails behind, influencing our run toward, or flight from, familiar terrains.

Every Christmas and Thanksgiving, whenever my work schedule permitted, as children eagerly awaited the unwrapping of gifts and the scent of roasted turkey permeated homes, I'd journey to visit my grandparents, aunt, and uncle. The laughter and warmth of these reunions were always treasured, but they invariably evoked the painful reminder of those missing from our gathering: my siblings and parents. Each vacant seat at the dinner table brought back memories of failed attempts to bridge our widening divide. As the years continued their relentless march, despite every twinge of rejection, my hope—steadfast and luminous—refused to waver.

The summer of 1997 dawned, marking many years since I'd had a meaningful conversation with my parents or siblings. My every attempt, every heartfelt letter, seemed to have vanished into an abyss of misconception and judgments. However, as the adage goes, "Necessity is the mother of invention," and soon, a novel, albeit unconventional, idea began to shimmer on the horizon of my thoughts.

My words, it seemed, fell on deaf ears, overshadowed by their perception of me as a "sinner." So, why not reach out with a voice they might respect? An idea took shape: to connect with pastors in Syracuse, specifically those whose faith aligned with my family's, such as the Baptists. My father, ever the religious skeptic, would likely dismiss words from a Catholic priest. But what if a symphony of voices, united in faith and doctrine, reached out to him? Would that chorus be strong enough to pierce years of silence?

With renewed purpose, I reached out to these shepherds of the faith, laying bare my story and my quandary. As the weeks passed, a group of pastors from various parts of Syracuse, touched by my narrative, joined forces. Following discussions about my family's complex dynamics, they united in their efforts, aiming to be the peacemakers, helping to bridge my family's long-standing rift. Here is a letter they wrote to my father.

June, 1997

Pastor Bob Mazur
Church of the Living Word
5963 Court Street Road
Syracuse, New York 13206

Dear Pastor Mazur,
Recently we received an email letter from you son Dan who lives in Florida. According to his letter, he desires to be reconciled to his family, but feels that it is impossible, since you have not talked to him for the past fifteen years. He also said that you no longer talk to or see your in-laws or other family members. Dan asked area Pastors for help in bringing reconciliation since he seems unable to do so.
Since we are only hearing his side of the story, we the pastors of the steering committee of the Central York Churches for Revival would like to set up a meeting with you at your earliest convenience to hear from you about your perspective on this situation. As fellow area pastors, who also have families, may be able to give you some counsel to help in this situation. Scripture affirms, "... in the multitude of counselors there is safety."

In Christ,
Brent Culver
Chairman of Central New York Churches for Revival

A month later I returned from work and headed straight to my mailbox. Sifting through the predictable flood of credit card offers and auto service discounts, a singular letter stood out—it bore the insignia of the Syracuse Pastors. Anxious and unable to wait, I found a comfortable spot and opened the envelope, careful not to damage the contents. A lone white sheet of paper greeted me, adorned with a single paragraph. It was so fitting given the brief responses typical of my lifelong quest. In mere moments I would learn whether my efforts had finally paid off, or if another opportunity had eluded my grasp.

July, 1997

Dear Dan,

Hello. I received your email but was unable to answer as we were away for 2 weeks on vacation. I apologize for the delay. On behalf of the Pastor's in CNY Churches for Revival, I wanted to let you know that I Did make contact with your father. We spoke briefly and we offered to meet with him to discuss some of your concerns and help in any way possible. He was not agreeable to meeting so we were unable to pursue it further. I do still believe that it would be helpful for us to meet with him and we will continue to pray about the situation and are available to help if we can. We pray that you would be aware of God's love and concern for you and your family during this time and we continue to believe God for reconciliation.

In Christ's love,
Brent C. Culver
CNY Churches for Revival

Once again my efforts bore no fruit, so I redirected my attention to the comforting diversion of my professional pursuits. Thus, my life unfolded for the remainder of the twentieth century: heartfelt visits with my grandparents, aunt, and uncle, treasured interludes with Claudia, and to fill the spaces in between, my ever-present work.

As the twilight years of the century approached, I was met with another sobering realization: my professional relationship with Ricardo in the flooring business was unraveling. He had accrued a significant debt to me and sidestepped all of my attempts to address it. In these trying times, I ventured into the burgeoning field of managed services in the computer industry, a pivot influenced by my background in the flooring business. My responsibilities in the company had, by necessity, extended to setting up and managing computers after we found external contractors unreliable. Drawing on what I had learned, I approached my contacts in the flooring business, presenting them with IT solutions. This initiative not only alleviated my immediate financial strain but also evolved into a thriving IT venture, which soon became my chief source of sustenance.

Despite the strains in my relationships with my parents, siblings, and now Ricardo, there was a silver lining. The growth of my IT enterprise, cherished moments with my family, and my intermittent yet meaningful encounters with Claudia, all bestowed a newfound equilibrium and purpose upon my life.

Months passed, each propelling me forward as I delved into the busy rhythms of business and various activities. These distractions became my refuge, providing a temporary escape from the tension surrounding my relationships with my parents and siblings.

This ephemeral period of tranquility was suddenly disrupted by a parcel from my brother-in-law, Frankie. When I opened the package, I unveiled a collection of cassette tapes, their handwritten sermon titles marked in black ink. I set them aside, intending to find the right moment to give them a listen.

The moment arrived when I finally had the opportunity to dedicate several uninterrupted hours on a Saturday to immerse myself in the sermons. As the final words lingered in my ears, an overwhelming storm of rage consumed me, and the true impact of my discovery settled in. Despite the passage of so many years since I left my family in Syracuse, my father persisted in speaking about me from the pulpit, branding me as poison, a snake. I listened in disbelief as he expressed gratitude for "faraway places like Tennessee and Florida" where my aunt, cousins, and I resided, rejoicing in the distance that shielded his flock from our alleged influence. The weight of his words struck deep, reopening old wounds that had never fully healed and reigniting the turmoil that had lain dormant within me.

I had reached my breaking point. I discovered that the pulpit had been used to discredit me over the passing years.

Its purpose, in part, was to disseminate a message about me that my father fervently advocated for my mother, siblings, his congregation, and others to embrace. Given his revered reputation, the title "man of God," and his position as pastor, he commanded immediate respect. His dynamic, and persuasive personality, combined with his unwavering dedication to delivering four sermons weekly and intensified by the isolation enforced within the school and campgrounds, made me wonder what chance I ever had of being heard amidst such formidable circumstances.

However, with the advent of the Internet and the relentless advancement in technology, emerging opportunities presented themselves, offering a unique opportunity for my voice to find an audience. Having recently delved into the realm of computers, I was well aware of the vast array of websites and knew that I could create one of my own. So, I seized the opportunity and created "The New Forum," subtitled, "Destroyed by a Cult."

In its nascent stages, the website showcased a compilation of quotations from Kay Marie Porterfield's book *Blind Faith, Recognizing and Recovering from Dysfunctional Religious Groups.* I handpicked dozens of quotes from her book, each one resonating with my own experiences and the challenges faced by my mother, my siblings, and fellow members of my father's church. Allow me to share a selection of these thought-provoking quotations.

> Believers can get so wrapped up in twisted religious systems that they lie.
>
> They loudly talk a good doctrine, while at the same time subtly nurturing dependency and suffocating independent thinking.
>
> Dysfunctional religious groups often claim to own the sole way to salvation or enlightenment. If members choose not to believe part of the creed or if they display signs of individuality, they are quickly, even forcibly, brought back into the fold or they are banished.
>
> Time commitments required for meetings may be enormous,

and demands are made to give up friendships outside the group.

The more a group isolates members from the world and the more exclusionary it is in drawing lines between its members and outsiders, the greater the potential for dysfunction. Thick boundaries and black-and-white thinking intensify group interactions. This intensity is often mistaken for spiritual energy.

Members begin to feel that they are the elect, the chosen, and voluntarily pull further away from the rest of the human race.

When individual members exercise too much critical thinking or freedom, rumors may be started about them as a way to ensure control.

Ends justify the means. Whenever a group focuses on mission instead of the spiritual needs of members, a great temptation exists to achieve the mission by any means, including lying. These practices are accepted, even though doctrine may explicitly forbid them.

Some of the doctrines may conflict with one's own deeply held sense of what is true.

We stop questioning, because without input from the world outside our group, we find it difficult to even formulate questions.

With an intent to awaken the Syracuse community to the unsettling truths chronicled on the New Forum, I took to the *Syracuse New Times*, placing a conspicuous advertisement. It showcased a portrait of my family, underscored by the stark words "Destroyed by a Cult," the website address. The response was swift. As curiosity was piqued and site visits surged, an influx of letters began landing on my desk. These included heart-wrenching accounts from former church members, detailing tales of abuse that parents and children had endured, some of them backed by documented court cases linked to the school and the church. Armed with their approval, I incorporated these raw narratives into my website. My intent? To peel back the layers of secrecy and shed light on the organization's veiled machinations.

Months melded into monotony, each day mirroring its predecessor, the air thick with a yearning for something—anything—to break the cycle. With nothing in the headlines compelling, I immersed myself in addressing my past. On my website I established a bridge to former Living Word members, fielding their questions and enriching the site with pages, documents, and evidence. I was building my case, laying out the truth with the precision of a seasoned attorney, crafting my argument, which was poised to shift public perception.

From my family in Syracuse, I received nothing but deafening silence. There was neither whisper nor word about the impact of the New Forum. Their absence was highlighted by the complete lack of phone calls, letters, or emails.

As the fall of 2001 neared and August wound down, I returned from a trip to Washington DC, where I had been visiting a friend. I shared details of my journey with several people, underscoring the beauty and spirit of our nation. In one of my emails, I included a photo caption that alluded to an unsettling feeling I had experienced in Arlington—a pervasive sense of malice, almost as if emanating from the shadows of the tombstones. At that time, I had no idea how eerily prophetic that sentiment would be, considering the tragic events of 9/11 the following month.

Twelve days after sending that email, I stood frozen on the polished marble floor of my Bal Harbour residence in Florida as my mental preparation for the day's first appointment was abruptly interrupted. It was September 11, a date destined to cast a haunting shadow on the annals of history. The lobby's typical serenity was shattered as a television, perched high on a shelf blared breaking news, ensnaring a swelling crowd of residents and visitors. Their faces portrayed a mélange of disbelief and horror, their chatter thick with shock, as they grappled with comprehending the evolving tragedy: a plane had just slammed into one of the Twin Towers.

I paused for a moment, observing and absorbing the discussions, but I did not participate. Instead, I continued toward my car, determined to embark on my scheduled journey. As I tuned in to the emerging events on the car radio, I gazed out of the window, witnessing a world that appeared different, forever altered by the weight of the moment. I made eye contact with other drivers, realizing that they, too, were engrossed in the heart-wrenching news. Little did any of us know that day would mark the beginning of a profound shift, one that would leave an indelible impact for years to come.

As if September hadn't already been eventful enough, two Fridays later, my phone interrupted my thoughts with its persistent ringing. It was Aunt MaryJane, her voice heavy with lament. "Danny, your Aunt Sue has passed away," she said, her words filled with the weight of our loss.

At the time, Aunt MaryJane and Uncle Gary were in the midst of building their new home in Columbia, Tennessee. While it was under construction, they lived in a nearby trailer. My grandparents, having recently sold their home in Syracuse, were staying with them, awaiting the home's completion.

"Danny, I don't know what to do," Aunt MaryJane said, her voice heavy with concern and the weight of responsibility. "I can't bring your grandfather to his sister's funeral."

"Don't worry," I said. "I'll take him to Syracuse."

The next morning, I set out for Tennessee, taking two connecting flights along the way. Little did I realize the taxing challenges awaiting me in the series of trips ahead!

When the time came to escort my wheelchair-bound grandfather to the airport, we mistakenly boarded the wrong plane. Although it may not have been an extraordinary mishap on its own, it complicated matters and added to the fatigue we were already experiencing. After rectifying our error and boarding the correct plane, we still had another connecting flight ahead of us before reaching Syracuse.

While in Syracuse, we stayed at the same hotel as my cousin, Timmy. He was doubly related to my grandfather, Carmen Fortino. On the one hand, Timmy's mother was my Aunt Sue, Carmen's sister. On the other, Timmy's father, Joe Ragonese, was the brother of Carmen's wife, Gertrude. Such a dual relationship in the family was truly distinctive.

At the time, Timmy resided in West Palm Beach, Florida. He played a pivotal role as one of the founders of the Living

Word Church. Alongside several other cousins, he took out a second mortgage on his home to fund the venture. I understand that this decision, among others of a similar nature, strained his relationship with his wife, Marsha. Although Timmy was once close to my mother and our family, their bond had been broken long before I became estranged from my family.

I remember a chance encounter with Timmy at the New York State Fair one year when I was a young, impressionable child, still involved with the church.

"Danny!" he called out to me, extending his arms for a warm hug. But I turned away, avoiding any interaction and depriving my cousin of the chance to engage with me. To me he embodied the adversary, someone I believed had wronged my father. My siblings, who were present with me that day, took my cue and also rebuffed his gestures of goodwill.

Despite my regrettable behavior toward him that day, I'm pleased to recall many fond memories with Timmy and his wife, Marsha, in Palm Beach County. I cherished the weekends spent in their company, frequently attending their church on Sundays during my overnight stays. Moreover, I became acquainted with some of their church friends, as we often congregated at local restaurants following the services.

Given the strained relationships—Timmy's with my parents and my own estrangement from them—it was unlikely that either of us would reach out to them while in Syracuse. Additionally, I had promised my aunt to protect my grandfather from any potentially uncomfortable encounters.

It was a Sunday morning, the day before my birthday, as I dressed in somber attire, preparing for the occasion ahead. While attending to my appearance, I couldn't help but notice my grandfather's fragility, his hands trembling as he struggled to put on his tie. Sensing his need for support, I stepped in to assist, helping him with his tie and attending to other tasks, ensuring that he looked his best for the solemn occasion. Alongside Timmy, a trusted companion on our shared journey, we embarked on a solemn pilgrimage to the hallowed grounds of the funeral home for the wake.

Upon entering the mournful venue, I took my rightful place, standing by my grandfather's side on the elevated platform. The room transformed into a kaleidoscope of mourners, the air heavy with whispered condolences and shared memories as familiar faces enveloped us. Amid the crowd, a flicker of surprise ignited as my brother David materialized, appearing like an apparition amidst the sea of mourners. My parents' absence was no surprise.

As the service drew to a close, a profound and tender moment took shape. Attendees rose from their seats, their steps guided by empathy and respect as they approached the elevated platform to extend their heartfelt sympathies to my Aunt Sue's grieving family.

Amidst the tide of mourners, my grandfather stood resolute, refusing to be seated. With every outstretched hand, he embraced the opportunity to connect with each guest, offering a warm, firm shake as a testament to his gratitude for their presence. There was a remarkable grace in the way my grandfather conducted himself, his aging hands extending consolation and compassion to those who approached.

And so, there I stood, positioned behind my grandfather, my arms enveloping him in a tender embrace, providing the support he needed as his legs faltered, rendering him unable to stand unaided. The procession of well-wishers seemed endless, a testament to their love for my aunt and for those left behind to mourn her loss.

And then it happened. Amidst the crowd, another figure materialized before me: my former girlfriend, Susan. The news of my aunt's passing had reached her ears, drawing her to the vigil. A mixture of emotions engulfed me as I beheld her presence—a blend of surprise, gratitude, and a long-overdue realization and confession.

When the final condolences had been given, I sought out Susan, yearning to express my gratitude for her support during my darkest days.

"Susan, I want you to know that I never properly thanked you for what you did. You stayed with me until I was on my feet again, and I was too messed up to notice the burden I placed on you. I'm deeply sorry for not expressing my appreciation and acknowledging your selflessness until now." As the weight of my words settled in, tears welled up in Susan's eyes.

We were about to depart, preparing to put the casket into the hearse and proceed to the graveyard, when David approached me. The words he spoke carried a particular sting, filled with unkind accusations hurled at me in that most inappropriate moment. However, I managed to look beyond his bitterness, and without a defensive retort, I stepped away from the conversation. As I continued conversing with others on our way out, my thoughts drifted back to David. I considered that his brief moment alone might have given him time to reflect on his comments. With this in mind, I approached him, extending an invitation with a simple question: "Would you like to join us at our cousin's house after the funeral?"

Remarkably, this seemingly mundane invitation blossomed into an opportunity to restore connections with my family. It had been twelve years since my last excommunication, and the possibility of rebuilding bridges emerged yet again against the backdrop of profound loss.

After the funeral at my cousin's home, David appeared at the front door. Little by little, he worked his way into conversations, mingling amongst the crowd of people, many of whom were cousins he hadn't seen or spoken with in many years. Before the gathering came to a close, David approached me once again and extended an invitation for my grandfather and me to visit his home and meet with his family—him, his wife, and their kids.

The mere thought of it triggered a flurry of thoughts and emotions within me. *Oh my goodness!* I mused. *How should I approach such a delicate situation?* After all, I had promised to protect my grandfather from any challenging or distressing situations. However, upon receiving the invitation, a sense of intuition guided me to accept it. Despite my initial uncertainty, I knew that accepting was the right course of action. While I might not have possessed the perfect words at that moment, I trusted in my ability to find the eloquence needed to explain my decision to my aunt.

And so, we embraced the opportunity and visited my brother and his family. It turned out to be the right decision. The sheer joy that illuminated my grandfather's face as he was surrounded by a circle of his great-grandchildren, my nephews and nieces, hands held and lifted toward the heavens in prayer, was so powerful to behold, justifying my acceptance of the invitation.

After spending time in Liverpool with David and his family, I drove my grandfather back to the hotel, where we rested for the night. The next day we made our way back to our respective homes. The first two flights brought us back to Tennessee, where my aunt greeted my grandfather at the airport, and the next two flights took me back to my home in Miami. This marked the beginning of another endeavor to mend and restore strained relations.

Back in Miami, I initiated communication with David via email, and we exchanged heartfelt video messages, particularly with his children, who radiated sheer delight upon hearing from me.

Against the backdrop of the September 11 tragedies, my return from Syracuse continued with a positive momentum, as the bridges of communication with my family started to strengthen. My first action was to take down my website, a gesture toward reconciliation. The renewed connection with David and his family also paved the way for reopening dialogue with my parents. Phone calls and emails began with them as well.

Not long afterward, a trip to Kiev, Ukraine, presented an opportunity to select gifts for my family in Syracuse, especially for my nephews and nieces. These gifts were meant for personal delivery during a planned visit in early 2002. The upcoming journey held significant personal meaning for me. It was the first time since moving to Florida in 1989, nearly thirteen years earlier, that I would return to Syracuse with the primary purpose of spending time with my parents and siblings.

In early March 2002, after returning home from my trip to Syracuse, my long-distance communication with my family resumed. Conversations with my father often focused on familiar subjects, particularly camera technology, such as exploring the shift from film to digital photography. However, as the days progressed, I yearned for more profound and meaningful exchanges with him. This longing culminated on March 8, 2002, when I composed a heartfelt letter to my father, seeking to share the innermost depths of my thoughts and feelings.

Despite the hurdles and unpredictable twists of fate, I persisted. At that time I was committed to my role as the IT specialist for the Holiday Inn Hotel on South Beach. In my inaugural year as a computer technician, it was the first enterprise I collaborated with. I oversaw the technology and systems infrastructure for the offices in the 253-room hotel. Securing that contract came from an introduction to the hotel's owner back in 1999, three years prior.

Miami presented a stark contrast to Syracuse, with its vibrant Latino culture and distinctive architectural styles posing both challenges and opportunities. As I delved deeper into these differences, I realized an important aspect I had overlooked when considering my move from Syracuse: the unique flooring in Miami. I encountered a variety of materials like Mexican and Spanish saltillo, terracotta, and travertine, which were new to me. These surfaces required specific maintenance, often using water and oil-based sealers. With time, exposure to the elements led these sealers to deteriorate, resulting in a lackluster finish. Upon delving into these differences, I discovered a technique that countered these effects, delivering pristine results that won significant customer acclaim. This method was not widely used, which worked to my advantage. This discovery became the bedrock of my business endeavor throughout the 1990s as I specialized in tile restoration for homes. Instead of hiring and managing a team, I decided to use other companies as subcontractors. After assessing various candidates, I chose the one that was best aligned with my standards and agreed to work with them exclusively. Thus began my nine-year relationship with Ricardo, the owner of "Perfection Industrial Services."

By the summer of 1998, our growing business expanded into the fields of installations and fabrications, establishing us as a premier installer for a large retail outfit known as the Expo Design Center. During that transformative period, I helped Ricardo modernize his paper-based business and transition it into the digital realm. We recognized the immense potential of incorporating computers to enhance efficiency and overall performance, embracing the evolving trend of adopting technology for everyday business use. This transition marked a significant technological adaptation, revolutionizing the ways of conducting business and carrying an equal, if not greater, impact than the earlier adoption of mobile phones in the early 1990s. Initially, we hired IT professionals to handle our computer needs, but we found them to be unreliable. As a result, as mentioned earlier, I took it upon myself to learn the necessary skills.

In 1999, almost a decade into our working arrangement, Ricardo found himself inundated with an excessive workload, which caused significant issues for him, the business, and me. Years earlier we had come to an agreement where I conveyed my lack of interest in any form of business ownership. My sole focus was on selling and accumulating contracts, and I found contentment in earning a commission based on the percentage of my sales, as I had unwavering confidence in my abilities. Throughout that period, my primary goal remained steadfast: to distance myself from additional responsibilities such as managing the labor force and dealing with personal matters. I wanted to concentrate my efforts exclusively on selling and maximizing my commission while entrusting Ricardo with the other facets of the business.

However, as months passed and our workload increased, I realized that despite diligently collecting payments from clients and submitting them to Ricardo, I hadn't received a single commission check in return. At its peak, Ricardo's debt to me reached $60,000, which presented a significant problem. With no savings and a growing sense of desperation, I turned to the only other skill I possessed, one that I had recently acquired. I started paying close attention to my clients' conversations regarding their computer problems. Recognizing an opportunity, I began offering my assistance, saying, "I can't guarantee a fix, but if I can help, would you be willing to offer me a few dollars?" It was crucial for me to take action, and through my sideline computer work, I managed to generate enough income to cover my expenses. In fact, I achieved so much success that when I discovered Ricardo was unable to meet payroll for his workers, I loaned him thousands of dollars to prevent them from leaving his company.

This went on for months, as I held onto the belief that Ricardo would eventually repay me. I feared that if I stopped working in the flooring business, I wouldn't be able to meet my financial obligations, including bills and rent. However, as time passed, reality revealed a different truth. It turned out that I could manage my expenses through computer work alone. So, when Ricardo's debt to me reached its peak, I reached a breaking point and decided that enough was enough.

Interestingly, when I first started working with Ricardo, I encountered some difficulties of my own and ended up owing him a sum of money. During that time I was living in Naranja Lakes, and Kyle was working alongside me in the business. Things were not going smoothly between Kyle and me during that period. As a result, we found ourselves in a situation where we owed Ricardo $10,000.

As described earlier, during the week of August 9, 1992,

a significant turn of events emerged. Kyle announced that he would be moving out and staying with his friend, Rick, in Kendall while he figured out his next steps. In the weeks leading up to that moment, Kyle had been feeling uneasy about our relationship as friends and business partners. Without engaging in any discussion for a mutually agreeable resolution, he decided to walk away from both aspects of our connection. The next day I had a lunch meeting with Ricardo, during which I filled him in on recent events. "Ricardo, I'm fully aware that I owe you ten thousand dollars," I said. "I don't have the money, and with Kyle leaving the business, he won't be assuming any responsibility for the debt. However, I want you to know that I am committed to repaying every penny. I can't provide an exact timeline, but I promise that I'll make it happen."

Much to my surprise, Ricardo didn't appear overly troubled by the revelation. Instead, he seemed appreciative of my honesty and the way I handled the situation and expressed a willingness to maintain our working relationship despite the debt.

After Hurricane Andrew, work recommenced, and money started to flow. With a steady stream of income, the moment arrived when I was finally able to repay Ricardo the $10,000 I owed him.

As fate would have it, however, in 1999 when I approached Ricardo about the $60,000 he owed me, there were no promises, no follow-up calls, and no invitations to reconcile over lunch like I had extended to him. Instead, he simply said, "Do what you have to do." Those few words pierced me, leaving behind a hollow feeling of sadness.

It was disheartening to realize that my perception of our relationship differed so markedly from his. I had considered Ricardo not just a business partner but also a friend. To discover that he did not view me in the same light was a profound disappointment. However, having met his wife and children, I believed it was best to let him navigate the challenges of supporting them without my interference.

Amid this disappointment, I chose to shift my attention to my new role at the hotel. This transition proved beneficial, providing a much-needed diversion from the developing disillusionment and the ongoing challenges arising in my family life.

Securing the Holiday Inn contract as an IT professional was an unusual and intriguing adventure. Enter Edith Anne White, the supervisor of a young woman named Karla. It was through Karla, who had hired Perfection Industrial Services to strip down the Mexican saltillo floors in her home, that I was introduced to Edith. Interestingly, it was the second time I had worked on that house, having performed the same service for a couple residing there eight years prior. Impressed with the results, Karla shared her positive experience with Edith, which led to our initial meeting. Through Edith, an agreement was reached to install travertine flooring in the lobby of her client, the Holiday Inn, on Miami's South Beach, where she was overseeing its renovation.

As our relationship evolved and upon recognizing the urgent need for an IT infrastructure overhaul at the front desk, I discussed the issue with Edith. She recommended that I meet with Clair, the hotel's owner, to present a proposal for the required upgrades. In a meeting attended by Edith and Clair, I admitted to my limited experience in this realm but conveyed my enthusiasm to embrace the challenge. To assuage any potential reservations, I proposed a payment structure contingent on the project's successful completion. After contemplating the offer, Clair consented to my terms.

From that point forward until the hotel underwent a transformation and was replaced by high-rise apartments, I assumed complete responsibility for all IT-related tasks. It was a significant undertaking, one that allowed me to further develop my skills and establish a reputation as a reliable IT specialist.

I formed a friendship with Clair, and our trio, completed by Edith, delved into a myriad of shared activities. From attending the Miami Open Tennis match in Key Biscayne with fervor to cheering on the Miami Heat during an exhilarating basketball game, we reveled in our collective experiences. Our exploration extended to the enchanting setting of the Vizcaya Museum, where we immersed ourselves in an event, and to accompanying Clair's circle of friends and family in their homes. Then, in the fall of 2001, our bonds led us to embark on a journey together: a trip to Orlando, a destination set to offer an unexpected encounter.

It was after my return from Syracuse, following my Aunt Sue's funeral, that I found myself in the company of Clair and Edith in Orlando. While we were there, Clair mentioned her interest in visiting a psychic whom she had known for several years, insisting that I should partake in a reading too. Intrigued by the idea, I readily agreed.

Several weeks later, in December, I was sitting in the living room of my Bal Harbour home, awaiting a taxi to take me to the airport for my journey to Kiev. As I sat there, the telephone rang. Expecting it to be the taxi company confirming their arrival, I answered. Instead, a mysterious voice said, "You are on a dangerous journey that you need to avoid." Startled, I asked for the caller's identity. To my astonishment, it was Susan from Orlando—the psychic to whom Clair had introduced me.

Susan elaborated, saying that my aunt wanted to thank me for taking my grandfather to visit her.

"What?" I replied. "You know my Aunt MaryJane?"

"No, your Aunt Sue," she said.

"But Aunt Sue is dead," I replied. "She passed away three months ago."

"Yes, I know," she said with calm certainty.

At the conclusion of our conversation, I felt torn, wondering if this was some cruel prank or a sincere warning advising me to forgo my trip. The timing of the message couldn't have been worse, wrapped as it was in layers of ambiguity. Its absence of clarity and thoughtfulness raised doubts about its true intent.

After much reflection, I decided to push past my apprehensions and stick to my plans. I was resolved not to succumb to fear, to overthink the enigmatic caution, or to dwell on the potential truth behind such a cryptic warning.

When my phone rang once more, this time confirming the taxi's approach, I was on my journey to Ukraine. Despite encountering a potentially troublesome situation involving an encounter with the police during my time there, I handled the trip without any major complications.

Upon my return, I approached Clair on several occasions, trying to discern any possible role she or her friend from Orlando might have played in the potential disruption of my trip. I suspected she might have shared information about my travels and Aunt Sue's passing. She fervently denied any involvement, assuring me she had no insight or link to the eerie call. I'm still plagued by doubts regarding that experience, unsure of how to piece together the perplexing events of that phone call.

Chapter Thirty-Seven

CHAOS ENSUES

A FTER RETURNING FROM AUNT SUE'S FUNERAL AND MY TRAVELS in Ukraine, the fragile nature of family bonds continued to haunt me, lingering for several months beyond my 2002 trip to Syracuse. It was in the fall of that same year that another hiatus ensued, as my communication with my siblings and parents once again ceased. Consequently, over the next few years, I diverted my attention to work and other more pleasant pursuits.

Then, five years later, on a Saturday afternoon in early 2007, my frustration reached a tipping point. While working on my laptop, I discovered that sermons from the Living Word were being uploaded online. They were available for download, a stark contrast to the days of waiting for cassette tapes in the mail. Driven by curiosity, I immersed myself in these sermons, especially those given by Bryan Rocine. As I listened, a wave of anger overtook me, overwhelming my thoughts and propelling me toward an inevitable confrontation.

Ten years prior, back in 1997, I had reached out to pastors in Syracuse in the hope that they could bridge the gap and help me communicate with my father and family. During that search, I had also contacted Bryan Rocine, who was the assistant pastor of the Living Word Church. However, my letters and phone requests had been dismissed.

After listening to a few of his sermons, I managed to stay composed and refrain from any immediate reaction. However, as I delved deeper, going through seven or eight of them, I became increasingly aware of their damaging content and widespread dissemination. This troubling realization pushed me to the brink of tolerance. My mounting frustration became uncontainable, driving me to take decisive action.

In July 2007, compelled by the troubling elements I had identified in his sermons, I felt it necessary to contact Bryan again. This time, my focus was on specific aspects of his sermons that had caught my attention. Over the ensuing weeks, I sent him a series of letters, each pinpointing my specific concerns and observations.

For instance, in a letter dated August 11th, 2007, I wrote:

Bryan,

I listened to your sermon "Godly Sorrow." Still you're telling others separation is not only necessary, but required by God. You say that Christians need to "cut off" relations, from even loved ones, sometimes even with those from family. You say that it is temporary sorrow, that joy and prosperity will come as consequence . . .

This letter was the third in my series of correspondences. The next day, I received Bryan's response. It was inflammatory and evasive, sidestepping the issues I had raised. Even more troubling was the tone—disparaging and accusatory. He labeled me as a manipulator, a hater of God, narcissistic, and described my teenage years as rebellious. He went on to paint me as an unhealthy, incorrigibly competitive individual, embittered with God, whom I allegedly perceived as an archenemy. His derogatory comments seemed to know no end.

In my response to Bryan, I questioned how he could form any opinion of me, considering he had never truly known me, having never even had a conversation with me. To offer him a chance to understand who I am, I invited him to visit and meet people who had known me for years. His response was dismissive: "You should not be so obsessed with justifying yourself to me," he said, followed by several more disparaging remarks.

As 2007 neared its end, the flurry of letters between Bryan and me showed no signs of slowing, extending our exchange well into the following year. Amid this whirlwind of emotions and correspondence, a glimmer of hope emerged in my family life. My sister Debbie and her husband Tom decided to visit me for the grand opening of my Broward store, a gesture of significance that stemmed from a phone call I received the previous year from Debbie and my other sister, Pam. They had begun to see things from a new perspective, realizing that I was not the person they had been led to believe I was. This shift in their views occurred after they withdrew their children from the Living Word Academy due to concerns of abuse and mistreatment. Consequently, they too had ceased communication with my parents, and their perception of me had changed. We had reconnected and were once again on speaking terms.

Though personal tempests threatened, a glimmer of hope emerged on my professional horizon. I had landed a sought-after lease at the Shoppes of Arrowhead plaza in Davie. Far more than just another strip mall, it shimmered with the potential to reinvigorate my computer business, filling me with a renewed sense of excitement.

In the early days, as the twentieth century had just drawn

to a close, my office was a humble space, merely a converted storage room tucked away in the parking garage of the Holiday Inn. During that time, it served as a space to store spare parts and allowed me to be reached while working on computers amidst a clutter of tools. As I sought new customers and witnessed the growth of my business, I became determined to enhance my working environment and establish stronger connections with other businesses. This aspiration led me to relocate to the Keystone Corporate Building on Flagler Street. Interestingly, the building's owner, Mike Mouriz, who was also one of my clients, expressed an interest in hiring me as a full-time technician for his personal and professional technical needs. However, instead of accepting the offer, I proposed a compromise. I would provide my services free of charge in exchange for an office space in one of his buildings—the same building where his office was situated. This arrangement proved to be mutually beneficial and thrived for many years.

A couple of years later, I decided to expand my business by opening another office in Miami Lakes. This new office shared a similar size, style, and purpose, which allowed me to tap into a growing list of customers in the area. However, I couldn't help but notice that the two offices lacked the presence and allure of larger establishments like Best Buy stores. Although my business was profitable, I couldn't shake the desire for a more appealing and inviting presence.

During one of my visits to Gateway Title Group, a newly acquired client located at the Airport Executive Tower on NW 12th Street, an unexpected opportunity presented itself. After a few hours of work and engaging conversations with the friendly staff, fate took an intriguing twist when I bumped into a man named Jesus, one of the three subcontractors I had hired back in the early 1990s during my time in the tile restoration business. Recognizing the value of our renewed connection, we decided to exchange contact information. Our initial meeting was followed by regular phone conversations, and we made plans for visits on multiple occasions. Over the years, Jesus became a close friend, and I grew to admire his sharp business acumen. His achievements in the janitorial business and wise investments in several properties, including his beautiful, spacious home in Pembroke Pines, were a testament to his exceptional business savvy.

As our friendship flourished, it seemed fitting to involve Jesus in my pursuit of opening a retail store. Together, we solidified an agreement and embarked on a mission to find a suitable property. After an extensive search, we discovered the perfect location and decided to sign the lease.

With unwavering determination, we set out to transform the retail space into a place that would captivate our customers. We embarked on a comprehensive renovation project, starting with replacing all the ceiling tiles and implementing special lighting to create an inviting atmosphere. The floors were torn up and replaced with new tiles and luxurious carpeting, enhancing the aesthetic appeal. To ensure utmost comfort and functionality, we commissioned custom-made furniture for the reception area and the lab at the rear.

Understanding the significance of branding and visual identity, we entrusted our advertising agency to handle the meticulous details. They took charge of designing our eye-catching logo, selecting a harmonious color scheme, and ensuring consistent backlit signage above the front of our store. Their expertise extended to creating captivating graphics within the store, utilizing innovative glass-printing techniques on the storefront, and crafting compelling advertisements that were showcased in prominent magazines and various media outlets.

Through collaborative efforts, we transformed our vision into reality, crafting a retail space that reflected our aspirations and conveyed a sense of allure to customers.

Just before our grand opening, Debbie and Tom and my Aunt MaryJane and Uncle Gary came to see me at the store. Brimming with pride, I gave them a tour of the facility. Unfortunately, their time in Miami was limited. After enjoying a pleasant lunch together at a nearby restaurant, we bid farewell, and I returned to the hustle and bustle of work.

I can't overstate my deep appreciation for the unwavering focus demanded by my business endeavors. Over the years, the intensity and time commitments have served a dual purpose, not only providing for my physical needs but also serving as a welcome distraction from personal worries, particularly concerning family relationships that could otherwise overwhelm and weigh me down.

Throughout my days of correspondence with Bryan Rocine, I remained in constant contact with Debbie. As I review the emails I sent her, now spread out before me, a rush of memories returns, reminding me of the deep disturbance I felt, provoked by Bryan's sermons. His unsettling words were not confined to his church congregation alone; they extended far beyond, criticizing and permeating the broader community. That, in itself, was deeply troubling. However, what ignited my rage was the personal dimension—the chilling realization that his harmful messages had infiltrated the ears of my brothers, sisters, and mother.

In an earnest attempt to caution my family about the potential consequences of heeding Bryan's misguided instructions, I shared selected excerpts from his sermons with Debbie. Within the text of my messages, I emphasized the troubling nature of his rhetoric. I never expected her to confront these issues directly or to approach Bryan to address his wrongdoings. Instead, my sole intention was for her to recognize the incorrectness, harm, and danger associated with his words. My hope was that by acknowledging these realities, she would be empowered to protect herself from becoming a victim of his manipulation.

One example that stands out is his unwavering insistence on branding those outside the Living Word Church as sinners while simultaneously demanding unwavering loyalty and exclusivity from his members to adhere to his specific doctrine. This extremism reached such alarming levels that not only were sinners in Syracuse unjustly labeled as dangerous, even Christians who didn't attend the Living Word Church were shunned.

With this unsettling background in mind, on January 21, 2008, I shared an audio clip with Debbie that contained a troubling statement made by Bryan from the pulpit. In the recording, he proclaimed, "And I'm telling you, the Christians in the churches nowadays, I know it's true in our own community, I can speak for our own community. They are under the heavy influence of Satan. They are under the heavy influence of Lucifer." This statement highlighted the depth of his divisive and harmful beliefs, and it was proof that the presumed rift between The Living Word and other churches in the community had moved beyond mere insinuations.

Nine days later, on Wednesday, January 30, I forwarded Bryan snippets of his most recent sermon. Within one thought-provoking segment, he made the statement, "I can't give you scriptures to support the idea of making more churches when you differ with the church you're at . . . but one thing you didn't do, at least it's not shown in the Bible, go make a new church." He emphasized the importance of unwavering commitment, perseverance, and the necessity of working through differences while remaining devoted members of the Living Word Church.

I was surprised that, despite the numerous critiques expressed in my messages to Bryan, he would occasionally respond, although he rarely addressed any of the multitude of questions I posed. Nonetheless, this ongoing interaction played a role in my continued engagement, as I regularly downloaded and listened to the sermons posted on the Living Word website.

At this juncture, after devoting countless hours to listening to Bryan's sermons and witnessing his unwavering refusal to address any of the concerns I raised, my anger reached its zenith. Moreover, a renewed sense of awareness dawned upon me regarding the profound harm inflicted on my family throughout the years by such rhetoric, solidifying my determination to take decisive action.

In a renewed and earnest endeavor to inform the public and foster awareness about the prevailing situation, I decided to send a copy of my correspondence with Bryan to members of the press in Syracuse. It was my conviction that the community needed to be made aware of what was transpiring within their midst. To ensure Bryan was fully cognizant of my intentions, I CC'd him on the message.

From: Daniel Mazur
Sent: Monday, February 04, 2008 9:07 AM
Subject: Danger in Syracuse

My name is Dan Mazur. My father is Robert Mazur, Pastor and founder of The Living Word Church in Syracuse NY.

I've been separated from my parents and two of my siblings for about 20 years now. I never had a drug problem, trouble with the law, not even an argument or fight with a brother to blame. I simply stopped attending my father's church, and refused to disown my Grandparents who left long ago.

Why Should you care? Well, if you know someone who becomes a member of the Church, someone from your family, a neighbor or friend, there's a chance you may never see that person again. But don't take my word for it, I have dozens of letters from people this happened to.

For the past year I've been corresponding with Bryan Rocine, the assistant pastor of The Living Word Church. I've been questioning him about the separation in my family, in other families, his tactics, sermons posted on the Church website encouraging division and more. A copy of the correspondence is attached for your review.

I recommend you provide this information to family and loved ones; any good hearted, trusting person in Syracuse that may be vulnerable to those dishonest who misuse the title of Pastor.

Thank you

That same afternoon, I received yet another response

from Bryan.

> From: B. M. Rocine
> Sent: Monday, February 04, 2008 4:16 PM
> To: Daniel R. Mazur
> Subject: Re: FW: Danger in Syracuse
>
> Hi Danny,
>   Any email I have sent or will send to you may contain legally privileged and/or confidential information. Any unauthorized disclosure, use or dissemination of this email message or its contents, either in whole or in part, is prohibited.
>   Thanks for your anticipated compliance with this prohibition!
>
> Regards,
> Bryan

Bryan's continual evasion of responsibility for his words, coupled with his deliberate efforts to conceal his actions, struck me as sheer cowardice. But his behavior didn't surprise me. I was keenly aware of the culture of secrecy and suppression that was rooted in the core tenets of his dogma—tenets that formed the bedrock of his church's beliefs and practices.

Moreover, his approach was telling. Throughout our correspondence, he never hinted at any legal or confidential repercussions. Only afterward did he broach such matters, revealing his true intentions: a continuous attempt to suppress information and a readiness to use tactical maneuvers to achieve his objective.

After sending the letter, I engaged with several individuals in the Syracuse media community. One significant connection I made was with Renne, a prominent figure at the *Syracuse Post Standard,* known for her insightful editorials on religious topics. As events unfolded, the confluence of my conversations with Bryan and the media's involvement led to developments that went beyond our individual feelings. These events carried profound implications and consequences.

Amidst these unfolding events, my sister Pam contacted

me to recount an unsettling encounter she had with an un-expected visitor—a reporter who unexpectedly arrived on her doorstep. As time has passed, the details of that incident have become somewhat hazy, leaving me uncertain wheth-er it was one of the reporters I had been in contact with or an entirely different individual. Nevertheless, a reporter did show up at her door and began questioning her about the Living Word Church, my involvement with it, and its assis-tant pastor Bryan Rocine.

News of the reporter's visit quickly spread to my sister, Debbie. As if by a stroke of providence, shortly after my initial contact with the media in Syracuse, I received a letter from Debbie's husband, Tom.

Tom had recently visited me in Miami with Debbie, per-fectly timed with the grand opening of my Davie store. While I consistently kept my sisters informed about my ongoing correspondence with Bryan, I never broached the subject with Tom or my other brother-in-law, Mark. Discussions about family matters remained strictly between my sisters and me. In fact, I never communicated with my two brothers-in-law; we never exchanged letters or had phone conversations. They also never approached me with questions or showed any in-terest in discussing matters.

However, the situation and their interests shifted unex-pectedly. Just three days after Bryan's warning regarding the confidentiality of our correspondence, I read Tom's letter. Upon learning that the media had inquired about the church, where he had once been a devoted member, Tom felt com-pelled to share his perceptions with me.

After deliberating over his letter, I took two days to com-pose my response.

Date: 2/9/2008
From: Dan Mazur
To: Tom Conena

Tom,

You were never asked to offer an interview with the Post Standard because, as far as I know, no one has expected you to do such a thing. I certainly didn't give your name to anyone. And if I chose to, I would first make sure it would not be problematic for you, you know, out of respect. And as for vengeance, I'm glad it has no place in your home, that it's not your practice when you feel harmed. But are you sure? Did you feel harmed by me before saying "you're a spitting image of your father," and "blow it out your ass"? Sounds extreme, excessive, with the force of vengeance. I'm curious, did you ever speak to Bryan or my Father showing a similar respect?

Like you said, this is America, where we are free to speak. So, though you have the right to talk to me or anyone this way, and though you insist I be respectful to you, I'm not so sure you're showing the same. And while on the topic of revenge, as you say "all you want is for those barriers to come down, and for you to be a normal family with everyone talking," which is it you're saying I say? Do I want family or revenge?

Look, I'm not trying to make you or my sister think anything, I just hope I'm giving you something to think about. There's a difference in this statement that needs to be noticed. Yet you go as far as to say I'm trying to "force" you and others, in this land of the free. This is how you are taking my questions, not to you, but to my sister? And as for my sister, I believe she spoke very well for herself. Are you so sure you need to speak for her? I'd be content to simply know how you feel, in this, my first letter from you. I "detest" my Father? "CHANGE!!!" Have I ever spoken to you in this way? Me, the guy defending you when Gary simply pointed his finger at you? Have I really been telling you what to do, like you're telling me? And do I have to be a "diplomat" to communicate with my family; with anyone? Where does this come from? I'm not a diplomat, and never claimed to be, and like I told Bryan I'm not very bright. But should either keep me from asking some questions? For taking the words of your family seriously, I don't know how sincere Debbie was for what she said, about killing herself. You'd be a better judge of that. My message was simply that I cannot understand how someone saying her Father's Church has Cult like tendencies would not want to protect others from devastating experiences that you appear to believe are a consequence. You interpret what I say as detest for my father, of disrespect for you, as revenge and hatred – even though you took a moment to flip to a better and more accurate meaning. If it's true, if you really feel that badly about me, then if I were you I'd consider your community to benefit from knowing this. Maybe there is an interview with a reporter that should be held, where you can speak of my hatred and need for revenge. And if you do, you can tell the reporter I'll agree to an interview, because anyone on earth can ask me anything. But in case I'm not being clear, let me make it clear I'm not telling you what to do, to do this or anything, simply to think about and consider it.

"a spitting image of your father" "ignorance" "loose cannon ball" "forced to do certain things" "lifelong tirade" "badgering" "leave us alone" "CHANGE!!!" "dwell on the evils" "ignorance" "hate campaign" "blow it out your ass" "I don't give a damn" "destructive way you live your life"—These are pretty harsh words for the first letter I ever got from you, from someone saying I'm vengeful—like my Father.

Evidently, you're pretty pissed about what I wrote to my sister. But Tom, I'm not even upset with you; by your letter. I'm not sure why. At the chance you might look back and think it's a little tough, don't worry about it. You've been good enough to me, so it's OK.

There's something I need to say that will sound as harsh as your letter has actually been to me. I think you were angry, and you meant me some harm when you wrote, and like I said that's OK. I promise that what I'm about to write I mean with no harm or revenge. And I hope that if you don't agree with what I say, you read it again, and again until the day that you do.

Consider to never tell me again what I can or cannot say to my sister or anyone else. I will not listen, and I don't care who it is, or what it is you think you are. I will write to Debbie all I want, anytime I want, and will say whatever it is I feel like saying. There is only one thing you may be able to do that will ever change that. I take this very seriously, this type of control you are trying to impose. To me, you do not have to show the same respect you insist I return because you can insult me all you like and I really don't mind. On this you get a pass. But if you want to control my conversations with my sister, or even an ADULT daughter, I suggest you forbid them to speak with me, or do your best to influence, to control them and others instead of attempting to control me. They will be the ones telling me to stop, not you. This is a risk that on principle I'll take.

If you never want me to write to you again, all you have to do is ask.

After receiving my letter, he wrote back. This time I found him more reasonable, and I believed we had moved beyond the potential rift. Months later, during a visit to my aunt and uncle's home in Homosassa, Tom and I maintained a pleasant, amicable relationship, enjoying our time together. However, an incident later on, on September 21, 2008, led me to reevaluate my decision to overlook his past actions and reassess my relationship with Tom.

This reassessment was influenced by a letter from another brother-in-law, Mark, under similar circumstances. Mark's comments, much like Tom's, were in reaction to my communications with his wife, my sister Pam. He sent a harsh, disparaging letter, similar in tone to that from Tom and Bryan. Frustrated by this recurring pattern, I resolved not to respond to Mark and decided to cut ties with both of my brothers-in-law.

Before receiving Mark's incensed and acerbic letter, other unsettling events occurred. Merely two weeks following Bryan's cautionary words about revealing his letters, I was surprised by an unexpected visit from the police at my doorstep. They were investigating allegations that I was building a bomb targeting the Living Word Church. I cooperated fully, allowing them to search my house. After their thorough inspection, and once they had left, I felt compelled to contact my father, Bryan, and others, to express my dismay and concerns about this alarming and baseless accusation.

From: Daniel Mazur
Sent: Thursday, February 21, 2008 9:49 PM
To: B. M. Rocine
Subject: Pastor in Syracuse has Police sent to my home this evening—claims I threatened to bomb The Living Word Church
To: Robert Mazur/Bryan Rocine – Pastors of The Living Word

Church in Syracuse

(Bryan – Please give my father a copy of this as I don't have his email address)

The police came to my door this evening, February 21st, down here in Miami. A Miami officer said the Syracuse Police contacted his department, said Robert Mazur (my father) claims I was threatening to "blow up The Living Word Church."

Both of you—your attempts to shut me down began long ago, with consulting, influencing psychiatrists in your Church as you were successful having me committed into Hutchings Psychiatric Center. And when I was released, you wouldn't have it, the police came to take me away again, at my apartment 1AM on a Friday for reevaluation. You cannot imagine how hard, how torturous that was, handcuffed and all, in the back of a squad car. Having my sanity questioned, again and again, my thoughts interrogated at a difficult hour, when I was having trouble sleeping, when I was released and told I needed to be home and rest. The Doctors eventually let me go that same morning, but not after asking "Who had this kid come here?" "His Father" Aunt MaryJane said. "Well, where is he?" Like the other times, though you had me committed under the guise of helping me, you were nowhere to be found. I was off to a kind of jail, locked up and out of both of your way. Shut down, mission accomplished, right? And after that morning, did it all stop? No, you kept calling the police trying to have them take me away again– but they wouldn't. And like a shake down, every now and then you still do it, make your phone calls to have me interrogated. Not very nice for me, as it continued when I moved to Miami – was away from you all. The FBI coming to visit me at my door. How did you manage that one? Now, again, it's back to the police. How is it you have people believing your stories? Oh, I forgot, that's your craft, my controlling manipulative father. A real shrink, not one of those that left your Church after "finding you out" long ago, would tell you you've not been so nice to me. I nearly killed myself over all this insanity years ago, remember?

You and Bryan can continue preaching from your pulpit about demons possessing me, about how evil I am, and they will always be in the back of my mind, those pictures of people practically running away from me in fear, when I lived there, when at a mall or gas station they'd cross my path. You won, no one wanted anything to do with me, no one would hear what I had to say, or believe me if they did. But neither of you can control me anymore. I'll

talk to anyone who calls me, and answer any questions I'm asked.
I fixed my life. I have nothing to hide.

I was overwhelmed by the cascade of events. The concoction of lies and the baseless accusations about plotting to blow up the church all weighed heavily on me. Then Mark's letter arrived, exhibiting the same attitude that Tom had displayed seven months prior. It felt as if everyone was swift to pass judgment, neglecting to understand who I was, what I believed in, and what actions I had taken.

Throughout my life, I had faced a litany of misunderstandings and misinterpretations. The most recent of these, as noted above, involved Tom and Mark, who seemed to perceive me largely through the lens of their spouses. Ironically, they faulted me for the very offenses they themselves had committed: passing judgment without sincere conversation and never granting me the benefit of the doubt. Their haste in adopting a viewpoint without pondering its potential inaccuracy, only to then cement that belief in writing, was disconcerting.

By September 2008 when Mark's letter arrived, my patience had worn thin. I chose not to engage with him directly. Instead, I waited a few weeks, allowing time for Pam to digest her husband's actions. When I finally contacted her, I sought her take on Mark's letter, hoping the elapsed time might have fostered some clarity.

Her response, while surprising, perhaps shouldn't have been. She not only aligned herself with Mark's position but also emphatically supported his sentiments, asserting, "I am 100 percent behind what he said, and the manner in which he said it." Stunned by her firm stance, I pressed her further, asking, "Don't you think there's even a slight possibility that there might be something amiss with it?" Despite my inquiries, she held firm: "No, I fully support his actions."

Reeling with a mix of disbelief and frustration, I asked her to reiterate her position. As she confirmed her stance without hesitation, a profound realization dawned on me. I could no longer tolerate such treatment from her or anyone else. With a newfound resolve and resolute conviction, I decided to distance myself from anyone who condoned or justified such behavior toward me.

"Under these circumstances," I declared, "I see no reason for us to continue moving forward together." It was at that moment she uttered words that pierced my heart: "What about my daughter, Rafael? She will grow up without any uncles in her life." It was an agonizing realization but also a confirmation that my decision was correct. She had demonstrated her understanding of the importance of kind and caring relationships for those she loved, but her actions suggested that I wasn't included on her list of those who deserved such care, driving home the need for me to prioritize my own well-being and act accordingly.

Instead of acknowledging the repeated harm she had observed being inflicted upon me, Pam focused solely on the potential impact on herself. It seemed she expected me to prioritize the interests of others, specifically hers and her daughter's, above my own.

This experience influenced my approach in a subsequent conversation about Tom. I voiced my disappointment, pointing out that his first letter had laid bare his authentic feelings toward me and that his follow-up letter was merely a façade. I suggested he abandon his pretense of amicability and embrace the truth within the sentiments he initially expressed. I stressed that, had he stayed true to his initial sincerity, my respect for him would have been greater.

Regrettably, my own actions exacerbated the tension in our relationships, further complicating my efforts to build meaningful connections with my siblings and their children.

THE JOURNEY TO MIRAMAR

SINCE MY INITIAL MOVE TO SOUTH FLORIDA IN THE FALL OF 1989, I have had the opportunity to live in various places. The first relocation was not a result of careful planning but rather a fortunate stroke of luck. It happened on Friday, August 21, 1992, just three days before Hurricane Andrew devastated the region. By pure coincidence, I found myself seeking temporary refuge with Gaston in Miami Lakes, which turned out to be a fortunate turn of events given the impending storm.

As the following year unfolded, my improved financial situation presented me with the opportunity to settle into a new apartment in Hialeah, conveniently located near Gaston in Miami Lakes. Despite the demanding nature of managing my business and the personal turmoil I was experiencing, my connection with Claudia remained steadfast. Aware of the high cost of long-distance calls during that time, I resorted to sending her letters via fax to her father's company, where the helpful staff ensured their delivery. With the acquisition of my first computer, I expanded our means of communication by corresponding through emails, which served as an additional bridge to overcome the physical distance between us.

Whenever Claudia visited me in Miami, I made it a priority to carve out precious free time to spend with her. Our excursions often led us to the lively and colorful locales of South Beach or Hollywood Beach. There, a charming collection of shops and eateries awaited us just a short stroll away from the ocean. Claudia cherished those moments, seizing every chance to delve into meaningful conversations about her family and friends. As she basked in the sun's gentle warmth, she found a sense of peace in the serene and mesmerizing views that embraced us.

Regardless of whether she was in Miami or back home in Buenos Aires, her unwavering love for the beach, the ocean, and her profound longing to reside by the coast resonated in her words, making a lasting impression on me. Circumstances brought us together, and I cherished every moment I spent with her.

After a couple of years had passed, and my financial situation continued to improve, I became resolute in my quest to find an apartment by the ocean. While the specific location was not my primary concern, two crucial factors guided my search. First, I aimed to find a place that was conveniently situated, allowing me to reach my customers and office without unnecessary difficulties. Second, I wanted to create an environment that would enhance my time with Claudia, providing her with more reasons to visit and embracing the surroundings she cherished.

With these goals in mind, I embarked on an earnest search for the perfect abode. Finally, in 1996, my efforts bore fruit as I secured a rental agreement for an exquisite high-rise apartment on the twelfth floor of the Harbour House located on Collins Avenue in Bal Harbour. It proved to be an exceptional choice, fulfilling my practical needs and desires and creating a setting that complemented my relationship with Claudia.

One of the standout features of that apartment was its proximity to the beach, which added a touch of perfection whenever Claudia visited. Just a few steps outside and through the pool gate, she could access the inviting sandy shores. The convenience made her times with me even more enjoyable. Meanwhile, for me, the nearby beach offered a convenient five-mile trail that became my go-to route for invigorating early morning jogs, accompanied by the rhythmic crashing of waves. It was a rejuvenating experience that I cherished.

My life followed this path, marked by delightful visits from Claudia and my daily commute south of my home to the Holiday Inn farther down Collins Ave., where I carried out my IT tasks. A couple of years later, I found myself heading to my office, located ten miles east of the hotel in the Keystone office park on the corner of Lejeune and Flagler. Throughout that time, I dedicated myself to serving my numerous small business clients scattered across Miami, ensuring that their technological needs were met with the utmost care and attention.

Living in Bal Harbour for seven years brought me immense satisfaction. The serene surroundings and the delightful experiences it offered enriched my life. Given the chance, I would have extended my stay without hesitation. However, my contentment was interrupted by the unfortunate news of the impending demolition of the pristine building situated on the intracoastal waterway of Bal Harbour. It was slated to make way for the development of a Ritz Carlton luxury hotel, compelling me to embark once again on a search for another place to call home.

Consequently, in August 2003 I relocated to another highrise residence. I found myself on the twelfth floor again but this time at the Intracoastal Yacht Club in nearby Sunny Isles Beach. Though I wasn't directly on the ocean, a five-minute bicycle ride brought me to its shores. This proximity allowed Claudia to continue relishing the coastal beauty both during our time together and in my absence while I was engaged with work.

However, from the outset, I faced multiple challenges with the building's management. On my first day there, I was dismayed to discover another vehicle in my designated parking spot. When I sought assistance from the security team, they advised me to use an alternative spot, which I did, albeit hesitantly. To my astonishment, the following day a large warning sticker with a tenacious adhesive was plastered on my car's window, cautioning me about potential towing if I continued to park there. Eager to sort out the issue, I approached the management in person and in writing. In my letter, I highlighted not just the parking problem but also other issues like cracked tiles and other unexpected discrepancies in my apartment.

Regrettably, this marked the beginning of a turbulent relationship with Patty, the property manager. Subsequent months were filled with numerous issues that I raised, highlighting Patty's incompetence, her team's inefficiency, and the overall lack of care for tenant and property relationships. The situation became increasingly frustrating as I struggled to receive proper attention and resolution for the persistent problems.

Two years later, in August 2005, Miami faced the fury of another catastrophic hurricane. Katrina tore through the city, leaving a lasting impact on the cityscape and its residents. Fortunately for me, the building where I lived remained largely unscathed, a stark contrast to several nearby buildings that suffered extensively from the hurricane's wrath. In the aftermath of the hurricane, our building faced a period of chaos and disorganization, particularly evident in the management of the Intracoastal Yacht Club. It was during this challenging time that I found myself witnessing a heated altercation between a fellow tenant and Patty right in the lobby.

The incident occurred as the tenant's car was in the process of being towed from a no-parking zone located just outside the lobby, where an argument ensued. Despite my fellow tenant's plea for understanding, given the formidable circumstances following the hurricane, Patty remained firm and showed no signs of sympathy or consideration. Observing this lack of compassion and drawing from my own experiences of similar mistreatment, I couldn't resist making a passing comment. "It's like talking to a wall. She simply doesn't care." Then I redirected my attention and proceeded to attend to my own affairs.

Later that evening, I was disheartened to return home and discover a "non-renewal notice" attached to my apartment door, indicating that my residency would not be extended once my current lease expired. Determined to find a resolution, I woke up early the next morning and made my way to Patty's office. Knocking on her door, I held out hope for an opportunity to resolve the matter. I offered my apologies for my behavior the previous day and made additional gestures of goodwill. Unfortunately, despite my efforts, Patty remained unwavering in her decision.

Feeling desperate, I conducted some research on the building and made a significant discovery—the owner had a business connection with one of my clients. Considering the strong rapport I had with that client, a glimmer of hope emerged. I reached out to him, explaining my predicament and imploring him to intervene on my behalf, urging the building owner to instruct Patty to reconsider her decision. Understanding my situation, my client acted on my behalf. However, he informed me that the building owner was hesitant to challenge Patty's authority, fearing potential consequences and a strain on their professional relationship. Despite our collective efforts, it became apparent that all available avenues for resolving the situation had been exhausted.

So, I was soon on the hunt for a new place to live. Fortunately, I found a suitable apartment just up the street at the Porto Bellagio Condos. Moving there meant only relocating my furniture; there was no change in travel time to the beach, the Holiday Inn, my Flagler office, or client sites.

Several months later while I was at a client's site—a title company on Lincoln Road at the heart of South Beach—I had an unexpected encounter with Laura, the business owner's wife. As it turned out, she was a real estate broker. She took the opportunity to discuss my living situation, suggesting that I might be unnecessarily spending on rent when I could be investing in my own home. Intrigued, I met with her a few days later to explore some properties that she believed would suit my needs. Among them was a tiny home that consisted of a kitchen, a living room, two bedrooms, and a bathroom, all within a mere 703 square feet. Laura insisted that it was the perfect fit for me. Originally built in 1968, the home had undergone a complete renovation, boasting new flooring, fresh paint, and updated appliances. Despite my initial reservations, Laurie's persistence persuaded me to purchase the property in the "up and coming" neighborhood, as she described it, that very day.

However, upon further reflection and consideration of my preferences, I realized the house was not suitable for me. Despite already giving Laura my word to proceed with the purchase, I found myself grappling with the decision. Nevertheless, feeling a sense of obligation to honor my commitment, I proceeded with the purchase at her office three days later. Following that, I met with Jay, who handled the title for the property, and we completed the closing procedures. In line with my principles of fairness and equality, I insisted on paying him for his services, declining his offer to waive his fee. This practice had become a personal standard for me, starting from the time I first declined special parking privileges at the Holiday Inn and insisted on working directly under the supervision and orders of the hotel manager, Mr. Orland Vazquez.

Interestingly enough, in addition to being a real estate agent, Laura also owned a tanning salon on Lincoln Road. She, like her husband, had become a client for whom I provided IT services. Approximately a year after acquiring my home, I found myself entangled in a vexing predicament with Laura. To my dismay, not only did she fail to provide compensation for the services that I had rendered, she and her husband displayed a complete disregard for my attempts to reach out through calls and messages for several months thereafter. This unexpected turn of events left me deeply unsettled, particularly since there had been no prior indication of any dissatisfaction or wrongdoing on my part. In fact, we had shared an enjoyable social dinner together.

For the first time in my journey as an IT professional, I found myself in a position where I felt compelled to apply pressure on a client to settle an outstanding payment. Although the amount in question was relatively small, totaling only a few hundred dollars, the significance of the matter lay in maintaining the principles and preserving the integrity of our professional relationship. It was particularly frustrating for me because I had reluctantly agreed to make a significant purchase from Laura, solely because I had given my word. Considering these circumstances, I believed my request for payment was reasonable and fair.

While in the vicinity of Jay's title company one day, attending to a client in an office building across the street, I decided to pay Jay an unexpected visit. Disregarding the response from his secretary, who informed me that he was not present or available, I bypassed her and the others in the vicinity, proceeding to open the door to Jay's office. My abrupt intrusion interrupted his meeting with one of his clients, as I expressed my grievances in a loud and assertive manner, asking why he didn't answer my calls and the failure of his wife to fulfill her payment obligations.

"This can't be happening," Jay said, then he summoned security to escort me off the premises. Sensing the escalating tension and having achieved the intended impact of the scene, I chose to depart of my own volition.

A couple of months later, after my business partner, Jesus, persuaded me to enlist the help of a collection agency to recover the outstanding payments owed to our company, I received an unexpected call from the courthouse. Much to my surprise, Jay was present, representing Laura in the arbitration proceedings. With little interest in anything more than putting the matter behind me, I agreed to a settlement, accepting only a fraction of the original amount owed to our company.

With the matter involving Jay and Laura resolved, I returned my attention to completing the finishing touches at my new home. To elevate its aesthetic appeal, Jesus, who owned a janitorial company, arranged for his floor team to apply a fresh coat of glossy oil-based sealer to the travertine flooring. Additionally, Jesus and his team provided invaluable assistance in the smooth transition of moving my furniture from my previous apartment at Porto Bellagio to my new home.

Once the relocation was complete, Jesus and I embarked on the exciting journey of opening our computer store in Davie. Our roles were clearly defined. Jesus would oversee the physical planning, development, and day-to-day management of the store as well as handle administrative responsibilities for the company as a whole. I devoted my efforts to ensuring the work performed by our skilled technicians maintained a high standard of quality while nurturing positive relationships with our valued customers. The costs associated with expanding the company were to be covered by the profits I had already generated, and we agreed that Jesus would forgo a salary until his contributions resulted in increased profitability.

However, much like my aspirations in Syracuse, our carefully laid-out plan did not unfold as anticipated. The emergence of mass production and the declining prices of computer systems greatly impacted the demand and profitability of the custom-built systems we offered in the store. Furthermore, the substantial investment we made in magazine advertisements and other marketing endeavors, which Jesus believed would substantially expand our client base, did not yield the desired results.

As expenses continued to mount, including the hiring of a

full-time employee, the store faced a formidable challenge in generating profits. We found ourselves heavily reliant on the earnings from pre-existing relationships with small businesses in Dade and Broward Counties to cover ongoing expenses. These mounting difficulties, combined with the realization that Jesus's involvement in the company fell short of my initial expectations, further complicated our business venture.

As our business relationship progressed, I followed through with my agreement to entrust Jesus with the responsibility of invoicing customers and collecting payments. To align with this change, I consented to redirect payments from my Flagler office to a more convenient location, which entailed setting up a designated PO box near Jesus's residence. Subsequently, Jesus decided to delegate the tasks of invoicing and collections to his wife, Tamara, despite her existing responsibilities for his janitorial company. This additional workload placed an increased burden on Tamara as she had to manage tasks for both companies.

In due course, Tamara expressed her belief that her contributions warranted a formal position and inclusion on the weekly payroll. Although I struggled to comprehend the need for this change, I agreed, and Tamara was added to the company's payroll. It was disheartening for me to realize that, apart from Jesus, I was the only one not receiving regular compensation. As the company was my sole source of income, this situation weighed heavily on me. I found myself in a situation where I had inadvertently agreed to receive payment only when Tamara and Jesus deemed that funds were available after fulfilling all other financial obligations. Unfortunately, this arrangement became increasingly challenging over time. While Tamara consistently received her weekly payments, I found it hard to justify compensating her for tasks I had handled by myself during my spare time.

The situation deteriorated when I faced extended periods, sometimes spanning a month, without any income. As a result, my financial stability was shaken to the point where I could no longer manage my monthly mortgage and car payments.

At the onset of our partnership, I had an excellent credit rating with only my car and home loans as outstanding debts. When my income halted, and I couldn't keep up with my mortgage commitments, I turned to Jesus and Tamara for understanding and support. Unfortunately, they didn't view the situation with the same sense of gravitas. To them, missed payments or accruing credit card debt was a typical and tolerable way to navigate financial troubles. This perspective was deeply unsettling for me, as I had always prioritized timely payments and had avoided any related penalties.

During this challenging period, I couldn't help but notice that Jesus and his family were indulging in extravagant luxuries, such as lavish vacations, cruises, and expensive purchases like cars and jewelry. I had no objection to their enjoyment of these indulgences, as I understood that it was their prerogative to spend their money as they pleased. However, their extravagant lifestyle and manner of living gave me pause and raised doubts about our shared commitment to the success of our business and our common goal of achieving profitability.

Shortly thereafter, Jesus decided to sell his cleaning business and venture into the air-conditioning industry, establishing a new company of his own. As time went on, I grew increasingly disappointed with the lack of business acumen and involvement from Jesus that I had anticipated and expected within our partnership and shared interests. The absence of meetings or discussions about his activities left me in the dark about his contributions to the growth and development of our joint business endeavor. This lack of transparency intensified my concerns about the future of our partnership.

As time went on, my situation grew increasingly dire, reaching a point where I went an entire year without being able to make any mortgage payments. It was a challenging period, and I found myself becoming numb to the situation, accepting the reality of living without money as my new normal. Jesus and Tamara were fully aware of my struggles, and

I often found myself relying on their generosity, including being invited to their home for dinners when I couldn't afford a meal. I also resorted to using credit cards to get by, which only deepened my financial burden. In an unsurprising turn of events, they even invited me to join them on a vacation to Las Vegas, despite my financial constraints. I declined initially, explaining my inability to afford such a trip, but eventually, I gave in and joined them, even though I had no means to enjoy the activities there.

As my situation continued to deteriorate, I reached a crucial point where I felt an overpowering need to assert myself more forcefully and convey the urgent need for change in our circumstances. With a determined mindset, I arranged a meeting with Tamara and Jesus to address the matter head on. As we reviewed and discussed Tamara's tasks, it became glaringly evident that she was investing an excessive amount of time in unnecessary activities. One notable instance was the substantial number of hours she dedicated to repetitive data-entry tasks each day. Recognizing the inefficiency, I introduced her to software solutions that could eliminate the need for redundant data duplication, such as a ticket system that would alleviate her burden of retyping technical task details performed by the technicians. However, Tamara exhibited resistance to the idea and displayed no inclination to pursue it further. She expressed contentment with her current responsibilities, deriving a sense of value and accomplishment from "keeping busy." While I acknowledged and respected her sentiments, I emphasized the importance of prioritizing efficiency and avoiding unnecessary expenses, particularly given my own dire circumstances. Regrettably, my words failed to carry the necessary weight. Consequently, without a clear vision or a viable path to a solution, I continued sinking deeper into debt without witnessing any improvements to my situation.

A few months later, I found myself on the brink of eviction. I shared this distressing news with Jesus, who suggested converting a room in his garage into a living space for me. Unsure of what to do, and with limited options, I decided to consult with a lawyer to explore the possibility of filing for bankruptcy. In the midst of this process, I approached Jesus and expressed the urgent need to discuss my unpaid wages and the misappropriation of company funds. To my disappointment, Jesus refused to engage in a conversation or sit down with me and Tamara, citing her unwillingness to discuss the matter and expressing concerns about straining their relationship. His refusal was a pivotal moment for me, as it highlighted their disregard for my concerns and showed that their approach was neither morally acceptable nor sustainable.

As I continued my consultations with the bankruptcy attorney, it became clear that proceeding with filing for chapter 11 bankruptcy was a prudent step. This process involved monthly court fees and a long-term commitment to repay my debts at reduced amounts. I believed that this course of action was the right decision. Not only would it let me persist in my business activities, it also opened the possibility of founding a company exclusively in my name again, all the while reducing the risk of a bank seizure.

This routine persisted for a couple more months until I received an unexpected phone call from Jesus. Finally comprehending the gravity of my circumstances, he made a momentous decision to step away and dissolve his and Tamara's involvement in the company.

A few days later, on June 7, 2012, I established a new company, Computer IT Solutions, Inc. I contacted all of my clients, notifying them about the transition and assuring them that our relationships would remain unaffected amidst the changes. Furthermore, I convened a meeting with my technicians, informing them about the new company and ownership structure while emphasizing that future payments would no longer be facilitated by Jesus and Tamara. Surprisingly, the transition unfolded smoothly, causing no disruptions to our day-to-day operations. To bolster our efficiency, I made an investment in ticketing system software, allowing me to accomplish in just two hours on a Saturday what had previously taken Tamara an entire week. This transformative shift, placing the organization entirely under my sole control, significantly boosted company morale and alleviated my financial burdens.

During this challenging time, I shared my experiences and sought counsel from Veronique, a longtime friend whom I had met over twenty years earlier at a client's office where she was employed. Having progressed from being a comptroller for a developer to establishing her own business providing bookkeeping services for small companies, Veronique was among the few individuals I confided in about my predicament. She expressed genuine concern and disbelief upon learning that I had been working for months without pay. Despite her warnings regarding the arrangement of my former partnership, I maintained my belief that prioritizing customer satisfaction was paramount, whether or not I was paid. And as fate would have it, my convictions eventually proved to be fruitful. With immense gratitude, I accepted Veronique's offer to handle the bookkeeping tasks for my new company, and she has continued to support me in this capacity ever since. Her unwavering friendship and support have been invaluable to me, and I cannot imagine navigating the unknown challenges that lie ahead without her.

Two months after the conclusion of our business relationship, I received an unexpected phone call from Jesus. During our conversation, he inquired about how I was doing. The call brought back memories of the frustrating dynamics we had faced during our collaboration. I had lacked access to checks and bookkeeping data, and despite my repeated requests for us to discuss vital matters like cash flow, income, and expenses, such discussions never took place. Every time I inquired about our monthly expenses and income, I was met with silence.

However, the situation took a significant turn for the better as I regained complete control over my affairs. I gained comprehensive knowledge and access to all incoming and outgoing transactions. When Jesus expressed curiosity about my current circumstances, I provided him with an accurate account of my monthly expenses, reported my total financial receipts from the past two months, and conveyed the note-worthy achievement of attaining a net profit of $20,000 since our separation. Furthermore, I elaborated on the positive outlook, explaining that all indicators pointed toward a high likelihood of consistently earning no less than ten thousand dollars in personal income each month going forward.

"If you're accusing me of stealing from you when I was with you—"

"I'm not accusing you of anything," I replied, cutting him off. "You asked how I'm doing, and I'm simply being precise in my response."

As a consequence of the bankruptcy, my credit took a se-vere hit. However, I accumulated cash at a rapid pace and managed to secure a debit card that I backed with ample cash deposits. Alongside fulfilling my monthly payments to the courts, as mandated by my bankruptcy obligations, my life improved rapidly.

As part of the bankruptcy agreement, I was required to vacate the condo I resided in. After conducting an extensive search, I came across a delightful two-bedroom apartment that captivated my interest. The apartment was situated with-in the Crescent House complex in Miami Lakes. Determined to secure this new living space, I met with the management and submitted my application. Unfortunately, my application was rejected due to my unfavorable credit history and recent bankruptcy. In a bid to overcome this hurdle, I offered to pay a year's worth of rent in advance, but this proposal was also declined. While this outcome wasn't unexpected, I remained undeterred in my pursuit. Over the next few days, I engaged in conversations with multiple individuals within the organi-zation, showcasing my determination. Through tenacity and unwavering effort, I managed to persuade them to reconsid-er their initial decision and offer me tenancy under standard terms. Consequently, six months after regaining sole owner-ship of my company, I moved into Crescent House.

For the next several years, my dedication to my business remained steadfast. Throughout this time, there was a notice-able absence of communication from Jesus, and I refrained from reaching out to him as well. However, one day I received a letter in the mail, informing me of Jesus' own bankruptcy filing. I suspected I had received it because of our former company's shared address. Filled with concern, I called and engaged in a heartfelt conversation with Jesus, inquiring about his well-being and that of his family. He assured me that everything was alright.

The nostalgic feeling of missing my dear friend, his wife, and their children flooded my thoughts. We had shared countless unforgettable dinners and joyous moments to-gether, and I had frequently stayed overnight at their place. Occasionally, I would even pick up his parents, who resided near my former residence, and drive them over for visits to see their son and grandchildren. As I contemplated the past, I envisioned a delightful reunion, brimming with amusing stories to reminisce upon.

Despite the curiosity that arose, I decided not to delve into the intricacies of our past or seek any further information. My intention was never to investigate, as I had no desire to un-cover what had transpired between us.

Then in late November of 2016, an unexpected letter ar-rived from the management of Crescent Apartments, inform-ing me of a considerable increase in my monthly rent for the two-bedroom apartment, now totaling $2,000. This sudden de-velopment prompted me to engage in profound contemplation regarding my living situation. Recognizing that I had accumu-lated ample funds in my bank account, I viewed this as an ideal opportunity to shift gears from renting to purchasing a home once again, this time with the intention of finding a residence that aligned with my personal preferences and aspirations.

I sought the guidance of a trustworthy realtor who helped

me explore a diverse range of appealing properties within the vicinity. Within just two weeks, I discovered a captivating townhome, the construction of which was almost complete, situated in the charming locale of Miramar. As December drew near, I concluded the relocation process and settled into my new dwelling.

The townhome boasted an expansive layout, consisting of three bedrooms, three bathrooms, and a spacious two-car garage. Driven by my strong desire to personalize my new space, I indulged in various upgrades. I enhanced the interior with stone flooring, granite countertops, and stainless-steel appliances, creating an ambiance of sophistication. Once settled, I replaced the carpet on the stairway and upper-floor loft with wood flooring, infusing an additional touch of elegance by installing crown molding throughout.

Leveraging the expertise of my trusted friends and clients from Electric Shade Corp., I entrusted them with the task of installing motorized window blinds, creating convenience and aesthetic appeal. Moreover, I selected new furniture to complement the home's aesthetic. Recognizing the need for efficient storage and improved functionality, I installed cabinets in the garage, creating ample space to organize my belongings. The garage itself underwent a remarkable transformation, with meticulous installation of special tiling over the concrete floor, enhanced by the addition of wood baseboards, creating a visually appealing and functional environment.

Remarkably, the burden of my previous bad credit was completely lifted, as I had the financial means to fund all these endeavors with cash. The acquisition of the home, furnishings, and even my new vehicles—a luxurious Cadillac and a sleek Buick—was accomplished without any worries or constraints related to credit.

And then, in the midst of installing the new flooring in my garage, an unfortunate and all-too-familiar incident occurred. FirstService Residential, the property management company in charge of overseeing the townhomes in my community, had my two cars towed from the streetside parking lot where I had left them overnight. This unexpected turn of events left me feeling puzzled and frustrated, especially considering my efforts to adhere to all the community rules and regulations. I had even obtained the necessary stickers to park my cars streetside within the community.

Motivated by a sense of bewilderment, I contacted different individuals and submitted letters expressing my concerns. To my astonishment, I received written and verbal responses confirming that the stickers I had obtained and placed on my cars' windshields were not meant for street parking. This revelation prompted me to revisit the paperwork I had been given, only to discover that the writing within the documentation was remarkably ambiguous, failing to provide clear guidance on the purpose of the stickers.

Recognizing the requirement and obligation for the property management company to address the situation and reimburse me for the towing fees, taxi expenses, and related charges, I filed a written complaint. However, they refused to provide compensation, fearing that it would establish a precedent and obligate them to reimburse others in similar circumstances. Their response reads as follows: "Mr. Manzur, I send your email to the Board and they understand your concern but they fill that if they make an exception for one owner then we would be opening a door to have to refund all the owners who have had their cars towed for the same violation. Sorry for the inconvenience and delay. Have a great day!"

It was disheartening to witness their approach, which appeared to lack the care and attention I was accustomed to providing my customers when matters of concern are brought to me. I have always been conscientious about spelling names correctly and proofreading my messages, as I want to leave no doubt that my response is thoughtful and that I take their concerns seriously, no matter how frivolous they may seem. Despite their dismissive attitude, I remained resolute in my commitment, driven by the significance of the information

I had gathered. My determination to follow through on my threat of pursuing legal action if I was not promptly compensated persisted. However, to my surprise and delight, the atmosphere took a sudden turn during the court hearing when FirstService Residential relented and agreed to pay me the full amount I had requested without putting up a fight.

With cautious optimism, I proceeded to navigate through the necessary paperwork to finalize the payment. It was at this critical juncture that I asked to review the document before affixing my signature. To my astonishment, a plot twist unfolded before my eyes—a clause revealing a gag order that would silence me from discussing my case with anyone.

Confusion and curiosity intermingled as I grappled with the significance of this restriction. When I voiced my concerns, they were met with dismissiveness, as if they were trivial and unrelated to the matter at hand. Frustrated by the situation, I couldn't help but express my discontent. "Shouldn't this be a matter of importance?" I asked. "What if a collective legal action emerges against the property management company, and my community relies on my testimony to shed light on their wrongdoings?"

Acknowledging the gravity of my concerns, my vocal objections about the clause prompted the defendant to engage in several phone conversations with other legal representatives advocating for the interests of FirstService Residential, deliberating the matter outside the confines of the courtroom. This action resulted in prompt revisions being made to the agreement, leading to the removal of the gag order. With my objections resolved, I signed the revised agreement. After a delightful conversation with the legal counsel, two weeks later, I received my check.

Chapter Thirty-Nine

THE FRAGILITY OF LIFE

After moving into my new home in Miramar in December 2016, I upheld my usual tradition of driving to Homosassa Springs to visit Aunt MaryJane and Uncle Gary during the holiday season. That year, Christmas fell on a Sunday, and I took a few days off work before and after the holiday to extend my visit. As I entered their home, walking down the hallway adorned with framed photos capturing our treasured memories, a powerful surge of emotions overcame me. On every holiday since the passing of my grandparents, their absence was deeply felt.

During my delightful sojourn, I had the pleasure of savoring delicious meals, taking comfort in the fact they were crafted with love rather than merely chosen from a laminated menu. In those precious moments of respite from the demands of work, we immersed ourselves in movies, engaged in lively card games with neighbors and friends, and visited Gary's sister and brother-in-law, who lived nearby. While our playful escapades with BB guns and rifles, once an option of our holiday gatherings on Gary's sprawling land in Parish, NY, had become a thing of the past, we discovered other captivating objects to ignite our imagination.

Among my treasured possessions, my latest acquisition took center stage: a drone that I had obtained prior to my move to Miramar. Although my previous drone met an unfortunate fate on its maiden flight in Homosassa Springs during a previous holiday visit, straying beyond its battery range on a misprogrammed excursion to a golf course several miles away, this setback did not dampen our enthusiasm for further aerial explorations. With my new and improved drone, we embarked on thrilling expeditions, capturing breathtaking videos and creating hilarious moments to enjoy on Gary's expansive large-screen TV. One particular escapade remains vivid in my memory: a Rice Krispies dessert tethered to my drone by a string. It was a creation made by my niece, Justina, Debbie's daughter, who anticipated us enjoying it after dinner. And we did! The spectacle showcased the dessert's resilient and inedible nature as it swung through the air like a miniature wrecking ball.

The next two years passed without significant changes or surprises. As always, I dedicated most of my time to work and took an additional day or two off during major holidays to visit my aunt and uncle in Homosassa Springs.

During my Christmas visit in 2018, my aunt recounted details of her recent trip to Syracuse, where she had visited her friend, Sherley. Their friendship had begun back in Parish and had remained strong over the years. In fact, I joined them, along with my aunt and uncle, for a memorable cruise to the Bahamas aboard the Carnival Cruise ship, *Ecstasy*, in the summer of 2013. I fondly remember the laughter and fun we had together, with Sherley's husband Fred adding his own jokes and humor to the mix.

A memorable incident during a karaoke event occasionally resurfaces in our conversations, when I playfully and repeatedly shouted "Get off the phone!" to an event organizer who seemed disinterested as passengers took their turns singing. It was all part of the lighthearted atmosphere we enjoyed. While we often reminisced about such moments and shared them via the video screens of our Alexa Echo Show devices in our respective kitchens, certain sensitive topics, especially family matters from Syracuse, were best discussed in person.

During the Christmas holiday in 2018, I was reminded that everything continually evolves within the realms of time and space, regardless of the pace. While my aunt was in Syracuse, my mother became aware of her presence and expressed her desire to meet her. Before my Christmas visit to Homosassa Springs, I was aware of their meeting, but I hadn't been informed of the additional details my mother had shared with my aunt—notably, the decline in my father's health.

It had been a while since he had been unable to climb the stairs to his bedroom. Several months, perhaps over a year earlier, an electric lift had been installed on the staircase to assist him. Upon returning to Miami from my holiday vacation and resuming my daily activities, I became increasingly preoccupied with sporadic updates on my father's condition. The mere mention of his name, coupled with the realization that I might never see him again, compelled me to take action once more. Since I had no direct means of contacting my father, I turned to my aunt, who had recently reconnected with her sister—my mother—and requested her assistance in delivering a message to my father. I composed the message, typing it on the morning of Friday, May 17, 2019, at 8:00 a.m.

Dad,
     As Aunt MaryJane is on speaking terms with Mom, I asked her to relay a message. Not wanting to take the chance of mis-

taken interpretation, I've asked this brief letter be read to you. Throughout our lives, on the rare occasion the topic of our relationship arose, you consistently responded with four words: "I'm not ready yet."

I'd like to be able to forgive you, which is not to say I can. The only way I know of finding out is by seeing you, seeing how you respond to me. You will decide what is important to you right now, and I'll soon learn if anything has changed. I'm asking one final time; "Do you want to make peace with me and with yourself."

Your first son,
Dan Mazur

Within an hour of delivering the message to my aunt, she decided to forward it to my brother, David. Later that afternoon, David wrote a response to me: "Confirming receipt and will get this message to Dad in some form, but not verbatim because parts are inherently spiteful, at least that's how I read it."

It wasn't what I had anticipated. I'm unsure why my aunt forwarded my letter to David. I wasn't aware of any change in her relationship with my brother; I would have thought he would be the last person she'd ask such a favor of. Nevertheless, it happened, and the next day, Saturday morning, I replied to David's message.

From: Daniel Mazur
Sent: Saturday, May 18, 2019 8:23 AM
To: dcmazur; MaryJane Lawton
Cc: Paul Mazur
Subject: RE: If you can try to get this North

That's fine Dave, do what you like. Read it, send it, doctor it, whatever. Just remember that in doing so it becomes your message to him, not mine.

As I sit here at my desk on Saturday, July 8, 2023, at 2:30 a.m., working to finalize this manuscript—a process I em-

barked on decades ago—with the promise of a fitting conclusion within my grasp, given the unfolding events, I am
plagued with uncertainty regarding the fate of the message
I entrusted to be delivered to my father. David's silence and
lack of disclosure have left me in the shadows, persistently avoiding any discussion of significant matters. The mere
thought of my brother—or anyone else, for that matter—considering the idea of altering and delivering a message from
a son to his ailing father perplexes me. If I were in his position, facing a similar situation, I would never entertain the
thought of tampering or presenting falsehoods. However, I
cannot feign surprise, as subtle manipulation has often been a
tactic used by my family to achieve their desired outcomes—
a reality that underscores the urgency for a more ethical and
upright approach.

The next day, my brother Paul, who had also been included in the message thread, provided me with an update on our
father's condition, one much improved.

For the following eight months, Paul and I engaged in a
written dialogue. Our email exchanges covered a wide range
of subjects, often touching upon accusations concerning my
perceived hatred and anger, my reluctance to let go of the
past, and my supposed need for spiritual redemption. While
I expected him to include scripture quotations to support his
viewpoints, amidst his reproaches, there were also moments
when Paul expressed his desire for us to reconcile and rebuild
our brotherly bond. However, despite these fleeting glimpses
of hope, the overall tone of our conversation made it clear that
the path to harmony was clouded by the complexities of our
relationship and a shared history that Paul, along with our
father and our other brother, David, refused to address.

In a surprising turn of events, in a letter dated September 13, 2019, Paul admitted to fabricating an event involving
our grandfather, concocting a lie that he believed may have
contributed to our estrangement from him. These false words
were spoken to our father, driven by his misguided percep-

tion of what our father wanted to hear.

I made every effort to convince Paul to disclose the truth to our father, as the passing of so many years had not diminished the importance of doing so. However, it appears that he never took that crucial step. It became clear that my opinions, conveyed through months of correspondence, were unable to penetrate the ingrained doctrines and mindset that Paul had adopted. Moreover, after reflecting on his troubling messages, I realized that my communication with Paul was having a detrimental impact on his mental well-being. As a result, I made the difficult decision to end our correspondence.

BACK TO BUSINESS

FOR THE REMAINDER OF 2019, I SHIFTED MY FOCUS ENTIRELY TO MY business, dedicating my time and energy to its operations. Once more, my communication with my family in Syracuse dwindled, allowing me to immerse myself in various distractions. These helped me avoid ruminating on memories of past family challenges. It was a double-edged sword. While I was grateful for the numerous distractions that year offered, I also recognized their potential downside.

For several years I faced challenges with an employee who had a varied influence on my company. Hired in 2013, this individual initially received training from Marco, another employee who had joined us the previous year. Marco was responsible for overseeing my company's backend technical operations, which included maintaining our mail servers, virtual machines, and backup systems across diverse locations, including our offices, client sites, and colocation facilities, like the one we had in Michigan.

However, in 2015 Marco discovered a more appealing business opportunity and informed me of his intention to depart. Had I been in a position to offer him a more competitive salary and benefits, I would have done so, but circumstances didn't allow it. Consequently, prior to Marco's departure, he trained another employee to step into his role. Over the next four years while Marco was away in New York, this young man performed his assigned tasks. Although he demonstrated good technical skills, his interpersonal skills left much to be desired. In fact, his behavior became a significant challenge, with some clients going so far as to insist that he never set foot in their offices again. Due to his consistent and unamended behavior, several clients even opted to sever their business ties with us.

These circumstances placed me in a difficult position. While the young man had good intentions, he faced personal challenges that affected his professional conduct. Furthermore, matters were complicated by the fact that, since Marco's departure, I had become reliant on him as the sole individual capable of maintaining our intricate and unique systems. Finding someone else who possessed such a wide-ranging skill set would prove to be an arduous task. I engaged in numerous conversations and meetings with the young man, offering suggestions and providing support to address any deficiencies. However, despite my best efforts, nothing seemed to yield positive results. By 2019, my frustrations reached their peak. I had lost numerous clients, our systems were teetering on the brink of collapse, and the employee's deteriorating attitude was impacting other technicians within my company.

During this challenging time, a much-needed ray of hope arrived in the form of an unexpected phone call. Surprisingly,

Marco's work with the company in NY had concluded earlier than expected, reigniting his interest in working with me once again. It was an omen of potential reprieve, and I was beyond delighted to hear from him. Over the next few months, we reviewed what had transpired since his departure and held meetings to discuss and implement crucial corrections, redirecting my business onto the right course. Miraculously, things started to improve. With the other employee having submitted his resignation letter, Marco rejoined me full time. My company regained its momentum in 2019, finally allowing me to shed the years of worry I had carried about surviving the grave difficulties I had faced.

As I continued to forge ahead with my company, my primary focus shifted toward enhancing our infrastructure and collaborating with Marco on planning strategies. Concurrently, in 2019 and 2020, I introduced new offerings to our existing and potential customers, taking concrete steps to improve our operations. However, early in 2021, another obstacle emerged when one of my technicians, who had been working with me for almost a year, decided to depart, leaving a critical position vacant. Determined to find a suitable replacement, I embarked on an extensive search, advertising the job through various media channels, an employment agency, and other platforms.

While I was in the midst of scheduling interviews with several candidates from a vast pool of over one hundred resumes, my attention was diverted by an incoming phone call. It happened while I was standing in my kitchen, contemplating the contents of an empty fridge in an attempt to quell the growling of my stomach. On the other end of the line was a man named Angel, who introduced himself after randomly dialing my number while perusing a directory of computer companies in his neighborhood. Remarkably, he had made the call while seated in his car during his lunch break at the law firm where he worked. Angel, an ambitious young man with aspirations of becoming an IT professional, was seeking a job in his field of interest. I was captivated by his demeanor and attitude during our conversation, and despite his relatively limited experience, I agreed to interview him, recognizing the potential hidden within his determined aspirations. During our conversation and the subsequent interview the following day, I was impressed with Angel and offered him the position on the spot without any hesitation. "No, no, I can't believe this. I must be dreaming!" he exclaimed, gratefully accepting the offer.

On March 15, 2021, after completing the necessary formalities, Angel joined our team and was added to the payroll. I dedicated significant time to training him on our ticketing system and familiarizing him with our company policies. Together, we embarked on visits to our client base, where we performed various IT tasks, making it a regular part of our daily routine in the subsequent weeks. My primary objective was to ensure that Angel established strong connections with our clients, building a sense of comfort and fostering positive relationships. It was of utmost importance to me that my clients, many of whom had become dear friends, held a favorable opinion of our new team member. Initially, everything seemed to be progressing smoothly.

However, amidst these professional advancements, I received a distressing update concerning my father. I learned that his condition had taken a turn for the worse, and his health was rapidly deteriorating with no signs of improvement. Once again, family matters resurfaced, weighing on my mind and overshadowing the happiness that had accompanied the progress and improvements made in my company over the past two years.

Meanwhile, during one of our typical car rides to a client's office, Angel revealed a conversation he had with his father the previous evening at their dinner table. The words he relayed resonated deeply within me for many days to come. He expressed his enthusiasm about the companies I had introduced him to and how warmly I was received, often with hugs and affection. According to his perception, our work transcended mere business, and it felt as though everyone we encountered were my close friends who held a deep care and regard for me.

At that moment, my resistance to compliments and skepticism of others' opinions of me led me to respond with a hint of bitterness. "Tell that to my brothers, sisters, and mother who want nothing to do with me," I said, unable to fully accept Angel's positive perception. After a brief pause, I went further and questioned his belief, almost hoping to plant doubt. "Are you sure I'm such a nice person?" I inquired.

But my doubts and bitterness didn't end there. As I conversed with Angel, I delved into the details of the typical scene portrayed in movies where a parent and estranged child reconcile before the parent's passing. With unwavering conviction, I expressed my pessimistic thoughts. "I may not know much, but one thing I am certain of is that when the time comes for my father's final moments, he won't be seeking to see me or mend our strained relationship."

One month later, on Friday, May 14, 2021, Angel and I were hard at work for a client in Deerfield Beach, installing patch panels and other infrastructure as part of a company's relocation. It had been a long and exhausting day of physical labor at the site, and as the day drew to a close, we loaded our cars with our gear and equipment, preparing for the challenging Friday evening traffic, well aware that the journey back to our respective homes would take a couple of hours.

During the drive, my cell phone rang, interrupting the peaceful moment as I neared the end of an exhausting and demanding workweek. "Computer IT Solutions, can I help you?" I said, still in work mode.

"Hi, Dan, this is Dave," the voice on the other end replied. I took a moment to process, trying to recall the voice.

"Okay, uh, Dave who?" I inquired, seeking clarification.

"Your brother," he said. It took a moment to register, and then it finally clicked. "I've been talking with Dad," he continued. "He's in the hospital, in the intensive care unit, and he wants to speak with you."

Surprised and filled with eagerness to comply, I asked David to put him on the line. However, David explained that he wasn't with our father at that moment; he was at home. However, he assured me that he would call back when he was at the hospital.

When I arrived at home, I received another call, this time from my father.

"Hello, son. How are you?" he asked. After I assured him that I was fine, without wasting any time, he began speaking as if determined to convince me that my decision to reject him was understood and acceptable. "I understand you don't want to see me," he said. "It's okay, but I want you to know, I want to tell you I love you."

He continued speaking, expressing his understanding of my supposed refusal to see him, without taking a breath or pausing to listen for my reply. So, in the middle of his words, I interrupted him. "Whoa, slow down a minute. When have I refused to see you? Are you saying you want to see me?"

"Son, I just want to put my arms around you and tell you I love you." It was the affirmation I had been seeking for years, the knowledge that he wanted to see me. It was everything I had hoped for, all I had ever wanted to hear him say.

As I had always promised and reiterated on several occasions, I made a choice in line with his wishes. "Okay then, I'll see you tomorrow morning."

"Really?" my father said, overjoyed. " You'll come and see me? Oh, son, I'd like that so much."

"Of course, Dad. I'll be there bright and early."

ONE MORE TIME TOGETHER

AFTER OUR CONVERSATION, I ARRANGED A DIRECT FLIGHT FROM Fort Lauderdale to Syracuse. The flight was scheduled to board at 7:15 a.m. the following morning, which happened to be a Saturday, with an estimated arrival time in Syracuse at 9:45 a.m. Exhausted, I took a refreshing shower and then set my alarm clock, ensuring I would wake up early enough to pack my bags for the two-day excursion. I was grateful that weariness facilitated my swift transition into slumber, sparing me from being overwhelmed by thoughts of the ongoing events.

As I settled into my seat on United Airlines flight 1750 the following morning, leaving behind the frenzy of packing, parking, and rushing, I found myself alone with my thoughts and a handful of snacks. It was a moment of serene reflection as I pondered the impending reunion with my father. The news shared by David about Dad's hospitalization in the intensive care unit and his wish to talk to me had taken me by surprise, but it also instilled within me a profound sense of obligation.

My mind was swirling with a whirlwind of questions. Had my father ever received the message I wrote to him two years earlier? Could this long-awaited meeting be the opportunity I had yearned for, where we could finally engage in the conversations I had longed for? Conversations that would delve into the depths of the past, seeking genuine understanding?

Memories from my childhood flooded back, bringing with them a particularly agonizing episode, an enduring abuse that had weighed heavily on me for far too many years. I vividly remembered the neighborhood boy, five years older than me, who introduced me to sex at the tender age of eleven. My youthful naivety and eagerness to please made me an easy target for his advances. Despite my discomfort and attempts to resist, I succumbed to his manipulation. The weight of that experience and the burden of carrying it alone eventually consumed me.

Over the years as I cultivated my own comprehension of sexuality and my personal preferences, a profound anger began to smolder within me. Fortunately, this child predator, who had attended the Living Word church with his family, relocated out of town after graduating from high school. However, destiny orchestrated a disturbing reunion when he returned home and attended a church youth event at a camp. It was there that I witnessed, with growing unease, his predatory behavior toward younger boys who remained oblivious to the danger they were in. The burden of guilt for my silence, for failing to protect those innocent boys, continues to haunt me to this day.

As I progressed through high school and neared my own graduation, he made another visit with his parents and siblings. I had resolved to confront him, to address the injustices he had inflicted not only upon me but potentially upon others as well. However, when he stood before me, a different persona emerged, casting doubt on my decision—an outward appearance of goodness and normalcy. This veneer thwarted my intentions, serving as a lasting reminder that good and evil can coexist within the same person. It added another layer of complexity to my task of exposing the harmful truth and deepened the challenges I faced in seeking justice.

In a cruel twist of fate, a third opportunity for confrontation presented itself during another moment together. This time it unfolded in our home, with my mother unwittingly creating the situation, unaware of the true nature of his actions. While we were all gathered, he mentioned his plan to head to the village, specifically to the Bayberry Fish Cove, to grab a sandwich.

"Why don't you go with him?" my mother suggested. In her eyes, I was still his innocent childhood companion, a sentiment her words tenderly painted. Despite my hesitation, I agreed to accompany him, and we embarked on our journey in his Volkswagen minibus.

I found myself alone with him once again, presented with the perfect opportunity to confront him. Yet for reasons I couldn't explain, I remained silent. Even when he resorted to his old tactics, I lacked the strength to voice my objections. Instead, I brushed off his advances, pushing them away without uttering a word against him. I chose to bury my pain and anger deep within, opting for silence over confrontation. It was a decision that haunted me later, as I constantly wondered what might have transpired or possibly even been prevented if, during one of my many chances, I had mustered the courage to speak up.

Despite my previous silence, I vowed that if an opportunity ever presented itself again, I would confront him and address the pain and injustice that had haunted me for years. However, fate had different plans, and I never had the chance to see him again. He was on a trajectory parallel in time and circumstances to that of a famous musician whose talent and voice deeply intrigued me. Tragically, both he and Freddie Mercury passed away in 1991.

Anyone from the Living Word Church who believes I equate the actions of a molester with those of my father is deeply mistaken. It is important to clarify that we are in agreement that the harm caused by each individual's actions is not comparable. The deviant behavior of my former neighbor had a significant impact on me, but I have overcome its effects. From my late teens until now, I have developed an understanding of my sexuality and encountered no obstacles in embracing it despite the challenges stemming from my past. However, in contrast, my father's actions have had a profound and enduring impact, permanently altering my life's trajectory.

With this heightened awareness and my profound regret for failing to act upon the numerous opportunities to confront the molester for his lesser charge, I found myself in a deeply perplexing and challenging situation. I was faced with the chance to confront someone who had caused even greater harm to me. The gravity of these circumstances left me consumed by uncertainty as I grappled with the decision of whether to take action and confront the person or once again succumb to a veneer of goodness and innocence.

And what about the message I sent him two years ago? Did he read it? Was it read to him, and were my words manipulated as David said he would do? Was my father finally ready to engage in a conversation with me, to acknowledge his wrongdoings and seek reconciliation? It was disheartening to accept the fact that his remaining days in this world seemed to be drawing near. However, it is the inevitable fate for all of us. What troubled me even more was the possibility that, as a Christian and particularly as a pastor, it took the impending reality of his mortality, standing at the threshold of departure, for him to finally confront the truth about his life. I couldn't help but ponder the notion that he might be seeking reconciliation from me, hoping to secure his entry through the pearly gates with Saint

Peter's blessing. If that turned out to be the case, it would be a poignant illustration of a life spent in constant and unnecessary avoidance of self-created tragedy.

These were the thoughts racing through my mind, the contemplations that would influence my conversations with my father later that morning.

With my head resting against the window, I turned my gaze outside and recognized the familiar sights below. The distinctive outline of Onondaga Lake came into view, evoking memories of songs, including the school's alma mater, which mentioned its name during events at Liverpool High School. "On the shores of Onondaga, Hail our orange and blue. Towering toward our Alma Mater, Live forever true . . ." Soon, I knew, the runway of Hancock Airport would appear.

As I felt the plane descending, I couldn't help but envision my flight instructor beside me. He guided me through the proper methods for approach in a Cessna 172, emphasizing the correct use of instruments and effective communication with the tower. This was a memory from my training days at Opa Locka Airport, a time when my work wasn't enough to distract me from familial rifts, and I obtained my pilot's license. If my family relationships had taken different paths, that flight might have been a return from a vacation rather than from my home, where I had the opportunity to participate in such an experience.

Upon landing, the lack of diversity among the people I passed was impossible to ignore. Their homogeneous appearance stood out in stark contrast to the vibrant mixture of cultures I had grown accustomed to in Miami. The absence of a Latin influence, which was so prevalent in my everyday experiences, was evident in that seldom-visited environment. It marked a distinct departure from my usual interactions and local encounters.

As I made my way to the baggage claim area, my attention was drawn to my luggage, already present and distinguished by the two green cable ties I had attached to each handle. After collecting my bags, I retrieved my rental car. Then I relied on Google Maps to guide me to the hospital despite my familiarity with Syracuse and its surroundings from having grown up there.

When I arrived at the hospital's parking garage, I took a moment to gather myself, preparing for the forthcoming changes. When I felt ready, I made my way toward the hospital's front entrance, filled with determination.

"I'm here to see Robert Mazur," I said to the receptionist. With a gentle reassurance, she informed me that my scheduled visit was planned for later, precisely at 2:00 p.m. It dawned on me that I had overlooked my brother's message regarding the designated visiting hours. Feeling a tinge of disappointment, I apologized and made my way out of the hospital, assuring the woman that I would return at the appropriate time.

With ample time on my hands, I strolled through University Hill, a neighborhood that was home to Syracuse University students and a place I had frequented numerous times with my friend, Kyle. During those visits, we would often embark on mischievous adventures, leaving indelible memories as we cruised the streets in his hot pink 280Z. We would initiate spontaneous conversations with passersby, inviting anyone willing to engage with us on our exhilarating rides through the neighborhood.

Marshall Street, just a block away from the hospital, was a special spot that we would visit frequently. It was a bustling hub of activity, adorned with a diverse range of shops and eateries. As I strolled along the street once again, I took in the sights, savoring the vibrant energy and observing the passersby while admiring the merchandise on display.

My feet led me to Acropolis Restaurant, a familiar establishment where I had savored countless enjoyable meals. It was a few minutes past 12:00. As I stepped inside for a bite, the lingering effects of the recent COVID-19 pandemic became apparent in the sparsely occupied restaurant. Nonetheless, the owner greeted me warmly, and with the reduced activity,

I seized the opportunity to engage in a friendly conversation with him, exchanging anecdotes and discussing the changes that had occurred since my last visit.

I ordered a couple of tantalizing slices of pepperoni pizza and then settled into a cozy booth near the front window. With eager anticipation, I welcomed the arrival of the savory slices, relishing every bite as the flavors transported me back in time. From my vantage point, I observed the lively outdoor activities of the town, which evoked fond memories of my experiences exploring the vibrant streets of Syracuse and the lively atmosphere of the hill.

As the minutes ticked by and my departure loomed closer, I reached for my phone, intending to sift through my emails and tend to any last-minute business matters. However, to my delight, no pressing issues demanded my immediate attention. With a sigh of relief, I settled back into my seat, allowing myself a moment of respite.

As I cast another glance out the window, my gaze was drawn to the lively scene unfolding on the streets. Despite the bustling activity, I couldn't help but notice the students engaged in conversations, their voices muffled by the masks they wore. It was evident that their communication was hindered, even though I couldn't hear their voices myself. We were all facing similar struggles in adapting to the new norms imposed by the pandemic.

As the server placed a third slice of pizza before me, I savored it while continuing my conversation with the friendly store owner. With the hands of the clock inching closer to 1:45, a sense of anticipation swelled within me. It was time to bid farewell to the restaurant's welcoming atmosphere. I rose from my seat, expressing my gratitude to the owner for his hospitality. We exchanged warm farewells and then I made my way back to the hospital, a renewed sense of purpose coursing through my veins. Whatever awaited me, I was prepared to embrace it with an open heart and a determined spirit.

As I arrived once again, my attention shifted to the growing line outside the hospital entrance. While engaging in a brief discussion with some of those waiting, I discovered that, in accordance with COVID-19 restrictions, only one person was permitted to enter at a time. This revelation triggered a question in my mind: would the same restrictions apply to visitations inside? Would they be limited to one person at a time? The yearning for a solitary moment with my father briefly flickered in my thoughts, but then the harsh reality quickly set in. I knew it wasn't feasible. Undoubtedly, my family would insist on supervising my visits to him, leaving no room for the privacy I desired.

When it was my turn to enter the lobby, I approached the front desk once more. The receptionist checked her booklet and then provided me with the location of his room. Before I proceeded, she captured my image and then affixed an identification badge to my shirt.

In the meantime, uncertain about the hospital's visitation policy, I inquired if anyone else was already present or scheduled to visit. "Due to COVID, we only allow one visitor per day," she explained. I was shocked.

Well, that settles it, I thought. My family had no choice but to permit me to visit my father without supervision, so I could honor his wish to see me.

I stepped into the elevator and ascended to the upper floor where my father was receiving care in the ICU. After maneuvering through a network of hallways, I reached the designated area. As I approached the spot that I believed to be his location, my attention was captured by a blue curtain, which created a flicker of doubt if I had arrived at the right place. The details of the curtain—the particular hue of blue and its texture—seized my focus, coinciding with a heightened awareness of the rhythmic sound of my own heartbeat.

With determination, I extended my hand to pull the curtain aside. In that powerful moment, there he was, right before me, my father turning his head to meet my gaze.

"Son," he said, his voice filled with recognition and anticipation. "Danny," he continued, as if to affirm the significance of a specific child being in his presence. Instantly, I became acutely conscious of each step, moving with a sense of purpose as I approached my father. Soon, I found myself standing by his side, still silent, unsure of which words would escape my lips first. And then it happened.

"Hi, Dad," I said, the words flowing naturally from my lips.

He lifted his head slightly toward me, and I could see the desire for a hug in his outstretched arms. However, I couldn't bring myself to reciprocate. "I can't, Dad," I said. "But I'm here, as I promised, and that must count for something, right?" "Oh, how wise you are," he replied, his voice filled with understanding and gratitude. "Yes, I understand. I'm so glad you came."

The moment of tension and the potential for disaster that accompanied the long-awaited encounter had dissipated. I realized that my father had the ability to perceive my actions with openness and a willingness to accept them as intended, rather than responding defensively and viewing me as a threat. It wasn't just the words exchanged; it was also the unfamiliar expressions that accompanied them. As I write, I find it challenging to express my conviction that his demeanor was not influenced by drugs or medication. It could be the countless micro-expressions and their timing, subtly registered and subconsciously compared to past experiences in my mind, that contribute to this belief. This explanation, described to the best of my ability, depicts my state of mind at that moment as I beheld my father's wide-open eyes, locked onto me with an intensity and duration that surpassed any I had witnessed before. In that unfamiliar and surprising environment, our first conversation began with simple inquiries about my life in Miami and my business ventures. I replied by sharing details about my experiences, and he reciprocated by telling me about my brothers and their achievements in the business world.

As our conversation delved into the familiar and harmonious realm of our professional lives, there were pauses, during which my father would interject, seemingly astounded, saying, "How wise you've become." I contemplated the significance of his words, searching for any hidden messages they might hold.

The topic of our discussion changed just as two nurses entered the room. Seeing them, my father's face radiated with pride, and he introduced me to them, saying, "This is my firstborn son, Daniel."

He continued to speak in this unfamiliar manner, weaving words together in a way I had never witnessed before. But I held steadfast in my belief that his words were purposeful and measured, unaffected by external influences. Whether intentional or not, his behavior conveyed a message that contradicted his past demeanor, as he led me to perceive myself in a new and positive light. In doing so, he forged ahead with compliments rather than reprimands—a strikingly different and contrasting approach that disregarded the potential costs or consequences that he had meticulously weighed in his earlier years.

As we continued talking, one of the nurses raised Dad's arm to insert a needle for drawing blood. However, even during this procedure, my father's gaze remained fixed on me, and I don't recall seeing him blink throughout the process.

The entire experience was like a whirlwind. Each moment, brimming with surprise, left me trying to catch up and comprehend. In the rare moments of silence, I tried to make sense of the chaotic emotions and revelations. As I delved into my past and contemplated my upbringing, a painful realization resurfaced—I had been conditioned to believe that I was rebellious, an outcast who had rejected my father and his life's purpose. It felt as though I had been treated as an impediment, a malignant tumor, excised for the sake of the collective well-being. Constantly burdened with the weight of guilt, I had been made to believe that my every action confirmed my inevitable path toward eternal damnation.

Now as I stood face to face with my father, a pastor who had dedicated his life to a doctrine that deemed me foolish, I was perplexed by the contradiction. He was now proclaiming to me and others that I possessed wisdom, a sentiment that left me bewildered. Should I now assume the role of quoting scripture, reminding him that human wisdom is often regarded as foolishness in God's eyes?

While contemplating these thoughts, my attention shifted as I noticed the nurse requiring my father's assistance. Sensing the importance of her task, I diverted his focus. "Dad," I said, "they need to take your blood."

"Oh, that's okay," he said. "Let them do what they need to do. I'm talking with my firstborn boy."

Throughout our interaction, my father's attention was directed solely at me. He seemed oblivious to others unless their actions or words directly concerned my presence. It was a deeply perplexing experience. How could he prioritize me and shower me with compliments, considering our extensive history of continuous disagreement? He had consistently held radical beliefs, accusing me of being swayed by evil and cautioning others about the perils of associating with me. I had anticipated a conversation centered more around reprimands rather than the unexpected praise that unfolded during what might turn out to be our final moments together.

Amidst the swirling confusion, a powerful surge of emotion welled up inside me, eager to find release. It evoked memories of a similar incident that had occurred at the dining room table back home, where I had struggled to contain my frustration. It was when my sister Pam had mockingly criticized our neighbor as her dog roamed into his yard. An inner voice had compelled me to speak up, offering an opposing perspective to the situation at hand.

Unable to restrain myself any longer, the words burst forth from within me. "But, Dad, I'm an atheist!" He lay there, serene and composed, without lifting his head or revealing any disapproval. There was no furrowed brow or even a hint of reaction that indicated I had crossed a boundary. Then he responded in a tranquil and comforting tone.

"Oh, that's perfectly alright, my son. Everyone goes through their own unique journey and experiences that shape their beliefs. You are on your own path, and that is fine. We all have something valuable to offer each other."

While I held firm to my beliefs, expecting and, in a peculiar way, yearning for a response that would spark a heated argument, his words gave me pause. I realized I couldn't react in my usual reflexive manner. I felt compelled to halt and contemplate the significance of what he had just said. And that's precisely what I did. I immersed myself in deep reflection, not just at that moment but also in the days to come, still engrossed in the profound implications of his words. It was a glimpse into an unexpected manifestation of wisdom that I believe had always dwelled within him yet remained concealed out of fear of jeopardizing the long-sought-after accomplishments he had attained.

With my words off my chest, followed by his calm reassurance, a sense of relief came over me, allowing me to relax and continue our conversation. We carried on, delving into safe, neutral subjects, until the moment arrived for him to be moved from the ICU into a shared room with another patient.

After my father was transferred from his bed to a stretcher, I walked beside him as the nurse wheeled him to his room. Upon arriving, another nurse helped lift him into his new bed. Once he was comfortably situated, the nurse offered him a menu, indicating that it was time to place his lunch order.

As I stood beside him, I couldn't ignore the continuous moaning emanating from his roommate, a clear indication that he was in pain. I turned to my father, expecting a reaction, or at the very least, an acknowledgment that he too heard and was somewhat discomforted by the distressing sounds. However, it seemed that my father had grown accustomed to such noises during his prolonged hospital stay. He appeared unfazed, as if these unsettling sounds had become a new normal for him. It took effort on my part to tune out the sounds that lingered in my memory as I tried to redirect my focus to my father's menu selections for the day.

When his meal arrived, it became apparent that he was unable to feed himself. Without hesitation, I offered my assistance, making sure to wipe his lips and chin, as necessary. I never could have anticipated his willingness to accept such support in his vulnerable state, especially from me. As I carried out this gesture, which could have been seen as endearing and as a way to compensate for declining his request for an earlier embrace, he proceeded to open up further and share new stories.

At that moment, my father unveiled a past plagued by personal doubt and low self-esteem. He shared about a previously undisclosed relationship with a sergeant that had developed during his time in the military after high school, a story that had remained concealed from me until then. The interactions between my father and this influential individual had a profound impact on him, forging a deep personal connection. Through his kindness and guidance, this sergeant not only revealed to my father his hidden capabilities but also imparted valuable life lessons, resembling that of a caring mentor to his protégé.

This relationship held immense significance for my father, contrasting sharply with the troubled relationship he had with his stepfather, whom he had consistently denounced. However, during his military service, my father's physical limitations, stemming from a previous injury, were uncovered, leading to his premature discharge. The realization that his bond with the sergeant would be severed brought him overwhelming anguish and distress.

As a consequence of this relationship, which was abruptly interrupted during his short stint in the military, my father asserted that he had discovered his authentic self, surpassing the limitations imposed by his previous acceptance of low self-esteem. He believed that the impact of this relationship would be embedded in his memory forever. Proceeding to recount additional anecdotes, he highlighted his notable achievements in rifle shooting competitions and his exceptional performance in business and various other endeavors, consistently outshining his rivals.

As I listened, occasionally feeding him spoonfuls of rice and portions of chicken, his eyes widened to accentuate key moments in his stories. Every now and then a few grains of rice or other food would escape his mouth, finding their way to his cheek or chin. I would wipe them away, momentarily pausing his narrative.

Perhaps influenced by the heightened focus on his meal, he transitioned into his next topic, one that I had never encountered before: "the food pantry." I was about to embark on a journey of discovery, learning about it for the first time. The pride and joy on his face were unmistakable right from the start.

The purpose of the pantry was to provide food for the community, extending a helping hand to those who were less fortunate. It was heartwarming to hear such a positive story and understand the immense value this initiative brought to the community. Witnessing my father speak of it with enthusiasm filled me with immense pleasure and pride, knowing that he had played a crucial role in its development. I also realized that without his involvement the program may never have come to fruition.

As he continued to discuss the impact of the pantry and its positive contributions to those in need, I became keenly aware of my need to proceed with caution in our conversation, given the precarious nature of our relationship. I understood that a single misplaced word or misinterpreted intention could have adverse consequences. With this in mind, as I wanted to express my perspective on what he had revealed, I selected my words carefully.

"I want you to know that I think it's wonderful, and I would have been pleased to be here, involved in such a meaningful project with you."

He continued discussing the project, and I remained attentive. However, a voice of pessimism began to emerge, whispering in my ear, reminding me of the cost associated with this positive occurrence. The voice demanded recognition, as if to uphold my self-respect and integrity. Engaged in a harmonious conversation with my father, I yearned to suppress these persistent thoughts that would undoubtedly disrupt our exchange. As my father continued to speak, it felt as if his voice receded into the background, and I became overwhelmed with a flood of persuasive arguments, compelling me to remind my father of the sacrifices made for what he was so proud to have accomplished.

And so it happened; I interjected with a long-overdue comment that had burdened me for decades. "The positive impact you have achieved is commendable. However, you declared spiritual warfare, drew a line between those believed to be with and against you. What about the collateral damage, those who paved the way and paid the price for the existence of this project?" I could sense from his eyes and expressions that he grasped the allusion I was making to myself, family members, and others who had been unjustly accused and mistreated. However, the typical reaction I had grown accustomed to—a rebuke and insistence on my removal, escorting me from the premises for daring to make such bold statements, as had occurred in the past—was conspicuously absent. There was no outburst, no reprimand or scolding.

After a brief pause, seemingly lost in thought regarding my comment, he simply responded, "I did the best I could, son. I did the best I could."

It was evident to both of us that his response fell short of addressing my long-standing concerns. Nevertheless, I had received his answer, and while we both acknowledged its inadequacy, I realized that any confession or acknowledgment of his wrongdoings could not be coerced by me. Instead, it should be offered voluntarily, stemming from his own volition.

Furthermore, my father's ability to exert influence over others had reached its conclusion. Though receiving an apology from him would have been gratifying, I realized I had to focus on what remained within reach, within my control. I could offer my father moments of comfort and succor during our remaining time together. Consequently, I simply said, "Okay, Dad, okay," then let the matter rest.

Hours had elapsed since the start of my visit, and I was determined to steer our conversation back to safer topics. With a renewed resolve, I introduced new subjects, aiming to bring our exchange to a joyful conclusion. "Do you remember when you bought me a suit and trench coat when I started knocking on doors to find customers for my photography work?" I asked.

"Yeah, I remember. It was at Penn-Can Mall," he replied with excitement. "And I bought you shoes too," he added with a hint of nostalgia.

I continued, striving to evoke as many pleasant memories as I could summon. "Do you remember the time I rode on the back of the orange Honda motorcycle with you? I asked why you always said 'heads up' when we hit a puddle."

"Ah, no, I don't recall that one," he replied.

"Yes, I must have been around eleven, and I asked why you didn't say 'heads down' instead." This prompted a shared laugh between us.

"It's funny how certain memories stick with us," he remarked.

I mentioned a nature documentary that he took me to, a wildlife film in a theater featuring a grizzly bear and a bearded man with a weathered, rugged face. We also talked about the times we traveled together, staying in a hotel during an out-of-town rifle competition, and walking together to the elevated dirt mounds where we set up targets 600 yards away. I fondly recalled how we admired the tight grouping of holes made by his .308 rifle in his target, which we viewed through the binoculars he gave me. And I couldn't resist sharing the moment when he made me giggle while showing me the wider groupings of holes in the targets of his competitors.

I was cherishing our time together, engaging in conversations and sharing genuine laughter with my father. However, deep down, I knew that within the limited time we had left, a more serious and potentially uncomfortable matter would inevitably arise.

Having visited my father at the hospital and being fully aware of his condition, I grew curious about the extent of his previous hospital stays and the adjustments he had had to make at home before his current admission. One aspect that piqued my interest was the installation of an electric lift on the stairway, which I had heard about. It helped him ascend to the bedroom. I wanted to inquire about when it was installed and how long he had been relying on it.

I listened with great interest as my father responded to my inquiries, absorbing the explanations he provided. The information shed light on his well-being and personal journey over the past several years, leading to the realization that he was no longer able to fulfill his pastoral duties. It became evident that a transition was necessary, and the role of full-time pastor needed to be passed on to someone else who could assume the responsibilities.

Hearing this only heightened my curiosity, urging me to inquire about the process that led to Bryan Rocine being recognized as the most suitable candidate for such an important role. With a mixture of apprehension and determination, I posed the question that had been brewing within me. "How was the decision made for Bryan to take your place?" In the depths of my mind, I had imagined a tale of divine intervention, envisioning my father spending weeks in fervent prayer, seeking God's guidance, and ultimately receiving the undeniable answer that Bryan was the chosen one. However, my earlier thoughts and predictions about what I would be told that day were way off the mark.

"Well, no one else wanted it, and he was really after it," he said in the most matter-of-fact manner. There was no fabrication, no twisting of truth to make it seem like an act of God or anything of that nature.

Summoning courage once again, and risking the tranquility of the moment, I shared my candid opinion about Bryan. "I've had some correspondence with him, and I must admit, I don't believe he's an honest man. His interests lie more in what he wants rather than in what's true." To my surprise, my father responded calmly to my disapproving comments. He acknowledged the faults he had seen in Bryan and the disagreements they had had. However, he emphasized that we were all on a journey of learning and growth, suggesting that Bryan had the capacity to change and focus on personal development.

It occurred to me that he may have understood that my criticism of Bryan closely aligned with my views on him. I wondered if his response was, in some way, a confession of his realization that his own prioritization of personal desires over truth had been misguided. Although my curiosity yearned to delve deeper into this matter, a cautious voice within me warned against pushing the boundaries of our discussion. I knew that my reservations about Bryan's character and his disregard for truth were well founded, even documented and available to anyone. However, I was reluctant to probe too deeply into such a sensitive topic, one reminiscent of my father's own character flaws, as it might exacerbate the tension in our fragile relationship. Once again, I returned to an earlier thought: my father's influence and impact on others were over, and I questioned whether pursuing this line of conversation would serve any purpose beyond indulging my own pride and self-righteousness.

With a sense of resignation, I decided to keep these thoughts to myself, realizing that delving deeper into the matter would serve no good purpose. However, after another hour of discussing more benign topics, a moment arose when I felt compelled to pose another crucial question, one on which I wanted my father's insight before leaving that evening.

"Dad," I began, with a mixture of vulnerability and curiosity, "if you hadn't met my mother at Grandpa's camp, if she had married someone else, what do you think her future would have looked like? What do you think the likelihood would have been for her to be separated from her parents, sister, some of her children, and all of her cousins?"

My father remained calm and respectful, taking in my question as he had done with all the others without even a hint of anger brewing within him. He paused, seemingly reflecting, and then, with a composed demeanor tinged with discomfort, he replied. "Son, I did the best I could. I did the best I could."

In that instant, his words triggered a flashback to one of his sermons in which he had been filled with fiery passion, insisting, "I've done my very best. I've done everything humanly possible!" Though his words were different and spoken years apart, they held the same meaning, resonating with other phrases I had often heard from him, such as his declaration that he had no regrets about his life. At that moment, as in the past, I couldn't fathom how anyone could believe or have the audacity to say they had done everything right, without room for even a little more effort.

Although we had been separated for decades, my father and I shared an understanding, an unspoken knowledge of each other's honesty. There had been moments of deception between us where we both tried to conceal the truth. However, once face to face, we could detect the tells, knowing when the other was being less than truthful. This was one of those moments. Yet again I realized that pressing the matter would only cause unnecessary discomfort. So, I simply responded to his denial as I had done before, saying, "Okay, Dad, okay," and I let it go.

As the clock struck 6:00, the nurse granted me an exception to stay past visiting hours until 7:00. During that final hour together, our conversation remained pleasant. It was of utmost importance to me that when I left, my father would be left with a sense of contentment about the time we had shared that day. If my people skills were any good, then I had succeeded in leaving my father just as I had intended.

Earlier that evening, David had called and extended an invitation for me to stay at his house for the night. Retrieving my phone, I accepted his invitation via text and confirmed his address. Before bidding my father farewell, after exchanging heartfelt pleasantries, I leaned in and kissed his cheeks. With a tight embrace, I whispered wishes for a peaceful night and a promise of tomorrow's conversation. Then I headed toward the parking garage. My rental car awaited, ready to sail me through the night to yet another chapter—a rendezvous at David's abode.

VISITING DAVID AND HIS FAMILY

THE LAST TIME I SET FOOT IN DAVID'S HOUSE, IT WAS NESTLED amidst a sea of autumn hues, twenty years earlier. As I revisited the address he'd sent in his recent text, a wave of nostalgia hit me, intertwined with a nagging doubt: was it the same home? In 2001, Syracuse had greeted me with its frosty breath as my grandfather and I journeyed from the warmth of Tennessee. We were there to bid farewell to his sister, our beloved Aunt Sue, a cherished pillar in our vast family.

The funeral was a blur of familiar faces, but among them, David's stood out like a storm cloud on the horizon. Years of distance had formed a chasm between us, and to my shock, he bridged it with harsh words and pointed accusations. I bit back my response, choosing silence over confrontation. Later, amidst the soft hum of conversations at our cousin's cozy reception, he approached me again. This time, regret softened his gaze. "Why don't you and Grandpa come over to the house and visit with me and the kids?" he suggested, the rough edges of his voice having softened.

It wasn't merely about reconciliation. It was an opportunity for our grandfather, whose days were colored by age, to forge a precious memory with his great-grandchildren. I jumped at the chance.

Watching them together that day, sharing stories and engaged in playful antics reminiscent of my own childhood, filled me with a deep sense of fulfillment. For each of them, at their tender age, this would be a unique and cherished experience, likely to be remembered for many years, perhaps even a lifetime. For me it was a nostalgic joy, a cherished memory revisited and relived at every stage of my own growth.

As we prepared to depart that evening, I witnessed my grandfather and the children forming a circle, holding hands, and sharing a moment of prayer together. Their faces were filled with deep emotion, care, and love—everything I had hoped for. It reassured me that I had made the right decision to bring them together.

In retrospect, despite the difficult decisions I've faced in life, breaking my promise to my aunt to minimize my grandfather's exposure to those who had harmed him is something I harbor no regrets about. I knew that after a brief explanation when I returned with my grandfather, she would understand and even be grateful for what I did. Though it may seem like an easy decision, given the complexities within our family, my choice to accept David's invitation wasn't made lightly. My grandparents had suffered greatly, enduring their estrangement from my parents, siblings, and their great-grandchildren for decades. It has profoundly affected them.

While that visit might have offered only momentary joy and normalcy for my ailing grandfather, the impact on him and the opportunity for the children to cherish that joyful experience to carry forward in their memories was an outcome I was pleased to have helped shape. As I traveled to David's house twenty years later, I was keenly aware of the memories of those events.

Delving deeper into my thoughts at that time, my introspection wove together past experiences with considerations of the events leading to my disownment. A haunting chorus of whispers filled my ears, and questions emerged, hinting that their answers might have illuminated my understanding of my life and those dear to me. As I prepared for the conversations that lay ahead, three primary considerations about my nephews and nieces came to the forefront: the evolution of their character, the influences that had shaped them, and their views on the world they now navigated.

Unsure of my proximity to their home, I consulted Google Maps and discovered I was a mere nine minutes away. As the map zoomed in, detailing their area on my phone screen, recognition dawned; he lived merely five minutes from our parents' home. Then my train of thought was interrupted by an unfamiliar song emanating from the car radio. Glancing at the dashboard's LCD display, I realized I didn't recognize the station. Eager for an improvement, I toggled through channels, hoping to find a more fitting tune. Success! The iconic strains of Led Zeppelin's "Dazed and Confused" blasted through the speakers. While it might not have encompassed all of my emotions, the song's vibe and lyrics encapsulated the dissonance of that journey: my shock and awe juxtaposed against others' unruffled acceptance. I double-checked the station's identity. It was 95.7, or 95X as it was known, and it had been my go-to during my Syracuse days. It had once powered my workout sessions and fueled spirited drives with Kyle in his 280Z. It felt like a serendipitous nod to the past, reviving memories and stirring my creativity.

The song's end heralded my arrival in David's neighborhood, with streets twisting and turning like ribbons in a dance. Darkness clung to the corners, making the house numbers play a game of hide and seek. Memories of a past blunder in Homosassa surged to the forefront of my mind. There, in a comical mix-up, I'd pulled into a stranger's driveway, thinking it was my aunt's. I waltzed up to the door, rang the bell, and when an unfamiliar face greeted me, I mistook his puzzled expression for mere surprise and brushed past him, already weaving tales of my journey in my mind.

However, the unfamiliarity of the décor soon shattered my delusion. The stark realization that I was an intruder in a stranger's dwelling was amplified by the sight of the man still clutching the doorknob, eyebrows raised in bemusement. As I retraced my steps, a hurried apology tumbled from my lips, punctuated by his unexpected chuckle. It seemed he'd pieced together my comical miscalculation before I had. I vowed then never to have an encore of that embarrassing performance, and that night was no exception. I strained my eyes harder, ensuring I wouldn't invade another stranger's home.

After spotting their address and verifying it thrice, I glided into the expansive driveway. As I approached the door and rang the bell, Dianne, David's wife, welcomed me. Her inviting smile, immediate and genuine, illuminated the entrance. "Hi, Danny, come on in," she said, the nostalgia of our shared past evident in her eyes. Growing up, Dianne and Lisa, the Maloney girls from our neighborhood, frequently joined David and me in childhood play. Dianne was a regular at the Living Word Church, attending with her close-knit family—a commitment she still maintains with David and their offspring.

Years ago I harbored a crush on Lisa, Dianne's older sister. Memories flooded back of how David and I frequented the Maloney residence, battling it out in spirited ping-pong matches in their basement. I couldn't forget their mother, Lorain, distinctively tall for a woman. Her slightly stooped stance and penchant for flat shoes seemed like a nod to her self-consciousness about towering over many, perhaps even her husband. Taking after her mother, Dianne was also quite tall.

She ushered me into the living room where the family had

congregated. Given my exhaustion and sensory overload from the cascade of events since the prior evening, and considering the advanced hour, I find it hard to pinpoint exactly who was there. Throughout my stay at David's place, that family room frequently served as the backdrop for deep, heartfelt conversations. It feels as if all our discussions coalesced into a single continuous narrative, painting a vibrant mural of tales with my siblings, nephews, nieces, and mother.

Although the clock read only 8:00 p.m., my body, accustomed to a 2:00 a.m. wakeup, perceived it to be much later. Despite my fatigue, provocative discussions upon my arrival highlighted the key players in the room.

Taking the offered seat, I melted into its plush embrace, its supportive armrests cradling me. As I settled, I felt the weight of inquisitive eyes from my family, their attention drawn to me. Dianne, ever the gracious host, asked if I needed anything to drink. Before long, a flurry of inquiries filled the room, emanating from every direction. The younger generation, in particular, buzzed with curiosity about my life in Miami and who I'd become. And when I say "younger," I'm reminded that the "kids" weren't so young anymore. Audrey, at twenty-one, was the youngest. Davie and Natalie had already embarked on their own matrimonial journeys, complete with kids of their own.

Nibbling on ranch-dipped carrots and savoring the variety of treats Dianne brought back, I started sharing anecdotes from my life in Miami. I aimed for a lively, upbeat tone, wanting to keep the atmosphere relaxed and engaging for them and their parents. Two decades had passed since our last reunion, but some memories lingered. It might've been Natalie who brought up Claudia. I shared updates about our time in Miami and my memorable trip to Bariloche to visit her.

Before long my brother Paul chimed in, delighting in recounting tales of my mischievous antics where he often found himself on the receiving end. He fondly recollected a family portrait day when I persuaded him to keep a straight face.

To this day, his solemn expression stands out amid the sea of smiles, the picture displayed above our parents' fireplace. He also regaled everyone with the story of my nighttime routine, where I'd tap on my bed's wooden headboard using two fingernails, creating just the right amount of noise to irk my brothers and keep them awake. The room buzzed with amusement, and David's exaggerated eye rolls served as proof that he too remembered these antics, lending credibility to Paul's narratives.

Amid the lively atmosphere, a voice stood out—that of my nephew, Davie. He bore little resemblance to the ten-year-old boy I had seen two decades earlier. Showcasing his mother's genes, he towered over most at a commanding height well over six feet. But it wasn't just his physical stature that caught my attention; it was his distinct mannerisms. His voice lacked the Mazur family's characteristic breathy undertone. His expressions, inflections, and overall demeanor set him apart, not just from our side of the family but also from anyone on his mother's side whom I had encountered. Davie was a unique blend, an individual in his own right.

However, his demeanor bore a striking resemblance to someone I knew in Miami—Jozef. Our bimonthly rendezvous at a café, typically over a chilled beer, had made me well-acquainted with Jos's mannerisms. A successful business owner originally hailing from Belgium, he divided his time between the United States and Europe. Our conversations often delved deep as we shared personal stories and experiences. Amid these dialogues, we uncovered clear disparities between our life journeys, with one striking contrast being our relationship with our fathers. Jos, who is a tad younger than me, had the privilege of a nurturing bond with his father, a factor that I believe played a significant role in his financial success and other personal achievements.

Seeing Davie, who was reminiscent of Jos, made me ponder how different Jos's life might've been under different familial circumstances. Such thoughts grew more poignant when, after I had shared some light-hearted anecdotes from my past, Davie remarked, "Where have you been?" It wasn't posed as a question but rather a statement, revealing his astonishment that I didn't match the image that had been constructed of me in family tales. Far be it from me to be exposed as an ordinary guy, not living up to the expectations assumed from the unverified and popular narratives.

The conversations flowed effortlessly, sticking to light-hearted subjects until my nephew's inquiries ventured into more sensitive territory. I found myself navigating uncharted waters, shifting from the familiar position of asking questions to answering them. I addressed his queries with care, a dynamic reminiscent of my earlier interactions with my father. However, without the benefit of adequate time and energy to reflect, I felt somewhat off-kilter. Facing this unanticipated role reversal—something I'd longed for over the years—was both thrilling and daunting.

His questions delved into my beliefs and my perceptions of others. Unsure about the appropriateness of my answers, I sought a silent nod of approval from David before proceeding. Time had flown since I first set foot in his home that night. Many family members, including Natalie and Paul, had already departed. Their absence seemed to earmark this as a time for deeper, more intimate discussions. Davie, now thirty and a father himself, was very much an adult. When I met David's eyes, his silent understanding communicated that, while Davie was his son, he wouldn't intervene in a conversation between two grown men.

The scene evoked memories from decades earlier when I had confronted our father with a question, even though I suspected I already knew the answer. I had asked if he had ever dissuaded my siblings from communicating with me. In defense, he asserted that they were grown-ups, and he had no sway over their choices of whom to speak with or not. As I considered David's silent approval, I wondered about the layers beneath it. Did he feel compelled to let our conversation happen? Had he tried to stifle such interactions over the years? And if Davie and I delved deeper into our discussion, would David attempt to halt any future conversations between us?

Taking his response at face value, I deliberated on how to navigate Davie's questions. In my quest to find shared knowledge or insights that might aid our dialogue, I was surprised when he demonstrated familiarity with thinkers such as Sam Harris, Jordan Peterson, and Daniel Dennett. This paved the way for an enriched discussion, spanning topics from worldviews and free speech to naturalism, well-being, and the complexities of free will.

Refocusing our conversation to address his initial question about my beliefs, I sought to grasp his take on "well-being," a concept profoundly articulated by Sam Harris. After grasping a clearer picture of Davie's stance, I conveyed my own perspective, stating, "I believe well-being is of the utmost importance, and nothing else matters." I elaborated further on my definition of "belief," framing it as an inherent understanding, not a conscious choice. To emphasize this notion, I remarked, "You can claim to have twenty fingers, but no rational mind would genuinely believe it. You believe you have ten fingers; there's no choice in the matter."

Then the topic of faith emerged, when it was asserted that I needed to have faith in God. In challenging his mention—the inherent value of faith—I asked for tangible examples that demonstrated its indispensable nature. "The air you breathe, you can't see it," my nephew retorted. "The plane you fly in, you have to believe it won't crash. The chair you're sitting in, you have to trust that it won't collapse." I replied that these are not mere leaps of faith but are based on evidence and accumulated experiences. We have scientific explanations detailing the composition of our air, aircrafts undergo rigorous safety tests, and chairs are designed to bear weight. Our life decisions stem from evidence and past experiences, constantly guiding us toward the paths with minimized risks. Our daily choices are evidence driven rather than purely faith driven, simply because it's a method that has been proven effective.

"So," I said, "why deviate from such a practice now? And given that faith can validate any belief, doesn't it render it an unreliable tool for discerning truth?"

While our perspectives often diverged, our conversation was marked by mutual respect and civility. Things were progressing better than I could have hoped for. However, the tenor of our dialogue was about to shift. As we delved deeper into philosophical realms, our talk took a personal turn when Davie proposed that we embark on an exploration of our family's intricate past.

As he navigated our conversation into the intricacies of our family history, I felt the weight of the topic. While he delved into the era marked by family rifts, I kept a wary eye on my brother's expressions, bracing myself for any signs of discomfort or disagreement. Until then, David had been a silent observer, absorbing every detail of our discussion. But in the early hours, after I'd spent a significant time detailing the circumstances of my departure and sharing my views on why many of our cousins had distanced themselves from the church, David finally spoke.

He reacted in a way that suggested skepticism toward my account. Without offering concrete reasons for his distrust, he voiced an overwhelming fear of me, declaring, "I keep a gun under my bed while I sleep at night." He conveyed that for years he harbored an intense anxiety about me, fretting over the possibility of me intruding into his home, compelling him to resort to such drastic measures to defend himself and his family.

While his words about keeping a gun for protection against me were unsettling, what shocked me even more was the palpable indifference from those still in the room. I had anticipated that someone might probe into the origins of his fear or question the reasons behind his dramatic disclosure, but no one queried what actions of mine could have warranted such dread or what could have driven David to such an extreme sentiment. I glanced around, seeking reactions on the faces of those gathered. The room was steeped in silence, and not a single countenance betrayed any hint of alarm, inquisitiveness, or bewilderment. It was as if a void had consumed all emotion.

I couldn't pinpoint if it was David's evident doubt about me or some other undercurrent, but the heavy silence lasted only momentarily before conversations picked up again, on a course that spiraled my spirit further downward. The tables seemed to have turned as I, for the first time, experienced the discomfort of being subject to questioning. To my credit, I didn't shy away. Instead, I faced the questions head on, striving to respond with authenticity and honesty. Up to that moment, I hadn't jumped ship.

By that point in our conversation, it was well established that I was an atheist, and my nephew aimed to dissect the nuances between our beliefs. The subject shifted to the dynamics between Christians and "non-believers" or "sinners," as I had been historically labeled, and it put me at great unease. I engaged initially, but when Davie insisted that he could never form a deep bond with an "unbeliever," I withdrew. My family's stance on the interplay between "sinners and saints" was something I was deeply familiar with, and I recognized that this topic was at the heart of many issues I had sought to address in the past. While Davie seemed eager to explore these complexities, unaware that only the fringes were within his reach, I was painfully aware of the ingrained beliefs, their unsettling ramifications, and the longstanding presumptions that had driven wedges between family members and old friends.

Davie's fascination with the world around him was evident, but his perception seemed skewed for peering through a prism of dogma—rigid beliefs and principles accepted without critical examination. It has been a family tradition, this manner of "forward progress" spreading like wildfire, a way of thinking that had spread insidiously, leaving a trail of devastation and deeply affecting the hearts of generations.

Every path seemed to lead to that point, culminating from various origins into the dogma I've observed and ineffectively challenged since the latter part of the previous century. By 3:00 a.m., I felt the weight of the matter was too daunting and the hour too late for such discussions. While I'd long recognized the importance of discussing this topic with my family, I sidestepped it, believing that the setting and timing were not quite right. I employed evasive maneuvers, doing everything possible to avoid the subject.

When the late morning hour was mentioned, I bid farewell to Davie as he drove home, and I returned to the bedroom that had been prepared for me earlier. As I prepared for sleep, I pondered the length of the night's rest ahead.

BRINGING DAD HOME

THE BED HAD BEEN LAYERED WITH BLANKETS, AND THE ROOM matched the orderliness evident throughout the house. Always in motion, Dianne reminded me of my mom and aunt, eager to cater to others. As I settled beneath the covers, it struck me that I wasn't in Miami but in Syracuse, more precisely, Liverpool. My mind retraced the day's interactions and events. As I drifted to the edge of sleep, I found it odd that I had seldom dreamt of being in that town, within the homes of the family I was familiar with. Every so often, my dreams painted vivid pictures of characters from my past, occasionally featuring relatives from Syracuse. But the settings rarely spotlighted my parents' house on Black Oak Circle, my grandparents' abode, or my aunt and uncle's place not far from there. I couldn't shake the thought of what it might feel like to be back in my parents' home—if, indeed, I had decided to visit once more before heading back to Miami come Monday.

Positioning myself for a good night's rest, I sank into the comfortable pillow, much nicer than my one back home. The tranquility of the room enveloped me, reminiscent of the silence in my Miami residence. This peace contrasted with my stays at my grandparents' Oak Street home, where the din of every passing vehicle pierced the quietude.

As I neared the brink of sleep, I realized the room wasn't entirely silent. An old, familiar, and soothing melody permeated the air—the nighttime serenade of my hometown. The enchanting chorus of nocturnal creatures was just as I remembered: crickets singing their rhythmic lullabies reminiscent of warm summer evenings from my childhood. I recalled watching the silhouettes of trees sway on the curtains, performing their nightly dance, like a silent film just for me. Drawn into this tranquil memory, my thoughts faded, pulling me into a deep and restful slumber.

However, my tranquility was interrupted by the sound of my ringing phone. Chiding myself for neglecting to switch it off, I glanced at the caller ID—it was a client. Reluctantly, I answered, only to learn there was an issue with his email account. A look at the clock confirmed the early hour—just shy of 5:00 a.m. Although many clients know of my early riser habits and are comfortable reaching out, I had hoped that being out of town would grant me a brief respite from such pressing matters.

Booting up my laptop, I tried to access our Michigan servers, but I couldn't gain entry. "This can't be happening now," I murmured, the weight of being away from the office pressing down on me. Recognizing the severity, I dialed Marco, my senior tech in charge of our systems, to diagnose the issue. As I ended our call, I held my breath, anxiously awaiting his response with some hopeful news. However, the update was grim—our systems had been compromised by ransomware, and everything had ground to a halt. This nightmare scenario was the last thing I had anticipated, and its timing couldn't have been worse. I urged Marco to update me further once he had assessed the full scope of the damage.

With sleep now a distant thought, my mind raced, awash with decisions to be made. Even if I tried, sleep seemed unattainable. I pulled on my jeans and navigated to the kitchen, fumbling for the light switch in the unfamiliar space. Setting up my laptop on the table, I plugged it in, mindful that its battery had long given up. Just as I wished for a mug of coffee to get me through, Dianne materialized, seeming to anticipate my needs. Moments later, a steaming cup of coffee was in my hand. With each sip, the caffeine coursed through me, sharpening my focus and preparing me to tackle the havoc wreaked by the hackers' nefarious handiwork, making me their latest catch in an all-too-familiar cyber net.

The gravity of the situation was palpable, but I recognized the limited influence I could exert from my current location. Eager for any updates, I reached out to Marco once more, pressing him about the status of our backups and their accessibility, but he was still in the preliminary stages of his investigation. It was crucial for me to remain patient and composed while awaiting more information.

While the urge to spiral into worry was strong, I sought to quiet such unproductive anxieties. Though the present business crisis loomed large, I reminded myself that the day's familial interactions could have an even more lasting imprint on my life. After all, despite having dedicated my life to my business, some moments transcend occupational challenges.

As the nocturnal serenades wound down, a new symphony emerged, ushered in by the birds greeting the dawn. They chirped and sang, each with a mission: to communicate, claim their domain, or perhaps serenade a potential mate. With the clock nearing 6:00 a.m. and the sun starting its ascent, I knew another species, one among millions on this planet—the

Homo sapiens residing upstairs—would soon be stirring.

My earlier conversation with Dianne transitioned into the dawn. It had begun with her kind offer of a brewed coffee, and our light banter proved to be a welcome distraction from the pressing concerns back at my business. As morning took hold, familiar household sounds began to filter in: the unmistakable flush of a toilet, water coursing through pipes, footsteps on wooden floors, the occasional creak of an old floorboard, and the intermittent sound of objects being dropped or shifted. I found it strangely comforting to take note of such everyday noises. Even though they might seem mundane to some, they revived a sense of domesticity that once filled my daily existence.

The inviting scent of eggs and bacon wafted through the house, reaching me in the living room. I gazed out the window, trying to catch a glimpse of one of the early morning songsters. Before long a blue jay alighted on a nearby branch. It seemed to be mimicking the calls of another bird in the distance, and its proximity allowed me to observe the gentle rise and fall of its chest with each melodious chirp.

As I entered the kitchen, the sizzle and pop of bacon intensified, and I was met by the groggy eyes of my niece, Audrey. With a playful flair, I crafted a lighthearted jest aimed to coax a laugh out of her.

Wandering around the home, a coffee mug in hand, I took in the photographs adorning the mantle and the walls. These frozen moments from their history prompted me to ponder what chapters I had missed. The array of shoes tossed by the front door was reminiscent of our childhood home. It made me wonder about the more mundane similarities, like the kitchen drawer. Did they, too, have a jumble of spoons, forks, and knives, shuffled from their designated spots? I was taken back to those days of hastily cleaning up after dinner, when, as kids, our rush to finish kept us from taking the few extra moments required to put things in their proper place.

One observation led me down another rabbit hole of memory. I wondered about the state of the radiators in their bathrooms. My younger self, often too restless and hasty when answering nature's call, would sometimes misdirect my stream, inadvertently splashing the radiator next to the toilet. Over the years those incidents took their toll, leaving the once-shiny metal with a "rustic" patina.

As the morning progressed, we each went about our routines in different parts of the house. Eventually, we reconvened in the living room, most of us clutching our coffee mugs. It was Sunday morning, a time traditionally reserved for church service. However, that day my family had chosen to skip it.

I had distanced myself from the Living Word Church during my last couple of years living with my parents. So, being with my family on a Sunday morning, not amid the usual church hustle and bustle, felt surreal. The all-too-familiar sound of my mother and sister, Debbie, bickering over an occupied bathroom or a forgotten curling iron was expected. I'd often muffle their arguing by burying my head beneath my pillow. But being home during church hours? That was unfamiliar territory.

One Friday evening stands out in my memory. Amidst a personal crisis, I turned to my father for help. However, he was unwavering in his dedication to our church, insisting that no predicament, not even the one I was facing, could justify being late for a service. Thus, the urgency of my situation, regardless of its severity, was relegated to wait. In our family, consistent church attendance and punctuality were prioritized above all else.

Soon, my mother arrived. I recall Paul and his wife, Amber, being there too, but I'm not sure if they were already at the house. David and his family were certainly there. My recollections from that day are somewhat hazy, possibly clouded by a combination of having had only two hours of sleep and the weight of various challenges concerning my father and my business affairs in Miami.

Amidst a wave of flowing events, David's phone either rang or he made a call—the specifics are blurry. However, the ensuing conversation with my father at the hospital remains clear. He was yearning to be home, but his ongoing treatment and medication regimen kept him tethered to the hospital bed. And since it was a Sunday, the protocols required for his discharge were not in place.

I listened closely as David delved into the specifics of our father's circumstances and his rationale for wanting to leave. Our father was earnest, determined to leave not only the confines of the hospital but also, it seemed, this world itself. He expressed a profound desire to be home for his final moments, surrounded by family, and to discontinue the medications and life support that were sustaining him.

The mere thought of it burdened our hearts. Nevertheless, we endeavored to honor his wishes, communicating them to the hospital staff, his primary physician, and others involved in his care. We made several phone calls seeking to facilitate his homecoming while ensuring he'd still have access to essential medicines and care. But with every step we took, a new hurdle emerged, making his discharge seem increasingly elusive.

As the situation evolved, my determination to see my father's wishes realized only grew stronger. Whether I was advocating over the phone or being drawn into thoughtful discussions to contemplate alternative strategies remains unclear. In fact, I may have done nothing at all other than being prepared to intercede at the first indication of a misstep. Regardless of my exact response, one thing was crystal clear: if my father desired to leave the hospital, I was steadfast in my commitment, prepared to go to any length to ensure his wishes were respected.

Honoring his unwavering decision to forgo medication and life support, preparations were made to bring my father home, where he would face life's final chapter.

It was around this time that Pam made her entrance, appearing at the front door before joining us in the kitchen. She walked in just as the phone conversation concluded, when details and arrangements were finalized. David's children—Natalie, Davie, and Jesse—were also present, and the atmosphere seemed to shift as Pam's gaze landed on them.

For a significant span, Pam hadn't spoken with David, Dianne, or their children. Yet here she was with a palpable determination not only to vocalize her pent-up grievances but also to state her decision against joining us in welcoming our father back home. However, the depths of her emotions went deeper than that.

Amidst the presence of Davie, Natalie, and Jesse, Pam unraveled her reservoir of grievances. She didn't just pinpoint the church, the school, and David for mistreatment but also implicated her nephews and nieces. What had been a congenial ambiance transformed into a tense battleground. As Pam's voice, laden with accumulated pain, intensified, she recounted the perceived wrongs done to her daughter, Raphael. Natalie, previously cherished as a cousin, was squarely in the crosshairs of those accusations. Nevertheless, she maintained her poise, countering each of Pam's impassioned assertions.

I found myself an observer amidst this familial storm without the full context or the bonds to intervene. I was confined to reading their faces, feeling the tension as it swelled and ebbed with each claim and counterclaim. The denouement was abrupt. Pam, her eyes shimmering with unshed tears, stormed out, leaving a weighty silence in her wake, punctuated by the words left unsaid.

After giving everyone's emotions a few minutes to simmer down and ensuring an air of calm had returned, we slipped on our shoes and made our way to David's car, heading to our parents' home. I occupied the front seat beside David, en route to the house of our childhood, where we'd anticipate our father's arrival. As I gazed out the window, the familiar landmarks of our town intertwined with memories of my past. Drawing closer to our parents' driveway, a long-forgotten thought from my high school days resurfaced, casting a reflective mood over the journey.

During my sophomore year at Liverpool High, I was drawn to an electronics class, captivated by the art of crafting devices from circuit boards, diodes, and transistors. On my inaugural day, my eyes landed on an ancient radio resting in the corner. It bore a striking resemblance to those radios from films set in the pre-television era, radios around which families would gather, eagerly awaiting the next broadcast. This relic, with its wooden cabinet, rounded contours, and twin robust knobs, paradoxically belted out modern tunes. It was a juxtaposition. While its design had me anticipating melodies from the early 1900s, it played the unmistakable rock 'n' roll beats of the 1970s. This unexpected blend of old and new lingered in my mind. It was this sentiment that surged within me, when we approached my parents' driveway, as I half-expected to see a Ford Pinto or a Ford station wagon there, not the sleek, contemporary vehicles of the twenty-first century.

Upon stepping inside the house, I registered the changes in its interior. However, any surprise I might have felt had been preempted by my own musings on what might greet me. As we settled in, the doorbell chimed. A team materialized, burdened with the delicate task of transporting my father into the family room. The dimensions of his gurney seemed mismatched for navigating the doorways and corners of the house. Despite some initial struggles, the men showed commendable dexterity and care, ensuring every adjustment was made for my father's comfort.

They placed him across the room, facing the sliding glass doors that opened to the outside—a location that evoked memories of when I had asked my Uncle Frankie about his feelings toward Dad being his half-brother. The familiar sofa, where countless evenings were spent with family watching episodes of *The Waltons* and where I would occasionally indulge in solo *Star Trek* marathons, had been repositioned. I chuckled inwardly, recalling my playful antics during family TV nights—obstructing pivotal scenes by flexing my biceps in front of the screen, much to my sisters' chagrin.

Those moments of levity seemed distant now. The room had transformed into a solemn haven, capturing final memories with our father and offering a space for reminiscing about bygone days.

I stepped out for a moment, compelled by pressing concerns that went beyond family. As much as I yearned to stay immersed in the present, I had to address emerging issues back home. Before I knew it, I was on the line with Marco, eager for updates on the escalating business crisis. Given the time since our last update, I hoped he'd have a better grasp of the fallout from the ransomware attack. The news he delivered, however, was bleak. The initial blow came with the revelation that a glitch with our backups had rendered the system unrestorable. And to make matters worse, our virtual servers, including the compromised email servers, were decimated by the attack and were beyond recovery. The ramifications for my business were both immediate and severe, a crisis magnified by my physical distance from Miami.

Though wrestling with business concerns, I recognized that it was neither the time nor the place to dwell on them. I endeavored to compartmentalize the anxieties of lost clients and the looming difficult conversations with friends whose businesses would undoubtedly face interruptions. With renewed focus, I re-entered the house.

Once in the living room, I sank into the sofa, yearning for a moment of respite. As I attempted to calm my emotions amid the maelstrom of events, my phone signaled an incoming call. It was Claudia, reaching out from Buenos Aires. Opting for convenience, I switched the call to speakerphone. She was well aware of my current circumstances: being in Syracuse due to my father's summons and the ensuing journey. Her call was a warm gesture, a touchpoint to see how I was holding up.

I filled Claudia in on my whereabouts, explaining that I was at my parents' home, surrounded by family and that we had just brought my father back from the hospital.

While I was still in Miami and before the current predicament developed, I'd told Claudia about an unusual incident with my brother, Paul. According to the tale, Paul had discarded his clothes and dashed through the streets during a crisis. In a moment of impeccable timing, Claudia exclaimed, "Oh, so you're with Paul? The one who ran through the streets naked?" Her voice, amplified by the speakerphone's unadjusted volume, filled the room just as Paul walked in.

Wanting to deflect the awkwardness, I told Claudia I'd have to catch up with her later. As the call ended, I shot Paul an apologetic glance. To my astonishment, he responded with hearty laughter. As Amber, his wife, entered the room, he recounted the amusing exchange. I didn't catch her full reaction, but if I had to guess based on knowing Amber, it was likely an affectionate eye roll. Stories, after all, often get exaggerated. For all I knew, it might have simply been a hot day, and Paul had chosen to go shirtless.

One undeniable reality, however, was that Paul had been traversing a discrepant period that had affected not only him but also his entire family. From my own journey, I had gleaned profound insights, perhaps more intimate than I'd preferred, into the potential catalysts and factors amplifying his distress—challenges strikingly similar to those I had grappled with.

Soon, the doorbell began ringing incessantly. A steady stream of visitors from the church community began to pour in. They made their way to the family room, joining my family in paying their respects to my father. While many expressions of sympathy were similar, certain words struck a deeper chord within me. Most notable were the repeated accolades for my father's benevolent and honorable life, a legacy described as worthy of immense pride, satisfaction, and no regrets.

The notion of having no regrets irked me. Truly? No regrets? If someone had been brave enough years ago to present my father with a candid reflection of his actions, the visitors might have been more varied. Perhaps the ringing doorbell would then announce the presence of a cousin, an aunt, or even one of my father's siblings.

I anticipated kind words about him, but the sentiments from these visitors underscored their inability to see below the surface. My frustration swelled, and I felt myself sinking into a tumult of memories, burdened by the weight of past, unshakable disappointments.

How comforting it would have been for my grandparents to receive such kind words and gestures from my father when he was in the prime of life, particularly knowing their health was waning. But during those crucial moments, my parents chose distance, absent even as their final hours approached.

An age-old anger stirred within me, taking me back to a passionate outburst in the dining room of that very house years ago. At that time I felt like the sole beacon, the only one willing to confront and address the deep-rooted issues tearing at the fabric of our family.

Now, with the weight of years and wisdom, and even in my exhaustion, I mustered the composure to maintain a warm façade. Engaging in conversations, I navigated away from sensitive subjects, even jesting with Paul. He played along, pointing to the family portrait hanging over the fireplace and recalling the time I tricked him into keeping a straight face. With this collaborative effort, I broadened our tales, weaving in more memories, and infusing the room with much-needed levity and laughter.

As the afternoon progressed, I wandered into the kitchen to top up my coffee. I realized I had never indulged in the coffee ritual there before, unlike the rest of my family. In earlier years, hot chocolate was my go-to, and it wasn't until my thirties that I sipped my first coffee.

Seeking a brief reprieve, I stepped into the bathroom to cool my face with a splash of water. Afterward, I raised my gaze to meet the reflection in the mirror, pondering the visage that met my eyes. It was the same mirror I had consulted countless times before, occasionally steadying my gaze, calming my pulse, ever hopeful of catching a transient vision of my future self, eager to gauge if my endeavors would thrive or falter.

As my heartbeat steadied and my eyes fixed on my reflection, it felt as though I was conveying a message through time to my younger self: "This is who I've become."

When I rejoined the group in the family room with my father, he was oscillating between moments of sleep and clarity, conversing with visitors when lucid. I drifted in and out of the room, observing but opting to remain on the periphery.

Later, my mother approached me, asking if I would be staying the night. I felt a growing sense that I wasn't essential anymore. There were no signs from my father indicating a desire to engage, to address lingering questions or unresolved matters between us. An intangible divide seemed to keep our interactions shallow. Nevertheless, I valued being in a setting where, if he had chosen, profound discussions could have taken place. Living with the perpetual "what if"—wondering whether he wanted to reconcile before his imminent departure—wouldn't have been easy.

Feeling that I had done my part and seeing no need to witness my father's last moments, I decided to stick to my flight, scheduled for the next morning. "Let's see how the rest of the afternoon goes," I said to my mother.

As the day progressed without notable change, I let my mother, siblings, and their children know I'd be heading back to Miami early the next day.

THE FUNERAL

When I touched down in Fort Lauderdale on Monday morning, I was engulfed in a strange sensation—a mixture of returning and departing. Amid the airport hustle, spotting my car was like finding an old friend. After stowing my bags, I nestled into the driver's seat, its familiar curves grounding me as I embarked on the last leg home.

En route, my phone morphed into a vital link, narrowing the distance with my team as I sifted through the cascade of updates since my somber sojourn to Syracuse. As the highway sprawled out in front of me, the hours raced on, and it was just past 1:00 p.m. when my house came into view. Though much of the business day had flown by, a looming storm demanded my focus.

Little had changed; our primary systems remained in disarray, with Marco striving to reconstruct them from scratch. Armed with information about which clients had been approached and the specifics of those conversations, the strategy's contours took shape in my thoughts. Before diving headfirst into the fray, however, I took a brief pause, seeking comfort in a short shower, a tranquil retreat to cleanse the remnants of travel and steel myself for the impending challenges.

Revived and reenergized, I braced for the tempest ahead. With every phone call, my voice served as a conduit, reaching out to our clients, assuaging apprehensions, and addressing the havoc wreaked by the ransomware attack. In tandem with my team, we synced our efforts, retrieving whatever data possible, utilizing remote system access, and scheduling hands-on visits. As the hours melded together, my dedication to the mission drew me further into the intricate dance of disorder and restoration.

While I was engrossed in work that evening, a text message from David glowed on my screen, a brief yet momentous blip in the flow of the day. It read: "Dan, tried calling, didn't leave a message. Dad has gone home to the Lord. Call when you can, we are all thinking of you."

These simple words brought a profound and irreversible truth crashing down around me. My father was gone. The finality was absolute, and all that remained was a time for reflection. The world seemed to pause around me, suspended in a moment of stillness, as I grappled with the reality that any chance for a heartfelt resolution with my father had slipped away.

Following David's message, my thoughts didn't dwell on his words but shifted to a message of my own, previously sent to David. The gravity of my request—for him to convey a message to our father while he still lived—intensified. I remained uncertain if David had passed it on, modified my sentiments as he once mentioned, or neglected my plea altogether. Questions swirled like shadows in my mind, tormenting me with "what ifs" and "might have beens." Did my words reach my father's heart? Did they bridge the gap, even in the eleventh hour?

Exactly two years to the day before my father's passing, I had crafted that message, an earnest plea to connect with my father, with David's assistance. Once a beacon of hope, that message now lay adrift in a ruinous sea of unspoken words and lingering emotions.

I called David that evening, our voices crackling across the miles. Our exchange was succinct, guided by a silent understanding. Arrangements were made, and, true to his word, David sent a text the following morning, a concise blueprint for the farewell. The funeral service, the interment at Woodlawn Cemetery, the reception at the church—all were laid out with clinical precision. Embedded within the specifics of his message was an invitation to join a conference call with the family and funeral director.

I replied quickly, my fingers tapping out a commitment to be there in person. "I will catch a flight tomorrow," I wrote, adding that I would stay for several days, at least until Sunday. The decision was made, and the plans were set, but beneath the surface, a torrent of emotions roiled, a complex mixture of grief, regret, and the lingering remnants of words left unsaid. Once again, the universe had conspired to present me with a choice at the least opportune moment. There I stood, at the eye of the most catastrophic storm of my professional life, yet I felt a pull toward something deeper, something more human. I knew that if I didn't go, the regret would become a silent, haunting companion for the rest of my life. It was crucial not just for me but also for my entire family that I was there with them, strong and steadfast. I conferred with my team. My voice faltered as I tried to convey that the upheaval in my personal life was not yet over and that I had to depart again. Their response was a mixture of concern and empathy. To my relief, they rallied around me, their support a tangible force that buoyed my spirits. They assured me that they would handle everything in my absence.

Later that afternoon, I reconnected with David, my mother, and Debbie over a conference call. Our voices melded and clashed, not merely as family members but as decision makers confronted with a somber ritual none of us were truly ready for. The images of caskets that appeared on my phone brought the reality into sharp focus, their polished surfaces reflecting a truth I struggled to accept. As we navigated the proceedings, our voices danced a delicate ballet of grief and pragmatism.

While we delved into the conversation, the suggestion of partitioning the costs surfaced like a hesitant whisper amidst louder voices. The origin of the idea, the nuanced wording, and the contributors to the discourse faded into the background, but from that murmur rose a burning conviction within me, a passion blazing brighter than any preceding sentiment.

"Choose the very best, the most expensive of everything," I urged them, my voice strong and clear. "The flowers, the casket, all of it. Spare no expense; I will cover everything."

There was a brief pause, its length matching my own ephemeral wonder. Were they pondering why I'd make such a gesture for someone I'd spent a lifetime at odds with? To them my decisions had always seemed inscrutable, and this instance was no different.

Decades earlier, under a stormy sky and amidst raindrops that seemed symbolic, I had extended an offer. It was an earnest pledge to bear the full cost of the roof that shielded our family from nature's whims. But instead of gratitude, my gesture was greeted with jaded skepticism, casting a haunting shadow over my character. This unfair judgment burrowed deep, branding me with labels of selfishness and vanity—a scar I've long since tried to heal. Now, as memories stirred amidst fresh sorrow, an opportunity for redemption emerged. More than simply funding the shelter over my father's earthly haven, I would cover the expenses for his eternal one.

At 3:03 a.m., when most souls were deep in slumber, my phone stirred to life, carrying with it another missive from

David. "Would you be one of the pallbearers?" The odd timing of this request jolted me, but as I was already awake, traversing my own predawn rituals, I said I would.

The canvas of the morning was painted with hurried strokes of activity. Rapid-fire commands were sent to my team, and luggage was unpacked from one journey, only to be repacked for another. Each motion carried an undercurrent of haste, with every tick of the clock underscoring the impending departure for Syracuse at 9:00 a.m. Once I touched down in Syracuse, a change awaited. Instead of the customary impersonal comfort of a rental car, it would be Pam's familiar and comforting embrace greeting me at Hancock Airport.

However, even before I set foot on the plane, David's voice poured forth from my phone with a profound request—to be a voice in the eulogy. Moved and a touch startled, I agreed. The enormity of this honor clung to me, its weight shaping my musings during the impending flight. I found the request almost as startling as the earlier intimation of sharing solitary reflections with my father. Might I risk articulating feelings so candid they could fan the flames of familial strife, possibly resulting in my being escorted away once more? My imagination ran wild, conjuring countless scenarios, each pushing the boundaries of expression even further.

Upon touching down at 1:34 p.m., I powered on my cell phone, a tumult of anticipation and fatigue swirling within me. By 1:37 p.m., a message lit up my screen: "I'm here right out front of terminal B. I have a small red Mazda and big white hair!"

"OK, going to luggage," I replied.

The familiar ritual of retrieving luggage was oddly comforting, the green cable ties on my bags serving as reassuring constants in the midst of such an emotional tempest.

Outside, Pam stood vigil beside her car. Our eyes met, and in that brief exchange, so much was said. We stowed my luggage, our movements almost automatic, and soon we were navigating the familiar roads toward our childhood home.

That drive was drenched in silent camaraderie and shared sorrow, a tacit understanding that we were entering uncharted emotional territory. The ordinarily mundane took on a deeper resonance, and I braced myself for the extraordinary events that awaited.

Upon our arrival, my mother greeted me with an affectionate embrace on the doorstep, followed by a gentle kiss. The enticing aroma of freshly brewed coffee filled the air, welcoming us into the kitchen. Pam and I reached for mugs from the cabinet, letting the coffee's warmth melt our apprehensions as we delved into a heartfelt discussion about the upcoming day. Thanks to the detailed arrangements made for Thursday's funeral, we were afforded the luxury of spending the remainder of the day in each other's company.

Bathed in the warm embrace of the mid-80s sunshine, with fluffy cumulus clouds playing hide and seek overhead, we opted to visit David's home, just a five-minute drive away. The instant we neared his front door, laughter and animated chatter welcomed us. David, Paul, and their spirited kids were making the most of the picturesque afternoon by their shimmering pool. Laughter rang out, water splashed, and the tantalizing scent of delectable food beckoned from the kitchen.

Ah, that kitchen! It was an oasis of culinary delights—a harmonious blend of Wegmans' deli specialties and generous portions of chicken, courtesy of my nephew Jacob, from Chick-Fil-A. After embracing, exchanging pleasantries, and shaking hands, I soon found myself in the midst of that gastronomic haven. A plate was handed to me, and I filled it with an assortment of flavors, each as diverse and enchanting as the company surrounding me. The feeling of joy was palpable, with every jest and chuckle creating concentric circles of happiness, much like pebbles causing ripples in a serene pond.

Yet amidst the jubilant frenzy, one individual captivated my attention: Audrey, David's daughter. This introspective soul had listened to my discussions with her brother, Davie, the previous week—always present yet never imposing or interjecting. It wasn't long before the two of us gravitated to a quaint dual-seat wooden swing near the pool. As we settled in, Audrey began to unfurl her narrative, a tale that had been biding its time, seeking the right moment and the perfect listener—me.

With each gentle sway of the swing, set against the backdrop of distant family laughter, Audrey's voice found its cadence. Thoughts that had lingered behind her watchful gaze emerged, transforming into profound reflections and unforeseen viewpoints, relishing their moment in the spotlight. Her anecdotes were more than just stories; they acted as conduits, unlocking hidden realms and illuminating the intricate mosaic of our family's heritage.

As our synchronized movements on the swing fostered an ambiance of trust, Audrey ventured deeper into her personal odyssey. She introduced me to her boyfriend, someone unfamiliar with the tenets of the Living Word Church—an institution she had grown distant from. This admission laid the foundation for a heartrending revelation about the delicate ties with her parents, which had been wearing thin over the years.

The contrast between her reserved demeanor and the exuberance of her siblings resonated with me, pulling me further into her world. Treading a path marked by both bravery and vulnerability, Audrey shared episodes from her past, overflowing with pain and introspection—tales of traumas that had left an indelible mark on her psyche.

She recounted the sudden death of a fellow student at Living Word Academy and her own shock at the school's lackluster response. Her voice wavered as she shared haunting moments of self-harm, her coping mechanism amidst overwhelming depression, anxiety, and confusion.

As Audrey unraveled her story, every word connected with me, touching upon my own past traumas and confusions. Her journey reflected familiar crossroads from my own life, times when I too felt adrift, desperately seeking understanding in an indifferent world. In her words, I didn't just hear Audrey's story; I felt a deep connection that went beyond familial ties. Our dialogue became more than just words exchanged; it was a testament to enduring pain, resilience, and the quest for clarity through life's upheavals.

The sun began to dip, casting long shadows and bathing the poolside in a golden hue, but the connection we'd forged in those brief moments felt timeless. Lost in our shared revelations, the world blurred as we continued to sway on the swing, two souls opening up and finding comfort in shared experiences.

In my burgeoning relationship with Audrey, an innate curiosity drove me to delve deeper into her psyche, to understand her aspirations, her apprehensions, and her passions. I yearned to understand the essence of this young woman.

When our discussion transitioned to her boyfriend, I navigated the conversation with sensitivity, aware that her parents might disapprove of him for not adhering to their religious beliefs.

"What do you like most about him? How did you meet? What does he do for a living?" I inquired, replicating the unasked queries I had craved to hear in my own youth, particularly when introducing Nancy, my first love, to my family. Audrey's eyes sparkled, and her voice danced with excitement, opening a gateway to cherished and extended conversations.

Her response was a fusion of youthful exuberance and mature reflection. As she described her relationship, I felt a resonance with her joy, her trepidations, and her journey of self-discovery. Her words became more than just answers to my questions; they were a vibrant mosaic of her life, rich with textures and colors that I had not known before.

That day was a collage of emotions, filled not only with animated discussions but also with laughter, delectable food and drink, and an unexpected splash in the pool, courtesy of Davie's timely offer of shorts. I teased my brothers, noting how perfectly the borrowed attire fit me in contrast to their heartier builds.

As the evening hues enveloped the sky, we transitioned

into a more peaceful ambiance until fatigue guided me to my room, the impending funeral occupying my thoughts.

The morning greeted us with its familiar chorus of clinking coffee mugs and animated breakfast chatter. Beneath the surface, however, an undertone of anxiety bubbled within me. Audrey, ever intuitive, sensed my unease, and her consoling words reached out. "I'll be there with you," she assured me. That compassionate gesture pierced my apprehension, and at that moment, I saw a reflection of myself in her eyes.

In the church, a reverent hush enveloped the space as the last attendees approached for a final glimpse of my father. The room oscillated between anticipation and profound sorrow. As the attendees settled in, the ambient noise faded, giving way to a profound silence. Bryan, having risen to the role of senior pastor, stood ready to address the assembly of mourners.

I was unprepared for the emotional impact when the expansive viewing screens on the walls illuminated, showcasing videos and slides curated for the tribute. Waves of nostalgia crashed over me, evoking memories of my childhood when my father would retrieve his slide projector from the closet. I could almost hear the click and whir of the machine as he sorted the small two-inch-square slides into the slots of the projector's circular carousel.

Each image materialized one after another, evoking the cherished ritual of my past, now rekindled amidst the solemnity in that hallowed setting. It felt as though the church had morphed into our family living room, where we once congregated in shared memories. The essence of the ritual remained unchanged, but its context had shifted to a moving public tribute. Just as newer images at our home viewings reflected our changing lives and bonds, the ceremony equaled that sentiment, amplified by the gravity of the moment. The blend of yesteryears and the present, personal recollections, and collective homage forged a deep connection to those bygone moments, bridging time and drawing me nearer to my father's memory.

But the way I had perceived those images had shifted, shaped by the passage of time and my evolving perspective. Now older and having immersed myself in reflections on my past, each picture seemed to penetrate deeper, touching raw emotions within me. At times those sentiments were uncomfortably intense, resonating within a dark corner of my psyche. Perhaps it was the location of the viewing, the church from my earlier years, a place rife with contradictions and confusion that had unsettled me ever since.

Despite the emotional turbulence, I managed to maintain my composure. As the ceremony progressed, Bryan recounted cherished memories of my father, our family, and the church community in a tone that was both somber and comforting. These recollections persisted, filled with joy and suffering, until the end of the service when I took my place as a pallbearer beside my father's casket.

As we prepared to hoist the casket, an unforeseen incident jolted me from my cogitations. A solemn-faced man approached the pallbearers, offering pens to each of us. I exchanged puzzled glances with the others, all of us sharing the same confusion. Why were we being given pens at such a moment? Their shared uncertainty reflected my own; the purpose of these pens eluded us.

I addressed the gentleman, my voice tinged with irritation. "What are these for?" I asked.

"Nothing," he replied. "They're a gift."

Upon closer inspection, I discerned the funeral home's name engraved onto the pens, accompanied by contact details. A mixture of disbelief and anger swept over me. Capitalizing on such a profound moment for promotional purposes felt not only misplaced but also deeply disrespectful.

In solemn unity, we carried the casket to the hearse. Then the procession embarked on its measured path through the town I knew so well, heading toward Woodlawn Cemetery. With the sun blazing in a clear azure sky and the air pleasantly warm, nature seemed to be wrapping us in a consoling embrace on that sorrow-filled day.

When we reached the gravesite, silence draped over us. Bryan advanced, a Bible gripped in his hands. He recited several verses, and in his voice, I discerned an emotional layer that breathed life into the ancient scripture and his subsequent interpretations.

As we stood enshrouded in our collective grief, the casket descended, merging with the chilly embrace of the earth below. A palpable stillness spread through those gathered, each person grappling with the undeniable reality of the moment.

Then an unexpected realization seized me—Bryan, a significant presence from my father's yesteryears, had neither engaged nor addressed me since I arrived from Miami. With my mind's landscape altered by fresh memories and reflections, I felt a pressing need to speak with him.

With unwavering determination, I met Bryan's stoic gaze. I felt drawn to him, every footstep rekindling haunting memories of yore. When I reached him, he assented to my request to talk, and we sought a secluded spot away from the crowd.

The setting was saturated with tacit expectancy. As we settled into our secluded nook, I laid my emotions bare. Each word, drenched in feeling, detailed my recent visit to my father in the ICU at Crouse Hospital. I recreated the intensity in my father's eyes, the delicate quiver of his lips, and the pride that radiated from him as his hand cradled mine, introducing me as his "firstborn boy." I went on, the weight of my father's repeated affirmation, "You're so very wise," pressing against my heart, made heavier by our complex history, my label as sinner.

"But I'm an atheist!" I told Bryan, my words heavy, almost defiant. I shared my father's gentle reassurance that it was okay, that journeys differ, that we all have something to offer.

"I have something valuable to offer you," I told Bryan, my tone mellowing and my gaze piercing his, "And you have something of value for me." My words lingered, serving as both a bridge and a barrier, an overture and a test. They marked the commencement of a dialogue, one that I hoped would strip away years of hurt, leading us toward mutual understanding and healing.

"We'll have to talk," he replied, his face inscrutable and his voice guarded. Strangely, he asked no questions and expressed no curiosity about my profound moment with my father, a man with whom Bryan had shared an intimate relationship for many years. His response was almost dismissive, and in his silence, an empty chasm formed in place of the connection and understanding I was seeking. We simply parted, each of us walking to our vehicles, the silence between us growing denser, filled with an assortment of unspoken words and unresolved emotions just clamoring and lingering. The answers to my questions seemed to float in the air like a ghost trailing behind us, evading a reckoning that slipped further away with each step. The gravity of the moment pressed upon us, ending in ambiguity, leaving me with a gnawing sense of unease, like a puzzle with a few vital pieces forever lost.

As we drifted apart, ensconced in our mutual silence, Bryan finally found words. "We good?" he called out, his eyes meeting mine across the increasing distance.

I stopped, the query lodged in my mind, reminiscent of a cryptic puzzle awaiting deciphering. "Uh, yeah?" I replied, betraying more question than affirmation. He asked once more, his words slower and more distinct. However, in my confusion, silence was my only retort.

As I continued to walk away, the weight of his inquiry hung in the air, dense and inscrutable.

Then a piercing revelation struck me. To Bryan, our exchange was meant to be an ending, a period. He had granted me his ear, as others often did, treating their attention as a magnanimous offering—an act of grace rather than genuine engagement. His words weren't meant to pave the way for understanding; they were designed to shut a door.

To Bryan, and all too often to the rest of my family, my act of voicing concerns signaled the end of a chapter, suggesting everything was resolved and nothing more remained to be said. Yet for me, it was akin to teetering on the edge, gazing down into a vast, unfathomable abyss. "There, you've had your say," I imagined them thinking. "We let you voice out, and we didn't rebuke you," was the unsaid sentiment, as if dissent itself was a grave offense.

"We good?" implied a cessation of any further dialogue about our day at the graveyard and everything tied to it. Like many before him, Bryan evaded accountability for past indiscretions. His words bore the veiled sentiment of "Let bygones be bygones," a mantra frequently used by those dodging accountability. Now it stood before me like a chilling, impassable barrier.

Over the next two days, Friday and Saturday, opportunities abounded to bond with my family. Up to that point, my time had mostly been divided between David, his family, and my mother. However, I resolved to also spend quality time with Pam and her clan. My plan took shape on Thursday evening when Pam guided me to her daughter Domonique's residence. There, I reconnected with family members I hardly remembered, including Raphael, my niece whom I had once cradled as an infant. Upon reaching the entrance, Mark, Pam's spouse, ushered me into Domonique's tastefully decorated dwelling. I was struck by Domonique's poise and the infectious joy of her two radiant daughters. Not long after, Pam and her other daughter, Rafael, joined us, making the circle complete. Unfortunately, Salvador, Pam's son, whom I had never encountered, was away, robbing me of the chance to make his acquaintance.

As the evening deepened, harrowing tales began to surface. The ambiance grew thick with disturbing accounts linked to the Living Word Church and Living Word Academy. These stories also painted a grim portrait of our own family.

A potent blend of shock and empathy swelled within me upon discovering that Raphael, much like Audrey, had faced similar ordeals that had led her to engage in self-harm. Each disclosure seemed to fray the ties of a family I was just beginning to understand.

Unable to overcome the relentlessness of time, our gathering had to end. The sun dipped below the horizon, giving way to a contemplative darkness. I took my leave, my heart heavy with a burden of feelings and unresolved uncertainties. The drive back to David's place was introspective, marked by the profound impact of the night's unsettling truths. When I finally sought rest in my room, sleep arrived, but it was restless, interspersed with persistent questions and memories of a troubled past now unearthed.

The following dawn marked the countdown to my departure early on Sunday. With over two decades of absence weighing on our shoulders, the day presented a last-chance saloon for anyone harboring lingering curiosities about me. Our usual breakfast ritual took place once more, the aromatic promise of fresh coffee intertwining with chatter about the day ahead. By lunchtime, a lavish spread awaited us in the kitchen, inviting everyone to feast. The day's vibrancy continued unabated, both inside the house and by the pool. Cloaked in vibrant swimsuits, everyone reveled under the sun's generous warmth.

By early afternoon, spurred by the renewed family ties, I reached out to Paul. His amiable voice, rich with warmth, heightened my eagerness to see him. The allure of familial bonding was irresistible, so after noting down his address from a subsequent message, I set off, brimming with anticipation.

When I got there, Amber, Paul's eloquent wife, welcomed me. A seasoned school teacher, she exuded a sharp intellect and engaging charisma. Our conversation veered into her adventures within the public education system, a topic I remembered as a hotbed of controversy from my younger days. Her articulate insights held me rapt, each word reflecting informed clarity.

Meeting their children—Jonathan, Jacob, and young Rachel—evoked feelings of discovery and lament. Learning about Jacob's upcoming graduation and Jonathan's sharp intellect instilled pride, but I was also saddened for not having known them earlier. Jonathan's brightness revealed a side of our family I had been unaware of, and I could see Amber's nurturing touch in his remarkable abilities.

Interacting with the kids was a sheer delight. In the basement, our laughter bounced off the walls as I clumsily navigated an electric hoverboard, only to be outperformed by the boys. The chess matches with Jonathan, in which I was consistently outplayed, remain a treasured source of humility.

As the time came to depart, I felt a twinge of melancholy. This reconnection with family was like a brief spark, illuminating but quickly extinguishing. I said my goodbyes, determined to immerse myself deeper in such precious moments during future visits to Syracuse.

After returning to David's home, as the shadows lengthened and the evening progressed, David, Dianne, and their children reconvened with me in the comfort of their living room. The walls, adorned with memories, seemed to close in as we settled, anticipating what was to be our final gathering before my departure, a moment soon to be charged with an unspoken gravitas.

Our conversation began gently but soon surged into turbulent waters, sweeping across a wide array of subjects and unearthing memories of past experiences, some raw and sensitive. These topics emerged like specters, and whether they were summoned by reflections on earlier comments made by me or some other mysterious origin, I knew not.

Pressed to reveal the details of what had happened to me in the past, along with my heartfelt perceptions, I opened the gates of recollection. With carefully chosen words, I painted the picture of my history, a landscape marred by egregious treatment. The room seemed to freeze as I spoke, the weight of my revelations settling heavily.

As I looked into their faces, I saw expressions of shock and skepticism. Their eyes widened in disbelief, and their mouths fell open as they questioned the veracity of what they had just heard. The silence that followed my words was devoid of sympathy or understanding, and I felt a cold chill of doubt. David's eyes, especially, held a look that seemed to pierce me, suggesting conclusions he desired to be drawn.

These were the interactions that cast a shadow over my soul, a sense of discomfort and detachment that clung to me as I fell into a restless sleep later that night.

Come 4:00 a.m. on Sunday, May 23, Debbie was there, as punctual as a well-tuned clock, ready to drive me to Hancock Airport. The early morning air was crisp, and the world was still asleep as we journeyed through the quiet streets. Miami, with its daily routines and the analytical precision I was familiar with, invited me back. I was returning to a world of pressing business concerns, like mitigating the damages caused by the ransomware, far removed from the emotional maelstrom of the night before.

HOME IN MIAMI AGAIN

FRESH FROM SYRACUSE, THE ACHE OF TRAVEL SETTLED DEEP IN MY bones. I watched the world awaken as I left Hancock Airport, only to be held captive by a two-hour layover in Atlanta. The connecting flight? As smooth as silk—a small victory that served as a prelude to the progressing tale of my day.

Instead of the typical route home, I made a detour to Miller's Ale House. The place welcomed me like an old friend, each corner filled with memories of laughter. The staff, well acquainted with my habits, had seen me walk in countless times, phone in hand, eyes scanning messages, after those early evening meetings with clients. Or even on weekend afternoons, when I accepted the invitation of friends at LA Fitness (where I exercised each morning) to join them in watching a

Miami Heat or Dolphins game on a sports channel.

They filled my plate when I was famished, drained from the day's labor, just like the staff at the other two restaurants I frequented: the Outback Steak House and the Olive Garden.

"Hey, Dan, Cajun chicken pasta?" Linda teased as I walked in, her pencil poised.

"You know it," I replied, a knowing grin playing on my lips. We chuckled; it was our familiar dance.

I was a creature of habit. My world thrived on routines, from the punctual cooing of my morning clock to my ritualistic way of dressing and preparing breakfast. I even poured my power drink and peeled my banana with a flourish that was uniquely mine.

As I settled into my preferred stool at the bar, that familiar spot that felt like home, I started winding down. The hustle and bustle of travel receded, and I was left with reflections of my trip, the solemnity of the funeral, and the precious time of connecting with family members, some of whom I had met for the first time.

But not all of my memories played out in sweet melodies. Shadows lingered amid the pleasantries, striking dissonant notes that disrupted the harmony. My time with Audrey resonated well, sparking hopes for future duets. But when my thoughts drifted to her siblings, Davie, Jesse, and Natalie, I was confronted with a harsh and discordant reality. My potential relationship with them charted a complex course, one marked by my father's enduring legacy—as their revered grandfather, the guiding force in their father David's life, and as the pastor whose doctrines molded their beliefs.

Yet, the symphony of life continued, the composition still unfolding, laden with complexities, awaiting my contribution to the next movement. The melody was unpredictable, but the rhythm of life persisted, my hand poised to steer its course.

My father's words—sharp and divisive—had seeped into the minds of those I loved, poisoning their perceptions. He once likened being with me to a snake's bite—a slow, insidious poison. He warned his congregation to stay away from me, lest they backslide into sin. The magnitude of his deceit, the lengths he went to isolate me, was staggering, its impact undeniable and cruel. Even David, unable to cite a single wrong I'd done and who refused to discuss the matter with me, had been swayed. His trust, once solid in our childhood, had wavered for decades, suspended in the uncertainty that my father's words had sown. The wounds were deep, the healing distant, and yet I found myself clinging once again to hope, a faint melody in a sea of discord.

This sinister legacy, born from my father's pulpit, had been passed to Bryan, the new church pastor. From pastor to pastor, from parent to child, it was a chain of separation that threatened to mar future generations. How could I convince my nephews and nieces that I, their uncle, maligned and distanced, had something of value to offer their lives? The challenge loomed large, but within it lay a glimmer of opportunity, a chance to break the cycle and compose a new harmony. The next move was mine, and the music sat on the precipice of continuation, its rhythm frozen in a moment of eager expectancy.

As I finished my meal, I realized this was not merely a tale of routine and comforting habits. It was a saga of family, hope, and a struggle to bridge a divide that had been generations in the making. The taste of Cajun chicken pasta lingered, but so did the questions, the doubts, and the possibility that maybe, just maybe, love could heal those wounds.

Never one for dessert or a late-afternoon drink, I bid farewell to my friends, expressing my gratitude for their consistently excellent service.

The drive home was quiet, a reflection of my weariness. Once home, I mustered only enough energy to empty my luggage from the car, leaving it and its contents in my kitchen until the next day, or perhaps the day after, when I had the vigor to tackle it.

The remainder of the day found me in my living room, sinking into a comfortable chair and turning on the big-screen

TV to unwind. On the screen, the world's problems unfolded, presenting another set of challenges that drew my contemplative gaze. The hours dissolved, mingling my internal musings with the external narratives on display. However, the buzz of my phone interrupted this solitude as two text messages demanded my attention—one from Audrey and one from Pam. These messages pulled me back into the family narrative, a story that eagerly awaited its next chapter.

Pam's message was heartwarming. She credited me for my good behavior, saying, "If I was an atheist, you would have turned me into a believer." Audrey's message was equally kind, expressing her dismay that her family hadn't acknowledged the poor treatment I had endured in the past.

Night enveloped the city, and I was lulled into my routines, unfurling them like a well-choreographed dance. While preparing for sleep, I anticipated the rest that would empower me to face the daunting days ahead. The bustling world of business beckoned, but for the moment I surrendered myself to the realm of dreams, where possibilities seemed endless.

With the sun's rise over the Miami skyline, the delightful aroma of freshly brewed coffee welcomed me. I embraced the age-old ritual of ironing my corporate shirt, adorned with the signature green logo. Poised and ready, I gathered my team for the morning meeting, where we continued to craft strategies to combat the consequences of the ransomware attack. We refined our approach and stayed a step ahead of uncertainty.

The cycle of my working days resumed, and with it came a renewed sense of purpose. As I continued to navigate a maze of new and unexpected challenges, the sun set, signaling a time to shift gears. Transitioning from the demands of the business world, I delved into the realm of family life. The day's challenges were supplanted by a different battle, one where I had to wage war against the reputation that had unjustly held me captive. My path was clear: it was time to free myself to rebuild and breathe new life into the bonds that had fractured.

However, just as I embarked on this journey, an unforeseen

interruption arose. Two days after my return from Syracuse, a call from Pam reached me. "I was watching a video on the Living Word website. David's telling everyone from the pulpit that you think everything there is perfect," she informed me, moments before a text from her lit up on my phone, including a link to the video.

Pam was infuriated. She believed that our brother had overstepped, speaking on my behalf, making it seem as if I approved of everything that was happening at the church. I assured her I would watch the video, using the link she sent to see what David was up to. Compelled beyond curiosity, I clicked on the link and played the video. There he was, addressing the congregation from the pulpit of the Living Word Church, presenting my perspective as he saw fit to interpret it.

> Good morning, Living Word. That's all of you down here, and everybody up there, and who might be watching on the streaming service. You are the testament of the power of God working on this earth. Do you know that? I just want to take a moment to say on behalf of my mom and my family, thank you so much for that love that you showed to us this past week, and with my dad's passing at the funeral. Wow, it was powerful. It was so powerful, and if I told you it was perfect would you believe me? Was it perfect? Would you believe it if that came from a brother of mine who said that, who's not here today? The Lord's working in my family." [cheers, clapping, and applause] "If you are going through a struggle this morning, no matter what it is, worship your way through it. You will be an overcomer. God will deliver you from whatever your issue is. So on behalf of my family, thank you very much.

Hearing David speak from the pulpit of the Living Word Church stirred emotions too profound for simple expression. Still, I endeavored to capture the depth of what I felt after viewing that video.

Within the sanctity of that church, where my family had convened for generations, I'd been transformed into the epicenter of declarations, both proclaimed and insinuated. Such unfounded and divisive assertions, meant to alienate me from my family and fellow congregants, had doggedly trailed me, reaching as far as Miami. They'd even manifested in cassette tapes mailed to my doorstep, bearing irrefutable evidence of slanderous lies that had been spread about me for decades.

Now, even after my father's passing, a distorted caricature of me continued to be paraded before the congregation and my family. It was an image shaped by a brother who seemed to have no interest in understanding the real me. Yet in a twist of irony, his own daughter, Audrey—who only met me a week earlier—had pierced this façade, discerning a more genuine sense of my being. Her willingness to see beyond the surface allowed her to achieve what had eluded David's comprehension—she simply opened her eyes. Had she been the one at the pulpit, I don't believe she would have done what her father did, reducing my complex emotions and perceptions of the funeral procession into a one-dimensional portrayal. Unlike her seemingly cynical father, she would not have contorted my feelings to fit a preconceived narrative aligned with certain lifestyles and life choices.

If David had taken the time to truly see me, to look beyond the superficial impressions during that critical week we spent together, he might have understood that my reactions were driven not by admiration but rather by a mechanism of self-preservation. He had witnessed in our formative years how I could "pop," a reaction triggered by being overwhelmed by the toxic behavior around me. This potential behavior was not unfamiliar to him; after all, he was the one who escorted me out of our home and away from our family years ago. Yet his perplexing misrepresentation of me, attributing words to me that I have never spoken, was not entirely without explanation. Perhaps he was creating an image of me that aligned with his wishes, sculpting a version of me that fit his narrative rather than accepting and understanding who I was and how I perceived my surroundings.

This path of misunderstanding was not a novel one. It stretched back through time, originating with my father's injurious actions and persisting under the guidance of Bryan, the new pastor. This legacy, fraught with distortion and deceit, lingered, casting shadows that stretched beyond the pulpit and pews of the Living Word Church.

Having recently tasted the rare sweetness of genuine acknowledgment—validated by Audrey and Pam—my tolerance for renewed misrepresentations of my character were diminishing rapidly. I couldn't stand on the sidelines and allow such distortions to prevail. An urgency to confront the situation surged within me, steering me toward contacting David to clarify the truth. Fueled by this reinvigorated resolve, I was drawn to question him, to probe why he continued to depict me in this way, especially when he stubbornly adhered to a path he had pursued for years—a path laden with a refusal to see me for who I was, skepticism regarding my integrity, and a reluctance to engage in authentic dialogue about our shared past and present.

I approached my brother, articulating my concerns in both broad strokes and meticulous detail, using both spoken and written words. What I got in return felt like a half-hearted apology, an ambiguous promise of no future repetitions. However, this answer didn't measure up to my hopes. More than an apology, I yearned for a rectification—a public denouncement of the misleading narrative and its replacement with a more truthful version. Armed with the clarity I had provided about myself, I believed he should address the congregation and publicly rectify his misrepresentation. After clarifying my stance toward the congregation, he could lead them in prayer for me, hoping that on future visits, I might feel authentic warmth and kindness, drawing me back home more often. I didn't seek to dictate his words, but I insisted on integrity—a genuine shift in perspective that valued authenticity over invention, providing the right lens through which to tell my story. Instead of crafting unfounded tales about me, he should have either spotlighted the truths that characterized me or not spoken about me at all.

Despite my genuine and passionate efforts, the days drifted away without any semblance of closure, confronting me with bitter disappointment. My fervent call for honesty and rapprochement seemed to have fallen on deaf ears, thrusting me back into the sting of an all-too-familiar revelation amid the deafening silence. The bridge to understanding and reconciliation, which seemed traversable for a moment, was barricaded once more. The walls that I thought we had torn down during our time together had been rebuilt.

My connection with David turned cold, but conversations persisted with my other siblings, my mother, and the next generation—my nephews and nieces. In those times of distance, I found myself locked in a relentless pursuit of maintaining our newfound bonds. Text messages became my lifeline, peppered with occasional phone calls initiated with a warm "hello." This new mode of connection felt foreign and awkward. I fumbled around like a teenager trying to navigate the world of dating again.

A memory blooms in my mind: Tara, the pretty face that caught my attention at the checkout line of Switz's. Unsure and intrigued about the dating process, and having caught her eye in return, I found myself in a bookstore one day, engrossed in chapters of texts delving into relationships. I purchased one—a guide to love, filled with suggestions of adventures to embark on, such as picnics, hiking, and visiting museums—all to keep the interest of a newfound companion. That very book later betrayed me when Tara discovered it. Its pages, never hidden, were laid bare for her curious eyes, eager to uncover what I was interested in reading.

"Everything we've done together comes from a book?" Tara's voice quivered, her eyes widening with disbelief. "None of it comes from you?"

I attempted to explain, but her accusations hung in the air, forming a judgment I couldn't dispel. Perhaps her words contained some truth. She might have been correct; maybe I shouldn't have sought external advice on how to connect.

That same uncertainty haunted me now as I reached out to

my young nephews and nieces. I stumbled through conversations, using humor to mask my uncertainty, desperate not to sever the fragile new threads that were forming between us. Their voices, filled with tales of mistreatment and confusion, were unforgettable as they were a reminder of the struggles of my own youth. They'd faced adversities both unfamiliar and eerily reminiscent of my own, grappling with a dearth of guidance and the missing threads of wholesome communication that were vital for confronting such challenges. Lacking the wisdom to endure these hardships, the essential tools they needed to handle the intricacies awaiting them in adulthood seem frustratingly elusive. Their fears, their pain, and their hopes resonated within me. I was both elated and horrified, understanding their struggles yet burdened by the profound scars they bore. In their eyes I saw a reflection of my own past, a turbulent storm I too had to navigate.

I was convinced that I could make a difference in their lives and be a positive influence. I was uniquely qualified, having not only survived what they had endured but also thrived despite it. I could pass on what I'd learned to these kids. I could be a beacon of light.

With the passing of my father, the one who sowed discord in the family and led them to view me with suspicion, I sensed a readiness in my family to hear me. The barriers that once kept me estranged hadn't completely crumbled, but I discerned cracks in those walls that I could exploit. A new path unfolded before me, imbued with the promise of meaning and purpose. I was ready to offer the kindness, understanding, and guidance I once longed for myself.

That eternal question, haunting humanity for ages and wrapped in the enigma of our existence, "What is my purpose?" Some suggested people stumbled upon it like a hidden treasure, waiting to be found. Others asserted that we had to forge it ourselves, shaping it from life's raw materials. To me its origin was irrelevant; possessing a sense of purpose was what mattered.

I felt as though I'd been molded for this moment, prepared to make a significant difference in the lives of my nephews and nieces. It was as if all my life, even my most challenging encounters, had been training for this task. The choices I'd made during difficult moments, the relationships I'd nurtured in Miami, the small business I'd managed to grow, and the modest successes I had attained—all these have come through perseverance, hard work, and a commitment to treating others with kindness and fairness.

In the world of business, regardless of the terrain I traversed—whether it was the artistry of photography, the raw labor of building maintenance, or the technical aspects of computers—one truth always prevailed: it was all about relationships. This understanding extended beyond my professional life, integrating into the rhythms of my daily existence.

Within my family, in the workplace, and even in those rare quiet moments at home, I found myself immersed in the interplay of relationships. Watching a battle on YouTube between chess grandmasters Magnus Carlsen and Hans Niemann was about more than a game; it was an opportunity to contemplate honesty and integrity. Following the news about the invasion of Ukraine wasn't merely a matter of geopolitics; it was a diverse panorama of human alliances and conflicts. Observing a political dispute on TV, such as a disagreement between Ted Cruz and a Democrat, transcending party lines, was a reflection of our shared struggles and convictions.

Amid all these vast relationships, what often touches us most profoundly are the connections with those who are closest to us. Perhaps that's as it should be, as it's within our immediate reach that we can genuinely effect change. Nevertheless, it's clear to me that we are all intrinsically linked, regardless of our geographic locations or disparate experiences. We are brothers and sisters, bound together in a shared human experience, each of us of equal importance.

With this mindset, I turned my attention to my nephews and nieces, who seemed to be within my sphere of influence.

Whether there was a guidebook on how an uncle can best interact with this younger generation, I wasn't sure, and I hadn't looked into it. What I did know was that if I had explored that avenue, it would have been with the purest of intentions. I hoped that for this effort alone, I wouldn't be subjected to criticism or interpreted as insincere, as if my actions were anything but authentic.

As July rolled in, I discovered that Audrey would soon be celebrating her birthday. *Ah, an easy task,* I mused, envisioning bouquets, thoughtful cards, and a meticulously selected gift. However, a few days later, a conversation with Pam introduced a new facet to my plans: another birthday was on the horizon. Raffaella, too, was preparing to celebrate in August.

This revelation sparked a flicker of inspiration within me. These two young cousins, once tethered by close bonds, had drifted apart like leaves on a languid river. This image triggered an idea in my mind, and a plan began to form. What if I could seize this occasion to mend the fraying threads of their relationship?

Consequently, I decided to offer them more than just tangible gifts. Instead, I opted for an experience. I'd send them both an equal, generous sum of money but with a caveat: they had to undertake a joint shopping spree, sharing laughter over dress choices, and swapping opinions on shoes. Hopefully, amidst the hustle and bustle of busy stores and changing rooms, they might rediscover their kinship. What young girl of modest means could turn down such an adventure?

Some might have labeled it a bribe, a blatant ploy to coax estranged cousins back onto common ground. But the semantics did not faze me. I was confident that if I could engineer the circumstances for their reunion, it could signal a new beginning.

So, I took action, wiring the funds to Raffaella and entrusting her with the task of sharing them with Audrey during their joint shopping adventure. I also made a simple request, that amidst their shopping spree they take a moment to capture a snapshot of their rekindled camaraderie and send it to me.

Days passed, and I was in the midst of a meeting with a client when my phone vibrated. As I opened the message, there they were, Raffaella and Audrey, their faces radiant with joy, captured in the reflection of a department store's mirror. A grin emerged on my face, aligning with the joy radiating from them.

My abrupt shift in focus from the meeting didn't go unnoticed. After I shared the heartwarming backstory, my client's expression softened, blossoming into a smile as large and bright as my own, which only added to the delight of the moment.

Shortly after the first picture arrived, another followed, a prediction from a fortune cookie. During their shopping excursion at Destiny, the largest six-story shopping mall in New York State, the girls took a break for lunch at P. F. Chang's. The fortune, inscribed in black text on a slender white strip, read, "You will soon receive an unusual gift that you will greatly appreciate." Instantly, I recognized another promising opportunity embedded within the image.

The following day, I contacted P. F. Chang's and asked to speak with the manager. Although my initial attempt failed, I learned the manager's name. A day or two later, I finally got a chance to speak with Jennifer, the restaurant's assistant operating partner.

I explained to Jennifer that I had recently visited Syracuse for my father's funeral, which marked the first time I'd seen him in decades. After reuniting with my siblings and meeting their children, my nephews and nieces, I felt inspired to give two of them a birthday present—funds for a shopping spree. During their outing at Destiny mall, they stopped for lunch at P. F. Chang's, where a fortune cookie presented a message, "You will soon receive an unusual gift that you will greatly appreciate." I suggested to Jennifer that the serendipitous event presented P. F. Chang's with a unique opportunity that they should consider capitalizing on.

I referenced their company vision statement, "Our purpose is to celebrate life, family, food." To further pitch my idea, I quoted Wikipedia's definition of a vision statement: "A vision statement is an inspirational statement of an idealistic emotional future of a company or group. Vision describes the basic human emotion that a founder intends to be experienced by the people the organization interacts with; it grounds the group so it can actualize some existential impact on the world." Finally, I suggested, "Why not commemorate the reunion of my family, a moment forever marked by shared meals at P. F. Chang's? Let's narrate the story, inspired by the joy of a reunited family that found its way to your restaurant and was moved by the serendipitous fortune they found." As a response to this poignant narrative, I proposed a unique gift: a lifetime of dinner vouchers for my family to continue savoring their renewed bond. "Let's make this into a newsworthy event and an unforgettable gesture, with thirty thousand dollars in dinner credits," I said. "I am prepared to cover the cost, a contribution that doesn't require public recognition."

Our conversation, riddled with persistent static interference despite numerous reconnection attempts, was challenging. To make sure there was no confusion about my intentions, I decided to write down my words, and Jennifer reciprocated by doing the same.

> From: Jennifer
> Sent: Saturday, July 3, 2021 4:27 PM
> To: Daniel Mazur
> Subject: Re: A Story about a PFCHANG Experience
>
> Dan thank you for taking the time to put all of this in writing since we had such a terrible phone connection. Your story is extremely touching and I really appreciate you reaching to me to help you out. I had to think on how best to help you out and although I'm not sure how to quite yet I have personally reached out and spoken to the companies Regional Vice President. He and I have had a close bond for many years and share a passion for helping others as we live the PF Chang's message to celebrate life family and food. He told me that he needs to think on it also but rest assured

we have received your request and will do our best to help you in your endeavors. If you need me for anything in the interim, please don't hesitate to reach out.

Warm Regards
JENNIFER
ASSISTANT OPERATING PARTNER

In summary, I was informed that my proposal, particularly the aspect of accepting money from me, along with other considerations, complicated the situation and raised concerns. Despite several subsequent attempts, my idea didn't come to fruition.

Having already mentally committed to the financial investment, I started exploring other potential uses for it. One idea in particular caught my interest, which I discussed with Raffaella. I considered the concept of a debit card with the same amount of funds, accessible to all my nephews and nieces when they agreed to vacation together. I saw it as an irresistible incentive. The places they could visit, the experiences they could share, how could they resist such a proposition? They could travel anywhere in the world without it costing them a dime. Again, by hook or by crook, whatever would get them together. However, this plan also failed to materialize, largely due to various reasons that Raffaella elaborated upon, including their reluctance to be together, conflicting schedules, and more.

Perhaps I was being naïve. Raffaella never accused me of such, but it was possible my ideas were impractical, my plans outlandish, maybe even requiring a reality check from others, including some of my nieces and nephews. I detested the sensation of having made a mistake. To quiet my mind at night and facilitate sleep, in such moments, I often asked myself, "Was I anything less than honest and caring today?" As long as the answer was "no," I allowed myself to feel at ease, refrain from ruminating on my actions that day, and resist the temptation to berate myself. At least that was the plan.

Regarding the photograph of my nieces, I devised a plan that I wouldn't regret. I had the image printed and set in unique frames, accompanied by the caption "Mirror Mirror In The Mall, Who's The Fairest Of Them All?" in a vibrant pink Disney-style font. Bearing the fortune cookie's message in mind, I had the framed pictures wrapped and sent one each to Audrey and Raffaella.

Forever wary of my decisions being perceived as foolish and feeling awkward within every verbal and text exchange, it struck me that Raphaella and Audrey's siblings might have felt excluded. I was concerned that my actions could be perceived as favoritism, which might have stirred up unwanted complications. In the case of Audrey's family, communication with her father, David, had ceased. He continued his life as he always had, showing no interest in my primary concerns, and it seemed he had persuaded his other children to regard me with the same sense of skepticism and suspicion that he had displayed. Feeling as though I had no chance of overcoming this barrier, and recalling my many past failed attempts to re-unify the family, I decided to concentrate my efforts on areas where I believed I stood a chance.

Engaging in almost daily conversations with Pam, I con-centrated my attention there. I also began to consider the im-pact on Raphaella's siblings, Domonique and Salvador, who might have already been aware of my generosity toward their sister. I called Pam and asked for Sal's phone number, indicat-ing that I'd like to connect with him. A few days after I left a message for Sal, he returned my call. He greeted me warmly, and I employed my best communication skills, which were still evolving for interacting with younger family members. To my delight, our conversation flowed effortlessly, and we talked for almost an hour. We discussed his recent vacation, and I expressed regret for missing him when I was in Syra-cuse, showing genuine interest in getting to know him better. By the end of our conversation, I secured a way to send a sum via Zelle equivalent to what I gave his sister. A few days later,

I extended the same generosity to Domonique.

In the ensuing weeks, I remained committed to making optimal use of my time. The serious impact of the ransomware attack was ever present, and my focus remained on mitigating the damage while reassuring my clients that we were taking appropriate measures to prevent similar incidents in the future. Marco stayed immersed in addressing the technical challenges, "hardening" our systems to make them more resilient against future attacks. There was no 100 percent guarantee that a breach would never happen again; such was the reality for any company that maintained a connection to the Internet. Nonetheless, we were making significant changes. By incorporating new security measures, completing a full transition to Linux-based systems, and establishing a variety of diverse backup systems, we were strengthening our defenses.

Despite these actions and reassurances to our clients, we were unable to retain all of our customers. These losses hit hard, and I missed the weekly interactions that I cherished with the individuals who had chosen to no longer use our services. Regardless, I intended to provide any necessary support to facilitate their smooth transition away from my company. Moreover, I planned to keep in touch, reaching out to them in the future to maintain a friendly rapport.

The balancing act between my professional and personal life continued week after week after returning from my father's funeral. Text messages and phone calls with my family became a constant, and I suspected I was becoming more proficient at both. My conversations with Sal became particularly frequent. I learned about his college studies in computer science, his passion for programming, and his enthusiasm for building his own computers. Aware that I ran a small IT company, he asked numerous questions about my profession. I was more than happy to share my insights with him, and delighted to find common ground on which I could connect with my nephew.

As we transitioned into the latter part of August, the birthdays of my two nieces came and went. In addition to transferring funds, I sent dozens of roses, a bear, and balloons. I continued to make phone calls and send texts, but for some reason, I hadn't heard back from Audrey in a couple of weeks. I started to suspect that her father's behavior, and perhaps my reaction to it, could be the cause, a suspicion that was soon confirmed by her next and final email, informing me she wouldn't be in touch with me anymore.

While re-examining her text messages, along with others, I was reminded that my rekindled relationship with my mother was fraught with its own complexities. I discovered that the time she allocated to visit my siblings and her grandchildren in Syracuse was far from evenly distributed, and there were many reasons for this imbalance. My numerous conversations with Pam abounded with explanations as to why our mother hadn't visited her, her children, and two young, charming great-grandchildren. Aware of this, I endeavored to encourage our mother to be more engaged with Pam and her family. However, this had proven to be a challenging and sensitive endeavor, one that potentially jeopardized our own relationship. In contrast to my mother's other grandchildren, Pam's children displayed various lifestyles and unique personal choices, such as tattoos, cohabitation without marriage, and homosexuality. These were interpreted as indications of failure, expected outcomes of a life spent not adhering to their religious teachings or participating in the services of the Living Word Church.

It had been a challenging task to present an alternative perspective of life to my mother, one not viewed through the lens of my father's teachings. Any form of relationship with individuals perceived to be "living in sin," regardless of whether they were family or not, was taught to us as an act of leniency or even tacit approval. This contrasted with the concept of "tough love," which required not acceptance but rejection and was seen as the proper response. Despite my efforts to navigate this terrain gently, I may have pushed too aggressively, which resulted in my newly forged relationship with my mother starting on uncertain footing.

Audrey's decision to cut off communication with me, though disheartening, wasn't entirely unforeseen. Her father, David, ensnared in the intricate web of our father's teachings, may never fully grasp the profound effects of such an influence on his life, a pattern he continues to impose on his own children.

There exists within me a bountiful reservoir that I wish to share with his family, but he bars them from access. I also recognize there is a wealth of experiences and insights they could impart to me, all of which I may be forever deprived of due to this unfortunate chasm.

Two years ago, during Thanksgiving 2019, I found myself in Homosassa, Florida, celebrating with my Aunt MaryJane and Uncle Gary. The gathering was further enriched with the presence of my niece, Justina, and her husband, Adam. While Adam was a new face to me, memories of my last encounter with Justina took me back to a somber rendezvous in the same town, my grandfather's funeral in 2005.

Against the comforting backdrop of familial banter, I slipped into my familiar role as the jesting prankster, eliciting laughs and playful scoffs. I had recounted a story from that day: an evening when Justina exhibited her culinary skills by making Rice Krispies treats with an extraordinary crunch factor. In a playful move, I had tethered them to my drone, swinging them like a wrecking ball, aiming at objects on the street.

While out for an afternoon drive in my uncle's car, Adam regaled us with tales of his videography escapades alongside Justina. Their cinematic adventures took them to beaches, parks, and various scenic locales. Adam also shared stories of their digital endeavors, including the promotion of an online store specializing in healthy dog treats. Our excursion led us to Best Buy, where a GoPro caught Adam's eye, its price tag seemingly formidable. He spoke about the gadget with such passion, framing it as a dream perhaps forever out of reach.

As our group meandered, examining watches, printers, and a myriad of other gadgets, I returned to the GoPro section, adding it and an Alexa Echo Show to my basket. A quick trip to the cashier ensured they were mine to give. Now, despite the distance separating our homes, I can interact with Adam and Justina just as I do with my aunt and uncle. And with his new GoPro, Adam is equipped to create and share the captivating videos he's always dreamed of.

That autumn of 2021, a year forever significant, marked by my father's funeral, I gained a new client who owned an art gallery. This relationship soon transitioned from professional to personal, and it was hard to miss his ever-present, fluffy white Samoyed, Aspin, during my gallery visits.

An invitation to a dinner he was hosting sparked an idea that I believed could benefit Adam and Justina. I envisioned a petite, wall-mountable doghouse designed like an art gallery. I proposed the idea to Adam, suggesting he construct the piece and that we offer it as a gift to my new friend. Adam consented, and without delay, I transferred the funds for its construction, emphasizing the importance of completing it in time for the upcoming party.

Within a few weeks, Adam's creative flair transformed the idea into reality. The finished artwork was delivered to my residence, arriving on the morning of the dinner event.

At the close of the dinner, I unveiled the "TreatHouse" to Kenny. He was deeply impressed and quickly chose a prime spot for it in his gallery. Our ensuing conversations paved the way for its showcase at Art Basel, Miami's esteemed annual art fair, considered a must-attend event for anyone interested in the contemporary art scene.

A strategy session with Kenny, Adam, and me followed. Kenny, recognizing the piece's appeal, expressed his optimism about its success. Preparations were afoot for its debut and prospective sale at the fair, which was frequented by affluent art aficionados like Kenny, many of whom doted on their pets.

Before introducing Adam to Kenny, I rang him up. "When you join our conference call," I said, "remember our chat, and choose your words wisely."

Adam's voice crackled with confidence. "Don't sweat it, Uncle Dan. I can handle the high falutin' types."

I sighed, trying to impress upon him the truth of the situation. "That's not what I'm saying. Just be straightforward, honest, and genuine. Don't try to put on airs."

"I've got this," he promised.

Despite his assurance, on the day of the call, Adam seemed intent on portraying himself as anything but a novice. He adopted the voice of a veteran, engaging with every detail Kenny introduced. He missed the mark entirely. I had informed Adam of the intimate tales I'd shared with Kenny, especially regarding our family's turbulent and conflict-ridden history. Kenny was there out of genuine compassion, not business intrigue, wishing to support my endeavor to mend our broken family ties.

Observing Kenny gracefully navigate around Adam's misplaced bravado, all while maintaining a sense of decorum to avoid embarrassing him, I felt a strong urge to intervene. Without a moment's hesitation, I plucked the phone from Kenny's hands. "Adam," I said, "I think this is going to be too much for you. Let's call it off. We'll catch up during the holidays."

As time progressed and life carried on, our workload, true to the season, ramped up. We welcomed another new client, prompting the acquisition of specialized cryptocurrency mining equipment. This gear is crucial for deciphering intricate mathematical algorithms, ensuring transactions are validated and recorded on a blockchain network—a technical tidbit for the curious.

My ongoing communications with Salvador led me to extend an invitation for a Zoom session between my team and our client. Due to school commitments, Salvador couldn't participate live, so I provided him with a link to catch up on the meeting at his convenience.

It was evident that Salvador's curiosity about my field was burgeoning. With this realization, and knowing that a pair of technicians on my team were contemporaries of his, I saw a fitting opportunity for introductions. During a subsequent virtual meet-up, they acquainted themselves with one another and exchanged contact info. I expressed to them the importance of mutual support, urging my technicians to help Salvador with any IT-oriented endeavors he pursued.

My commitment to being involved in the lives of my nephews and nieces remained unwavering, and as the year wound down, I sought opportunities for meaningful connections with them. During a chat, Salvador surprised me with a proposal to fly to Miami and work with me for several months. While I mulled over his idea, I determined that the timing and logistics were less than ideal.

As he repeatedly brought up this desire, I proposed an alternative. Perhaps he could handle remote assignments from his home. Given Salvador's beginner status in the IT realm and his geographical distance, finding immediate, substantial roles for him proved to be a challenge. However, I reiterated my commitment to scouting out collaborative avenues.

In line with this, I soon floated the idea of probing the Syracuse region for IT opportunities suitable for him. The potential of establishing an office there arose, emphasizing its possible role as a hub for equipment handling and a base for our marketing endeavors.

Shortly after I shared this idea, Salvador responded with a series of texts. Apparently, the parents of one of his friends owned a real estate company, and this friend also had connections with local advertising agencies that would be able to help us too.

Throughout October and November, I dialed into the Syracuse vicinity, assessing the market potential there compared to locales closer to me. The indicators suggested a significant financial outlay. More questions arose. Would it be feasible to collaborate with a novice, remotely located in a less-than-ideal marketplace? Could I shoulder not just the monetary implications but also the investment of my invaluable time? Given that my primary motivation was fostering family ties rather than profit, I wondered if I should proceed.

As December approached, the question of how to celebrate Christmas lingered. For decades I'd spent the holidays with my aunt and uncle in Homosassa. However, with a renewed connection to one of my sisters and her family, I was contemplating spending Christmas with them. I reached out to my aunt to discuss my thoughts and gauge her feelings on the matter. She said it would be a wonderful gesture for me to reunite with my sister and her family for the festive season. So, I decided to do just that and finalized plans to visit them. After that I notified Salvador of my imminent visit, hinting at our ongoing discussions regarding potential collaboration.

Since my return from my father's funeral in December, I'd been in frequent contact via text with Pam, Salvador, Raphaella, and occasionally, Dominique. Pam shared glimpses of their home: family photos adorning her walls, the Christmas tree in their living room aglow with festive lights, and lighthearted YouTube videos where tech-savvy individuals outsmarted scammers targeting the elderly and others who were less adept with technology.

Amidst these cheerful exchanges, however, were stark reminders of our family's discord. Many messages touched upon the sensitive issue of our familial divide. In one of them, Pam informed me she would not allow our mother or Debbie in her home, at least not while Raffaella was present.

CHRISTMAS WITH PAM AND HER FAMILY

AFTER LANDING AT HANCOCK AIRPORT IN SYRACUSE IN 2021, I headed to baggage claim. Traveling light, I brought only two bags—one of them empty in anticipation of gifts I'll be returning with. The airport's subtle festive decor signaled that Christmas was just around the corner. I found the ambiance inviting, and the prospect of my weeklong stay excited me.

I eagerly anticipated meeting Salvador in person and deepening my bond with Domonique and Raphaella. The thought of the playful giggles of Domonique's daughters lightened my heart. This visit promised cherished moments, allowing me to unwind in their delightful company. I was also looking forward to spending time with other members of my family and Mark's family too, including his mother, brothers, and other kin.

The icy air, a stark contrast to Miami's tropical warmth, made me shiver. I fumbled with the rental car's controls before activating the windshield wipers, which cleared the intermittent snow flurries as I made my way to Pam's residence. The blanket of night settled in, the clock nudging 8:00 p.m. with remnants of a sunset fading.

As I pulled up to Pam's house, a light coat of snow on the driveway caught my attention. I deduced that Mark must've been at work with a shovel not long ago—a chore I once grudgingly performed and was now gratefully distant from.

Moments after I rang the bell, the door swung open, and Pam greeted me. We shared a heartfelt embrace before I stepped inside, shedding the outside chill. Leaving my bags near the entrance, we made our way to the kitchen, where the inviting aroma of fresh coffee filled the air. With mugs in hand, we settled into cozy chairs, our conversation flowing effortlessly as we reminisced about time gone by.

Shortly after, the sound of footsteps from a stairway intensified, reminiscent of the noises in my parents' kitchen when someone ascended from the basement. Salvador, my burly young nephew, greeted me with a grin. Though our face-to-face introduction was a first, our previous interactions on Zoom had bridged much of the unfamiliarity.

"Uncle Dan," he called out, his arms stretching wide. "Bring it in," and we shared a warm embrace. Then he headed to the kitchen, got himself a mug, and joined our ongoing conversation.

As the evening lengthened, a collective exhaustion from the day became increasingly apparent. With the onset of nightfall and accompanying yawns, we opted to call it a night.

The room designated for me was Raphaella's. As I unpacked, the mementos and decorations around provided a glimpse into her character. At the age of nineteen, she had chosen to live with her boyfriend away from her family, charting her own course through the nuanced journey of early adulthood.

As my night was drawing to its conclusion, I began to drift into sleep but was jolted awake by a shout, the origin of which was unknown to me. I lay still, waiting and wondering. A few moments later, it happened again. Then it dawned on me: it was Salvador. Earlier in the kitchen, he had shared stories about the computer games he played with his friends and spoke of the exhilarating world of virtual reality. He even invited me to experience it with him in the basement come Thursday. Clearly in the throes of the game's excitement, he struggled to contain his enthusiasm. Consequently, my sleep was disrupted sporadically by his impassioned outbursts throughout the early morning hours.

As dawn was yet to break, I found myself up and about, embarking on my morning routine of tidying up, showering, and dressing, and then making my way to the family room. Alone with my laptop, I checked my emails and then delved into a few games of online chess. As I grappled with the frustration of a close loss, Pam emerged in the kitchen, dressed in her morning attire, and began brewing coffee. I was entertained watching her trips to the refrigerator, the cabinet, and the sink. Moments like these embedded themselves in my memory, later invoking recollections of individuals in my life and times shared with them. Their distinct gestures and habits acted as signposts, much like index cards in a library pointing to a book's location. These moments were the milestones in my memory, which I often revisited to reminisce about our shared experiences.

Once the coffee was brewed, Pam offered me a cup, and we sat down together, beginning our day with conversation. I mentioned that I had heard Salvador during the night, the noise waking me. She acknowledged that it was an ongoing issue and agreed that it needed addressing.

The chilly air outside and the rhythmic sounds of radiators cycling on and off stirred memories from my childhood. As I wandered through the house, cradling my coffee cup in my hands, I was enveloped in the holiday spirit. The Christmas tree, adorned with bulbs and lights, stood majestically in the living room. I noticed the strings of popcorn, which we threaded together as children, were missing from its branches. Several red stockings hung from the fireplace mantel, each emblazoned with a letter. The one with the "D" belonged to me. These were nostalgic elements missing from my Miami townhouse. There I chose not to decorate, feeling that the decorations would be solely for my own appreciation.

As the morning advanced, Mark stepped out from his room, joining our gathering. Soon after, Raphaella, Dominique, and her two spirited young daughters arrived, infusing the home with warmth, laughter, and vivacity. By the time midday rolled around, Salvador stirred to life, adding to the energetic atmosphere. Our discussions naturally drifted to the day's activities. Recalling an earlier phone conversation with Raphaella, I mentioned my plan to go shopping, hoping she'd join. Staying true to her promise, she arrived prepared. I extended the invitation to Salvador, and shortly thereafter, the three of us set out.

Unsure of where to go, I asked for suggestions. They didn't hesitate; both immediately said "Destiny Mall," as if it was the obvious choice, and they were puzzled that I hadn't thought of it myself.

"Fair enough," I replied. "Let's head there."

Upon our arrival, I circled the parking lot, searching for the closest spot to the entrance. Ultimately, I had no option but to park a fair distance from the mall's doors, and we braced for the cold as we made our way to the entrance. I've always disliked shopping, and every time I'm faced with the task, I usually strategize the quickest exit before even setting foot in a store. However, this time was different. It was the holiday season, and I was looking forward to shopping for the family and enjoying time with my nephew and niece.

Having recently moved into a new apartment, Raphaella appeared to be an easy person to shop for. We first ventured into T. J. Maxx, identifying a few potential gifts, before moving on to Walgreens for additional options. While watching her, I marveled at her efficiency in navigating the aisles. She quickly evaluated each item, setting aside what wasn't suitable and selecting what fit her taste. Her brisk pace brought to mind memories of my Aunt MaryJane—her swift drives in her red Mustang, her rapid pace in bowling, and her efficiency in whipping up meals and desserts, especially when back-to-back guests were anticipated.

As for the others on my list, we discussed what might appeal to each. For Domonique's daughters, our stops included the Children's Place and Journeys Kidz. There, I picked out a range of items for them. From coloring materials to matching decorative iPad covers and purses, our bags were quickly filled. Then, for Pam, we made a special detour to Keys Jewelers. Assisted by Raphaella, I settled on a beautiful ring as a gift. We even shared a lighthearted moment with the sales rep, playfully haggling in hopes of a slight discount.

At the end of our shopping spree, we chose to indulge at P. F. Chang's. It was the perfect way to wind down the afternoon. Interestingly, it was the same restaurant where my two nieces received the fortune cookie foretelling "unexpected gifts." On a whim, I asked if their manager, Jennifer, was around. I hadn't intended to visit her, but given the situation, it seemed like a fortuitous opportunity. "Jennifer isn't here right now, but she'll be in later this evening," the waitress informed me. It felt like a lost chance. However, as we waited for our meals and I dove into animated conversations with my nephew and niece, my attention shifted. I was keen to explore their hopes and dreams. These moments, however precious, were transient. Before long we were making our way back to their mother's house.

Upon our return, Raphaella helped me carry the numerous presents to her room, where we engaged in a friendly competition, each of us claiming superiority in our wrapping skills while pointing out any apparent imperfections in the other's craftsmanship.

Meanwhile, sounds from the kitchen indicated that Pam was preparing the evening meal. I'd heard remarkable things about her culinary talents. Her brother-in-law, Dan Palladino, oversaw Heritage Hill, a beloved family-owned brewery and restaurant perched in the elevated hills of Pompey. A collaborative venture between Dan and Pam gave rise to the farmhouse café, a place where she often was when I chatted with her over my cell phone from Miami. Aunt MaryJane had visited the café during her latest Syracuse trip, praising the café's ambiance and Pam's delectable baked goods, crafted in the adjacent kitchen. It seemed I'd soon get to experience the extent of her culinary prowess firsthand.

In the evening, before Domonique and her boyfriend, Jordan, along with Raphaella and her boyfriend, Ryan, arrived, I shared a meal with Pam, Mark, and Sal. The food on my plate made me realize what I'd been missing back home. I'm not one for cooking, so I tended to visit the same restaurants, ordering the same food week after week. Pam, however, was a marvel in the kitchen, and her family was lucky to enjoy the dishes she crafted with such proficiency.

Upon their arrival, I seized the opportunity to engage Jordan and Ryan in conversation. Jordan worked with an event-production company in Syracuse, and I discovered we both held memberships in a health club. We scheduled a workout session together for Saturday morning. On our drive to the gym, I intended to delve deeper, aiming to get to know him better. In contrast, Ryan resonated with the persona of an entertainer. He hosted a podcast and held a position at a restaurant on Erie Boulevard. Their personalities contrasted sharply. Jordan, exuding a keen interest in Domonique and her two daughters, came across as someone with a clear vision of his life's path. Ryan, on the other hand, appeared to be on a journey of self-discovery, simultaneously navigating and evaluating various avenues.

As the evening progressed, filled with food and conversation, fatigue set in, and one by one, people began to depart, the joy of Christmas morning only hours away. I also retreated to my room, laying my head down in hopes of a peaceful sleep. But tranquility eluded me. Once again, Salvador's shouts from the basement woke me, making a tranquil night unattainable.

The following morning, I found myself the early bird once more, wandering restlessly in my room. The faint groans of the staircase indicated Sal retreating to his quarters, likely winding down from a late night. After a quick stop in the bathroom to freshen up, I moved to the living room. Just as I immersed myself in a fresh game of chess on my laptop, Pam entered, weariness evident in her eyes.

"What's wrong?" I asked.

"I didn't sleep much last night," she replied.

"Again? Because of Salvador's yapping?"

It was the second time since my holiday arrival that our conversation had centered on Sal. The scenario perplexed me. Growing up, any of us causing such a disturbance so late at night would have been told to "knock it off," and that would have been that. I could almost hear our father's admonishing tone: "No playing games in the basement when everyone's trying to sleep!" Disobedience wasn't an option; there were consequences. While I didn't voice those thoughts to Pam, they were on my mind as she discussed her strategy to address the situation. She seemed to be formulating a plan to persuade him.

A strategy? I thought. *Sal needs convincing? It's night; people need to sleep.*

I found the situation intriguing and puzzling.

Before long, the sun began its ascent, and soon Mark was up and moving. The inviting scent of coffee wafted through the air, signaling that breakfast was about to be prepared.

Cell phones came to life, with Pam becoming engrossed in a conversation with Raphaella and Domonique. The excitement in the air was tangible, evident in the animated voices of the little girls, Giovanna and Giada, which I could hear from Pam's phone. I could picture them jumping in anticipation of the numerous gifts that they would soon unwrap. And that's precisely what occurred. With everyone's arrival, we opened presents and reveled in the festive spirit of Christmas Day. Remarkably, for the first time in many years—perhaps since my early years—I found myself in Syracuse, celebrating Christmas alongside my sister, Pam.

On the subsequent Saturday, after a memorable early morning at the gym with Jordan, we journeyed to Heritage Hill: Palladino Farms in Pompey. Our initial stop was Pam's café, situated opposite the restaurant. The warm, inviting atmosphere took me by surprise. I found myself wondering why Pam hadn't shared pictures of this beautiful place earlier. Seeing her achievement firsthand filled me with pride. The café, teeming with activity, had been the setting for countless of our phone conversations as Pam navigated through her duties, whether baking or attending to her customers.

From there we decided to stroll over to the restaurant for lunch. While awaiting our meals, Mark guided me through the brewery, an integral part of the same complex. Once the tour concluded, I found myself back in the restaurant's dining section, which pulsated with the lively chatter of its patrons. Their conversations merged into a harmonious hum.

Laughter and light moments peppered the air as I made faces at Giovanna and Giada, drawing amused reactions from those around us. Not to be outdone, the kids reciprocated with their own playful expressions. Amidst all the joviality, Salvador remained anchored to his phone, likely lost in a game or caught up in a texting exchange.

As the day drew to a close, enveloped by the embrace of the coming night, the dawn of a sunlit Sunday morning was close at hand, heightening the anticipation of my mother's impending visit. For the past while, Pam and I had been navigating a deluge of texts and calls, considering the prospect of uniting the family under one roof. It was my brainchild, an idea teetering on the brink of dissolution, threatened by historical tensions and persisting sentiments. But amid the uncertainties, a viable plan emerged, even if it wasn't the perfect middle ground I had hoped for.

Wary of past undercurrents and apprehensive about a tempestuous reunion with our mother, Pam's daughters opted for distance. This reality was evident during my visit, as I approached both, hoping they might reconsider joining us, even as a personal favor to me. Already knowing full well her daughters would decline any gathering involving their grandmother, Pam devised a plan for a more intimate, serene gathering—just our mother, Pam, and me, an arrangement our mother graciously accepted.

As we awaited the meeting, set to delve into sensitive topics, the trill of Pam's phone interrupted the silence. She checked the screen—it was Mom. "Hi, Mom, are you on your way?" I heard a fragile blend of hope and unease in Pam's voice. She switched to speakerphone, a gesture that seemed partly to include me in the conversation and partly, perhaps, for me to hear any potential letdown firsthand. While I was still in Miami, Pam recounted numerous instances of inviting our mother over, always with the same pattern—an initial agreement, followed by a last-minute call filled with reasons for her absence. Once again, our tenuous peace teetered on the edge, and this time I was present to witness the escalating drama firsthand.

Then, in a tone as serene as a still pond, our mother said, "I'm stopping at the bakery, what kind of doughnuts would Danny like?" Pam's face conveyed her relief. The plan was still firm. "Chocolate eclairs filled with custard, if they have them," I chimed in.

These were the same treats I savored when Grandpa would detour to Harrison's Bakery, taking me with him for post-church macaroni dinners at his house on Oak Street, where we would gather with the family most Sundays. A whisper of curiosity touched me: does Mom ever think, as I do, about those simpler times?

As the heady aroma of freshly brewed coffee permeated the room, it mingled with a pronounced air of anticipation. In eager suspense, we awaited our mother's arrival. When she finally appeared, we were enveloped in the warmth of familiar embraces and the tenderness of cheek-to-cheek kisses. She handed Pam a box of assorted doughnuts, and like magnets, we were drawn to the kitchen.

We moved amid the clinks of mugs and the gentle glugs of the dark elixir being poured. As the ritual played out, Pam presented a feast for the senses, the doughnuts blending with her homemade culinary masterpieces. With an atmosphere thickened by nostalgia and expectation, I found my thoughts drifting. Beneath the soothing embrace of hot coffee and the seductive sweetness of pastries, a profound journey lay ahead. I steeled myself, sensing that we were teetering on the edge of delving deep into our family's narrative, with its blend of sweet memories and bitter tales.

Once we had taken our initial bites and sips, we progressed to the living room, sitting close together on cushioned chairs with our mother positioned between us. Unsure of how to initiate the conversation, I dove in, sharing the first thoughts that came to mind.

"Mom," I began, my heart in my throat, "I've always loved you, just as I have loved Dad. We've had our moments, rifts, and disagreements, but never did I harbor hatred. That is an emotion I've never held, not for anyone. And yet, for the better part of my life, there's been this distorted tale, one that casts me as distant, painting me as aloof, indifferent to the very idea of family. That story? It's a mirage, an illusion conjured by my father, and it strays far from the truth."

Taking a deep, steadying breath, I strived to maintain clarity, preventing a surge of emotions from clouding my thoughts.

"From my first breath in this world, I was immersed in the warmth of our family—your parents, your sister. How, then, could I cut those deep ties without a compelling reason? When I was instructed to distance myself from them, I reacted differently from my siblings, who adhered to our father's wishes. Instead of accepting it blindly, I challenged his decision. 'Why?' I persisted. 'What could they possibly have done to warrant this?' But the justifications I received were flimsy, insubstantial. Instead of tales of deep betrayals or unforgivable errors, I was told that Grandma simply wouldn't perpetuate certain versions of events or shield Dad's failings. Should I ostracize my family over such inconsequential disagreements?"

A fervor gripped me. "Do you recall, Mom, those days when you'd nudge me to call Grandma and say hello because she'd love to hear my voice? I recall reminding you, time and time again, of the warmth your parents always exuded. And I'd urge you, 'Call her. She'd love to hear from you just as much.' Does that sound like someone wanting to detach from his family roots?"

The bitterness swelled within me, impossible to contain. "For standing my ground, I was engulfed in a storm of rumors, the origins of which traced back to my own father. As the years wore on, those whispers turned into deafening roars, constructing an insurmountable wall that separated me from you and my siblings. The heartfelt letters I penned, yearning for understanding, mysteriously never reached you. My attempts to connect through calls and messages to the academy? Mysteriously thwarted. The deeply personal letter I sent to David in 1981, which detailed my painful ousting, remained unread. Its truths were conveniently ignored. I was likened to a venomous snake; to associate with me was to risk poisoning, ensnarement, and even being trapped by the devil himself, thereby jeopardizing eternal salvation. This harrowing isolation, more than any other factor, pushed me to the brink—not any perceived sin or supposed demonic possession but the sheer weight of that rejection. It's what landed me in a mental institution and drove me to that desperate act of trying to take my own life."

I met my mother's eyes, seeking to bridge the vast chasm of misunderstanding that had widened over the years. "Since Dad's funeral, you seem to perceive a new side of me, as if I've undergone some transformation, emerging kinder, gentler. But, Mom, there's been no metamorphosis. Look deeper, beyond the years of separation, the distortions from my father, and the pain. Beneath it all, it's still me, Danny, your son. Do you recognize me? I've always been this person."

My mother's eyes welled with tears, resonating with the words I had spoken. Sitting beside her, I lapsed into a quiet reverie, letting my thoughts meander. A memory from 2003 wafted in, transporting me to the sun-drenched Beach Club, an elegant high-rise on Miami Beach. In the midst of addressing the comptroller's email glitch, a quick peek at my chiming phone revealed my mother's name. Seeking a touch of privacy, I slipped outside to take the call.

Two months before that memorable day, she'd hinted at a longing to bridge the gap between us. Yet in the subsequent weeks, an unsettling silence fell, and I had no way to reconnect with her. "I'll be the one to call," she'd assured me, her voice laden with caution. "Dad shouldn't know we're in touch." Over those few conversations, I'd nudged her about this cloak-and-dagger approach. "I'm trying to spare your father's feelings," she admitted with a heavy sigh.

"Hello, Mom. What's the weather like up there?" was my icebreaker. We bantered about the contrasting climates—her crisp Syracuse chill versus Miami's predictable balmy eighty-five degrees. But our conversation had an untimely end. "I need to go; Dad's coming down the stairs," she whispered. And just like that, she receded into the backdrop, reemerging only when news of my father's declining vitality reached me earlier this year.

The bridge to my mother has been mended, yet I couldn't help but ponder its fragility against the relentless tide of time.

The intricate dance of our relationship, filled with nuances and challenges, never escaped me. Every rendezvous with her painted the canvas of past rebuffs. However, a profound transformation had taken root, its trajectory and consequences on the verge of being unveiled. That tale, which once remained locked within me, had found its voice. To see her tears and hear her apologies was a scene I hadn't witnessed, especially when she had negated any inkling of my distress. Now our conversations flowed unhindered, her maternal affections unchecked by past reservations.

Even as she continued to seek refuge in her church, the ominous cloud of my father's dominance, once intent on silencing my voice, had dissipated. The congregation, and the ideals of God were as integral to her as a heartbeat, much like they were for David Gentile. However, beneath this spiritual veneer lurked subtle undercurrents of falsehood, deceit, and manipulation. While faith may guide many to God, discerning these hidden flaws requires nothing more than a keen and observant eye.

She was ensnared in a realm that reeked of toxicity, but it was also where her roots ran deep. Nevertheless, I'd walk beside her, even within the confines of the Living Word Church. As I sat among the pews, I'd be privy to the distorted teachings, the artful deceits voiced by her spiritual guides. To her I might appear like the lost, the one spoken of who needed salvation. But in those moments, I'd guard my reactions, finding consolation in the understanding that our renewed connection, released from the weight of past judgments, was its own kind of salvation.

My mind sharpened on the present as I observed Pam endeavoring to console our mother. She shared my sentiments, emphasizing that any past anger attributed to me should be contextualized by the grave and unfounded accusations I faced. In that profound exchange, Pam not only spoke about the harm done but also unveiled the challenges her family had endured and the emotional tempests they'd been forced to weather. Her family, like me, had grappled with groundless allegations. They had felt the sting of alienation not only from our parents and siblings but also from their church community and her children's school. Witnessing our mother's palpable sorrow, I was torn between thinking our actions might be too forceful or perhaps just overdue. While it was evident that she needed to hear these truths from both of us, I remained ambivalent about the timing and the magnitude of our disclosures. However, then the dialogue between them eased, guiding us back to a more tranquil moment.

As the curtain fell on our Saturday evening, we bid our mother goodbye, then reconvened in the kitchen. We refill our mugs, the warmth a stark contrast to the emotional chill of the evening, and took a moment to reflect on the gravity of our conversation, its timing, intricacies, and the potential ramifications.

With the first light of Sunday morning filtering through the curtains, I once again found myself engrossed in a game of chess in the living room. It offered a quiet reprieve, but it was short-lived as Pam entered. Perhaps seeking more familiar territory, our conversation circled back to Salvador's nocturnal disruptions. She hadn't confronted him yet. However, as the early afternoon approached, and Salvador emerged from his room, I became a spectator to their face-off. In essence, she instructed him to abstain from gaming in the wee hours. Surprisingly, he offered no immediate pushback, leaving me to wonder why Pam had been so hesitant to broach the subject.

Throughout the remainder of my stay with Pam and her family, I deepened my acquaintance with Domonique's boyfriend, Jordan. Our private conversation en route to the gym served as a perfect moment to gain insight into his life. Additionally, I spent more time with Pam's daughters, visiting Domonique's home and checking out Raphaella's new apartment, where I spotted a Christmas gift I'd given her. Amidst these engagements, I also made time for a meaningful conversation with Salvador about his professional aspirations.

As the time came to delve deeper into Salvador's ambitions, I sensed it was the right moment. In response to my inquiries, he revealed his keen interest in programming, with a particular emphasis on an app he had pondered for several years. He envisioned it as a debate forum—an online arena where users could delve into various subjects like politics, religion, and other controversial topics. Salvador's fervor was evident as he explained the concept in depth. Then, in a burst of enthusiasm during our chat in the kitchen, he rushed to the basement, exclaiming, "I have a notebook with all the details," signaling his eagerness to share more.

However, he returned empty handed, unable to locate the notebook. It was clear that he was invested in the concept, and I aimed to delve into it to ascertain if there was any potential for collaboration between us—a chance for me to support and work alongside my nephew. Then I asked Salvador about his firsthand experience with computers. I'd taken note of the system he set up in his basement and listened to his explanations regarding the challenges he faced with it and the solutions he had crafted.

I was scrutinizing Salvador's mindset and character, seeking to understand all the factors that might influence a potential professional partnership with him. Despite being a somewhat disorganized and clumsy twenty-one-year-old—a Paladino trait, as my sister pointed out—I consistently emphasized to young professionals that technical prowess was only half the battle. Equally vital were interpersonal skills. Since tech experts often had access to a company's most sensitive data, their trustworthiness was non-negotiable. Furthermore, their capacity to make others feel comfortable, especially those apprehensive about their tech limitations, was indispensable.

When Salvador wasn't engrossed in his phone or lost in computer gaming, I recognized his warm and reassuring demeanor—qualities crucial for anyone representing my company and engaging with clients. This trait was certainly a point in his favor, tipping the balance of potential benefits and drawbacks toward the context of a successful partnership. However, gauging his honesty, the most critical evaluation, was something that only time could reveal. I'd come to realize that I shouldn't, and wouldn't, express my interest in this quality. It was an attribute that had to manifest naturally, not one that was contrived because of perceived expectations.

In the blink of an eye, Wednesday snuck up on me, the day I had to bid farewell. From my window seat on the plane, I watched the orchestrated dance of the ground crew below, their movements reflecting the rhythm of my own contemplative thoughts. The narrative of the past week, rich with experiences, played out in my mind. Memories with my sister's family painted vivid and cherished scenes. However, it was the complex, bittersweet moments with my mother that resonated most deeply, like a melody I couldn't quite shake.

A NEW HIRE

WHEN I RETURNED FROM MY VACATION WITH MY SISTER'S FAM-
ily, my phone greeted me with an influx of messages and photos. These snapshots beautifully encapsulated various moments spent with her family: from the
exhilaration of unwrapping gifts on Christmas morning to the
shared enjoyment of dinners to playful interactions with her
two endearing grandchildren. Among these treasures, I also
came across messages from Salvador, their content brimming
with anticipation for my response. These messages signaled
his keen interest in continuing our discussions to explore the
exciting possibility of collaborating in the field of IT.

I touched base with my team to ascertain if there was anything requiring my attention now that I had returned. It was

the week between Christmas and New Year's Day—a time typically characterized by quietude. I discovered that nothing demanded my immediate focus. I had no plans for New Year's Eve and found contentment in the prospect of staying home to unwind. However, I was about to put into motion an idea that had been brewing in my mind, an idea that was sparked during recent discussions with Salvador.

Considering his enthusiasm and keen interest in the development of his debating app, I was prepared to invest financial resources in it. Even so, I also made the decision, in alignment with the purpose of my involvement, to seek opinions on the app's feasibility from other entrepreneurial acquaintances—friends who had successfully pursued their own business ventures. More crucially, my intention was to involve Salvador in these discussions, exposing him to the mindsets of individuals who had flourished in the world of business. My objective was to grant him access to the fertile grounds of success that he might not otherwise encounter.

This was a good time to introduce my dear friend, Thomas. Once an integral part of a thriving construction company in Hollywood, Florida, he had since risen as the proud owner of a multimillion-dollar business. Years back, Thomas had been my primary liaison when my company clinched the contract to manage the IT operations for his then employer. Later, he was entrusted with overseeing my company's handling of all IT services required during the construction phase of Brickell City Centre, a sprawling project spanning multiple city blocks in Miami's financial district. Through our professional engagements, I got to know Thomas closely. As was often the case in my line of work, the hours I spent collaborating with Thomas fostered a deeper appreciation and understanding of the man, causing my perceptions of him to evolve. Thomas was a man dedicated to his job and his profession. His mind was constantly abuzz with ideas that he ardently pursued. But not everyone shared his fervor, and this discrepancy had led to his frustrations. Despite his accomplishments, which significantly benefited the company, he felt held back and underappreciated. As we grew closer, he saw in me a confidant, someone with whom he could share his frustrations and navigate through them. Thomas's character impressed me, and I was inclined to support him in any way possible. Interestingly, the support he required, perhaps unbeknownst to him, was simple: I recognized in him a person possessing all the tools necessary for almost any achievement. He simply needed someone to bolster his confidence, to champion his drive and his ideas rather than critique them. My newfound friend yearned for an experience similar to what I had with Dick Shutt, the owner of SSAC, in my early twenties. It was then that Dick guided me, assuring that the solutions I sought were already within me.

Over the following months, my conversations with Thomas delved deep into his circumstances and his growing aspiration to depart from the company and embark on his own entrepreneurial venture. He presented his plans for moving in this direction to me as though he were seeking my feedback on their viability or perhaps seeking any suggestions I might have. His respect for my opinion was flattering. Early on I recognized that Thomas possessed more business acumen than I did, and I was convinced that his capabilities surpassed even his own expectations and ambitions. I became a sounding board for Thomas, and while I might have offered an idea or two, my primary role was to reassure him that the day would come when he would look back and laugh at the frustrations and challenges he was then facing—a sentiment I shared with him using these very words.

And indeed, that was precisely what transpired. To this day, Thomas reminds me of how I insisted that he would eventually look back and laugh, finding it hard to fathom the extent of frustration and adversity he once endured, especially when contrasted with the sense of achievement he has now attained.

From the outset, Thomas had entrusted all of his IT needs

to my company. Even after its rapid growth and his move out of state, we continued to manage all of his systems. I maintained regular weekly contact with him and his team.

My conversations with Thomas had also extended beyond business. We'd delved into many facets of our personal lives. While I had yet to go too deep into the intricate dynamics of my family, Thomas understood the fundamental aspects: my prolonged estrangement from them and how my father's recent passing had provided chances for rekindling ties. He was also aware of my nephew, Salvador, whom I'd met for the first time.

Against this backdrop, I approached Thomas to introduce Salvador's concept of a debating app. More than the app itself, I communicated my hope of immersing Salvador in enriching professional environments. I aspired for him to recognize that in these settings, values such as empathy and concern for others could serve as cornerstones to financial success.

Thomas embraced the idea of collaborating and offering his insights. He agreed to arrange a Zoom meeting that would allow Salvador to present his app idea and gain insights from an adept entrepreneur.

Following my conversation with Thomas, I called another contact, Nicholas, a successful attorney who was a valued client and a friend whose integrity I admired. He was equally receptive.

I contacted Salvador to brief him on the arrangements and to confirm his availability for the Zoom sessions. Salvador indicated he would review his schedule and update me via text.

On Friday, January 7, 2022, we started our Zoom meeting at 9:00 a.m. I also brought in Angel and Edwin, two technicians who were the same age as Salvador. My goal was twofold: to enrich the conversation and to cultivate rapport among Angel, Edwin, and Salvador.

An hour into our discussion, I was deeply satisfied with the outcome. We were engaging in comprehensive evaluations of the app, discussing its strengths, weaknesses, and potential. Several questions directed at Salvador prompted him to consider certain nuances he had overlooked. The session was uncovering crucial insights, highlighting areas for the app's refinement. It also set a productive precedent for our upcoming Zoom session with Nicholas the following Friday.

Amidst these endeavors and the typical January business flurry, I sought to understand Salvador's ambitions further. One aspiration he consistently voiced was a desire to work alongside me in Miami.

Despite my diligent efforts and brainstorming to find a suitable role for Salvador in IT work in Syracuse, no viable options emerged. In all our interactions, Salvador's desire to join my Miami team was fervent, steadfast, and constant. While I highlighted the challenges and painted a stark picture of the improbability of bringing him here, his relentless enthusiasm, coupled with the apparent dead ends in Syracuse, compelled me to reconsider the possibility.

Over the years, the notion of expanding my operations a bit farther north, roughly an hour's drive, to cater to areas like Boca Raton and West Palm Beach had crossed my mind. With renewed interest, I took several exploratory trips to identify potentially suitable locations. The insights from these trips, combined with discussions with Salvador and my introspection about these prospective locations, led me to a pivotal decision: to secure a spot in Boca Raton and tap into my savings to inaugurate a new office.

I was acutely aware of the looming overhead—rent, utilities, equipment, furnishings, licenses, commuting expenses, time commitments, payroll—and the inherent risks. Slipping into a negative cash flow situation, where savings could rapidly deplete, was all too easy, a lesson I had learned from experience. However, when weighing these considerations, one driving factor became clear: even if this venture led to a financial setback or outright failure, the intrinsic value of deepening my relationship with my nephew justified the gamble.

This set the stage for a full-time position that I planned to offer Salvador within my company in Miami. The package included a full-time role with a salary. He would reside in my home, having a bedroom and the loft to himself, complete with a private bathroom. I wouldn't charge him rent, and his sole household responsibility would be to maintain the cleanliness of his space. I was insistent on this requirement, especially having observed Salvador's less-than-immaculate habits. Additionally, I would provide him with a brand-new car for personal and professional use, with the company covering comprehensive auto insurance. I empathized with his situation and intended to offer him what I would desire in his place.

This reflection led me to think of the numerous challenges I had faced in the past, challenges that this kind of opportunity might have circumvented. Perhaps such hardships were essential, serving as catalysts that fueled my drive and determination.

When I contacted Salvador with the offer, he responded with enthusiasm. However, before finalizing anything, I wanted his father's blessing; without it, we wouldn't proceed. That evening, I reached out to his father, Mark. I shared my intentions, expressing that I saw this as a chance not only to aid Salvador in his professional aspirations but also to contribute to his personal growth. I assured Mark that if he harbored any apprehensions, I would honor them without seeking justification. After a conversation that spanned around thirty minutes, Mark gave his full support.

At that point the real work began. I squared away arrangements with the property manager in Boca, securing the lease with a year's payment in advance for a slight discount. As I navigated through the bureaucratic maze of permits and licenses, I also embarked on a hunt for the ideal car. Recollecting my purchase of a Chevy Trax for the company a year prior, I aimed to secure a similar one for Salvador. However, my timing to venture into the auto market was far from impeccable. Due to a global semiconductor shortage, the industry was in turbulence, and acquiring a new car required a wait of nearly a year.

Eventually, I settled for a used Trax that was in pristine condition with a mere 5,000 miles on the odometer. Although the market compelled me to shell out an extra $8,000 compared to my prior purchase, the acquisition was essential. Following a strategy I employed before, I adorned the car with an eye-catching wrap featuring our company branding. This savvy marketing move reaped dividends, turning heads and often translating into business leads.

On February 1, 2022, I sent images of the cozy spaces in my home that Salvador would soon call his own and gave him a virtual tour of his new set of wheels.

Over the following days, our communication intensified through phone calls and texts. We covered a range of topics, from the company's dress code to the new phone I procured for him, with a special focus on its tethering capability for use at job sites. Technical responsibilities he would soon shoulder, such as setting up the Windows 10 operating system, also became a subject of our conversations. Furthermore, we talked about Linux systems, the process of password recovery, and the diverse functionalities and potential uses of Raspberry Pi.

Just days before his anticipated trip to Miami, I informed Sal that the car wrap was complete and sent him pictures of the final look. Then, on February 26, 2022, after what I was told was a sleepless night, Salvador began packing for his eagerly awaited voyage.

Upon landing at Fort Lauderdale airport, luggage in tow, Salvador spotted me at the designated curbside in the arrivals area. Setting his luggage down, he opened his arms wide and beamed. "Bring it in!" he said, just as he did when we met in Syracuse. His grin was infectious, and our hug was firm and heartfelt. After catching up beside my car, we stowed his luggage and set off for his new residence: my two-story townhome in Miramar.

The conversation in the car started with the usual icebreakers: inquiries about his flight and the weather back in Syracuse when he left. There was so much I wanted to do with Sal, perhaps even stopping at a nearby restaurant for a bite to eat and more conversation. But as the hands of the clock neared midnight, and my energy waned, our activities for the rest of the night were going to be limited.

Navigating through the dim streets, we soon approached the entrance of my gated community. I briefed Salvador on the entry codes he needed. After we pulled into my two-car garage, we unloaded his suitcases. Under the soft glow of the overhead lights, Salvador's eyes were drawn to his new Chevy Trax, poised in its sleek wrap, ready for his maiden drive the next day. It was a far cry from the battered hand-me-down he drove back home.

"Wow, it's really nice," he remarked, opening the driver's door and settling into the seat, perhaps already envisioning himself cruising down Miami's sunlit streets. Carrying a suitcase each, we ventured into the cozy embrace of my home. Recognizing the lateness of the hour and the fatigue in our steps, I assured Salvador that tomorrow would be filled with fresh stories and exciting escapades. But for the remainder of the night, rest was the only agenda.

Come Sunday morning, I woke not to the aroma of fresh coffee but to the realization that it was 2:00 a.m. Today was a gym day, and I had tasks to tackle before my 5:00 a.m. work-out at LA Fitness. One of the wiser decisions I made when living in Liverpool in the 1980s was purchasing a lifetime membership at Sundown Fitness Club. Although it cost me nearly $1,000 back then, that same membership today is valued at about $4,000. Fortunately for me, once Sundown Fitness closed its doors, I was able to transfer my membership to LA Fitness in Miami.

During the early morning hours, my activities often leaned toward business-related endeavors. I prepared my power drink, then moved to the living room and turned on my big-screen TV. Using my Apple TV remote, I searched on Google and explored various YouTube videos that offered engaging tutorials and insights. From time to time, I down-loaded some of these tutorials onto my iPad. On cardio days at the gym, I immersed myself in this material while on the treadmill. The topics I explored ranged widely, from intricate tasks like PowerShell scripting and Python programming to simpler updates on the newest features of word-processing programs. Often, my choice aligned with a recently surfaced client requirement. This autonomous approach to learning was crucial for my professional development, allowing me to earn certifications without turning to formal training courses. Adopting this method was essential when I started out with tight funds, but it remained practical, as the information I sought was almost always available at my fingertips.

Beyond the realm of business training, the early morning hours offered an ideal backdrop for my forays into debates. Regardless of the topic—be it religion, politics, healthcare, so-cial issues, economics, or the environment—my fascination was unwavering. I was enthralled by the dynamics of argu-mentative duels. There was a unique allure in observing and understanding the subtleties of persuading someone to em-brace a particular perspective.

I headed to LA Fitness for my typical ninety-minute work-out. Once done, I returned home to prepare my breakfast. Sal-vador was still sound asleep, so I treaded lightly to avoid wak-ing him. Once he stirred, I offered him breakfast, marking the beginning of our inaugural day with my nephew in Miami.

Throughout March, Salvador familiarized himself with Mi-ami: the diverse dishes and beverages from local eateries, the city's labyrinth of roads, its distinct culture, and his new ac-quaintances. Among them were Angel and Edwin, his cowork-ers at my office, and naturally, there was me, his uncle. Taking this step signified a monumental change for Salvador as he em-barked on his maiden journey of living away from home.

Choosing to inject some fitness into this new chapter, he opted to join me for my 5:00 a.m. workouts at LA Fitness. To my astonishment, on my first Monday with Salvador, he emerged in my kitchen, fully geared up for the session. I cautioned him from the outset not to emulate my regimen. He might have perceived me as an elderly figure—indeed, I was over sixty—but I had been dedicated to my fitness routine for decades and reaped the benefits. "Remember," I advised him, "it's not about pushing yourself to the limit at the start. The key is consistency: showing up and fostering a desire to return." During those initial days and in the sessions that followed, however, he exerted himself excessively, seemingly feeling a compulsion to outperform his limits. "Ease up. Pace yourself," I continually urged him. "Fitness is a journey. The aim is sustained dedication; progress manifests organically—don't rush it."

As for business, Monday morning kicked off with a meeting at our Miami Lakes Office. Over doughnuts and juice, the team got acquainted. I was especially pleased to see Angel and Edwin extend invitations to Salvador for activities outside of work. Given that they were of a similar age and shared many interests, they extended an invitation to my nephew for a gaming event.

Throughout March, I guided Salvador's immersion into client visits, working alongside his colleagues and me. These sessions, predominantly with small businesses, presented him with opportunities to engage with a myriad of owners and their staff. More than mere exposure to the technical realm of IT, Salvador started to grasp the complex dynamics inherent in diverse business settings. He was exposed to the relationships, the rapport, and the unique interactions that shaped each workspace. He gained insights into the relationships, camaraderie, and unique interactions that defined each professional environment. To deepen his understanding, during our personal interludes, I shared my accumulated experiences and insights. My objective was to equip him with a sophisticated comprehension of these landscapes, aiding him in his navigation, with the overarching ambition of ensuring mutual benefits in every collaboration.

As my first month with Salvador neared its end, my ten-day vacation with Claudia approached. On Wednesday, March 30, we reunited at the luxurious Lirolay Suites in Bariloche, Argentina. This was our second visit there. Our fond memories from that perfect retreat in April, four years prior, inspired us to return.

Claudia was fully informed about the recent shifts in my family dynamics, particularly Salvador's move to Miami to live with me. Her stance on this matter was clear. I shared with her the challenges my nephews and nieces faced, stemming primarily from their tumultuous upbringing, an upbringing she recognized had scarred me too. Nonetheless, she remained skeptical. I expressed my goal to uplift their lives, to show them there's an uncle who deeply cares and wants to support them. Despite Claudia's frequent declarations that she knew me better than anyone, she remained indifferent to the significance I placed on this issue. She disagreed with my decision to house Salvador and offer him employment. In her view, given the adverse impact my family had on my life, there was no reason for me to entangle myself further, and she was skeptical about the potential benefits of such involvement.

In the four weeks leading up to my departure, I was committed to preparing Salvador to manage well in my absence. Every day, whether on the job or at home after work, I engaged in extensive conversations with him. I was heartened by the feedback I received about his interactions. Corporate clients and homeowners alike commended his kind nature. They reported that he was considerate and attentive to their needs. I emphasized to Salvador that technical know-how was just one aspect of our work. "In our business, possessing people skills and earning the trust and respect of our clients is crucial," I told him. In terms of technical skills, Salvador made commendable progress. He always had the support he needed and never lacked resources to consult when faced with a problem. Everything proceeded as planned and aligned with my expectations and aspirations.

Sunday evening, April 10, 2022, arrived all too quickly, signaling the conclusion of my vacation. I was in Buenos Aires, preparing for my next flight on my return journey to Miami. The ongoing COVID-19 epidemic presented its own set of challenges. The test I took in Bariloche just two days earlier was unexpectedly considered expired. As a result, I was mandated to undergo another test at the airport before I could board my next flight. Further complicating matters, once we boarded, we were informed of an unforeseen issue: the absence of a pilot. This dilemma seemed to be yet another repercussion of the epidemic, with a notable pilot shortage. Having just settled into our seats, we were instructed to disembark. The initial boarding process was already strenuous. To my astonishment, I was among a few passengers randomly selected for an exhaustive body search. As I attempted to board for the second time, I was subjected to the same meticulous search and once again was confronted with questions in Spanish. Despite living in Miami and being exposed to the language for many years, I still didn't understand enough of it.

As I settled into my window seat, my phone buzzed with a new message. It was Salvador, who asked me to text him when I landed.

By the morning of Monday, April 11, I was back in Miami, facing a full workday. This week demanded extra attention, given all the tasks waiting for me after my time away. Additionally, the upcoming weekend celebrated Easter, and I had made plans to be with my aunt and uncle in Homosassa. My mother and Debbie were joining us as well, flying down from Syracuse. Consequently, the regular weekend hours I typically reserved for paperwork were not at my disposal. The workdays passed swiftly, and by the time Friday came, I recognized that I'd already collaborated closely with Salvador for over a month.

Pam had alerted me to some of Salvador's traits that she deemed concerning. In particular, she pointed out his lack of tidiness and his tendency toward clumsiness. True to her observations, these characteristics became evident quickly. The new car I provided for him turned into a repository for leftover food, candy wrappers, and empty soda containers, despite my repeated warnings about potential consequences. He even managed to damage the car by accidentally lowering the garage door onto it. Though he agreed to do laundry on Saturdays, Salvador consistently delayed the task until late Sunday evening, leaving me struggling to sleep due to the noise from the washer and dryer's location right outside my bedroom door.

In an effort to emphasize the importance of adhering to rules, I barred him from using the washer and dryer for two weekends, hoping the hassle of using a laundromat would teach him a lesson.

Moreover, I noticed other worrisome tendencies. Mornings usually found his alarm blaring several times before he eventually got up, and he didn't account for the time needed to shower. "Wake up a bit earlier," I advised. "Make breakfast, take some time to relax, and mentally gear up for your day."

"I'm not a morning person," he retorted, "and I don't do breakfast."

Every morning, by the time Salvador awakened, I had already returned from the gym and had finished my breakfast. He stopped accompanying me to the gym quite some time ago. While I assured him he was welcome to join me again, I tended to avoid the topic so as not to discourage him by drawing attention to his lack of commitment. After all, the goal to attend the gym together was his idea, not mine. As I sat in my office, engrossed in my work, I often heard him hastily getting ready. From time to time, I stepped outside my office to observe him. More often than not, his shirt was a crumpled mess, left untucked, and he seemed in need of a shave.

"You're going out, looking like that?" I would ask. "Your shirt all wrinkled, your face unshaved?"

"But I'll be late," he would protest, "and you always tell me it's important to be on time."

In the evenings, we would sit together in my living room, discussing his day. These sessions were not just casual chats; they were opportunities for me to offer guidance, especially on making his life more organized and efficient. Regarding his shirts, I advised, "The night before, ensure you have one ironed and ready on a hanger."

These conversations were frequent, as Salvador's challenges with preparedness were becoming increasingly evident. He often left home forgetting essential items. "Before stepping out in the morning, take twenty seconds to confirm you have everything you need," I would advise him.

At judiciously chosen moments, I encouraged Salvador to venture outside of his bedroom on weekends. I hoped he would engage more with the world beyond his bed, his phone, and his computer. I understood that it was his free time, though, and that he needed the liberty to spend it as he wished. Therefore, I broached the subject with care, ensuring that he knew my occasional advice was motivated by genuine concern.

I also conversed with Pam, filling her in on these occurrences. My intent wasn't to gossip or seek any form of reprimand or reprieve. Everything I shared was geared toward determining the best strategy to support Salvador, giving him the optimal opportunity to thrive. I solicited ideas and suggestions in every conversation. After all, she was his mother, and I was just beginning to understand him.

Moreover, I was not disconcerted by any of these instances. Salvador was good natured and embodied the qualities I expected and sought from him. Even as he persevered in his constant justifications, which often seemed to be the root of his struggles, I remained patient, investing countless hours in conversations with him. I listened to his cyclical arguments regarding his beliefs on why his chosen paths consistently led to personal challenges. For me, it was an intriguing experience, and it rekindled my fascination with the human tendency to argue and what hindered individuals from making choices that would enhance the quality of their lives and render them more manageable.

Based on my interactions with him, I had gleaned insights into some questions I had pondered back in Syracuse. There, I had noticed Pam considering how best to ask Salvador to keep it down during the early hours. Engaging Salvador in discussions about behavior adjustments required preparation; otherwise, I would unintentionally find myself conceding to his viewpoint. Salvador was astute and persistent in his discussions, arguing fervently. If allowed, he pressed his point tirelessly. I delved into numerous conversations with him, curious to gauge when he might relent, especially when he discerned that I couldn't be swayed by his arguments. Such interactions could be draining, given his incessant attempts to justify his actions and persuade others to see things his way.

After hours of explaining my rationale behind a specific decision to Salvador and consistently meeting opposition, there were times I felt compelled to insist, "We discussed this extensively. I clarified my position. I won't continuously restate my reasoning in hopes of either securing your agreement or having you persuade me otherwise."

Situations where discussions stretched as late as 9:00 p.m., especially when I had to be up by 2:00 a.m., were unfeasible. Despite my insistence to refrain from discussions at such hours, Salvador persisted. Even with the frequency and extensive time spent addressing issues, my stance remained unchanged, and Salvador continuously questioned my decisions.

Late into the night, Salvador's lively gaming sessions with friends occasionally disrupted my sleep. On weekends he seldom left his bedroom. From my neighboring office, a medley of sounds reached my ears: the intensity of marathon gaming, intermittent snoring, and the lively cadence of phone conversations with his friend. The combination of all these behaviors concerned me. However, I held onto the belief that, with guidance and support, Salvador would thrive in Miami with me and in other endeavors in the future.

As Easter weekend approached, I asked Salvador if he planned to join me at my aunt and uncle's home in Homosassa, as we had discussed. I believed it would be a meaningful experience for him, offering quality time with relatives, especially his grandmother and Aunt Debbie, who would fly in from Syracuse. However, knowing Salvador as I did, I suspected he might be accepting my invitation more out of a sense of duty than genuine enthusiasm. He might prefer spending his free time at home, gaming with friends and catching up on sleep. Nonetheless, he agreed to join me there for a few days. I was hopeful that the four-hour drive to Homosassa and back would pave the way for deeper conversations, giving us an opportunity to understand each other better.

Upon arriving at my aunt and uncle's home, I hoped that Salvador would engage with the family. While I understood he was under no obligation, I hoped that with me gently encouraging him, he would create cherished moments and memories. However, my expectations proved to be misplaced. During meals and various family gatherings, Salvador often chose to be elsewhere, or if present, was engrossed in his phone. To compound matters, he seemed to grate on Gary's nerves. In the mornings while everyone else was up and about, Salvador persisted in sleeping on an air mattress in the living room, seemingly unaware of the inconvenience, causing everyone to maneuver around him. He also left his drink by the mattress, which he might knock over. Gary's perception of Salvador was unmistakable. He saw my nephew as self-centered, showing little regard for his own family. Gary relayed this sentiment to me, and I tried to defuse any tensions, aiming to ward off any disputes during our visit.

During our drive home, I broached the topic of relationships with Salvador. I specifically mentioned his sleeping late in the morning, in the living room, the central gathering place. "It's where everyone comes together, sipping their coffee, tuning into the news, and sharing stories about their day. Did it cross your mind that, as a guest, you should have been up and out of the way?" Each of his answers, while immediate, bore a defensive edge.

"This is why I don't like being around people. I'm perfectly content alone," he retorted. But within his words, a deeper struggle surfaced: an underlying anguish stemming from the challenges in forming meaningful connections.

"We are social beings," I replied. "Finding comfort in solitude is one thing, but only when it's a genuine choice, not a refuge from relational challenges." Sharing my narrative, I spoke of my own battles. Despite my diligent work ethic, a significant portion of my life revolved around striving to heal family bonds, regardless of the previous rifts. His reply made me wonder if I had overshared.

"You're a workaholic, always buried in your work," he snapped. "That's no life. I'd never want a life like yours."

On a Monday evening, after returning from our Easter weekend in Homosassa, I was overcome by a peculiar sensation. Settling into my sofa to unwind with my big-screen TV, I pressed the button to activate the recliner. As I reached for the remote control on the armrest to power up my Apple TV, I found it was missing. Puzzled, I glanced to my right and spotted the remote resting on the sofa cushion beside me. A nagging feeling hit me—the sensation that I had knocked something off the armrest.

Indulging my intuition, I leaned forward, scanning the floor. Despite finding nothing, the feeling remained, prompting me to check behind the sofa. Still nothing. But the sensation refused to fade. Compelled by an inexplicable urge, I fully reclined the sofa and peered beneath it. That's when my fingers encountered a small, sharp object. Holding it up to the light, I examined the pebble-sized shard: white with specks of blue, revealing a part of a recognizable pattern. I headed to the kitchen and opened a cupboard. There, my eyes took notice of three white dinner plates, each adorned with the same pattern. One was missing, and it dawned on me what had happened while I was in Bariloche. Having gotten to know

Salvador fairly well, I believed it was likely that he had broken my plate, accidentally of course, perhaps because of a careless move while eating in the off-limits area of my living room. I also suspected he had cleaned up the mess, hoping the incident would go unnoticed.

I harbored doubts about confronting Salvador, expecting it wouldn't elicit an honest response. From my observations, Salvador avoided admitting mistakes and wrongdoings, especially if he believed they couldn't be substantiated. Keenly aware of occurring events, he navigated accepted facts to shape others' perceptions. If I chose to address the matter with him, I would need to be tactful and persistent, ready to invest the energy that such conversations demanded.

"While I was in Argentina, did everything go well here at home? Were there any problems?" I asked on Monday evening as Salvador headed to the refrigerator for some food.

"No problems," he replied. "Everything was okay. Why do you ask?"

Little by little, I continued to probe, asking about anything that might have occurred while I was away that I should be informed about.

"No, nothing," he replied.

I edged closer to what I know without revealing too much. "Do you recognize this?" I asked, showing him the shard from the broken plate.

"No, what is it?" he replied, which was unsurprising given how minuscule the fragment was.

"It's a piece of the plate you broke while I was on vacation, while you were eating and watching TV in the living room," I informed him.

"Oh yeah, that did happen," he conceded. "I forgot to tell you about it."

I couldn't have cared less about the plate. I was not upset that it broke, nor was I bothered that it was likely due to his clumsiness or that it happened in a place where he wasn't supposed to be eating. What troubled me was his penchant for deception, a habit that surfaced time and time again in a variety of contexts and situations. I wanted to delve deeper into the issue. Everything within me believed that he broke the plate and deliberately concealed the fact to prevent me from finding out. Honesty is paramount, even in innocuous matters, and it was important for Salvador to understand this.

"You forgot to tell me about it?" I asked. "Are you sure you didn't hide what you did because you didn't want me to know?"

"No, I just forgot to tell you," he insisted. I cast a skeptical glance his way, conveying my disbelief.

"What are you trying to imply?" he asked. "You can't read my mind. You can't prove that I didn't forget to tell you."

He was right, of course. I wasn't present when it happened, and there was no video evidence of the event. Nonetheless, his choice of words deepened my suspicions about him. My intuition about the situation seemed to align with the character traits he displayed. Determined, I pressed on, trying to discern how adamant he was in his denial. His unwavering stance, insisting that he simply forgot, accentuated the seriousness of the issue. Throughout our relationship, he had exhibited traits like clumsiness, forgetfulness, and sloppiness—attributes I observed and was forewarned about. I had the patience and understanding to navigate those traits. However, dishonesty? That was an unforeseen challenge, one I never agreed to accept or contend with.

As life resumed over the next two weeks, I dedicated extra time and energy to observing and communicating with Salvador. I became convinced of several alarming transactions taking place. While I discovered he wasn't being truthful about some of them, others remained merely suspicions. Regardless, I grasped the gravity of the situation and its impact on my life and felt uncertain about how to proceed. My conversations with Pam regarding Salvador were ongoing. However, the nature of those discussions shifted. I began sharing my concerns about Salvador's integrity.

"You know what Salvador is like," she said. "I warned you."

"Yes, you mentioned his clumsiness and sloppiness, but you never alerted me to his dishonesty. You asserted that your children never lie to you. Well, one of them is certainly being dishonest with me."

As scheduled, at the end of those two weeks, coinciding with the first week of May, Pamela, Mark, and Raphaella arrived in Miami for a visit. I suggested that Sal take Friday off to be with them. Due to a series of commitments, I remained at work that day. However, I joined them on Saturday. They visited my home, getting their first glimpse of where Salvador resided. Afterward, we made our way to a shopping district in northern Miramar. Unfortunately, I couldn't stay with them for long and parted ways to return to my responsibilities. But come evening, I was free again and took everyone to Chima Steak House, a renowned dining spot for tourists on Fort Lauderdale's Las Olas Boulevard.

After their departure, my challenges with Salvador continued for nearly two months. Considering what I knew about Salvador, coupled with the insights he had provided, his behavior didn't surprise me. Keeping these issues and his consistent seclusion during weekends in mind, and his seeming distance from anyone in Miami, my concern about potential long-term repercussions—for me and for Salvador—was growing. I was increasingly compelled to consider how to best address this situation.

However, as the close of two months' time with Salvador was nearing, I was scheduled to take another flight to Syracuse. I had committed to attending the high school graduation ceremony of my nephew, Jacob (Paul's son), on Saturday, June 25. Once more, I would entrust Salvador with my home in my absence, though not without a sense of apprehension.

A STOMACH CHURNS WHILE TASSELS TURN

As the clock struck 2:30 P.M. on the sunny Miami afternoon of June 24, I stepped onto flight 897, bound for Syracuse once more. The adventure was set for a tight three-day span, with my return scheduled for Monday. Thanks to Allegiant Airlines' direct weekly services, the hassles of connecting flights had become a relic of the past.

When I touched down, my mother—radiating a mixture of excitement and nostalgia—was there, ready to whisk me away. On past journeys, the familiar havens of my siblings, David and Pam, had been my refuge. But this visit promised a different backdrop. The destination? The very home that reverberated with the sounds of my childhood laughter and was haunted by the shadows of trauma. A chill coursed through me when she proposed the idea. The notion of being encompassed by those walls, reliving a torrent of memories, had felt almost unthinkable just a year ago. But fate, with its penchant for unpredictability, often catches us off guard. So, that night, within those familiar confines, I journeyed through dreamland, drifting off to sleep and waking up to the memories of my past.

As I emerged from Hancock Airport, a surprisingly warm breeze caressed my face, its warmth like a welcoming handshake. Within moments my mother materialized by the curb, her eyes a lively blend of joy and anticipation.

"Hi, Danny!" she called out, her arms open in invitation. I walked into the comfort of her hug.

"Hi, Mom. Nice weather here this evening."

Her reply came with a warm smile. "Yes, it was in the eighties again today and mostly sunny."

We stowed my luggage, and the car purred to life, heading toward the nostalgic lanes of Clairmont Park. An amused smile formed on my face as I reflected on the name's irony—from my home in Montclair to my past in Clairmont. The hum of the car harmonized with our light-hearted conversation, our chit-chat covering memories and mundane subjects alike. Soon, the familiar Liverpool house came into view.

"You'll be in Pam's old room," Mom said. Then, with a hint of excitement in her voice that made me giggle, she added, "But before that, let me show you around the house."

I nodded, anticipating a tour of the recent renovations.

The previous year, during hushed phone conversations with Pam about the ancestral house, a question tumbled from my lips: "Is she holding onto it or letting it go?" At first, Pam painted a picture of my mother gravitating toward a fresh start. The spacious rooms, which accentuated my father's absence, made the prospect of a cozier, more manageable place, perhaps a townhome, increasingly appealing. A place without the demands of tending to a lawn and myriad rooms. But as time moved onward, hints from my mother's heart-spilled stories revealed a patchwork of emotions tethered to the home. Beyond the bricks and mortar, it was the wooden treasures, handcrafted by my father in his basement workshop, that my mother said she was unable to part with. Anchored to the memories these items invoked, the idea of severing that bond was a mountain too steep to climb.

Pam shared this narrative with me, hinting at her belief that David convinced our mother to keep the home for his own benefit. Regardless of the motives behind the decision, Paul flooded my phone with photos of the house undergoing a significant renovation in January. Floors were stripped to the two-by-four framing underneath, with many of the interior walls removed entirely. As I ascended the stairs, fresh from my mother's tour, memories of those images resurfaced, prompting questions. While hauling my bags into Pam's old room, I wondered why her door wouldn't close properly. When pushed to shut, the door grazed the floor before reaching its frame. Might the craftsmen who had installed it overlooked potential swelling of the door due to ambient humidity?

Another oversight led to the formation of a small pond in the yard. In addressing the home's long-standing moisture problem in the basement—an issue that had escalated over time—a sump pump was incorporated to redirect water from the basement to the house's exterior. However, instead of channeling the water into a gutter or drainage system, it was directed into the yard beside the house. David, drawing upon his expertise, assumed responsibility for appointing and overseeing the contractors (that is, if the accounts I'd heard were true). Nonetheless, his choices were met with skepticism, especially considering his role as executor of the estate. Whispers about his management, especially concerning our mother's finances, had reached my ears. As for the veracity of these matters, I remained largely indifferent. I was confident that my mother would spend her twilight years in comfort.

If I discovered that my trust had been misplaced and things took a turn for the worse, I would simply intervene.

In yet another familial dispute, Debbie recounted her experience of organizing a garage sale to pare down the household clutter. My father, it appeared, had an inclination to acquire items reflecting his transient enthusiasms. For instance, when culinary arts caught his fancy, he'd buy a myriad of cooking tools and gadgets, only for them to lose their allure and gather dust. I'd heard tales of how the garage had evolved into a storeroom for these once-loved but long-forsaken passions.

Regarding the woodworking machinery, Debbie had committed to giving some pieces to a church member. This gesture, the reasons for which remained elusive to me, struck a discordant note with David. It appeared he also had a bone of contention with regard to Debbie's management of the garage sale and its proceeds.

While I had remained aloof from the details of these squabbles, I was aware of what concerned me—the perpetual rifts and disagreements among my siblings.

The following day, on the occasion of the graduation ceremony, my mother and I made our way to the church that was hosting the event. When I saw Jacob, my nephew, it was evident that he was in an environment where he was treated well, and he reciprocated that care to others—his peers, teachers, principal, and fellow Christians. Beneath this surface of harmony, however, I was privy to undercurrents of profound concerns and alarming realities. Suddenly, one such concern came into focus.

The commencement began with a speech from congregant Andrew Hockenberry, an alumnus of the Living Word Academy from the class of 2001. He opened with, "I just want to say something about why I'm thankful for the Living Word Academy."

As a teacher in the city's public school system, he drew a stark contrast between his daily encounters there and the environment at the academy. He talked of children consumed

by anger, a byproduct of homes where faith wasn't the cornerstone. Such children, he said, were traumatized by their home
lives, and resorted to violence as an outlet for their pent-up
anger. He noted they were undernourished and improperly
clothed and that they emanated a sense of hopelessness.

Then he transitioned to highlight how the academy, along
with the parents affiliated with Living Word Church, catered
to and addressed these pressing needs. "Our school is founded with that in mind. To get kids out of the public school system, into a place where they can learn about Jesus, day in and
day out, guided, helped, and given hope."

Aware this was only a taste of my nephew's daily con-
sumption, my memories surged, evoking the pervasive influences that shaped my early life. It was suddenly evident why,
on my first day as a freshman, apprehensively stepping into
what I believed to be the daunting world of public schools, I
found myself clutching a knife, as if preparing for some impending threat. Yet the irony was clear: my most profound
confrontations with anger, violence, and trauma weren't in
school corridors but within the confines of my purportedly
"Christian" home. This grave introspection deepened as I
recalled the heart-wrenching stories my nephews and nieces confided—their acts of self-harm and the inner chaos they
grappled with during their years at the academy.

While sitting there, I was overcome with a sense of disquiet. The one-dimensional views, monochromatic perspectives,
and oversimplified narratives my nephew's generation was
exposed to became glaringly apparent. Rather than being encouraged to explore a world resplendent with vibrant hues
and intricate patterns, offering a wealth of enriching experiences in its subtleties and complexities, they were ushered
down a constricting corridor. Guided by those who claimed
to have exclusive insights into absolute truth, they were gradually distanced from the world's intrinsic richness, day by
day, year after year.

Two large video screens dominated each side of the church

sanctuary. Videos appeared showcasing the teachers sharing reflections on the graduating class. Among these videos,
slides with bold white text intermittently appeared. One slide
in particular sparked my interest, posing the question: "Any
more advice for the Class of 2022?" The screen transitioned to
reveal insights from four teachers, each imparting their distinct words of wisdom.

1. I want to encourage them personally to keep serving God.
   When things get difficult their faith will be tested.
2. Don't become unequally yoked. Fellowship with other
   believers. Get to church as much as you possibly can.
3. There is absolutely nothing in the whole universe that's
   worth your soul.
4. You're going to be targeted, and it's going to be a real
   temptation for you. So, what you have to do is you have
   to stay connected to the body.

Did I symbolize a word of warning to my attentive nephew? "Proceed further with caution?" Surely, there was wisdom in this world—even from those perceived as sinners
like me—that held value, that was worth sharing with these
young graduates.

Or was it truly as I discerned and remembered: a doctrine
steeped in fear, a worldview boiled down to the stark contrasts of simplistic binaries, the virtuous versus the vile, the
saint pitted against the sinner?

I'd grown up and ventured into the very world they described, yet their depiction of it felt foreign. Did evil exist? Absolutely, and I'd witnessed it. But there was also beauty and
wonder, alive and pulsating amidst the pandemonium.

Why not highlight the enchantment and allure of these marvels, urging the students to seek them out? Why deprive these
impressionable young minds the knowledge of these wonders?
And where was the affirmation that individuals from diverse
religious backgrounds might bring invaluable insights? Phrases like "Be equally yoked" underscored alignment with those

of similar faith, overlooking the enriching contributions from those of diverse cultures who were equally compassionate and caring. Such oversights were not merely detrimental; my own experiences bore witness to the deep-seated damage such narrow-mindedness could cause.

Had I heard messages at the commencement that resonated with me, elements that I considered enriching? Without a doubt, there were numerous points—similar to the moment when my father spoke about the food pantry at the hospital. But akin to that day, the issues that deeply troubled me were what seized my attention. These were the matters crying out for focus and change, not the aspects already worthy of accolades.

As the ceremony concluded with the symbolic shifting of tassels from right to left and the graduates tossed their caps high in the air, we made our way toward the back, prepared to exit the church. Standing beside my mother, I noticed my brother David approaching. When he reached out and offered a handshake, I was caught off guard.

"Why are you bothering with me now, David?" I asked, my tone neither acrimonious nor biting but simply direct, unwilling to pretend all past grievances had been addressed. David's reaction, however, was incendiary. He insisted that I leave, asserting that I had no place there. While I stood my ground, I felt more embarrassed for him than for me, and I chose to ignore his outburst. Eventually, he departed.

A short time later, his wife, Dianne, approached with an apology. "David has been under a lot of stress recently," she said. The funny thing is, she said it to my mother, never looking at me. I wondered if she would ever realize the offense was made against me, that I was the one who deserved an apology, a gesture from David that I suspected would never come my way.

The next morning, we were up at the crack of dawn. Mom whipped up scrambled eggs for breakfast.

The day before, I had promised to accompany her to Sunday service, and despite David's recent actions, I had no intentions of backing out. As we finished our meal and engaged in light conversation, it was time to prepare for church.

The journey there was short. As I looked out the window, the familiar sights stirred memories of our numerous visits to the church. I recalled its humble beginnings in an office setting, where traditional pews gave way to rows of vinyl chairs.

Upon arrival, I took a seat beside my mother, presumably in her usual spot. Directly in front of us, David and his family settled in.

The congregation lifted their voices in praise. When the songs subsided, Bryan emerged, poised to share his sermon. It dawned on me that this was a live address, not a recorded message on cassette tape or a digital download. What would he say?

Bryan started by assuring the congregation that he was not a salesman. "Been a pastor more than thirty years, a rookie for a year now as a lead pastor," he said. "My duty is to preach the gospel, to warn, to teach, the maturity of the congregation being the goal."

Then he delved into a discussion about sales tactics, high-lighting the "bait and switch" technique. He recalled that the last thing he sold was fruitcakes during his Cub Scout days. Shifting gears, Bryan explored the essence of "being in Christ," juxtaposing it against the prevalent cultural mantra of intro-spective self-discovery. "Sigmund Freud's theories have been debunked," he declared.

I might have anticipated the term "debunked" linked to fig-ures like Charles Darwin, given that some audiences hold such beliefs. But Freud? His psychoanalytic theories, while having evolved and been scrutinized extensively over time, had never, in my experience, been described outright as "debunked."

And I would be remiss if I didn't mention that earlier, be-fore Bryan's sermon, a prophecy was shouted by a woman in the congregation, one I later discovered that my mother, among others, believed was intended for me. "Thus sayeth the Lord God, you have said to me, I wish that God would speak to me. And I say to you, I have spoken to you for years, but every time I send my servant to you with my word, you resist him. You dismiss him because you think you are yielding to the voice of a man. But I sent them to you, and it is my word that you have dismissed. And so I say to you again, again I say to you, I have big plans for you. I have plans for your good, for a full and overflowing life. You have big plans but my plans are bigger. What have you found in this life that has satisfied you? Nothing, nothing. Nothing will satisfy you except for me. So, stop resisting. Turn from your sin. Turn to me, and I will save you, and I will be your God."

If the prophecy was indeed intended for me and truly from God, it left me untouched. The music, the theatricality, and the insistent whispers all failed to sway me. I clearly saw the human intentions behind those acts, motives Freud might have deftly analyzed if he were beside me.

As the service concluded, Mark, an acquaintance from the church's early days, approached. "Do you have thirty seconds?" he inquired.

"Of course," I replied.

He started to share a "hunch" he had about me. I was intrigued, but time was fleeting, and his allotted thirty seconds passed quickly. In the background, I heard my mother's voice, reminiscent of times when I'd linger too long outdoors as a child, late for dinner.

"Sorry, Mark, I need to go," I said, promising to get back to him. A personal prophecy of my own, if you will.

On July 9, two weeks later, I made good on that promise and sent Mark a letter.

July 9, 2022

Mark Michaels,

Hello again. We didn't get to finish our conversation. If you ever want to, we can.

You said it was something like a hunch, the reason asking me for 30 seconds of my time. I wonder, where do such hunches, such ideas come from? We've never had a conversation other than the superficial as to tell you a day earlier I own a business. You probably can imagine, others, over the passing of dozens of years have ideas of me as well. Funny thing is they're all pretty much the same idea. When I just got back to Miami from my father's funeral, in my mailbox was an envelope containing a track from Tony Leader and his wife, asking me to make a choice to go to heaven rather than end up in hell. Under my nose, for me to read while just beginning to grapple with matters of family since my return, printed in color with illustrations of fire, the devil and such for what, to console me for my loss? These ideas, these hunches about me, do they come from a consideration of reality—real events occurring or do they come from someplace else?

You and your brethren, you claim answers to questions still being asked today, going back into the BC. You know there's a God (not gods), his (a male, gendered as humans and animals) name, that he expects from you (theism, not deism), and you know exactly what he expects of you (who to sleep with, associate with, what to drink or not, etc.). Me, I don't even know if there is a god, not to mention if it would care what we do or the church, synagogue, mosque, temple or other organization it participates with. But you and your brethren, Bryan and my father, you all have the answers, and while knowing nothing about me, without query or conversation approach me as if needing to fix or set me onto a correct path. If you want from me, shouldn't you know something about me first? How can you be so sure I'm broken or have gone astray? At least now you know and can say something relevant about me. You've learned I don't have the answer you claim to one of the world's biggest questions; "Is there a god?" And do you mind? Can it be OK, for you and your friends that during and after all these years "I don't know" is my answer?

Still think I need the god you follow? Where should I look to find him? Syracuse? Your church?

More than 36 years have passed since I was thrown out of my family for failing to claim as much as you, for questioning rather than following the dogma and demands made of me. Yes, that's what happened, because I refused to follow orders regarding family, specifically to make no mention, not even of the names of my grandparents and aunt to my siblings and mother. I was already being lied about, people like you were already buying into false ideas about me, but that's when the most damaging fabrications about me began, when after being told to leave I was said to have left on my own, for the world, to live in sin, shack up and all the rest, you know, that binary choice of heaven or hell your church speaks of. The truth, the irony is that I was tossed away for refusing not to care. I wanted my family to stay together, but Dad didn't and his lies and manipulations were enough for my siblings and Mother to cut away from me "for good." I mean it wasn't the sole selling factor, there was the dogma, need for Christians to separate from sinners as myself and others were made to appear. Which reminds me, do you really think those not believing as you are all headed for trouble? What I heard Saturday from one of the graduates, to either continue following the Lord (e.g., attend the Living Word Church) or slip away into sin, living for lust, drugs, etc. These are the only options? It's not possible someone like me can be living a good life, one caring and with meaning? I find it alarming. I've heard this for years, the binary choice of the Living Word way or the roadway to hell, and I've seen its impact on many finding themselves unable to continue attending your church. Awareness of some of the destructive consequences of your organization, this may be reason enough to leave, but further reasoning is required to consider there are better places to be. Good or evil, serve the Lord or the devil, the Living Word or man's word, exposed for years to this binary mentality, what chance is there to leave for a better life? Seeing the wrong, as rife as it is within your organization, this alone does not bring awareness that better options exist. For years you've heard it said it's sin that waits for you on the other side, right? And often, as I've seen it, that's what's chased, even if believing it's only for temporary relief or pleasure. What better can be expected when unexposed to reality, trusting in the experience of others selling you what to believe by presentation of only a portion of the facts. It's wrong, you may even say sinful to use an omission of what's true to influence someone, be it a church selling their theology, a political party its ideology, or a dealership a car.

I wasn't surprised after asking where your ideas about me came from. You know practically nothing about me and I didn't expect our dialog could be substantive. Since being there long ago, you, as with every other member of your church never chose to contact the oldest son of the founding pastor, someone capable and willing to speak with you, with anyone for hours, weeks even months providing facts and evidence as opportunity to be knowledgeable and intelligent in conversations about goings-on in your church. Instead, 36 years later you approach me with a hunch that

I assume you'd have me see in a better light than that Leader's track. But isn't it really the very same thing?

Sunday's sermon, the one I listened to closely before your request for my time, what did you think of it? Bryan, he's not a salesman, not selling anything? Every day, my friend. He told me in writing that I'm a God hater, that God is my archenemy. He said I am a loser, a wretch, unhealthy, narcissistic, that I was a rebellious teenager and went on with other ad hominem attacks. How can this be when like you and others He's never had a conversation with me about anything? Maybe he too had a hunch? About what, having me be what he needs me to be to make what he's doing right? I offered to introduce him to my friends, people who've actually experienced me for many years. But Bryan's response, he only attacked me, disparaged me more. My approach, maybe he considered my comments too thoughtful? Don't think, don't reason, just give it up to God at times appears to be his approach, that is, aside from characterizing me as hateful and all things bad. "You shouldn't be obsessed with justifying yourself to me . . . arguments, complaints about mitigating factors, rehashing history, the Lord isn't going to play verbal chess with you . . . cry out to Jesus for mercy, find peace in your obsessed soul." Funny thing is though, Bryan, like my father, uses reason when he thinks it's working for him. It's ok then, but when it's not getting him where he wants to go, then it's like Bryan said to us Sunday—"Sigmund Freud was debunked years ago." His wording was a bit messy, maybe Bryan was conflating psychology with Charles Darwin's theory of evolution? Regardless of his grammar, as Dad did, Bryan reasons to convince, to sell. That's when psychology, when reason is just fine and escapes criticism. But when in a dialog rife with reason, one where Bryan finds himself losing an argument, that's when he turns, when reason gives way to substance-less remarks like "cry out to Jesus for mercy," when other techniques like straw-manning—defaming character begins. You don't have to take my word for it, it's empirical fact that's been documented, available to you and others for years if ever wanting to know something substantive, something honest about our experience in a place once together.

I'll tell you a story providing some insight about my father's view of psychiatry. During my stay at Hutchings Psychiatric Center where I was committed, my father was informed it was necessary to meet with him. He refused. My mother explained to me years later that Dad "is too busy a man to just jump up and run when some psychiatrist asks him to." I digress, but those years I waited, dying to know why my father refused the meetings I so deeply craved is engraved in me. Ok, so Dad spoke degradingly of psychiatrists, of psychiatry for years, at the dinner table and in the church. But I had to hear it and make whatever connection I would between his refusal for participation and claims of disbelief in the reasoning process. And if true, if Dad thought psychiatry was nonsense, then for what reason after my release did he seek Joseph Mastrelio, a psychiatrist and member of your church to be my outpatient therapist? Proof was piling up that what troubled me, what got me committed in the first place, it wasn't my imagination or hallucinations, rather that all was fair game with people having titles like pastor or elder, people respected, followed and listened to that will do just about anything when it comes to getting what they want. Awareness of this behavior and its impact on myself, on my family, on people I cared for, that's what broke me. It's what I wanted Joe Mastrelio to know long ago. "Dr. Mastrelio, you said I'm so bad off that I'll likely die if I don't see you for therapy" "Yes I did." "Ok, if you tell my father you believe this, if he agrees to pay half your fee I'll see you." On my next visit I asked if he told my father how necessary it was I see him. "Yes, I told him it was a matter of life and death." "Did you tell him I'll see you if he pays half your fee?" "Yes." "What did he say." "He won't do it."

If there is your god—the god of the Living Word, He knows apologies are long past due. And from the pulpit, where the lies all started, let the truth finally be told. Let them end and be corrected. Wrong from the past has not been addressed, has not been corrected. Sunday morning services, Bryan will talk about putting trust in God, having faith he's in control of matters out of hand. He'll preach about it, he'll talk about it, there's "lip service" for sure. But Bryan will lie, manipulate, tell half-truths, do whatever's necessary to get his way. Faith, really? An apology for wrongdoings is long overdue and known by Bryan within, as you may say his heart of hearts. And that pitch of his Sunday, that he doesn't sell, is not a salesman is hogwash. Did you buy into that? From what you've read so far, can you imagine my mindset that Sunday morning? How about near the service end, during the tongue talking, calling for lost souls to approach the alter? My mother was impressed, in fact she told me the calling was for me "Danny, this is for you, can't you feel God calling you?" What if I spoke my mind? "Mom, it's not me, if God's out there calling someone it's Bryan, he wants him to repent!" The irony. The pulpit of the Living Word is where my father disparaged me, fabricated stories scarring, remaining with me on more than several cassette tapes. Treatment from "the world" has been so much better, a walk in the park compared to the way Living Word Christians have treated me past and present. The twisting of truth, lies spun, the secrets kept about real goings-on, this has been my life hardship, my nightmare and what put me into a mental hospital many years ago. It's the truth, one about me that should be known by you and your congregation as things true should be known, as falsities need to be exposed and corrected when discovered.

After returning home from my father's funeral, I was told about a video on the Living Word Website that may interest me. There he was, my brother David speaking from the pulpit of your church. "The Lord is really moving in my family." He mentioned an observation of mine while there. "Would you believe me, my brother, the one that's not here said it was Perfect?" Without asking what my experience was while there, while refusing all his life to sit with me and discuss anything, David had an idea about me and decided to tell you all about it. It's bad enough he refuses to hear me out, to know who his brother is, but to double down telling others about a brother he doesn't even want to know, now that's special. If there is a god, a just God, it would understand why such behavior keeps anyone honest from joining your church. What my brother said, it couldn't have been further from the truth. Still, I gave him the benefit of any doubt, contacted him with an opportunity to explain. Problem is, like I said, David won't talk, never has about matters of importance such as our relationship and that of our family. Predictable, but I do what I do anyway, let the chips fall where they may, maybe someday I'll be surprised. Anyway, I called my brother. He refused to discuss anything about what he said that day. So I took the time to write him, to explain in great detail exactly what my experience was while there, ensuring if ever he cared to know he would clearly understand the truth, the difficulties I encountered while there, the challenges I faced, the courage I sought and found to simply be in his presence and that of others. It took a lot of self-control, a lot of focus, every minute there an effort to remain silent, kind during my visit to the very place causing me and those I care for a great deal of harm. The decades of separation, the consequences of lies and deceit present in my awareness has never left me, challenged me then, challenges me now. The reasoning within myself it took, to resist speaking my mind defending myself and others. I bit my tongue many times when hearing how wonderful, how perfect my father's life was. If someone, anyone only had the guts to speak out long ago, to say what was true, maybe I wouldn't have been there that day for the first time in dozens of years. I fought to resist saying such things, especially when invited to speak at my father's funeral. David and Paul had words from the pulpit to say. I did too, but I was somehow able to remain in the pew, my objective simply to contain myself. God has anything to do with this? The video, David up at the pulpit that day had more to do with what's keeping us apart than anything that will get us back together. I get it, my brother wants to believe God's involved, answering prayer, moving in our family, changing our lives for the better. But putting his hands and mouth into it, making up stories to get us there, like our father did for years and Bryan's doing today just won't get it done. I asked him, "David, now that you know what I was going through while there, can you fix your mistake and tell the congregation something true about me, anything else just something true?" How many more times will I watch my brother, a Living Word Christian refuse to correct wrongdoings made aware of? This is it, what split my family and keeps it apart. A shoddy hand-me-down process of responding passed through generations that is taught in your church. A refusal to communicate resulting in stunted growth, a shelter for lies and coverups your church finds preferable to the exposure of uncomforting truths.

Ok, so Dad was frail, needed to be in control, the center of attention, was abused as a child feared death and all the rest. But there's no excuse, only indications, clues, warning signs he wasn't qualified for the job. His way of doing business ensured I would never have a relationship with my family for dozens of years, and that others like me, interested in what's true, what's contrary to his interests pay a price as well. I've begged him to talk with me for decades, he always refused with the same response; "I'm not ready yet," that is, until the Saturday before his death when he came a little bit clean. One such mention was telling me Bryan came to his position because he was very much after it and nobody wanted it. I expected to hear a story about weeks in the closet praying to God for an answer. But it wasn't about God, it was slim pickings instead. And what to expect, who would take his place other than another amoral man claiming a godly life? I told my brother what our father said about Bryan, but he wouldn't discuss it. Not to me, probably never will with anyone. The truth? My brother, the leaders of your church, they don't care what's true, it's comfort they're after. And fabricating the narrative, well that's fair game to get it and the made-up reality they live by. You can say there are valuable lessons in your church that are preached, but as a child learns from a parent's behavior, so too the congregation learns from its pastor. These demonstrably selfish people are driven by COR values (Comfort Over Reality) as I call it. Godliness, truth, honor, courage, these are not characteristics they admire or treasure, not what they seek or what guides their decisions. It's comfort they're looking for, that's at the core of life changing decisions made in your church.

I'm said to be running, hiding from the truth. But the truth is if I'm hiding from anything it's my disgust for what I've seen. I've often said, if I become a Christian one day my life will hardly change. But the life of some of your friends, Christians at the Living Word, their whole world would have to change.

If you asked my mother why she disowned me, why she hasn't had a relationship with me for most of her life, what do you think she'd say? Ask her why she didn't see her parent's for over thirty years, didn't go to their funeral, left their care with her sister who was also cut out of her life. My father was successful, that's why. When I learned my grandparents and aunt were told to leave the church, I drove to the school where my father studied for the evening's service, where he told me he'd make it so my mother and siblings would never see them again. I explained how wrong, how vindictive that was, and for a brief moment there was consideration, there were tears. But the truth of my words, of that of other wrong doings I spoke of, as obvious as it all was, wasn't enough to change the course that was for years in the making.

Today, since my father's passing, Mom visits with some of her cousins who years ago she was very close to. It's very strange, her behaving as if she never stopped seeing them. But it's likely no one will mention it to her, no one will talk with her or amongst themselves about this because remember, talk about the past, talk about goings-on is taboo. Problems, complications within relationships, these are matters reserved for the wiser to address; "Stop the railing and the murmuring. Don't muck up the waters dealing with matters you don't understand." And today, dozens of years later, why bother anyway? My mother's thinking process has been tampered with for so long, she wouldn't know how to face or discuss such matters anyway. And her stunted growth, it's not the only obstacle creating difficulty addressing, resolving problems. She's a nurturer, not the "A" type personality of my father. That Saturday at the hospital, I asked my father; "If Mom didn't marry you, say she married just about anyone else, what do you think the chance would be that her relationships with cousins, parents, sister, an oldest son would all be severed?" "Son, I did the best I could, I did the best I could." It's what he said in response to every five or six pointed, relevant questions I asked about our past. I always responded to him saying "Ok Dad, OK." His answer was poppycock, we both knew it, but I thought it better to have him laughing, to find as much enjoyment as possible in my first and last eight hours alone with my father that day.

I don't believe there's a god, which I hope you've noticed is different than saying one doesn't exist. I'll keep making mistakes, in much I do, and when recognizing them, if choosing not to repeat them I'll learn, get closer to the truth of matters. Where I spend my time and who with is important. Limiting my time, my involvement with dishonest people matters. Participating in your church as everything is, to get closer to God and eventually finding him, if doing so is possible the process may be as simple as sticking to this—to not doing what I know I shouldn't do.

You may have heard it said that eyewitness testimony accounts for as much as half of wrongful convictions, a demonstration of our inability to accurately account for what we see. How much worse we must be at understanding the truth about the unseen, you know, all that stuff I'm expected to accept by faith. The anecdotes told, by you and others speaking of their hunches, speaking in tongues and their interpretation, how much stock should I take of all this? We've a lot of work ahead of us when it comes to understanding what's right under our noses, yet I'm expected to decode unobserved supernatural events, to conclude the same as you by explanations riddled with logical fallacies. One person's epiphany, for all I know is another's revelation from God. A light bulb moment or bad thought, can I know it's not God or the devil talking instead? Two men from New York duping their community, one using religion the other a Ponzi scheme, a predictable Nostradamic calculation because their initials are BM? Where should we start and stop?

The leaders in your church claim many answers. Am I the one gone wrong? Such answers decades from my grasp come effortlessly, without appeal or request to those like my father. Dad shut Josephine Ottman down, stopped her dead in her tracks one day shortly after beginning a prophecy in the Phoenix church. How did he know so quickly what she said wasn't from God, that her claims, her statements came from someplace else? Such supernatural events occurring or not, is it possible my father simply didn't like what Josephine had to say? This situation, on its own merits in isolation from others similar, maybe the answer would be difficult to say. But considering history; my father's reputation, isn't the truth simply within reading between the lines? Your pastor, these teachers are not honest people. I said something similar while there, at my nephew's reception party to another Living Word Christian. "Nobody's perfect" I was told. "But who's asking for perfection? Aren't we supposed to take responsibility, make matters right when we discover what we've said or done isn't true, is wrong?" People like Bryan have been lying, deceiving and covering their tracks for many years. Remember the sermons, when my father preached about lying, how difficult, how complicated it becomes because you have to remember the lies you lied about? It's bad enough when it's corrupt politicians or businessmen doing it. But this is about leaders of a church, teachers of morality, about God and family. Pay attention to the goings-on in your church. Have high expectations of your leaders and sufficient understanding of the implications for not doing so.

I've a lot to say about the phony and fake, but at times I also think about what something real, something true might look like. Where are the prophecies about a god that's watching, angry his message is being ignored? Where's the outcry for those ungodly, for the leaders of your church to repent and change? Did you see Bryan approach me, the former pastor's son to say hello while I was there last week? He didn't, but I approached him with something to say, "I told my father I'm an atheist, he said it was OK, that everyone has to find their own way. I want you to know Bryan, we have something to offer each other."

My brother David approached me in your church, after our nephew's graduation ceremony. He reached forward to shake my hand. Since moving to Miami in 1989 I've never created a façade, pretended to be other than I am or to think other than I do. But my family, my mother and others you know, it's what they've done quite often. I could tell you stories about run-ins with former Living Worders in restaurants, gas stations, grocery stores and other places, uncomfortable moments causing my parents at times to stay home and not leave at all. Unlisted phone numbers and out of reach, a lifestyle accustomed to for decades that I suppose can be OK if you don't conflate terms like pastor and public servant. My life in Miami is different. Without secrets to cover up or behavior to be ashamed of, what need have I to cower? But my brother David has many secrets he continues trying to hide. "Leave it behind, there's nothing to be gained from discussing the past." A pretty convenient option for those behaving badly. What about the Bible, nothing to learn there? Most of it is just that, talk about the past. If Judas Iscariot lived today, maybe he too would hide what he did or tell his story differently. Yet there it is, written in black and white for centuries, discussed by theologians and others to learn from. As I said, I wrote David explaining in great detail how I felt about his talk of me from the pulpit. Months had passed and his decision to treat me, his flesh brother was without care or consideration, or shall I say in a manner unbecoming of a Christian? There he stood in front of me, long after lying in that very place about me, amongst the congregants of your church reaching to shake my hand. We weren't on good terms, nothing was settled. Without a plan or goal, not even a thought about what to do should such a situation occur, I did as I would in Miami, what came naturally, what occurred to me at that moment; "Why bother with me now David?" I asked. I was honest, spoke my words gently and waiting for his reply as I sincerely wanted an answer. But the calm in the air, of the moment soon turned. The reason, my best guess is he perceived the handshake a peace offering, one I rejected which to him was simply intolerable. I mean I'll never know for sure why it was he became so upset because there will never be a discussion about it. Nevertheless, after a pause of hardly more than a second or so, while pointing to the front doors of the church he yelled out "leave now! " several times in flashes of rage. Years earlier there was a similar moment, when my brother escorted me out of our Liverpool home, when again I was told to leave. I sat on a milk can on the front porch of our home, putting my shoes on. There was such a rush to get me out the door I wasn't allowed the time to put them on while inside. My mother swung the door open, began speaking words apologetically, promising to call me later to work things through. But she didn't finish, was interrupted by my father reaching through the door, pulling her arm saying "Fanny I want you inside now, don't talk with Danny, let him go." At the church, David's wife Dianne approached in a similar way, to console, to apologize for her husband's behavior. He's been going through a lot lately" she said. But David wasn't having any of it, in fact like Dad years earlier, now he appeared even more upset because she wouldn't let it—let me go. And there it appeared again, the tug of a wife's arm to get her away from me, followed by another "don't talk to Danny," a finger pointing to the door and a "leave this church now!" The next day, Sunday I was at the church again, this time for the morning service. David was with his wife and daughter, in a row just ahead of me. There he stood, singing, waving his arms to the heavens, oblivious to the ruminating in my mind of his antichristian behavior in plain sight for all to see the day earlier, another addition to a plethora of matters unresolved—to never be discussed.

I had the opportunity to talk with my mother about many things while there. Remember Bob Dean? My mother does, but has no recollection about his ever leaving the church. She was so emphatic about his never leaving that I began to wonder myself. But it happened, as I was later reminded. Bob was close with my Father and family, going fishing together and more that I personally experienced. My mother's recollection of the past appears a bit wishful, more about what she wants it to be than what it actually was. I get it, maybe she needs to believe all has been fine and rosy. My Aunt MaryJane ran into Bob Dean a few years back, at another church in Syracuse. She approached Bob and was fairly forthcoming, criticizing him for his treatment of her parents the day they were told to leave the Living Word Church. "You're right, you can punch me in the face right now, I deserve it" he said. I told my mother about this, one of several unwelcoming realities about our past. My brother Paul also spoke to me about the day of my grandparents' departure. He too expressed his regret about something he did, a secret revealed to me last year. "I did something terrible, unforgivable, and it's my fault Grandpa was told to leave our family and the church. I lied to Dad about what happened." Paul said he made up a story, accused our grandfather of doing something terrible because "I thought it's what Dad wanted to hear." "You should get this off your chest, tell our father about it." I told him. As far as I know he never did. It's another uncomfortable but important story I tried as gently as possible to have my mother know about.

A pushing aside of reality, a fabrication of stories made possible when comfort is the objective and attempts are made to create the outcome instead of discovering it. COR values—it's the vehicle that gets you there. It's cowardly, selfish, and a critical message missing from the prophecies and sermons I've heard.

Just look at my family and the mess my father left behind.

I have a business that keeps me very busy. My involvement and influence in your circle is tiny if anything at all. However, if I may ask, as I asked other leaders of Christian churches in Syracuse years ago who your organization refused, how about a conversation, a dialog to work matters through?

The Sunday morning I was there, the prophecies about God calling someone, watching several people up front spinning, waving their hands to the heavens. The music, the congregation swaying left to right in place, my mother nudging me, saying "Don't you feel the Lord calling you Danny? This is about you." "No, Mom, I don't" I said, followed by "Please allow me my free will" after the fourth time hearing her repeat herself. Could I have allowed myself to get caught up, carried away, influenced by my feelings, the environment? Maybe. But with all I know, the truth about what's going on up there, for my own good shouldn't I be afraid of becoming involved?

I spoke with my mother about many things while up there, but it's so scratching the surface. There was a letter I wrote to my family 36 years ago about the day I was told to leave. My mother never read it, that is until this year. She cried, expressed great regret and sorrow about what was done to me. For the very first time in decades, someone in my family heard me out, believed me, wasn't calling me a liar. It's a glimpse my mother has of me, of who I was, who I am today and of what I've been put through for dozens of years. It's a departure from contrived versions, character assassinations used to sustain my banishment from my siblings, from my mother for years, all to keep people like you from believing anything I say. It's going to take a long time for my mother to really know me, for who I am and have been, as it should, the ticking of a clock not yet started with my brother David. And your pastor Bryan, he's dug in deeply, his eyes on the prize, the comfort he enjoys created by the faulty dogma he inherited, modifies and protects. It's easy enough to say you believe in God, but to live the life of a true Christian, one with honor, with honesty and godliness can be another story. It's the record of our lives that speaks for who we are, what we really believe in, and it alone is worth paying attention to.

THE NEPHEW CHRONICLES

MY VISIT TO SYRACUSE WAS A JOURNEY OF CONTRASTS. IT RE-kindled memories of the past, bringing forth a maelstrom of unresolved issues that remain to this day. Yet amid the shadows, the trip was illuminated by the creation of new, heartwarming memories.

A standout was meeting Levi, my sister Debbie's grandson. He was nestled in my mother's home, living with his parents—Jocelynn, Debbie's daughter, and Trever. The pair met back in California during their college years and have since relocated, a progression in their own familial lives. When I visited, Levi was just four months shy of his third birthday. It was a joyous first encounter, filled with playful moments that I had never experienced before despite having thirteen nephews and nieces.

Interestingly, the only other child of my siblings I'd met who was near Levi's age was his mother, Jocelynn. She was Debbie's eldest and the pioneer among my parents' great-grandchildren. I recall that one day spent with not-yet-one-year-old Jocelynn in the living room of my parent's home. I have footage from that event, which I captured in anticipation of bridging the chasm between my kin and me.

On the morning of my return to Miami, history whispered once again. In that same living room, I was graced with precious moments alongside Levi, drawing once again from a pool of warm memories spanning Syracuse and Miami. A pile of Lego blocks evoked recollections of playful times in Miami with my friend Veronique's daughter, Amelie. For Levi, I built a towering Lego edifice, almost reaching my own height. Imitating my playful antics with Amelie, I nudged Levi to bring it crashing down. While with Jocelynn our moment together was captured on an antiquated VHS tape, this time the lens of my Galaxy 9 was the silent witness.

Our day unfurled with a nostalgic jaunt to Clairmont Park, the place where I once played as a child. Our exchange of words danced gracefully, mingling observations and questions as we meandered through our surroundings.

Once ensconced back in Miami, I was embraced by the world I had molded for myself, a realm seemingly eons apart, and not just geographically, from Syracuse. No church bells were chiming for me there, and there were fewer reminders of the shadows from the past that still cast their pall on my family. However, one connection to my past remained: Salvador.

As the rhythms of my daily work returned, my quandary—what to do about Salvador—dominated my thoughts and weighed on my heart. The allure of Miami, its balmy embrace, the promise of a clean slate, and Sal's initial fervor for the bounty of opportunities before him seemed to be waning.

Just a few weeks prior, before I headed to Syracuse for Jacob's graduation, Sal expressed a desire to vacation with friends for a week.

"You've barely settled in," I said. "I'm not sure it's the best move."

Maybe I should have been more flexible. Perhaps the promise of that break was the morale boost he needed.

Despite my previous decisions, Sal seemed to be drifting into a groove that aligned more with his innate disposition, molded by his life's experiences to date. He seemed to be resigning from the hope of a new trajectory. His growing reclusiveness was disconcerting—evenings and weekends locked away, lost in slumber, video games, and endless phone chats. This behavior, seemingly set on a path divergent from his expressed ambitions, felt intractable, leaving little room for any deviation. Even so, I persisted in my optimism, unwilling to accept this as a predetermined downfall.

I recognized it wasn't productive to press him on the fitness routines he had abandoned. However, there could be alternative pursuits that not only engaged his interest but also promoted his physical health, which, in my eyes, was pressing. I had introduced Sal to the exhilaration of wakeboarding and the charm of Amelia Earhart Park in Hialeah. I painted a vivid picture: the inviting warm waters tailored for relaxed strolls and adrenaline aficionados enticed by the thrill of challenging ramps. I mentioned the cozy café, tempting treats, and the unmatched joy of reveling in Miami's sun-kissed outdoors. To my joy, he gave it a shot—but just for one day. Sadly, the experience didn't resonate with his preferences.

Being a perpetual optimist, I kept looking for opportunities to engage with Sal. Our conversations continued to deepen, delving into his life's progression and future hopes. It seemed his self-imposed isolation had reached a tipping point, another topic that I was more than willing to discuss with him. He had been looking for an apartment, eager for independence. While I supported this move, it came with challenges.

Sal shared that many potential landlords required a cosigner. Eager to assist, I offered my backing, but it was clear there were deeper hurdles. The recent pandemic had wreaked havoc on Miami's housing market. It was no secret that apartment prices, already steep, had skyrocketed, sometimes by a staggering 50 percent or more. My associate, Marco, recently disclosed his plans to abandon his longtime apartment, pushed out by a steep rent increase. Given this situation, Sal's quest for affordable housing felt like a daunting challenge.

Adding a layer of complexity, Sal confided his friend's intent to join him in Miami.

"Great, shared expenses!" I replied. However, then I learned that his friend was jobless and residing with his mother. While there was vague talk of potential gigs like Uber Eats upon his relocation, nothing was set in stone. And Salvador's next remora only served to heighten my apprehension.

"I don't want him to work; I want to take care of him."

As I reflected on this, pieces of our previous conversations began falling into place.

Sal hinted at wanting the same support for his friend that I had extended to him—specifically, a position within my company. I questioned Sal about his friend's qualifications and tried to convey the importance of making business decisions that safeguard the interests of the company, its staff, and its clientele. Despite these dialogues and the absence of a clear business case for hiring his friend, Sal remained relentless in advocating for his inclusion. It was now clearer to me the motives behind his persistence.

Sal's quest for an affordable apartment that fit his budget—without my concession to add another employee to my payroll—continued for weeks, but it bore no fruit, much to his dismay. This frustration manifested in various ways. One day he confronted me about it. "You promised my salary would be doubled by now."

"What?" I replied, taken aback. "Sal, you haven't even been here for five months."

Days passed, and as life proceeded, Sal approached me again. "Dan," he said, "we need to have a conversation."

I nodded in agreement. "Sure, what's on your mind?"

He paused for a moment before responding. "I've been in touch with some friends in Syracuse. There's a job opportunity there that would enable me to afford a place and live with my boyfriend."

I took a deep breath, collecting my thoughts. "Sal, when you decided to move to Miami and join the company, you described this role as your 'dream job,' a golden opportunity, remember?"

He stared back at me, a hint of defensiveness in his eyes, but nodded in acknowledgment. "Yes, I do."

I had been under the impression that Sal was in Miami to solidify his footing in the IT industry, which he professed a deep passion for. I believed he wanted to construct a sound financial foundation, with my mentorship aiding him in achieving his aspirations.

"Sal, wasn't your intent to focus on building a steady career and financial trajectory? Was I wrong?"

His response left no room for doubt. "My top priority right now is to be with my boyfriend."

If I had been privy to this sentiment, I might not have invited him to join me in Miami. However, I didn't believe he misled me during our initial discussions about working together. It was plausible that his intentions were genuine at the outset, but as he delved deeper into the business world, his priorities shifted. In hindsight, perhaps my own work ethic and the apparent intensity of my profession might have been intimidating to Sal. After all, he did once admit that he wouldn't desire a life like mine.

When Salvador requested time off to interview for the position in Syracuse, I granted it.

One Friday evening as I settled into my living room, engrossed in international news, an unmistakable aroma permeated the room—the distinct scent of cannabis. My suspicions homed in on the lone source of this unwelcome aroma. With mounting consternation, I navigated my way upstairs and knocked on Salvador's door. When he appeared, his glazed eyes paired with the strong scent left no doubt.

"Were you smoking pot in my house?" I asked, taken aback by the audacity. He responded with a casual shrug.

"Yeah, what's the big deal?"

What followed was a strained exchange. Sal posited that in the absence of a direct prohibition from me, his behavior was within bounds. His demeanor wasn't just dismissive; it was outright belittling. He evaded accountability at every turn. From his viewpoint, his actions were perfectly defendable.

This incident only intensified my apprehensions about Sal. Up until then, I had shared my concerns with his mother. I didn't shy away from detailing numerous disconcerting interactions with Sal, seeking her insight and counsel. However, each time these issues came to light, rather than proposing solutions, she offered justifications, seemingly suggesting that Sal's behaviors were somewhat predictable, even permissible.

"You're two grown men, butting heads," she said. Her words hinted at a conviction that her son was on par with me. However, he was not my equal, and although I acknowledged my own fallibility, I found her inference in response to my detailed accounts of Sal's misconduct both inappropriate and unsettling. However, I kept my concerns to myself, fostering a growing apprehension that she might be reluctant or unable to acknowledge the true nature of the issues at hand.

As I moved forward with Pam, a narrative began to unfold within our discussions and written exchanges. This account, marked by a continuous search for external factors contributing to Salvador's troubling behavior, took precedence in our conversations. Eventually, it led to the characterization of Sal not as the originator of problems but rather as an individual grappling with ADHD.

Upon uncovering Sal's actions, I instructed him to dispose of all drugs and associated paraphernalia in his possession. With an awareness of his craftiness, I articulated my instructions clearly: "This includes from your car, on your person, pockets of every piece of clothing, this room, and all its drawers. Furthermore, I want to ensure there are no drugs anywhere in my home. Let me be unequivocally clear: no drugs, whether legal or not, are permitted in my residence. Do you understand?"

As the evening settled down, I considered my approach and how I was going to inform Pam. While I may not have been a therapist, doctor, or a father, some argued that I lacked the credentials to voice judgments or opinions on certain issues. However, I contended that my capacity as a thinking person, coupled with firsthand observations, granted my insights a validity that merited at least some consideration.

Sal was an exceptionally bright young man. Over the five months I had known him, he had consistently showcased the ability to achieve anything he was passionate about. Every interaction I had with him underscored his unwavering persistence and tenacious drive.

As I got to know him better, though, I began to see more layers of his personality. I observed his moral principles, his capacity for empathy, and his sense of fairness. Like everyone, Sal had goals, and he navigated through these traits to reach them. Unfortunately, sometimes his journey, marked by shrewdness and astuteness, obstructed a crucial goal that I had urged him to embrace, one he agreed to adopt, ensuring that all parties involved benefit. From my observations, he undoubtedly grasped this foundational goal, and that it went beyond mere understanding, that it called for active participation.

If Sal ever decided to engage with a therapist, my curiosity would be piqued about the possibility of ADHD being identified as a contributing factor to his intermittent indifference toward other people's feelings. This curiosity stemmed especially from situations where individuals had unfailingly shown him nothing but kindness and concern.

Putting aside for a moment the symptoms such as forgetfulness, clumsiness, a penchant for solitude, and detachment from family, how did a diagnosis like ADHD or any other medical condition intersect with a person's character? Was there a medical or psychological explanation that could shed light on an individual's apparent insensitivity to the impact of their actions on others, or their seeming reluctance to consider fairness in their dealings with others?

After taking a day to reflect on Salvador's actions, I felt composed enough to engage in a thoughtful conversation about our future path. In the evening, I spoke candidly with Sal, acknowledging his astuteness and shrewdness and how he had wielded these traits to his advantage in various situations. I emphasized to Sal that his behavior suggested a predominant focus on his own interests, with concern for others only when it served his immediate goals. This observation led me to reiterate the principles I had tried to instill in him: everyone's well-being and interests were paramount.

Considering his cunningness and his propensity for deception, I also expressed my discomfort with his continued stay at my home, urging him to persist in seeking alternative living arrangements. Additionally, I offered him reassurance. Unlike the treatment I endured at his age, I assured him of sufficient time to transition to a new living situation. He was under no pressure; there was no established exit date.

"While you continue to reside here," I concluded, "I will not revisit this topic again, and I will extend to you the same respect and kindness as always. Nevertheless, do not misconstrue my kindness as acceptance. Based on what I have come to understand, your presence here is no longer cherished, and my patience and generosity have their limits."

His reply was brief, ending our conversation almost as soon as it began.

For the ensuing week, each morning as he emerged, I posed the question, "Are there any drugs in your room?"

"No, Dan," he replied without hesitation.

Once every day, I asked him the same question, holding his gaze intently, letting a brief silence linger after his answer. Through the steadiness in his gaze, I sensed a begrudging acknowledgment of the respect I demanded.

"No, nothing," he reaffirmed, making it seem as though my daily check-ins, however calm and succinct, might be unwarranted.

As Friday evening opened its welcoming arms, nestled in the embrace of my living room, I immersed myself in global news. The burdens of professional rigors began their slow dissolve, granting me a brief sanctuary to gather strength for what lay ahead. But just as the ambiance settled into a harmonious rhythm, an insidious whiff of that unmistakable cannabis aroma tangled with my senses. My pulse quickened, my indignation stirred.

Propelled by a newfound urgency, I ascended the staircase, each step amplifying my mounting fury, until I reached Salvador's room. Disregarding any semblance of courtesy, I thrust the door open.

"You can't do that!" Salvador cried. But the sight before me—him nearly undressed, his eyes mirroring a distant realm—spoke more than his words ever could.

I stood there shrouded in silence, my eyes embarking on a quest for clarity. There had to be something within my gaze that could elucidate my nephew's behavior. If it had been me caught red-handed, standing before another man I had been deceitfully reassuring, I wouldn't have been able to bear his scrutiny. Where was the expression of guilt, the manifestation of remorse? Where was the boy who once texted me, effusively expressing his gratitude for the opportunity I was offering him?

"What?" he asked, as if my silence had lingered too long.

My mind inadvertently meandered to the moment I was escorted by two policemen to the psychiatric center. I recalled my posture in that moment—head lowered in submission, shoulders slumped in defeat, feet dragging across the floor beneath me as I was guided to a place designated for my reckoning and atonement. I was a spectacle of defeat. Though my eyes were glued to the floor, the murmured words and gasps I overheard betrayed the onlookers' shock at my dismal state.

I felt like I was drowning in guilt, shouldering the blame for the punitive circumstances and the ordeal I was facing.

But now as I observed my nephew, I saw no trace of my past surrender. His posture bore no shadow of shame. He stood as he had claimed to be, proud and unyielding, and my astonishment felt unfounded. The words "You're not paying me what I'm worth" resounded in my mind as a potential counter from him, a drop in the ocean of fabricated excuses for his unkept promises. In that revealing moment, my mind clung to a swirl of rationalizations likely dancing in his own thoughts, allowing him to face me with such unwavering defiance. If in his mind he was already poised for departure, dreamily envisioning a life with his friend and eager to cast off the shackles of responsibilities and disappointments in Miami, then why not embrace irresponsibility? Set to leave soon, what did he have to lose?

I stood there observing a figure before me with whom I no longer desired any association. It was a stark revelation: you never truly know someone until you share time and space with them. I've uttered these words before, primarily after hiring young individuals to serve as technicians. Despite the resumes, the interviews, extensive conversations, and referrals, and regardless of any acumen for reading between the lines, the real essence of a person unfolds only when you engage with them for a substantial period. In regard to Salvador, it felt as though this very moment had unveiled his authentic self to me.

"Put on some clothes, and call a cab or an Uber," I said. "I want you out of this house tonight."

His response was a laugh, followed by a dismissive and mocking tone. "Oh, big man in charge, in control, giving me orders."

Full disclosure? The fantasy of thrusting my fist through his smirking face bloomed within my mind. I would never act on such a thought, of course, but the urge resonated with what I felt the situation demands. I was swamped with curiosity about how this boy managed to muster the audacity, the gall, to address an uncle, or anyone for that matter, with such blatant defiance. Had he not faced consequences for such behavior before, or was this a shocking debut? It didn't seem like the latter; his demeanor was too assured, too at ease, and too practiced in its insolence.

Still, he remained unwavering. "You're just jealous because I'm leaving you, and you want me to stay," he declared. "You don't want anyone to know I don't want to be here. You want them to think I'm gone because you got rid of me."

And there it was, a glimpse into the intricate workings of his mind, long shrouded in secrecy. His pronouncement matched the image I had reluctantly crafted of him, solidifying my apprehensions about his character. He was spinning his own tale, constructing a version of reality that absolved him of all faults, aligning with his aspirations.

As I stood there, threading my way through the fragments of reality entangled in his expansive web of self-deception, a question arose in my mind. If Pam could exonerate her son by attributing his actions to ADHD, why hadn't she insinuated that, in her view, our father and Bryan Rocine were also merely victims of circumstance, their deeds drifting beyond the moorings of personal accountability? This notion plunged me into a churning sea of uncertainty, compelling me to confront the profound depths of denial and self-justification.

Amid the tempest's roar, clarity sliced through the chaos, emerging as a formidable savior. *That's it,* I thought. *My nephew, like my father and Bryan, is irrefutably COR, prioritizing comfort over reality.*

The acrimonious exchange limped on, with Sal hurling derisive comments, caricaturing me as an authoritarian uncle intoxicated by control. I retaliated, my words sharpened with the single aim of expelling him from my home posthaste. Finally, after an agonizing five minutes that felt like eternity, he disappeared into the obsidian embrace of the night, leaving relief and despondency in his turbulent wake.

I sank into a chair, relishing the newfound calm and silence enveloping my home. With Sal's departure, clarity pierced the fog, allowing contemplation to unfurl its wings. The revelation of Sal being COR cast a new light on the landscape of my understanding. My years, rich with interactions with those adept at contorting reality, nudged me to ponder the far-reaching implications.

Ahead lay another phone call to Sal's mother, and I braced myself for the probable fallout from Sal's distorted narrative. In his crafted universe, he was the victim, exploited and unfairly used. While I couldn't gauge the extent of his COR-infused influence on Pam's perspective, the signs lay scattered everywhere, hinting at his deception.

Undoubtedly, she'd been introduced to tales of my unfair treatment toward him. It was a new consideration I was now aware of, a lens through which our forthcoming conversations must be viewed. However, for the moment, I needed to address the issue of his belongings, which I'd have to return to him.

Before dialing Pam's number, I veered toward Sal's bedroom. Beyond the occasions of reprimanding him for his trysts with cannabis, where our glares intertwined in silent confrontation, this marked my initial venture into his private space since his advent nearly six months prior. Upon my entry, my gaze descended to my feet, meeting a mysterious stain on the carpet. Kneeling down, my fingers grazed its surface, attempting to discern its origin—perhaps a spilled soda or some other substance? A peculiar scent assaulted my senses amidst this exploration, steering my gaze sideways. Beneath the bed, a panorama of disbelief unfurled, stealing my breath: mountains of discarded bottles, both water and soda, some still containing their liquid contents, accumulated in an overwhelming mass. Their exact tally was veiled in obscurity, conjoined in a seamless mosaic of clutter, sprawling from the carpet to the bed's underbelly.

How deceived I had been. My trust in Sal had been unwavering for months. His responsibilities were minimal: to maintain the cleanliness of his room and his car. Each morning as he prepared to step out, I would inquire, "Is everything in order with your room?" Without fail, his response was a confident, "Yes, all set." And naively, I never second-guessed him, never ventured into his space to verify.

I stretched my arm under the bed, initiating the laborious task of extraction. Behind the initial barricade of bottles, a further vista of neglect unveiled itself. Candy wrappers, half-eaten morsels, sticky substances adhering to the carpet, and heaps of detritus came into view. "Remember, no food in your bedroom. Eat in the loft," was among the few rules he had consented to abide by. And now, what was this? A propane tank? A likely apparatus for igniting his cannabis, I surmised.

The discoveries didn't end there. Behind the nightstand and beneath the dresser, further heaps of discarded items were laid bare. The magnitude of the situation was beyond words.

I dialed Pam, detailing the situation and the disarray unveiled. Her response was laden with apologies and regret for the hidden chaos. Beyond that, the conversation was limited, centering on the logistics of returning Sal's possessions.

I had to step back, to find respite from the overwhelming sight. Surveying the mountains of refuse unearthed from beneath the bed, I marveled at how such a volume could have been stowed there. I resolved to complete the transfer of the remainder to the loft the next day.

After completing this arduous task and engaging in another conversation with Pam, I sent her a photo of the colossal heap, a testament to the astonishing neglect and deception revealing itself within the confines of those four walls.

Ahead of me loomed the unenviable task of packing his belongings. I approached the closet, a muted light revealing the array of shirts on hangers, shrouding his luggage beneath.

I removed his clothes from their hangers, folding shirts to place them in the suitcase. As the rhythm of my task lulled me, a stark realization jolted my thoughts. Why this meticulous care? Why this unearned diligence for a nephew who has filled my space with more trash than clothing, showing scant regard for my property and generosity? There I stood, packing each item, ensuring safe transit for his belongings, while he'd left a trail of discarded wrappers and half-eaten food in his wake.

The incongruity of the situation stirred a resolve within me. Seeing as the clothes and the trash belonged to him, I decided a fitting departure gift would be to reunite him with both. This revelation emboldened my steps, infusing a rhythmic energy into my actions.

I treaded upon the hardwood of the loft, each step a confident assertion amidst the quietude. My hands, guided by unwavering purpose, dove into the mosaic of discarded remnants, a vivid tableau of his disregard. Gum wrappers were mixed in with fragments of half-devoured food and bottles partially filled with forgotten liquids. A motley treasure in my arms, I navigated back to the epicenter of his occupancy, his suitcase lying open and expectant.

The items tumbled into the suitcase, mingling with the folded clothes. The stubborn confines of the suitcase rebelled against this newfound alliance, its bulging seams crying out in protest.

Undeterred, I descended to the kitchen pantry. There, a choir of trash bags awaited, their whispering forms extending a silent, welcoming embrace. Their ample folds stood ready to cradle the discordant medley of belongings and refuse, a harmonious melding in their gentle grasp. The sight ignited a flicker of nostalgic remembrance. Visions of my younger self, embarking on a journey into the world's uncertain embrace, my belongings ensconced in trash bags.

In this reflection of past and present, a harmonious circle completed itself. Sal's possessions, both cherished and discarded, found a shared abode in the humble yet embracing folds of the trash bags, ready to accompany him on his journey, a silent, bundled testament to his sojourn within these walls.

Within the span of an hour, Sal's garments and the mounds of refuse melded together, ensnared within the unyielding embrace of the trash bags, a clothing basket, a suitcase, and a carry-on bag. Nestled behind his corporate car, they reposed in patient anticipation of their retrieval. With a nimble flick of my fingers, I seized a visual testament of this seamless confluence, dispatching it across the boundless digital expanse to Pam. The photo, illuminated by the ethereal glow of early afternoon sunlight, was like a memorial to Sal's triumphs and trials, offering a stark revelation of the concealed realities that lay in wait as I endeavored with boundless goodwill for my sister's son.

The evening shadows had just settled in, casting a peaceful hush that contrasted with my turbulent thoughts. In the aftermath of ushering Sal out of my home, the glaring screen of my phone shattered the silence at precisely 9:07 p.m. with a text from Sal: "When can I get my stuff?"

With a heavy sigh, I typed a reply, desiring to sever all direct communication with him. "We can talk through your mom. Don't text me."

His reply was swift, a palpable tension crackling through each word: "No. Don't get my mom involved in this more than she has to. I'll get my stuff tomorrow and then we'll stop talking afterwards."

Again, Sal wanted to control the situation, to have his way. "You're not calling the shots here. Give it up. I am blocking you now." The words were sharp, a final barrier to further communication. And there, in the luminescent glow of the screen, rested Sal's last words to me, a sarcastic sneer embedded in each letter: "What a power play. Hahahahaa."

The "Hahahahaa" in his text reverberated in my mind, conjuring a vision of his laughter, his face twisted in a mocking smirk, just as he had looked when he sauntered away to his waiting Uber. I could hear the disdain in his chuckle, feel the sting of his condescension prickling my skin. A surge of disgust filled me, a tide of revulsion that solidified my resolve. The thought of facing him again, of hearing his voice, filled me with aversion.

Honoring my words, I blocked him, severing the tenuous digital thread that connected us. The cold finality of the act, a silent declaration of my boundaries, resonated within the quiet spaces of my heart. I turned instead to his mother to organize the final details of his departure.

However, only minutes after conveying my wishes to Pam, her response arrived. Eager to avoid any further discord with her son and urging the placement of his company phone at my front door, I was met with disappointment. "He had already left when you texted me. Of course he forgot your phone. He said he will bring it tomorrow," her message read. Her words, tinged with a note of exasperation, added further complexity to the already entangled series of exchanges.

Exhaustion nipped at the fragile edges of my fraying patience, eroded further by Sal's persistent disrespect for boundaries. He consistently circumvented any established channels to meet his obligations, thrusting relentless turmoil into the once orderly flow of my life. I resolved I could endure it no longer.

As I crafted a text to his mother, I stood at the base of my garage under the imposing hold of the sun-soaked sky. Suddenly, an all-too-familiar figure broke through the tranquil scene. Sal materialized before me, rounding the corner with an effortless ease that belied his trespass. How had he breached the secure boundaries of my gated haven? The uninvited question imposed its weight upon my burdened mind as he entered without the expected notice or permission.

"Do you have my phone?" I asked, a frail hope whispering within the question.

"No, I'll bring it tomorrow," he replied, his words carrying the familiar undertone of unfulfilled promises.

"Leave then. Come back when you have the phone," I replied, aiming to end the tiresome encounter.

In defiance, he stood immovable, a steadfast pillar

amidst the gathering storm of our discord. A torrent of accusations cascaded from his lips. He labeled me as insane, suggesting a return to a mental institution, uttering the words with calculated malice.

In the face of our verbal maelstrom, my focus narrowed to a singular yearning—a desperate desire to expunge his presence from my existence. Amid the clattering cacophony of our parting, I surrendered his bags, his belongings, into his eager clutches, the forgotten phone now a mere whisper swallowed by the gale of our confrontation.

In the quiet calm following his departure, my fractured world embarked on its fragile healing. In the hallowed journey of recovery, a firm vow unfurled—his shadow would never again shroud my doorstep.

After his exit, I drew a deep, purifying breath, a gentle whisper of relief. I looked forward to the slow return of tranquility, though marred by the scars of recent turmoil. But the chapter had not yet concluded; the reverberations of the conflict lingered in the new wounds within my heart's chambers.

Scarcely an hour after Sal's departure, an unforeseen message shattered the tenuous peace. It was from Pam, seeking to probe into the crevices of my actions, into matters divorced from Sal's deeds. I was left bewildered, trying to decipher how her morning church service could have prompted her to revisit and scrutinize my letter to Mark in response to his request for thirty seconds of my time. Considering the day's unfolding drama, it seemed more pertinent to address Sal's conduct rather than to be critical of my own actions. It was curious, her decision to impart religious insights and quote scripture to me, a non-believer, particularly amidst the day's tumult.

While I understood her deep Christian faith, the sermon's resonance, and the influence of biblical teachings on her perspective, I was still puzzled. Why direct these religious views toward me, and why now in the midst of Sal's disruptive actions? The timing was perplexing. I couldn't shake the feeling that I was overlooking an underlying message. Could it be that she viewed my interactions with Sal as the core issue needing resolution?

Additional discussions with Pam further illuminated Salvador's actions. I discovered personal property borrowed that had not been returned. His phone, another forgotten return, was eventually handed over but only after all its data had been erased.

Witnessing Pam's reaction to these disclosures was also disheartening. Her predisposition to provide excuses for Sal and absolve him of responsibility amplified my concerns that she was not only avoiding addressing her son's issues but may also have been intensifying them. I felt like the lone voice recognizing the urgent need to hold Sal accountable for his own benefit.

Time moved forward, and life began to return to normalcy. Sal was out of the picture, which brought me relief.

Throughout my life, I had always acknowledged that "we go through things." I could have extended forgiveness to Chris, the child molester, had he permitted me to. My father, who relentlessly strived to exclude me from the family, could also have received my forgiveness, had he approached me with an acknowledgment of his misdeeds and a request for pardon. The same grace lay in wait for Salvador despite the harm he too had inflicted upon me.

My capacity for forgiveness was something of which I was acutely aware. It was crucial for Pam to recognize this sentiment within me as well. Despite the prevailing chaos, I held fast to my conviction that all was not beyond repair. A pathway lined with reason stretched ahead, offering a beacon of hope for reconciliation and the reinstatement of mutual well-being.

But walking this path necessitated a readiness to confront reality head on. It mandated that those who had committed wrongs must acknowledge their mistakes and shoulder full responsibility without resorting to excuses or shifting blame by citing the faults of others.

Days slipped by, coalescing into weeks. As time flowed onward, I was left wrestling with burgeoning questions. I pondered the path that led Sal into the mire of such deplorable behavior. In the days of Pam's and my youth, such conduct from any of us children would have been unfathomable. Our father's stern gaze alone would have been enough to set us straight, his leather belt ensuring the correction of our wrongs. What form of discipline, if any, had been applied to Sal to deter his descent into his current state? This question settled into my mind as the days drifted by, days marked by a notable silence from Pam.

After a few weeks of silence, punctuated by my internal musings, my phone finally rang. It was Pam. "Hi, Danny," she began, then plunged into a sea of small talk. While I didn't mind the trivial conversation, an unmistakable elephant loomed in the room. Unable to dance around it any longer, I cut through our banter about local weather.

"Pam, I need to know. How did Sal end up this way? Surely, he must have shown you and Mark the same disrespect he showed me. You know well what Dad would have done to us in such a situation. What actions did you take with him?"

Her flurry of responses was non-committal and elusive. Statements like "You're two grown men" and "You just didn't see eye to eye" dodged the issue.

Hearing this, clarity dawned on me, helping to unravel the mystery of Sal's demeanor.

Sensing the futility of my approach, I pivoted the conversation. "I'll be in Syracuse again, and I want to visit you and your family. How can I be in your house with Sal there considering how things were left?" I expressed to Pam my consistent inclination to forgive those who had wronged me, a sentiment I had extended to our father, our mother, and even to her. "Everything I've done for Sal, I did for you, Pam."

How could she refute this? She knew the emphasis I placed on compensating for the adverse family experiences that my nephews and nieces encountered. Her awareness of my dedication to this cause should have accentuated the authenticity of my words and intentions. "All I'm asking for is an apology from Sal for his inappropriate behavior and his failure to uphold the agreements," I continued, clarifying that satisfying these terms would permit me to persist in my family visits without feeling suppressed or uneasy.

"He's a grown man; I can't tell him what to do," she replied, revealing her desire to refrain from accepting responsibility.

"Now that he's back in Syracuse, where is he living?" I inquired.

"He moved back into the house; he's staying here with me and Mark," she replied.

Grown man, I mused. Once again, my thoughts gravitated toward the concept of discipline, the teaching of consequences for one's actions, and I wondered, where was the discipline now? With this in mind, I probed further. "You allowed him to return and reside in your home? Why didn't you say, 'Not until you apologize to your uncle first'?"

My disbelief swelled, wrestling with the harsh reality. Despite Pam's awareness of my extensive efforts to aid her son—efforts I now feared she misconstrued as exploitation—she refrained from using her influence to secure an apology from him, an act that I had emphasized as a crucial step for the continuation of my support and involvement with her family.

"Danny, I told you, he's a grown man," she reiterated. "I can't make him apologize."

"Sure, a grown man who runs home suckling at his mommy's breasts," I retorted, my reply burgeoning with frustration. "You wield influence over him, and you should have utilized it. Measures need to be taken."

The conversation unwound further. With unwavering persistence, I conveyed my sincere desire to sustain a relationship with her family. I also highlighted the essential need for substantial change to make this continuity possible. I floated the idea of her and Mark engaging in a candid conversation with Sal. My hope was that they could emphasize the genuine purpose behind his time with me, making it clear that my initiatives were in no way for my self-interest but solely for his progress. I clung to the expectation that this dialogue could cultivate understanding and repentance in him, steering him toward recognizing the importance of taking responsibility, and ceasing to blame others for his actions.

However, at every juncture, Pam's reaction was defensive, as if she felt compelled to shield Sal from my allegations.

From this discourse, the situation became increasingly unambiguous. A problem clearly existed, but Sal wasn't the sole proprietor of it. The excuses for Sal's behavior proliferated, expanding as voluminously as the clutter that had crowded under his bed, leaving no corner unoccupied. When the absurdity of Pam's remarks could no longer be confined within the boundaries of reason, she resorted to shouting. "Bob Mazur, Bob Mazur, Bob Mazur!" Her words seized me, her invocation of our father's name pulsating with desperate intensity. The implication of her exclamation pierced me, casting a cold, dim light over our conversation. Through her eyes, my intentions, however noble, were nullified, leaving me shrouded in the dark specter of tyranny, resembling our father.

Perhaps the letters from her husband, Mark, and my brother-in-law, Tom, reflected more truthful sentiments about my character. As Mark suggested, without the experience of fatherhood, what insights could I possibly offer regarding the treatment of children? Tom's letter, declaring me to be the spitting image of my father, now resonated in harmony with Pam's words. I was branded as the one needing to apologize, the one with a "sick, twisted concept of what family is." As Mark expressed with stark clarity, "Pam is a stubbornly protective mother whom strangers show more care for than my father, myself, or any other idiot."

In the repeated outbursts of our father's name, laden with accusation, I sensed the attack on my character. Acknowledging her glaring overstep and recognizing the futility of any potential rebuttal, I opted for silence, severing the connection with a click.

After that day, not a word was exchanged between Pam and me. However, in the following months, my dialogue with my mother, Debbie, and Paul and his family persevered. Our discussions were harmonious and positive, unhindered by the influence of any external figure aiming to sow discord among us.

As 2022 came to a close, whispers of a shared vacation began to permeate our text exchanges. The concept of a cruise held everyone in its enticing grasp. Within a week or two of our vibrant discussions, we firmed up our plans, booking an eight-night adventure aboard Royal Caribbean's *Explorer of the Seas*. Set to embark on this journey were my mother, Debbie, Aunt MaryJane, Uncle Gary, and me. Despite the gathering excitement, I felt the hollow absence of a crucial missing part: Pam.

I racked my brain for various strategies to entice her participation. I held onto the belief that she would seize the chance to join us if she could only surmount the barriers stifling her communication. Unable to conjure a compelling or inventive approach, I settled on sending her a text in which I outlined the excursion and offered to cover her expenses, ensuring that financial constraints wouldn't pose a barrier to her acceptance. Sadly, my message was met with silence.

The sting of rejection deepened as it became apparent that Pam's withdrawal was not confined to me alone. More unsettling was her decision to sever communication with our entire family. She distanced herself from our mother and our siblings, a chasm that yawned wider with time. It was disheartening to anticipate that this rift would extend to her children, as she abstained from encouraging them to maintain family bonds, reflecting her own choices.

In many interactions, I noticed Pam's consistent portrayal of herself as the perennial victim, a narrative I observed unfolding over a considerable span of time. Although I did not address this directly with her, I shared these observations with our aunt. Pam's unwavering assertion that she had faced the harshest adversities among us amplified this tale. Despite the adversities we all faced as a family, her steadfast belief that she alone had endured the worst treatment was unyielding.

If I ever hinted at this perception in conversations with her, it was only to highlight the numerous advantages I had gained in my life as a result of facing adversity. My experiences and introspection endowed me with skills and insights that I was convinced I would not have otherwise. I did not perceive myself through the lens of victimhood; instead, I regarded my experiences as necessary steps that shaped me into the person I had always aspired to be.

Chapter Fifty

CHOOSING COR

T WENTY-NINE YEARS AGO, IN MARCH 1994, AT THE AGE OF THIR-ty-two, a profound realization dawned on me: I was inadequately prepared to navigate my life toward realizing my aspirations, overcoming past harm, and averting its unwarranted continuation. Eager to confront any challenge to attain peace and tranquility, my ambitions soared. I was driven to enhance my personal life and my financial standing.

My lifelong reliance on learning through trial and error guided me. This journey was undertaken with a wholehearted acceptance of my strengths and my weaknesses, regardless of their proportion. Despite possessing average intelligence, my indomitable spirit of persistence and grit, coupled with a resolution to face reality, served as the safety net needed to transform my fallen dreams into stepping stones toward achieving my goals.

In my eagerness to improve and increase my chances of realizing my aspirations, I contemplated a fresh strategy. I resolved to sit down, calm my mind, and jot down pertinent "data" for later reflection and examination. It was a novel and unexplored technical approach, one that aligned with the onset of my new career as an IT professional.

On the horizon, set to reveal itself in hindsight decades later, was another realization that I hadn't considered: exploring beyond the realm of absolute truth and the boundaries of reality. This has emerged as yet another alternative path in pursuit of what might more succinctly be termed as my happiness.

Overall, my journey through life has underscored one fundamental understanding: the most effective pathway to knowing others begins with knowing myself. Just as I understand the jolt from biting into a lemon, I can grasp the sensations others experience in doing the same. Through introspection, I glean insights into the emotions and thoughts that others might encounter on similar self-reflective journeys.

Despite our unique paths, we remain bound as human beings, united in the grand tapestry of evolution, sharing cultural exposures and life experiences within our communities. This shared heritage and experience provoke a compelling question: why wouldn't they be like me, and why wouldn't I be like them?

However, through this decades-long process, I've noticed something I had previously overlooked: the diverse ways in which each of us responds to our feelings. This is something I realize I have not adequately considered; in fact, I haven't given it any thought at all.

For me, to move forward in life with genuine intent, addressing the actualities of my experiences is fundamental. I must face the truth without fear of embarrassment, exposure, or repercussions, acknowledging and addressing any faults in my character. This approach will eradicate all influences that prevent my access to reality.

Convinced that this process is the only method for those who are honest and well-intentioned toward their own and others' improvement, I made a grave error, especially since I considered it self-evident that anyone who is sincere understands that evaluating truth, not falsehoods, leads to betterment.

After writing hundreds of pages and reviewing my past, I have realized that my approach to self-improvement is one I have seldom seen in others. Although I consider it self-evident that truth is the road to improvement, it seems that most people are inclined to do the reverse. Instead of using what's true to discover reality, they deny the truth and create their own reality.

I am also reassessing my assumption that everyone believes in an independent reality, waiting to be discovered, a belief I once held as self-evident. After examining my life and observing others, I've found the contrary to be true. Many people live as if reality is malleable. This perspective has been especially hard for me to grasp because it contrasts so starkly with my personal experience and my approach to life. As I've tried to express, my view of others fundamentally reflects my view of myself. I had naively presumed that everyone seeking the truth does so honestly. This assumption, however, begs the question by presupposing their honesty and straightforwardness without providing any evidence to support this belief.

What I observe in the masses is individuals altering their surroundings to reflect not their true selves but the image they desire to convey to others.

How I came to embrace the opposite approach is unclear to me. Years ago I embarked on a journey of writing to discover myself by observing the actualities within my environment. This might have been a consequence of my mental breakdown. Having realized the futility of "shaping my reality," I chose a different path. Maybe this is why I do things differently now, or maybe not.

Before being committed to Hutchings, I was raised in a

Christian family and felt compelled to mimic their behavior, contrary to my convictions. This façade made me a hypocrite, as I feigned belief in a deity simply to fit into a familial and societal narrative. Though being punished for faking my belief was a lesson learned, the pivotal revelation was recognizing that I wasn't alone in donning a false persona. I discovered that everyone else was doing the same. Their claim to believe in God may have been sincere; however, every step along the way, they have shaped their God into something unlikely to exist, a being compatible with the fabrications and deceptions used to obtain and maintain their interests.

I recall years of guilt, my self-imposed punishments for behaving contrary to the truth about my beliefs—or rather, disbeliefs—that I hid, buried deep within me as if exposure would ruin me. Little did I know then the possibility that I would escape this pattern of existence, a trajectory that some people, like my father, likely never escaped. How else can his refusal to come to grips with his lifelong treatment of me and others, even on his deathbed, be understood? To this day, this stands as the most credible explanation I have discovered. My father meticulously constructed his world, his reality, fashioned for the person he longed to be. My deepest hope, when all is said and done, is that he remained unaware of the damage he caused. I cling to this hope, yearning to believe he would not have perpetrated such acts had he understood the profound pain and suffering he inflicted upon others. If he was indeed ignorant of this overwhelming impact, my heart mourns my persistent failure over the years to illuminate this reality for him—a realization that could have arrested his harmful deeds and unveiled to me a true and worthy display of repentance, transforming into something concrete and observable, something I could evaluate and respect.

The trait I have termed "COR," which stands for "comfort over reality," the act of creating a reality tailored to one's comfort, manifests to varying degrees within many. In its milder form, I've illustrated this trait in "The Story of a Salesman."

In this narrative, a salesman, eager to portray an image of honesty and competence, inadvertently reveals a contrasting reality through his actions. Much of my writing delves into exploring such individuals, predominantly family members, who exhibit diverse levels of COR. In every situation, a cost emerges, and a penalty unfolds, seemingly in direct proportion to the extent of their self-deception.

My aim is to illuminate this linkage for such individuals, elevating their understanding that straying from reality does not go unpunished. This penalty, emerging in diverse forms, reveals itself to everyone regardless of their realization of its correlation with their behavior. Recognizing this bond and accepting the self-generated origins of the anguish that escapes their notice could lay the groundwork for transformation. In making this change, if they are truly benevolent beings, they can choose to avoid misplaced reprisals, thus shielding others from the repercussions of their actions—a turmoil unknowingly conjured not by facing reality but by manufacturing it.

The self-imposed weights emerge from their disregard of urgent matters, transforming their environment into a realm that aligns with their mistaken routes. This alteration perpetuates damage to themselves and others by neglecting to address the altered realities they have sculpted.

Without awareness of those entrenched in COR, individuals remain vulnerable to its harsh and destructive effects. Within numerous organizations today—religious, political, and otherwise—deceptions thrive. For the sake of integrity and the well-being of good people, these falsehoods must be recognized. But the question remains: who will shed light on them? The individuals themselves or someone else?

In the United States, the freedom to make personal choices is cherished. While I hold no sway over anyone's decisions, I stress the inevitability of consequences. Grasping the intricate details of these repercussions may not always be crucial, but for individuals like me, gathering some evidence is essential. However, delving into such matters can be a prolonged and intricate endeavor, and the investment of time and resources may not assure significant insight.

The most effective route is to embrace the simple truths we've all known since childhood—play nicely in the sandbox, and embrace truth wholeheartedly. This clear-cut strategy, regardless of how one arrives at it or from whom it originates, may emerge as the most invaluable insight of all.

Our dominion over our existence is inherently bounded. Instead of embedding deceptions in the framework of our futures, it is wiser to permit their legitimate evolution and submit to the odyssey of uncovering. This mindset resonates more closely with the biblical interpretation of faith, a confidence that acting in harmony with truth will naturally lead you to your rightful place, a destination to be discovered, not crafted. Embarking on this route requires bravery and a sincere pursuit of truth, a longing that each person must realize for themselves.

I am realizing that this preference cannot be imparted to others; it stands as a personal revelation to either accept or repudiate.

In conclusion, I want to reflect on the gift that my father left me. As I culminate this literary endeavor, a newfound assurance envelops me, a conviction that comes from having successfully navigated the expedition I embarked upon. I asked myself, who am I? What is true and significant about me? Is my identity merely a reflection of others' perceptions, or can I discover something about myself that either corroborates or contradicts what I've been told?

Through this journey of introspection and while pondering my father's words, a revelation has unfurled. I stand enlightened, realizing my own worth and the substantial contributions I am capable of offering.

In every aspect of our daily lives—from our professions and religious practices to casual walks in the park and routine trips to the grocery store—we constantly intersect with a vibrant mosaic of individuals, each enriching the world with their unique perspectives and beliefs. This colorful array of differing viewpoints and ideologies unfurls endless opportunities for personal enrichment and growth. Let us not allow baseless prejudices to obfuscate our judgment, leading us to the fallacy that there is nothing valuable to gain from those who differ from us. Let us remain receptive, wholeheartedly embracing the abundant knowledge and understanding that our multifaceted world generously extends.

Furthermore, it's crucial to challenge the belief that meaningful relationships and cherished moments cannot flourish between individuals of differing beliefs or backgrounds. This principle applies across all spheres of life. In every religious community and throughout the extensive political spectrum—from Democrats to Republicans and from libertarians to the Greens to members of the Constitution Party—individuals can be found either championing or rejecting the truth. The narrative extends further. It would be remiss to overlook other facets of our culture, including our interactions with various races, intellectual levels, and physical appearances, whether perceived as beautiful or ugly, thin or heavy, tall or short.

Reflect also on familial bonds. I once faced a situation where a former brother-in-law declared he could no longer see me because his girlfriend deemed my family detrimental. Unbeknownst to her, I shared a similar sentiment but will never have the opportunity to convey it to her due to her assumption that my familial connection determines my character.

The idea of demonizing or avoiding associations with diverse groups is not only irrational but also fundamentally detrimental. It inhibits the growth of understanding, empathy, and shared humanity that binds us all together, transcending our disparate backgrounds, beliefs, and characteristics. In these connections and shared experiences, we find the richest moments of life, fostering mutual growth, learning, and enrichment.

A time will undoubtedly come—and maybe it already has—when you will glean wisdom, empathy, and insight from someone whose life path markedly diverges from your own. Let us ensure our hearts and minds remain unbarred, receptive to the boundless opportunities for learning, growth, and connection proffered by our extensive global family.

Concerning my family, as my experiences have illuminated, overlooking the inherent value in each member culminates in a painful loss, a squandering of the limited and cherished time we are allotted together.

As the final words of this book sound a gentle parting, may my life and the accounts contained within these pages resonate within the recesses of your mind. Visualize a tale of two facets: on one, a clear warning against the subtle allure of division, a tempting whisper that urges us to sever the precious threads of unity and understanding.

As for the other, as your eyes traverse this textual tapestry, envision a brilliant beacon piercing the veil of division, its luminous rays illuminating the expansive horizons of opportunity. Within this effulgent glow, boundless opportunities unfurl, eager to be grasped by valiant souls embarking upon the majestic voyage of exploration and self-discovery. May the resonance of these tales waltz within your spirit, kindling the flames of courage and hope as you embark upon the boundless odyssey of exploration and self-discovery.

May my life, along with the entirety of my written words, stand as a dual testament: a solemn warning against the divisive maneuvers of those set on fostering division and a luminous beacon that underscores the remarkable opportunities awaiting those valiant enough to undertake a continuous journey of exploration and self-discovery.